Professionalism in

POLICING

AN INTRODUCTION

Professionalism in
POLICING

AN INTRODUCTION

FIRST EDITION

David J. Thomas

Australia • Brazil • Japan • Korea • Mexico • Singapore • Spain • United Kingdom • United States

**Professionalism in Policing:
An Introduction**
David J. Thomas, PhD

Vice President, Career and Professional
Editorial: Dave Garza

Director of Learning Solutions:
Sandy Clark

Acquisitions Editor: Shelley Esposito

Managing Editor: Larry Main

Product Manager: Anne Orgren

Editorial Assistant: Danielle Klahr

Vice President, Career and Professional
Marketing: Jennifer Baker

Marketing Director: Deborah S. Yarnell

Marketing Manager: Erin Brennan

Marketing Coordinator:
Jonathan Sheehan

Production Director: Wendy Troeger

Production Manager: Mark Bernard

Senior Content Project Manager:
Betty Dickson

Art Director: Joy Kocsis

For product information and technology assistance, contact us at
Cengage Learning Customer & Sales Support, 1-800-354-9706

For permission to use material from this text or product, submit all requests online at **www.cengage.com/permissions.**
Further permissions questions can be e-mailed to
permissionrequest@cengage.com

Library of Congress Control Number: 2009942334

ISBN-13: 978-0-4950-9189-9

ISBN-10: 0-4950-9189-8

Delmar
5 Maxwell Drive
Clifton Park, NY 12065-2919
USA

Cengage Learning is a leading provider of customized learning solutions with office locations around the globe, including Singapore, the United Kingdom, Australia, Mexico, Brazil, and Japan. Locate your local office at: **international.cengage.com/region**

Cengage Learning products are represented in Canada by Nelson Education, Ltd.

To learn more about Delmar, visit **www.cengage.com/delmar**
Purchase any of our products at your local college store or at our preferred online store **www.CengageBrain.com**

Printed in the United States of America
1 2 3 4 5 6 7 14 13 12 11 10

This text is dedicated to my family:

Mabel, John, Diane, Patricia, Erika, and Champ

for their unwavering devotion and support

CONTENTS

3   CRIMINAL LAW   51

4   POLICE SOCIALIZATION   95

5 THE POLICE ORGANIZATION   129

ABOUT THE AUTHOR

David Thomas, PhD, is an assistant professor at Florida Gulf Coast University, currently teaching in their criminal behavioral analysis program. He was a police officer for twenty years and retired from the Gainesville Police Department, Gainesville, Florida, in June of 1998. Unlike many officers, he did not spend his entire twenty years with one department; during his tenure as an officer, he worked for five different agencies in Michigan and Florida. As a police officer he has worked patrol, training, SWAT, Hostage Negotiation, Detectives, and served as a Field Training Officer. David has been training police officers since 1980 and has served as the Director of the Criminal Justice Training Center at Grand Rapids Junior College as well as academy coordinator at St. Petersburg College and St. Johns River Community College, both of which are in Florida. He holds a doctorate in forensic psychology and criminology from The Union Institute, a master's degree in education from National Louis University, and a bachelor's degree in psychology from Mercy College of Detroit. David maintains an active role in police recruit training and is certified as a use-of-force expert in the Florida courts.

PREFACE

T he idea for this text was born from teaching two different audiences: police recruits and university students. Each wanted access to a text that would help them in understanding a police officer's role in American society. At the request of both groups of students, this text was designed for the primary market of university and community college criminal justice students as an introduction to policing or law enforcement. The secondary market that it was designed for are police academy recruits to be used as a reference text and offer information that they will not be able to find anywhere else.

TEXTBOOK DEVELOPMENT

This textbook was written because of a frustration I had with the current books on the market. They discussed the concepts and philosophy of policing very well, yet they did not provide the student with information about what it is like to be a police officer. There was very little or no discussion of the law because many of my colleagues believe that this is not important to policing and should be taught in a criminal law course. Yet, the very foundation of policing is not only grounded in the law but also governed by the law.

As mentioned, the idea for this text was born from teaching two different audiences, police recruits and university students, with each wanting access to a text that would help them understand a police officer's role in American society. Beginning with the police recruits some thirty years ago, I developed calls for service in my lectures known as 10-65s, meaning "Prepare to Copy." The 10-65s were designed to help the students develop problem-solving skills and apply the law in their decision making.

When I began teaching at the university level, I utilized the Socratic Method and supplied students with anecdotal information from my law enforcement days. However, there was little or no challenge for the students, and many were reluctant to participate in the discussion. To enhance their participation, I integrated the 10-65s at the university level. Each week the students were given a call for service and were required to research the call and the law, to determine the best course of action, and to present a solution that met the legal guidelines. This project was presented in six classes, with my students suggesting that I write a textbook with the 10-65s as an offering. Before moving forward with the text, I prepared one chapter with the 10-65s and posted it online for my students to review; they all agreed that this made the text engaging and something that they would read.

TEXTBOOK ORGANIZATION

The text is designed as a series of building blocks, beginning with the history of law enforcement and closing with a discussion on the future of law enforcement. The concept of the text is for students to examine information, grasp some of the tools, and understand the complexity of policing and police decision making. The text contains twenty-four scenarios that are integral to achieving the objectives presented in each chapter. This is more than an introductory text to law enforcement; it is an introduction to professionalism that introduces the student to the challenges of policing. Professionalism has been at the core of policing since the Peelian Reform. The text also introduces the student to chapters that are rarely seen in an introductory text such as ethics, law, education, and career development.

To the Reader

Following are descriptions of each chapter to introduce you to the topics discussed and what you can expect to learn from the chapter. This brief overview illustrates the scope of this text.

Chapter 1, entitled *The History of Policing,* provides you with a brief history of policing and then explores the historical challenges policing has faced in attempting to become a profession. A discussion about the ideas of August Vollmer indicates that problems in modern policing stem back to its humble beginnings. Vollmer stresses two important points regarding the challenges: politics and the lack of quality personnel. Today officers receive quality training; many have college degrees when they enter the profession, and the screening process is designed to weed out those who are unfit. The unknown quantity remains the human psyche. Police are human beings, and therefore they are influenced by a number of variables in and out of policing that impact their actions. In essence, we cannot predict the future. As a result, this textbook addresses a host of issues that police face on a daily basis. The challenge after completing the text is for you to define professionalism.

Chapter 2, entitled *Ethics,* provides you with what can best be described as the perfect foundation for ethical decision making and the cornerstone of professional policing. However, what may be ethically sound in many cases may be in direct conflict with our moral values. The questions that many officers face and which challenge their value systems are:

1. Can I kill someone? Under what circumstances would I feel comfortable in taking a human life?
2. If I saw my partner take money, would I turn him or her in, or would I become a part of the blue wall of silence?
3. What role will peer pressure have on my ability to make decisions, and how will that influence my decision-making ability?
4. Can I be fair and impartial, or will I allow my personal biases to enter the equation?
5. Finally, will I safeguard the rights of those who I know are guilty, even those who are guilty of the most heinous crimes?

From a theoretical perspective, we would like to believe that we will always do what is ethical. However, the real world provides officers with opportunities, temptations, and pressures that challenge all that we believe to be moral and ethical. Simply stated, being a little unethical is akin to be a little pregnant: there is no such thing. Either you are or you are not ethical. Unfortunately, the issue of ethics has been a part of policing in the United States since its inception, and it is something that continues to stain the fabric of the profession.

Chapter 3, is entitled *Criminal Law.* The law is the greatest tool that officers have at their disposal. In fact, it becomes the foundation of all decisions that are made. The Constitution provides that each state has the ability to self govern and develop a series of laws that govern and protect the population of that state. In doing so, we have developed fifty different criminal codes.

The challenge for police is to know the law to such a degree that they can make reasonably good decisions on the spot. This is necessary when it comes to determining if someone is to be arrested. In addition, it becomes an excellent tool when investigating a crime, or even if you want to stop a vehicle. Knowledge of the traffic laws will help you decide whether you have probable cause to make a traffic stop. The stop might be for something as simple as a "license plate light out" or an "obstructed license plate."

The greater problem for police appears to be the rules associated with such things as Miranda warnings and when *Miranda* applies during interrogations. Other issues that continue to plague the profession are the rules of evidence, search and seizure, and probable cause. When examined, each appears to become an issue because officers have their own interpretations of the law or because they have violated the rules before and gotten away with it, so doing so becomes a common practice until a defense attorney catches a violation.

Besides ethical conduct, the law and the procedural rules associated with enforcement are the only tools that separate the police from the suspects. As a student, you will be challenged to make decisions based on the law and evidence through a host of scenarios and reflective questions. You will also be challenged to consider: Are interpretation and enforcement of the law issues in policing today as they were in our past?

Chapter 4, is entitled *Police Socialization.* The public has a perception of police that is dependent on the type of contact citizens have had with them in the past (e.g., community perceptions in African American and Latino communities) or media interpretations of past incidents. The question for many is: how does policing impact individuals professionally and in their personal lives? The profession is rife with high rates of alcoholism and divorce, and suicide rates are almost twice the national average.

The process of socialization begins with the decision to become a police officer. As a student, the question that you will have to answer most often is: Why do you want to be a police officer? The profession has a different meaning to every person. In your reflection, attempt to avoid this answer: "I want to help people." The decision to become a police officer is usually much deeper than that.

This chapter explores every aspect of the police career from selection to retirement. As a student, you will explore preemployment screening, the academy, field training, career development, stages of a police career, politics, and police suicide. The goal of this chapter is to show how each of these issues acts independently as well as collectively to impact the police profession.

As a student and future law enforcement officer, it is important to understand that your personal convictions and constitution must be strong to maintain balance in your life. Policing is an identity that consumes you and requires that you become a model citizen 24 hours a day, 7 days a week. It is so ingrained that when officers retire, they lose a formidable piece of their identity. In this chapter you will be faced with a number of challenging scenarios representing dilemmas that those who have gone before you have had to resolve.

Chapter 5, is entitled *The Police Organization*. Vollmer argues that criminals have the ability to cross jurisdictional boundaries and that the police are unable to continue their investigation because the criminals continue their activity in other jurisdictions. Because of this, Vollmer believes that all police should have national jurisdiction. This argument is in direct conflict with the U.S. Constitution, which established jurisdictions to keep us from having a police state. In fact, the only limitation on police organizations is in their desire and ability to share information; thus, our system of policing is fragmented.

With that said, an organization is judged, in whole or in part, by its leadership and their guiding vision. If the leader has an excellent relationship with the public, communicates not only the good but also the bad, and is the first to step up when there is a problem, then the organization is first-rate. Anything less than that leaves doubt and reservations in the minds of the public as well as the troops.

A good leader provides his or her organization with a guiding vision and core values. The core values are the heart and soul of the organization. The core values define what will be tolerated within the ranks as well as during public interactions. The core values are fundamental to the agency's many subcultures. For example, African Americans and women have had a difficult time assimilating and are seen as lesser than their white male counterparts.

As a student, you will have an opportunity to examine the various subcultures within agencies, their impact in policing, and the issue of affirmative action. The scenarios will make you angry and challenge your belief systems regarding fairness. The questions you need to ask as you complete this chapter are:

1. Are these issues related to the history of policing?
2. Were any of these problems hidden in the past before they became issues?
3. If I were a police chief in Vollmer's time, would I have hired blacks and women, or would I have done what was politically correct, knowing that my job depended on making the "right" decision?

Chapter 6, entitled *Patrol Operations,* discusses patrol, which is the backbone of a police organization. In fact, it is the one division of the agency with which the public is in constant contact. The public forms most if not all of their opinions based on how they are treated during a traffic stop or during the investigation of a burglary. As much as we would like to think that presentation has nothing to do with police, the reality is quite the contrary: image is everything and, in many cases, the key to success. In essence, patrol style defines an agency's image.

Besides communications, patrol is the only division of an agency that provides services 24 hours a day. The one constant that remains with patrol is officer safety; from an administrator's point of view, it is visibility and officer safety. This difference creates the great debate: one-person versus two-person patrol units. For economic reasons, some agencies have been forced to acquiesce and settle for one-person units to avoid layoffs. The greatest question facing police in our society is: what is our role in society? As you read this chapter, attempt to answer that question.

As a patrol officer, you will be faced with many of society's evils, including drugs, prostitution, child abuse, and homicide. One's success in patrol has to do with a working knowledge of all the skills associated with policing. As a student, you will be exposed to a host of scenarios that will challenge your decision-making ability. The scenarios are designed to task your leadership ability and knowledge of the law.

Chapter 7, is entitled *Investigations.* Patrol is the point of contact for every crime committed in the United States. It is rare that an investigation begins with detectives. In fact, most cases are closed by arrest if patrol completes the investigation and makes the arrest. The key to any successful investigation is being thorough and answering basic questions. Here you will be exposed to the investigative process and work a case from the beginning through the arrest. The chapter is designed to lead you to ask relevant questions and to help you understand the pieces of a puzzle and how they relate to criminal charges.

Chapter 8, *Use of Force,* covers the controversial topic of force. No other area of policing has created such fear and animosity because of its use in policing history. Force is an interesting concept because it is totally subjective and based on an individual officer's belief. Although subjective, it is nevertheless often the center of great debate, and it has resulted in numerous lawsuits.

Police do not have a magic pill that renders a subject helpless during a physical confrontation. The bottom line is that when an officer has to resort to hands-on contact, it is both dangerous and often perceived as brutal. Variables that impact an officer's ability to use force include background, academy training, defensive tactic skills, and the subject's actions. Survival in such incidents is based on an officer's ability to assess a threat and respond appropriately.

As a student, you will be exposed to a number of scenarios that should challenge your thought processes in regard to the use of force. Try to relate these incidents to history, and think about what it must have been like to be an officer in the 1960s and 1970s.

Chapter 9, is entitled *Terrorism*. Before September 11, 2001, we all thought that terrorism was something that happened in other countries. Since 9/11, counterterrorism is another role that has been thrust upon police as first responders and, more importantly, as intelligence gatherers. It is clear that this is necessary, but as a citizen, what role do you want your local police to have in the fight against terrorism? As a student, you will explore ideology, methods, and the problems with intelligence and local police. You will also look at the history of policing and see how simple it was then, and how complex it has become today.

Chapter 10, entitled *Education,* is designed to show you the importance of education and what it means to a police career. Most if not all states require only a high school diploma; however, most agencies require a minimum of 60 credit hours, and others require a bachelor's degree. It is important to understand that a college education is the foundation of an officer's career development. This chapter stresses the importance of getting a degree from an accredited college or university and warns you to stay away from degree mills. Remember, if it sounds too good to be true, then it is. The concept of education is in line with August Vollmer's belief that all officers need a degree as a foundation. This chapter also challenges you to answer the question: What will I do at the end of my career?

Chapter 11, entitled *Career Development,* is designed to take you beyond a college education and offer insight into the many specialties in policing. It provides you with a short list of in-service courses that prepare officers for future assignments beyond patrol. It is important to understand that career development is your responsibility and that you need to have a plan for where to go after the first year in patrol. Depending on the size of an agency, the specialties may be unlimited: aviation, mounted division, canine, investigations, street crimes, training, terrorism task force, intelligence, internal affairs, personnel, communications, beach patrol, and so on.

Chapter 12, entitled *Future of Law Enforcement,* begins with the following quotation:

Law enforcement hasn't changed in the last fifty years. There is an expectation by the public that when they need service, police will respond. However, the future of policing is predicated by its past; the problems remain the same, with additional responsibilities.

As a student, take a moment and reflect upon this quotation. Policing has made very few changes. The advances that have been made are based on legal mandates and technology, with technology having the greatest impact with new tools for crime fighting. The same tools that police covet as advancing their cause in crime fighting are the very same tools that criminals have used in the development of new criminal enterprises such as transnational crime, cybercrime, the exploitation of children, human trafficking, white-collar crime, and narcotics. As a student, you will understand the limitations of policing based on the U.S. Constitution. The question that you will need to answer is: How do we become effective at battling crime when it has no boundaries?

FEATURES

One unique feature that is consistent throughout the text is the number of scenarios. All of these scenarios were taken from actual police cases. Following the scenarios is an analysis and reflection section with a number of thought-provoking questions and answers. From a learner's standpoint, this feature allows students to examine the difficulty that is associated with certain decisions and to explore possible outcomes. In many of these cases, students will examine moral dilemmas such as those associated with the use of deadly force, affirmative action, and politics. These are the real challenges of policing.

In addition to the scenarios, each chapter begins with a quotation described as "Doc's Words of Wisdom." These are reflective statements that are relevant to the subject matter at hand. I developed this feature while teaching in the academy for police recruits as a point of future reference.

Chapters 10 and 11 allow students to explore the benefits of education and assist them in making sound decisions regarding their educational and career goals. The discussion on education provides insight into college accreditation and diploma mills. It also provides the student with understanding of the importance of a college degree and upward mobility. The concept of career development is rarely discussed in policing but is very important, since the average length of stay as a new hire is 34 months. This discussion provides students with the necessary information to determine whether an agency is the right fit for long-term employment. One major issue here is opportunities: the larger the organization, the greater the opportunities. This is one of the many variables for students to consider in choosing an agency.

ACKNOWLEDGMENTS

Thanks to Pricilla Doyle, who took the time between her graduate studies to proof and make suggestions regarding the text.

REVIEWERS

The author and publisher would like to thank the following reviewers whose input helped to shape this text:

Beth Bailey
Charleston Southern University
Charleston, South Carolina

James J. Lauria
Pittsburgh Technical Institute
Oakdale, Pennsylvania

Mengyan Dai
University of Baltimore
Baltimore, Maryland

Bobby B. Polk
Criminal Justice Professor
Omaha, Nebraska

Douglas Davenport
Truman State University
Kirksville, Missouri

Dr. Jacqueline L. Schneider
University of South Florida St. Petersburg
St. Petersburg, Florida

John F. Doherty
Marist College
Poughkeepsie, New York

Pamela Spence
Holmes Community College
Goodman, Mississippi

George R. Franks, Jr.
Stephen F. Austin State University
Nacogdoches, Texas

Harrison Watts
Washburn University
Topeka, Kansas

CHAPTER 1

THE HISTORY OF POLICING

OBJECTIVES

After completing this chapter, the student will be able to:

- Describe the concept of deviance as it applies to civilization.
- Describe the tithing system.
- Discuss the importance of the Peelian Reform as it relates to modern policing.
- Describe the history of the New York City Police Department.
- Describe the outcomes of investigative bodies beginning with the Wickersham Commission and ending with the investigation of the Rampart Scandal.
- Discuss the court cases that have had an impact on police conduct.
- Discuss attempts to professionalize policing and describe the role of CALEA in modern policing.
- Define professionalism.

KEY TERMS

Christopher Commission – a commission established in 1991 to investigate the Los Angeles Police Department after the beating of Rodney King and the Los Angeles riots.

Commission on Accreditation for Law Enforcement Agencies (CALEA) – a credentialing body with the purpose of credentialing law enforcement agencies that meet CALEA's established standards.

communication down the urban hierarchy – a method that cities use to inform each other of advances; in the history of American policing, used to describe the development of uniformed police departments in small cities even when there was no need for them at the time.

crews – noted by both the Mollen Commission and the Rampart Scandal, crews were described as groups with five to ten members that participated in acts of violence in order to earn respect, extort profit, relieve frustration, and administer street justice.

dangerous class – the faceless in U.S. society—the paupers, tramps, and criminals—comprised of five groups: urban criminals, rural criminals, rural paupers, urban paupers, and tramps.

grass-eaters – a term developed by the Knapp Commission to describe officers who took small amounts of money and made corruption respectable within the ranks of the New York City Police Department.

hue and cry – an alarm system used by members of a tithing to alert neighbors that they needed help; most often associated with criminal activity or fire.

Kerner Commission – a commission established in 1967 to examine the causes of inner city riots, the two most violent of which were in Detroit and Newark. There were a total of twelve common complaints assigned to three levels of intensity; police practices were the number one complaint assigned to the first level.

Knapp Commission – a commission established in the 1970s to investigate widespread corruption in the New York City Police Department in response to a *New York Times* article.

Law Enforcement Assistance Administration (LEAA) – an organization established to professionalize policing by offering monies for education, training of local officers, bomb squads, pilot programs studying alternatives to incarceration, drug treatment programs, and state court organization.

meat-eaters – a term developed by the Knapp Commission to describe officers who took large sums of money without hesitation and pushed for the big dollars.

Metropolitan Police Act – the first piece of legislation in modern policing; enacted in 1829, the law made police public servants and not private actors.

Mollen Commission – a commission established in 1992 to investigate corruption within the New York City Police Department; the commission had three mandates: to investigate the extent and nature of corruption within the NYPD; to evaluate the department's ability to detect and prevent corruption; and to recommend changes to enhance their effectiveness.

professionalism in policing – the ethical conduct of officers who meet the challenges and the needs of the communities in which they serve.

professional police model – defined by the LAPD as a model of policing that is focused on crime fighting with minimal contact with the public.

Rampart Scandal (LAPD) – an investigation in 2000 of an antigang unit known as the Community Resources Against Street Hoodlums (CRASH), which was very successful in reducing violent crime but which also prompted several scandals.

rotten apple theory – a theory that corrupt officers will infect the rest of those they associate with if they are not removed.

shire – a cluster of one hundred families or ten tithings; equivalent to a county in American society.

shire reeve – a position created by English noblemen and landowners; this person was responsible for law violations within the shire; equivalent of a modern sheriff.

Sir Robert Peel – considered the father of modern policing, he was responsible for the Metropolitan Police Act; his most notable contribution was deterrence of crime through preventative patrols.

Tammany Hall – a part of the New York political machine, which held a certain number of police jobs in exchange for political favors.

tithing – organized after the Norman Conquest in 1066, a cluster of ten families whose sole purpose was to protect each other; the promise of support was known as a pledge; equivalent to a neighborhood in American society.

Wickersham Commission – established in 1929 and formally known as the National Commission on Law Observance and Enforcement, the commission published "Report on Lawlessness in Law Enforcement" in 1930, which detailed police misconduct in the forms of protracted questioning, threats and methods of intimidation, physical brutality, illegal detention, and refusal to allow suspects access to counsel.

DOC'S WORDS OF WISDOM

The need for police in society can be found in a social contract giving up some freedoms for safety and protection from those who prey. Historically, policing has evolved. However, the problems of the past remain ever present in its future.

INTRODUCTION

The role of police in American society will be discussed at length throughout this text. However, it is important to understand the history of policing before we can even begin to appreciate how far policing has come as a profession. Practitioners as well as students must understand that the future of policing is deeply entrenched in its past practices and the perceptions of citizens. If policing were a person, it would have been forgiven a hundred times over for its transgressions, but as an institution it continues to make the same mistakes no matter how progressive it appears to be.

The opening quote is quite clear; as a society we need police as part of a social contract, for without police and the criminal justice system the world in which we live would be in total chaos. Historically, American policing has not been the most desirable of professions and has been associated with corruption, political influence, racism, ineffectiveness, abuse of civil rights, and brutality. In fact, the nature of these incidents is deeply ingrained in the American psyche. In America, police are viewed with a cultural bias: one community believes that their police department does an excellent job, and minority communities view the police as being racially insensitive, and at times as an occupying army. This chapter provides a brief history of American policing, with emphasis on the evolving institution.

DEVIANCE AND CIVILIZATION

Tromanhauser (2003) argues that deviance is a characteristic of civilization and that if we were isolated on an island with no social interaction, there would be no need for police or the law (p. 82). In examining Tromanhauser's statement, we must be cognizant of the following:

1. The growth of societies and the human need to interact are foundations for deviant behavior.

2. As a result of deviant behavior, which is considered a violation of social norms and/or law, there is an inherent need for society to respond to such violations.

3. Hence, there has been the need for and development of a protective force, be it sentries who guarded the city's walls, night watchmen, sheriffs or town marshals, or, finally, law enforcement as we know it today.

BRITISH BEGINNINGS

The concept of policing grew out of the need for safety. There was no such animal as police until the British government began to organize in 1066 after the Norman Conquest. Policing was not a formal institution, but consisted of neighbors in clusters of ten families known as **tithings**, who had taken an oath to protect one another. The promise of support was known as a *pledge* (Holdsworth, 1922, pp. 13–15). Unlike today, there was no technology; if a crime occurred, members of the tithing would be alerted with what is known as a *hue and cry*. The **hue and cry** was nothing more than a series of loud shouts designed to alert others in the tithing that a crime had just occurred and that a neighbor needed assistance (Holdsworth, 1922, p. 294).

The next level of organization and enforcement involved grouping ten tithings into what is known as a *hundred*. The hundred, defined by the land mass sufficient to sustain one hundred families, was known as a **shire**, which is equivalent to what is known as a county in the United States. The English noblemen and landowners created the position of **shire reeve**, who was responsible for law violations within the shire (Fuller, 1661, pp. 60–65). The shire reeve is the equivalent of a modern sheriff.

URBAN POLICING

Urban policing became an issue as a direct result of the Industrial Revolution. With the growth of industry, employment opportunities moved from farms to factories. To follow the jobs, what had once been the rural populations of England now migrated to London and other urban areas. With the population boom came a host of urban issues. Two of the most common were, and today still are, poverty and crime (Hobsbawm, 1999; Monkkonen, 1981). In essence, there were not enough jobs for those who sought them.

As the cities of England grew in population, the system evolved into a watch system. The watch system was designed to protect the property and populous from crime and fire. The structure of the watch system was that private citizens were organized to patrol city streets; they were the eyes and ears of the local constable. If a watchman witnessed a crime, he was to alert a constable and other watchmen with the hue and cry.

Reform of the watch system did not occur until the 1800s. The first major step into modern policing began with Sir Robert Peel in 1829 and legislation known as the **Metropolitan Police Act**. The reasoning behind

tithing

organized after the Norman Conquest in 1066, a cluster of ten families whose sole purpose was to protect each other; the promise of support was known as a pledge; equivalent to a neighborhood in American society.

hue and cry

an alarm system used by members of a tithing to alert neighbors that they needed help; most often associated with criminal activity or fire.

shire

a cluster of one hundred families or ten tithings; equivalent to a county in American society.

shire reeve

a position created by English noblemen and landowners; this person was responsible for law violations within the shire; equivalent of a modern sheriff.

Metropolitan Police Act

the first piece of legislation in modern policing; enacted in 1829, the law made police public servants and not private actors.

Peel's reform was that policing had become corrupt. In fact, the era before the *Peelian Reform* saw the rise of private police whose motive was purely profit, and thus the system became corrupted. The most noteworthy issue to come from **Sir Robert Peel** as it pertains to modern policing is that of crime prevention or deterrence through preventative patrols (Lentz & Chaires, 2007; Peak, 2006; Walker & Katz, 2005).

Sir Robert Peel

considered the father of modern policing, he was responsible for the Metropolitan Police Act; his most notable contribution was deterrence of crime through preventative patrols.

If we take a moment and reflect on the beginnings of policing, the elements of the systems are not much different from those of modern policing. The main difference is the use of technology. The tithing system could be considered a neighborhood or one block of a city street. The system of protection was the hue and cry. Today many neighborhoods in the United States participate in a neighborhood watch. Each neighborhood watch has a block captain. When there is suspicious activity, the neighbors are alerted by telephone. The goal is to obtain as much information as they can without intervening and relay that information to the police. The shire reeve is equivalent to our modern-day sheriff.

LOCAL POLICING IN AMERICA: THE 1800S

The American system of policing in the 1800s was very similar to that of the British. However, it also was different because the United States had a component in its culture that was unique: slavery. Walker and Katz (2005) provide the following hierarchy of law enforcement: sheriff, constable, watchmen—day/night, and finally slave patrol. As unique as the advent of the slave patrol was, it had its place in the southern states, with the purpose of quelling slave uprisings and recapturing runaways.

Although the Peelian Reform was introduced in 1829 and in theory policing in the United States was making strides toward professionalism, it is clear that there were major differences in each country. Miller (as cited in Carte & Carte, 1975), in comparing the origins of the London and New York City police departments, pointed out that each had to be defined in accord with public demands that the maintenance of order be limited by protection of civil liberties. London police were professional, applied the rule of law and due process, were impartial in their decision making, and were supported by the middle-class.

The first municipal police department in the United States was the New York City Police Department. An article in the *New York Times* dated January 27, 1895, outlines the progression of the police department, dating back to the 1600s, with the first police officer being called a *schout*. The schout never made an arrest but recommended punishment to the *burgomaster*, who was considered the mayor or chief magistrate. Beginning in 1665, the system made several changes from what was known as the "ancient Charlies," "leatherheads," and "marshals" to what we now know as police officers. In 1844, New York City established the first uniformed police department in the United States.

From an observer's standpoint, it would be logical to argue that a host of serious crimes was the catalyst for the growth of urban policing in the United States. New York and other major cities had a set of unique circumstances in that they had large numbers of immigrants who entered the United States, many of whom stayed in cities such as New York, San Francisco, and Boston. The immigrants came to the United States seeking opportunities they did not have in the European countries. Once again, the conditions for many were deplorable, including poverty, poor or no housing, and crime.

Monkkonen (1981) questions two hypotheses in relationship to the growth of American policing. One hypothesis is that the growth of American policing was in response to a rise in crime and civil disorder. The other is that the growth of policing was in response to the need of the elite in American society for the police to act as a buffer between them and what he describes as the dangerous class. The **dangerous class** is defined as the faceless in U.S. society—the paupers, tramps, and criminals—and is comprised of five groups: urban criminals, rural criminals, rural paupers, urban paupers, and tramps (p. 87). Monkkonen argues that either of these hypotheses could be correct except that U.S. cities seem to follow suit through a process described as **communication down the urban hierarchy**, a method that cities use to inform each other of advances. Smaller cities did not have the problems of New York or Boston, and yet they formed uniformed police departments. The argument is that the police uniform became the symbol of social control and order for local governments and that is why these smaller cities opted to create police departments (Greene, 1996; Maguire & Radosh, 1996).

That policing was a form of social control in its early origins can be seen in how it was influenced by rule of politicians and corrupted by the local political leadership. One example is the history and influence of **Tammany Hall** politics, the New York City "political machine" that always had a certain number of police jobs in exchange for political favors. Even in 1936 August Vollmer recognized that reform was almost nonexistent except for large police departments that had the ability to provide training. Vollmer (1971) argued that the poor quality of the personnel was the weakest link in American policing and described political influence as a burden (pp. 4–6).

dangerous class

the faceless in U.S. society—the paupers, tramps, and criminals—comprised of five groups: urban criminals, rural criminals, rural paupers, urban paupers, and tramps.

communication down the urban hierarchy

a method that cities use to inform each other of advances; in the history of American policing, used to describe the development of uniformed police departments in small cities even when there was no need for them at the time.

Tammany Hall

a part of the New York political machine, which held a certain number of police jobs in exchange for political favors.

PROFESSIONAL POLICING

Policing from the 1880s to today can be chronicled in many different ways. Germann, Day, and Galatti (1976) describe three hundred years of policing prior to 1978 as "operations that have ranged from the most sordid to the most splendid, and with practitioners whose capacity and character have spanned a continuum from the most incompetent and corrupt to the most brilliant and edifying" (p. 74).

The observations of Germann et al. (1976) and Vollmer (1971) in regard to professionalism help us to understand that policing does not happen in a vacuum independent of society. In fact, it is just the opposite: what has happened in America culturally has had a direct impact on the profession of policing. The history of modern policing can best be examined by looking at a host of commissions that have demanded change. The other form of oversight that needs to be examined in relationship to the history of policing is the landmark court cases that have mandated change and provided guidance.

Wickersham Commission, 1930

The Wickersham Commission was formed after a decade of criminal influence in policing that was directly related to the enactment of the Volstead Act of 1919 (Prohibition), followed by the Great Depression of 1929. It was during this time that organized crime rose to power, with tentacles that reached politicians, judges, and police in the form of payoffs and threats.

Wickersham Commission

established in 1929 and formally known as the National Commission on Law Observance and Enforcement, the commission published "Report on Law-lessness in Law Enforcement" in 1930, which detailed police misconduct in the forms of protracted questioning, threats and methods of intimidation, physical brutality, illegal detention, and refusal to allow suspects access to counsel.

The **Wickersham Commission**, formally known as the *National Commission on Law Observance and Enforcement*, was appointed by President Herbert Hoover on May 20, 1929. The commission, which completed its work in 1930, published fourteen reports on subjects such as prohibition laws; criminal statistics; prosecution; enforcement of deportation laws; child offenders in the federal system; criminal procedure; penal institutions, probation, and parole; crime and the foreign born; costs and causes of crime; and the police. Another report on the controversial Mooney-Billings case was submitted to the commission but not officially published. Most of the commission's reports had little impact except for one entitled "Report on Lawlessness in Law Enforcement." According to Walker and Boehm (1997), that report detailed police misconduct in the forms of protracted questioning, threats and methods of intimidation, physical brutality, illegal detention, and refusal to allow suspects access to counsel (p. 9).

Kerner Commission, 1967

The 1960s in the United States was a time of social change on all fronts. The generation we now know as *baby boomers* was on college campuses opposing the Vietnam War; then they were known as the hippie generation, draft dodgers, and the counterculture. Some were members of groups like the *Students for a Democratic Society (SDS)*, which initially promoted civil rights, voting rights, and urban reform, although they were most noted for their opposition to the Vietnam War. Students marched on college campuses, burned their draft cards, and participated in peaceful protests such as sit-ins; in some cases, groups such as the *Weather Underground* participated in acts of terrorism. Finally, illegal drugs such as marijuana, LSD, and heroin were introduced into college campuses. The theme of the day was "Make Love Not War!" (Barber, 2008; Leen, 1999).

The antiwar protests of the 1960s were marked by years of civil disobedience and many clashes with the police. One of the most violent clashes with police was during the 1968 Democratic Convention in Chicago. There were five days of riots with protesters attempting to march to the convention. Rioters and innocent bystanders were beaten by the police. The police action was televised around the world (Kush, 2004; Walker, 1968). The most haunting conflict of the time was the *Kent State shootings* in 1970. College students were protesting the Vietnam War, more specifically the U.S. bombing of Cambodia. Ohio National Guardsmen opened fire on the protesters, killing four unarmed students (Hensley, 1981; Rosinsky, 2008).

In the south, the civil rights movement was beginning. The movement officially began with the landmark decision in *Brown v. Board of Education of Topeka, Kansas,* in 1954, and a number of significant events during the years that followed forced the issue of equality: 1955, Rosa Parks refused to move to the back of the bus; 1957, Central High School in Little Rock, Arkansas, was integrated; 1960, in Greensborough, North Carolina, four black students peacefully staged a sit-in at the local Woolworth's lunch counter; 1963, in Birmingham, Alabama, police turned fire hoses and police dogs loose on peaceful protesters; 1963, at the March on Washington, Martin Luther King delivered his "I Have a Dream" speech; 1964, the Civil Rights Act was signed by President Lyndon Johnson; 1965, the Voting Rights Act was passed by Congress; 1965, the Watts race riots took place in Los Angeles, California; and in 1965, President Johnson signed Executive Order 1146, which was the beginning of affirmative action (Bullard & Bond, 1994; Dierenfield, 2008).

It is interesting that each of the movements in the United States moved in parallel ways and often supported one another. The media played a significant role in bringing these events to our living rooms. The Vietnam War was the lead story at 6:00 P.M., offering daily body counts of both the enemy and Americans. The civil rights movement also played out in the media. Although the protesters and leaders usually were peaceful and had taken a vow of nonviolence, their oppressors used violence as a tactic of fear to maintain control. There were bombings, assassinations, murders, and hangings—all of which were played out in the media for all the world to see.

The 1960s is often described as a time of turmoil in the United States. The protectors of the day, as they are today, were the police. America viewed police action that included beating students with batons, the use of tear gas to disperse protesters, and the use of police dogs and fire hoses on civil rights protesters. The bottom line is that the police action was less than professional, and often the police used excessive force. It is because of this that the police were seen as oppressors and not protectors of all in American society.

Kerner Commission

a commission established in 1967 to examine the causes of inner city riots, the two most violent of which were in Detroit and Newark. There were a total of twelve common complaints assigned to three levels of intensity; police practices were the number one complaint assigned to the first level.

The **Kerner Commission** was established by President Lyndon B. Johnson in 1967 to examine the causes of the inner city riots, the two most violent of which were in Detroit and Newark. The commission was to answer the questions: What happened? Why did the riots happen? and What could be done to prevent them in the future? The commission created a hierarchy of common complaints. There were a total of twelve complaints, with each complaint being assigned to one of the three different levels of intensity. Police practices were the number one complaint assigned to the first level of intensity.

The commission noted: "The abrasive relationship between the police and the minority communities has been a major—and explosive—source of grievance, tension and disorder. The blame must be shared by the total society" (Kerner Commission, 1968, p. 14). The real cause of the tension was the demands on police service as a result of a higher crime rate, aggressive patrol practices, and no effective mechanism for grievances to be heard because of poor police practices.

A summary of the commission's findings included a review of police operations and recommendations to eliminate a sense of insecurity within the community, provide a mechanism for complaints, develop policies to assist in decision making, recruit more Negro officers and promote them accordingly, and develop a "Community Service Officer Program" to attract Negroes to the profession of policing (Kerner Commission, 1968, p. 15). The commission's recommendations are important because these same issues, as well as others, seem to be central to the lack of professionalism that dates back to the beginning of the profession.

FBI Counterintelligence Program (COINTELPRO), 1956–1971

The FBI's COINTELPRO was charged with targeting foreign intelligence agencies operating in the United States during the Cold War. However, the mission changed in the 1960s and it became the political police in the United States. The FBI mounted counterintelligence programs to disrupt, misdirect, discredit, or otherwise neutralize the civil rights, black liberation, Puerto Rican independence, antiwar, and student movements of the 1960s (Churchill and Vander Wall, p. x). Churchill and Vander Wall (2002) show the actual letter sent by the FBI in 1964 in an attempt to get Martin Luther King to commit suicide (p. 99), other forged letters to activists and their supporters in an attempt to destroy their credibility and sway their followers, FBI-authored articles that were published in friendly media as if they were their own, and cartoon leaflets pitting one group against another (p. xi).

Many may wonder why some Americans are leery of the Patriot Act, which gives law enforcement unfettered access to personal records, allows wire tapping without warrants, and gives police the ability to declare individuals an *enemy combatant of the state* and place them in jail without due process. It is because of the aforementioned acts. The FBI has been a strong organization with a reputation of being professional and above reproach, but conduct such as this has made the average American question the professionalism of the organization.

Law Enforcement Assistance Administration (LEAA), 1968

In response to the Kerner Commission's findings, the **Law Enforcement Assistance Administration (LEAA)** was formed. The LEAA was funded due to the passage of the Omnibus Crime Control Act of 1968. The goal of the LEAA was to professionalize policing by offering monies for education, training of local officers, bomb squads, pilot programs studying alternatives to incarceration, drug treatment programs, and state court organization. The LEAA was disbanded in 1981 and was the forerunner to the National Institute of Justice.

Knapp Commission Report on Police Corruption (Knapp Commission), 1970

The **Knapp Commission** was established by Mayor John Lindsay to investigate corruption within the New York City Police Department (NYPD).

Law Enforcement Assistance Administration (LEAA)

an organization established to professionalize policing by offering monies for education, training of local officers, bomb squads, pilot programs studying alternatives to incarceration, drug treatment programs, and state court organization.

Knapp Commission

a commission established in the 1970s to investigate widespread corruption in the New York City Police Department in response to a *New York Times* article.

The commission was established in response to a 1970s *New York Times* article that detailed widespread corruption within the NYPD. The article, entitled "Graft Paid to Police Here Said to Run into the Millions," presented a survey in which officers spoke to the *Times* with complete anonymity and provided chilling accounts of the corrupt practices. Burnham (1970) states the officers discussed how they paid to work good patrol zones on Sunday and how businesspeople and criminals alike paid police to operate. Those who had paid the police included builders, numbers operators, and liquor dealers; the pay totaled in the millions (pp. 1, 18).

Upon completion of a two and one-half year investigation, the commission determined that corruption within the agency was widespread. They noted that there were two types of officers: *meat-eaters* and *grass-eaters*. The **meat-eaters** were officers who took large sums of money without hesitation and pushed for the big dollars. The **grass-eaters**, who were more prevalent and were considered a scourge of the department, were officers who would take small amounts of money all the time. The commission noted that the grass-eaters made corruption "respectable" (Knapp Commission, 1972, p. 4). Such conduct destroys both public confidence and morale within the organization.

Another concept discussed by the commission was the **rotten apple theory**. Simply put, if the department acknowledged that an officer was corrupt, then that officer would have to be removed from fellow officers and categorized, which would cause the organization to look at all the other officers who associated with the "rotten apple." The commission noted that the NYPD ignored the existence of corruption in the department because there was no way to determine how many of a rotten apple's associates had become tainted, and trying to do so would destroy or tarnish the agency's public image (Knapp Commission, 1972, pp. 6–7).

Failure of the FBI Crime Lab, 1989

The FBI Crime Lab was known for its excellent work. In fact, many agencies sent their evidence to the FBI Crime Lab for processing because of the quality of work. However, in 1989, the Crime Lab was given notice that there were problems with its lead bullet, DNA, and explosives analyses (Bergman & Berman-Barrett, 2008; Pyrek, 2007). Beecher-Monas (2007) notes that an investigation into the FBI Crime Lab revealed substandard work, inadequate training of lab technicians, rendered opinions that exceeded the findings, testimony tailored to meet the needs of cases, and a lack of objectivity in report preparation (p. 102). This type of behavior is far from professional.

---

meat-eaters

a term developed by the Knapp Commission to describe officers who took large sums of money without hesitation and pushed for the big dollars.

grass-eaters

a term developed by the Knapp Commission to describe officers who took small amounts of money and made corruption respectable within the ranks of the New York City Police Department.

rotten apple theory

a theory that corrupt officers will infect the rest of those they associate with if they are not removed.

O'Hara (2005) argues that such findings must be classified as an institutional failure and that such organizations draw a curtain around themselves, refusing to allow outsiders to view or challenge their conduct. Ultimately this behavior is supported by professional privilege and political power (p. 149). However, this privilege is far from professional and should be considered destructive entitlement.

Thomas (2008) describes destructive entitlement as a belief that we as individuals should be treated fairly and with a sense of justice. This expectation is understood in a host of relationships, including husband-wife, employer-employee, government-citizen, teacher-student, and doctor-patient relationships, to name a few (p. 177). Because of the FBI's reputation, the organization was entitled to respect, and it was assumed they would be fair and just; however, because they failed to meet the professional standards, they have lost their credibility.

Independent Commission on the Los Angeles Police Department (Christopher Commission), 1991

The **Christopher Commission** was established in 1991 after the beating of Rodney King by the Los Angeles Police Department and the Los Angeles riots. The commission was charged with investigating the agency's failure to supervise in regard to complaints of excessive force, the culture and officer attitudes toward the minority community, the inability of the community to redress complaints against officers, and the lack of leadership, both sworn and civilian.

Christopher Commission

a commission established in 1991 to investigate the Los Angeles Police Department after the beating of Rodney King and the Los Angeles riots.

The commission completed a survey regarding ethnic bias and excessive force that included 960 officers. The results were as follows:

- 24.5% of the 650 officers who responded agreed that racial bias (prejudice) on the part of officers toward minority citizens contributes to a negative interaction between police and the community; 55.4% disagreed; and 20.1% had no opinion.

- 27.6% of the respondents agreed that an officer's prejudice toward a suspect's race may lead to excessive force; 57.3% disagreed; and 15% had no opinion (City of Los Angeles, p. 69).

- The commission also noted that this issue dates back some twenty-five years to the 1965 Los Angeles riots. The McCone Commission in 1965 observed that there were many reasons for the riots; however, police brutality in the African American community was a recurring theme and one of the causes. In 1965, the McCone Commission recommended open communication between the African American community and the police.

Commission to Investigate Allegations of Police Corruption and Anti-Corruption Procedures of the Police Department (Mollen Commission), 1992

The **Mollen Commission** was established in 1992 by Mayor David Dinkins to investigate corruption in the New York City Police Department. Mayor Dinkins authorized the commission with three mandates: to investigate the extent and nature of corruption within the NYPD; to evaluate the department's ability to detect and prevent corruption; and to recommend changes to enhance the department's effectiveness. The commission's investigation, which lasted twenty-two months, stated that corruption extended far beyond the corrupt cop. The commission discovered that corruption was allowed to exist because of officers' fears of being labeled a rat and of the potential consequences for being honest, and because supervisors were willfully blind, fearing scandal more than the acts of corruption (City of New York, 1994, p. 14).

The commission also noted that there had been a change in the type of corruption within the ranks of the NYPD. The new generation of corrupt officer was influenced by the drug trade and the explosion of crack cocaine. Those who participated were no longer grass-eaters but had become the meat-eaters and were involved in brutality, sale and distribution of narcotics, and robbery of their competition. The commission described the officers as working in **crews** ranging from five to ten members each. These crews participated in acts of violence that were used to earn respect, extort profit, relieve frustration, and administer street justice (City of New York, 1994, p. 34).

The commission's investigation of violence was quite interesting because the commission opted to address this subject, whereas other commissions such as the Knapp Commission had focused solely on corruption. The Mollen Commission found that brutality was common, although difficult to quantify, in large drug-infested minority communities. Even honest officers were reluctant to report or discuss brutality; officers were more open when it came to the issue of corruption (City of New York, 1994, p. 58).

The issues presented in the Mollen Commission's report mirror those in the 1972 Knapp Commission report, with one distinct difference: the type of corruption in the NYPD had changed to include crews who were now the major players/meat-eaters, as opposed to grass-eaters. This change meant that the NYPD had become an agency of good cops with a few bad apples. In response to the Mollen Commission findings, it was recommended that the city of New York establish a permanent independent commission to oversee corruption in the

NYPD. On February 27, 1995, Mayor Rudolph Giuliani established the Commission to Combat Police Corruption.

Rampart Scandal (LAPD), 2000

The **Rampart Scandal** was investigated by the Rampart Independent Review Committee. This committee was sanctioned by the Los Angeles Board of Police Commissioners to investigate the operations, policies, and procedures of the Los Angeles Police Department as a result of the Rampart Scandal. The investigation was an examination of an antigang unit known as the Community Resources Against Street Hoodlums (CRASH). CRASH was very successful in reducing violent crime. The officers were given great latitude in order to accomplish this goal, but doing so cost the LAPD due to a host of scandals that shook not only the law enforcement community but also the citizens they served. The bottom line is that there was no trust because of the unit's actions.

The behaviors of the officers in CRASH were exactly the same as those investigated by the Mollen Commission in New York City five years earlier. After the Christopher Commission's report, the LAPD had set out to change from what they described as the professional police model to the community policing model. The **professional police model** is defined by the LAPD as being focused on crime fighting with minimal contact with the public (Rampart Independent Review Panel, 2000, p. 7). The transition to community policing, however, never took place. The administration was never sold on the concept and never made it an agency priority. As a result, it was business as usual, with the community advising that the LAPD had never utilized community resources to create partnerships. The most notable observation regarding management was that they managed the department from the top down, rather than promoting collaborative partnerships and problem solving (p. 7).

Because the LAPD's style of policing had never changed and CRASH was given great latitude, a particular type of officer and culture had been bred. Three separate incidents brought CRASH officers to the forefront: a bank robbery committed by Officer David Mack; the theft of narcotics from an evidence locker by Officer Rafael Perez; and allegations of excessive force by Officer Brian Hewitt, as well as other members of the unit (Rampart Independent Review Panel, 2000, p. 44).

The Rampart Independent Review Panel had a host of findings, but the one that stands out most is number three, which focused on the agency's relationship with the community. In fact, the committee noted: "LAPD's failure to treat communities as full partners in law enforcement is

Rampart Scandal (LAPD)

an investigation in 2000 of an antigang unit known as the Community Resources Against Street Hoodlums (CRASH), which was very successful in reducing violent crime but which also prompted several scandals.

professional police model

defined by the LAPD as a model of policing that is focused on crime fighting with minimal contact with the public.

related to its failure to treat its officers as partners" (Rampart Independent Review Panel, 2000, p. 99).

Movement Toward Professional Policing

Vollmer (1971) argued that policing needed to become professional. Today the standards are higher and more stringent than ever. The selection process is arduous, with many steps—each of which can lead to elimination from the process if a candidate does not meet the standard. Then there is the academy, which has a minimum of a 20% attrition rate, and finally the field training program. Yet the profession still has a host of issues (Ervin, Flores-Macias, Lee, & Taylor, 2002, p. 6). Each of the commissions discussed has examined the actions of officers in either the LAPD or NYPD, but the problems found are not limited to those departments; they are problems that are associated with the profession as a whole.

Educational standards, administrative oversight, policy manuals, and codes of ethics all contribute to the professional conduct of law enforcement officers. Policing conduct has another form of oversight as well. The courts have handed down a number of decisions that limit the power of the police officer and ensure that citizens receive due process. Law enforcement has faced a number of challenges since its inception in 1066 (see Figure 1-1).

COURT CASES ADDRESSING POLICE CONDUCT

Many court cases have addressed police conduct and have become the mainstay of a citizen's due process rights. The most famous of the cases is *Miranda v. Arizona,* which gave birth to the Miranda rights an officer must cite when a citizen is arrested. These historic cases are so numerous it would be impossible to discuss each one. What you will find here is a brief outline of selected cases that provide a historic timeline.

The mandates of the court demand a change in officer conduct, with ultimate goal being professionalism. The rules are the only thing that separates government from the criminal element, and without them there would be chaos. The need for such guidance and rules can be found in the findings of each of the aforementioned commissions.

- *Carroll v. United States,* 267 U.S. 132 (1925): created the automobile exception in warrantless searches of vehicles if the officer has probable cause.
- *Brown v. Mississippi,* 297 U.S. 278 (1936): using force to obtain a confession makes the confession inadmissible.

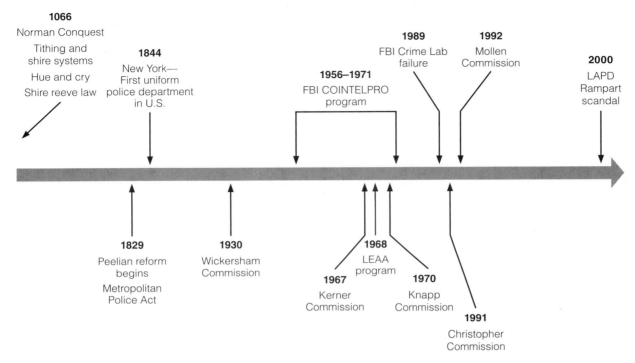

Figure 1-1   Historical Timeline of Police Beginnings and Professional Challenges

- *Mapp v. Ohio*, 367 U.S. 643 (1961): evidence obtained in an illegal search and seizure is inadmissible and a violation of the Fourth Amendment.
- *Escobedo v. Illinois*, 378 U.S. 478 (1964): Sixth Amendment's guarantee of a defendant's right to assistance of counsel while in custody. Any statement obtained after the request is inadmissible.
- *Miranda v. Arizona*, 384 U.S. 346 (1966): while in police custody, a person must be read the Miranda warnings and waive the right to an attorney before questioning can begin.
- *Katz v. United States*, 389 U.S. 347 (1967): provided that police must have a warrant to wiretap a phone booth.
- *Terry v. Ohio*, 392 U.S. 1 (1968): authorized police to pat a suspect down for weapons with the burden of proof being less than probable cause.
- *Tennessee v. Garner*, 471 U.S. 1 (1985): abolished the long-standing fleeing felon rule and limited the use of deadly force to only situations in self-defense or the defense of others.

Such findings of courts are not meant to be punitive. They are at best guidelines and rules established to address the needs and concerns of the community. In addition, the courts develop what can best be described as a series of best practices for law enforcement. With that said, the term *professionalism in policing* has many different definitions; there are no clear-cut universal standards by which an agency or an officer can be judged.

Professional Standards for Police

The greatest failure of policing as a profession has been the failure to establish a universal set of standards or guidelines. Policing is a profession where an individual can still be hired with a high school diploma or GED, depending on the agency and its individual requirements. There are as many different definitions and standards of professionalism as there are jurisdictions and agencies in the United States. Baker (1995) supports this assertion and suggests that officer skills differ radically from state to state and often between adjoining jurisdictions within the same state because there is no universal standard (p. 1).

In 1979 this lack of consistency was addressed when four law enforcement associations decided to meet and develop a process to professionalize policing. The participants were the International Association of Chiefs of Police (IACP), the Police Executive Research Forum (PERF), the National Organization of Black Law Enforcement Executives (NOBLE), and the National Sheriffs Association (NSA). The end result of this collaboration was the **Commission on Accreditation for Law Enforcement Agencies (CALEA),** with the purpose of credentialing law enforcement agencies that meet CALEA's established standards (Baker, 1995; Medeiros, 1987). Even though CALEA was established in 1979, today it still has its detractors. McAllister (1987) observed that the most common argument against accreditation is that the standards mean nothing and they represent the lowest common denominator in policing.

CALEA is a nonprofit private organization that has established 924 standards for an agency to become accredited (Baker, 1995; CALEA, 2007). The goals of CALEA are to: strengthen crime prevention and control capabilities; formalize essential management procedures; establish fair and nondiscriminatory personnel practices; improve service delivery; solidify interagency cooperation and coordination; and increase community and staff confidence in the agency (retrieved November 2, 2008, from http://www.calea.org).

The concept of CALEA is excellent, but the organization has limitations in that it is unable to hand down meaningful sanctions against an

Commission on Accreditation for Law Enforcement Agencies (CALEA)

a credentialing body with the purpose of credentialing law enforcement agencies that meet CALEA's established standards.

officer or agency. This is because CALEA is not a governing body. If an agency loses its accreditation, it is still a police department and still provides service to the community. Only two bodies have the ability to provide meaningful sanctions. The first is the Justice Department, which can oversee an agency if it is found that the agency has consistently violated the civil rights of the community, and the other is usually the governing criminal justice body of the state in which the agency is located, which can strip officers of their standards if they are involved in criminal activity. This argument is supported by Kultgen (1988), who outlines five responsibilities of the professional corporation. The two that impact CALEA and its lack of enforcement ability are:

- *Standards of competence:* includes education, tests for admission to practice, and reviews to ensure that practitioners maintain expertise. A licensing agency needs the power to censure, penalize, fine, suspend, or revoke services.
- *Standards of conduct:* includes a code of professional behavior, rules, laws, and their enforcement. In order for an organization to support ethical practitioners against pressures to violate standards, it needs the power to sanction clients and employers who exert pressure.

CALEA has none of these powers that are required for enforcement.

Defining Professionalism

The larger question is: What makes an officer or agency professional? Is it educational standards and the requirement of a college degree? Is it academy training and a set of minimum training standards established by the state criminal justice governing body? Is it strict adherence to agency policies and procedures? Or is it the hiring standards established by the agency? Numerous attempts have been made to professionalize policing. After the reading you have done, what is your definition of a professional police officer? Or better yet, what makes an officer professional?

Professionalism in policing can be defined as the ethical conduct of officers who meet the challenges and the needs of the communities in which they serve. Kultgen (1988) offers that skill in interpersonal relationships varies based on the profession, that it is a moral obligation of every professional to be proficient, and that professionals should have a vision of the human condition and the personal welfare of those that they serve (pp. 356–357). Finally, Maister (1997) argues that real professionalism has little to do with education; rather, it is dedication and the desire to help (p. 17).

professionalism in policing

the ethical conduct of officers who meet the challenges and the needs of the communities in which they serve.

CONCLUSION

The beginning of modern policing dates back to 1066. In its earliest form, it was similar to what today is called a neighborhood watch, incorporating the tithing system and the hue and cry. Sir Robert Peel looked to professionalize police with the introduction of the Metropolitan Police Act and the use of preventative patrols as a deterrent; these remain as the foundations of modern policing today. However, even with the innovations of Sir Robert Peel, the one remaining constant has been the challenge of turning policing into a profession.

In the history of policing in America with its meager beginnings in Tammany Hall of New York, the many court cases that have established rules of conduct for police, the establishment of CALEA in 1979, and the LAPD Rampart Scandal of 2000, two issues have remained in the public purview: police behavior and the lack of professionalism. In regard to *professionalism,* the term has many different meanings; some argue that the lack of college degrees has created the problem, while others argue it has resulted from a lack of supervision and leadership. This text has defined *professionalism in policing* as the ethical conduct of officers who meet the challenges and the needs of the communities in which they serve. With this definition in mind, ask yourself: Who becomes the responsible party in creating a professional police organization? What tools become the binding forces in defining professionalism in policing?

The remainder of this text is designed to challenge you, the student, by examining the positive and negative aspects of the profession. The text offers a number of scenarios and case studies as food for thought. Reflect on the scenarios, and ask yourself: What would I do in this or a similar situation? Or better yet, ask: what is the ethical thing to do?

 ## DISCUSSION QUESTIONS

1. Describe an event in history, either recent or further in the past, that you believe had a significant impact on policing. What implications do this event and its resolution have on the future of law enforcement?

2. Why was the hue and cry important? Think of how that system has evolved with technology into the present system we use today. What type of "hue and cry" warning system can you imagine might develop with future technological advances?

3. Describe the two hypotheses discussed by Monkkonen and their relationship to the growth of American policing.

4. In the history of American policing, there have been a host of investigations related to police misconduct. Based on the recommendations of the various commissions, do you believe that policing has learned from its mistakes, or will there always be some form of aberrant behavior in policing? Defend your answer.

5. What is the difference in the definition of *professionalism in policing* as described by the Mollen and Christopher commissions and as defined in the text?

 ## RESEARCH TOPICS

Following are two topics that are central to this chapter. Choose one, and research the topic based on the instructions of your professor.

- *Professionalism in policing.* What measures would you institute to change the image of policing, while knowing that no matter what you do, there will always be some rotten apples hired, or the profession itself will always influence some behavior negatively. Defend your answer with research.

- *History of policing.* Policing has evolved over the years to meet the challenges of the public that it serves. Examine the history of policing, and determine if there is anything you would adopt from the past that would assist today in changing the public's perception of police. Defend your answer with research.

 ## BIBLIOGRAPHY

Baker, S. A. (1995). *Effects of law enforcement accreditation: Officer selection, promotion, and education.* Westport, CT: Praeger.

Ball, J. R. (2008). *Professionalism is for everyone: Five keys to being a true professional.* Reston, VA: The Goals Institute.

Barber, D. (2008). *A hard rain fell: SDS and why it failed.* Jackson: University Press of Mississippi.

Beecher-Monas, E. (2007). *Evaluating scientific evidence: An interdisciplinary framework for intellectual due process.* New York: Cambridge Press.

Berg, B. L. (1999). *Policing in modern society.* Boston: Butterworth-Heinemann.

Bergman, P., & Berman-Barrett, S. J. (2008). *The criminal law handbook: Know your rights, survive the system* (10th ed.). Berkeley: Nolo.

Brown v. Board of Education of Topeka, Kansas, 347 U.S. 483 (1954).

Brown v. Mississippi, 297 U.S. 278 (1936).

Bullard, S., & Bond, J. (1994). *Free at last: A history of the civil rights movement and those who died in the struggle.* New York: Oxford University Press.

Burnham, D. (1970, April 25). Graft paid to police here said to run into millions. *New York Times,* pp. A1, A18.

Burnham, D. (1971, May 2). 15 police trials begin tomorrow: City's largest corruption case in almost 20 years. *New York Times,* p. A1.

Carroll v. United States, 267 U.S. 132 (1925).

Carte, G. E., & Carte, E. H. (1975). *Police reform in the United States: The era of August Vollmer.* Berkeley: University of California Press.

Churchill, W., & Vander Wall, J. (2002). *The COINTELPRO papers: Documents from the FBI's secret wars against dissent in the United States.* Cambridge, MA: South End Press.

City of Los Angeles. (1991). *Independent commission on the Los Angeles police department.* Los Angeles: Author.

City of New York. (1994). *Commission to investigate allegations of police corruption and the anti-corruption procedures of the police department: Commission report.* New York: Author.

Commission on Accreditation for Law Enforcement Agencies (CALEA). (2007). *CALEA process and programs guide.* Fairfax, VA: Author.

Dierenfield, B. J. (2008). *Civil rights movement.* United Kingdom: Pearson Publishing.

Ervin, A., Flores-Macias, G., Lee, H., & Taylor, B. (2002). *Reducing attrition at the cadet training academy: Recommendations for the North Carolina highway patrol.* Durham, NC: Terry Sanford Institute of Public Policy.

Escobedo v. Illinois, 378 U.S. 478 (1964).

Fuller, T. (1661). *The history of the worthies of England: Vol. 1. Introduction to law enforcement and criminal justice.* London: J.W.G.L. and W. G.

Germann, A. C., Day, F. D., & Gallati, R. R. J. (1976). *Introduction to law enforcement and criminal justice.* Springfield, IL: Charles C. Thomas.

Greene, J. R. (1996). *The encyclopedia of police science.* Boca Raton, FL: CRC Press.

Hadden, S. M. (2001). *Slave patrols: Law and violence in Virginia and the Carolinas.* Cambridge, MA: Harvard University Press.

Hensley, T. (1981). *The Kent State incident: Impact of judicial process on public attitudes.* Westport, CT: Greenwood Press.

Hobsbawm, E. J. (1999). *The age of revolution 1789–1848.* New York: Random House.

Holdsworth, W. S. (1922). *A history of English law.* Boston: Little, Brown.

Katz v. United States, 389 U.S. 347 (1967).

Kerner Commission. (1968). *Report of the national advisory commission on civil disorders: Summary of report.* Washington, DC: Author.

Knapp Commission. (1972). *The Knapp commission report on police corruption.* New York: George Braziller.

Kultgen, J. (1988). *Ethics and professionalism.* Philadelphia: University of Pennsylvania Press.

Kush, F. (2004). *Battleground Chicago: The police and the 1968 Democratic National Convention.* Westport, CT: Praeger.

Leen, J. (1999, September 27). The Vietnam protests: When worlds collide. *Washington Post,* p. A7.

Lentz, S. A., & Chaires, R. H. (2007). The invention of Peel's principles: A study of policing "textbook" history. *Journal of Criminal Justice, 25*(1), 69–79.

Maguire, B., & Radosh, P. F. (1996). *The past, present, and future of American criminal justice* (2nd ed.). Lanham, MD: Rowman & Littlefield.

Maister, D. H. (1997). *True professionalism: The courage to care about your people, your clients, and your career.* New York: Simon & Schuster.

Mapp v. Ohio, 367 U.S. 643 (1961).

McAllister, B. (1987, March 17). Spurred by dramatic rise in lawsuits, police agencies warm to accreditation. *Washington Post,* p. A7.

Medeiros, K. H. (1987). Accreditation: Expectations met. *Police Chief, 54,* 14.

Miranda v. Arizona, 384 U.S. 346 (1966).

Monkkonen, E. H. (1981). *Police in urban America, 1860–1920.* New York: Cambridge Univertsity Press.

New York police history. Growth of the department and its present proportions. Its origin the single Schout. The "ancient Charlies" and the "leatherheads"— The London system tried—reorganization of 1870. (1895, January 27). *New York Times,* retrieved October 17, 2008, from http://query.nytimes.com/mem/archive-free/pdf?

O'Hara, P. (2005). *Why law enforcement organizations fail: Mapping the organizational fault lines in policing.* Durham, NC: Carolina Academic Press.

Peak, K. J. (2006). *Policing America: Methods, issues, challenges* (5th ed.). Upper Saddle River, NJ: Pearson/Prentice Hall.

Pyrek, K. (2007). *Forensic science under siege: The challenges of forensic laboratories and the medico-legal death investigation system.* Burlington, MA: Elsevier Academic Press.

Rampart Independent Review Panel. (2000). *A report to the Los Angeles Board of Police Commissioners concerning the operations, policies, and procedures of the Los Angeles police in the wake of the Rampart scandal: Executive summary.* Los Angeles: Author.

Rosinsky, N. M. (2008). *The Kent State shooting: We the people.* Mankato, MN: Compass Point Books.

Tennessee v. Garner, 471 U.S. 1 (1985).

Terry v. Ohio, 392 U.S. 1 (1968).

Thomas, D. J. (2008). Culture and the hostage negotiation process. *Law Enforcement Executive Forum, 8*(6), 169–184.

Tromanhauser, E. (2003). Comments and reflections on forty years in the American criminal justice system. In I. A. Ross & S. C Richards (Eds.), *Convict criminology* (pp. 81–94). Belmont, CA: Thomson/Wadsworth.

Vollmer, A. (1971). *The police and modern society.* Montclair, NJ: Patterson Smith.

Walker, D. (1968). *Rights in conflict: The violent confrontation of demonstrators and police in the parks and streets of Chicago during the week of the Democratic National Convention of 1968.* Washington, DC: U.S. National Commission on the Causes and Prevention of Violence.

Walker, S., & Boehm, R. (1997). *Records of the Wickersham Commission on law observance and enforcement. Part 1: Records of the committee on official lawlessness.* Bethesda, MD: University Publications of America.

Walker, S., & Katz, C. M. (2005). *The police in America: An introduction* (5th ed.). New York: McGraw Hill.

CHAPTER 2

ETHICS

OBJECTIVES

After completing this chapter, the student will be able to:

- Define the terms *ethics, meta-ethics, normative ethics,* and *applied ethics.*
- Describe the relationship between discretion and unethical behavior.
- Explain the conflict that exists between ethics and law.
- Discuss the term *integrity* and its importance in policing.
- Discuss the importance of organizational ethics in controlling police behavior.
- Describe the five typologies associated with police brutality.
- Discuss Kohlberg's theory of moral development.
- Describe the internal affairs process and the role of the *Garrity* decision.

KEY TERMS

applied ethics – a branch of ethics that attempts to answer practical ethical questions, meaning issues to which the answer is an action. The common professional fields that are most often researched are: business, education, the media, science and technology, human genome projects, medicine, police, the law, and the environment.

domestic violence – in American culture, violence in the home that, until the mid-1980s, was considered a personal issue and a misdemeanor.

early warning systems – a data-based management tool used to identify problem officers before their conduct gets out of control.

ethics – the philosophical study of morality or, more specifically, the study of what is morally right, wrong, good, bad, obligatory, and permissible.

Garrity v. New Jersey – 1967 legal case (385 U.S. 493) providing that an officer must cooperate with an administrative investigation; however, information provided to Internal Affairs during the investigation cannot be used against the officer in a criminal investigation.

honor killing – in Muslim culture, an act of murder to defend the honor of the family, usually by a father who kills his daughter because her honor has been infringed upon.

integrity – the basis of trust; the one quality that cannot be acquired, but must be earned.

Law Enforcement Code of Ethics – an ethical code developed in 1956 and revised in 1989 that exemplifies the philosophical aspects of policing.

meta-ethics – a branch of ethics that asks the bigger questions; it is seen as evaluating specific claims and arguments made by the other forms of ethics. Philosophers theorize with a focus not on what we should do but on the status of ethical theories.

normative ethics – a branch of ethics that attempts to arrive at conclusions regarding moral standards or, in essence, what is right and wrong.

organizational ethics – those principles and value systems that have been established by an agency's administration and to which agency employees are expected to strictly adhere.

progressive discipline – officers who violate a department policy may be counseled for first violations, and then receive progressively strict discipline if violations persist, until possible termination.

racially biased policing – occurs when law enforcement inappropriately considers race or ethnicity in deciding with whom and how to intervene in an enforcement capacity.

DOC'S WORDS OF WISDOM

Ethics is the foundation of a law enforcement officer's convictions. To violate the Law Enforcement Code of Ethics is to violate the public's trust and the kinship of the profession.

INTRODUCTION

Before you begin to examine this chapter, take a moment to reflect on what you believe ethics are and how they relate to the profession of policing. Ethics is the cornerstone of policing, and there is an expectation by the public that law enforcement officers will act in an ethical manner. Champion (2001) equates immoral behavior with police misconduct, asserting that it is illegal, immoral, or both (p. 3).

As discussed in Chapter 1, a number of issues have affected the public perception of police over the years. The image of policing has been tarnished by acts of poor judgment, theft, bribery, brutality, drug dealing, protection, gang affiliation, and even acts of murder. The end result of these acts means that the public trust is no longer automatic. In fact, this lack of trust is especially apparent in minority communities and among the poor and disenfranchised, as well as the young (Bradley, 1998; Palmiotto, 2001; Reisig, 2002).

POLICE MISCONDUCT

Champion (2001) argues that police misconduct is a result of the abuse of police discretion. The concept of discretion is hampered by police officers' roles in the communities in which they serve (Goldstein, 1977; Keeling, 1999; Wilson, 1968). Police misconduct is associated with many violations that can range from violations of departmental policy to those as serious as murder. Some of these acts are drinking on duty, leaving a duty post, sex on duty, brutality, bribes, tampering with evidence, illegal searches and/or seizure, false arrest, theft, robbery, and murder. Klockars, Ivkovich, Harber, and Haberfeld (2000) argue that policing is a discretionary profession with much of the business conducted in private, providing opportunities for misconduct for those who so choose (p. 2). Such encounters/opportunities challenge the officer's human nature.

Schmalleger (2005) provides a ranking order of the different forms of misconduct from the lowest to highest: receiving gratuities such as a free cup of coffee; playing favorites, including selective enforcement of the law; accepting minor bribes; considering oneself as being above inconvenient laws such as speeding or smoking marijuana; role malfeasance protection of crooked cops or destruction of evidence; major bribes; property crimes; criminal enterprises such as the resale of confiscated drugs; denial of civil rights and circumventing constitutional guarantees; and the commission of violent crimes (p. 330). Kleinig (1996) argues that crossing the line once, such as accepting a free cup of coffee, opens the door for more serious forms of misconduct (p. 180).

No matter how we define or characterize forms of misconduct, the final question regarding an officer's conduct or behavior can be summed up in one word: *ethics*. The litmus test is: Was the officer's conduct ethical? Although there is a common belief that police behavior is universal, however, nothing could be further from the truth. This is supported by the examinations of the Los Angeles Police Department and the New York City Police Department discussed in Chapter 1; every few years, the same issue is being investigated. The one constant that stands out is: no matter how many measures are put in place, there is always a subculture that allows misconduct.

WHAT IS ETHICS?

ethics

the philosophical study of morality or, more specifically, the study of what is morally right, wrong, good, bad, obligatory, and permissible.

Williams and Arrigo (2008) define **ethics** as the philosophical study of morality. More specifically, ethics can be described as the study of what is morally right, wrong, good, bad, obligatory, and permissible. Ethics is not just a study of morality; it also attempts to evaluate moral beliefs, principles, and practices and to state what should or should not be done in light of these evaluations (p. 5). The key to this definition is that it is philosophical and does not take into account the operational definition of ethics. In law enforcement, we have the *Law Enforcement Code of Ethics*, which exemplifies the philosophical aspects of policing.

Law Enforcement Code of Ethics

an ethical code developed in 1956 and revised in 1989 that exemplifies the philosophical aspects of policing.

Most officers are introduced to the **Law Enforcement Code of Ethics** upon entering the academy (see Figure 2-1). Many of the recruit classes are required to recite the code each day before class begins. The Code of Ethics was developed in 1956 by the Peace Officers Research Association of California in conjunction with Dr. Douglas M. Kelly of Berkeley's School of Criminology. The International Association of Chiefs of Police (IACP) reviewed and finalized revisions to the Code of Ethics at the IACP conference in Louisville, Kentucky, on October 17, 1989. In October 1991, IACP members unanimously voted to adopt the new code (see Figure 2-1). Read the code and reflect on the values that it prescribes. Are there any operational values in the code? Does it offer the difference between right and wrong, good and bad, the obligatory and the permissible?

Law Enforcement Code of Ethics

As a law enforcement officer, my fundamental duty is to serve the community; to safeguard lives and property; to protect the innocent against deception, the weak against oppression or intimidation and the peaceful against violence or disorder; and to respect the constitutional rights of all to liberty, equality and justice.

I will keep my private life unsullied as an example to all and will behave in a manner that does not bring discredit to me or to my agency. I will maintain courageous calm in the face of danger, scorn or ridicule; develop self-restraint; and be constantly mindful of the welfare of others. Honest in thought and deed both in my personal and official life, I will be exemplary in obeying the law and the regulations of my department. Whatever I see or hear of a confidential nature or that is confided to me in my official capacity will be kept ever secret unless revelation is necessary in the performance of my duty.

I will never act officiously or permit personal feelings, prejudices, political beliefs, aspirations, animosities or friendships to influence my decisions. With no compromise for crime and with relentless prosecution of criminals, I will enforce the law courteously and appropriately without fear or favor, malice or ill will, never employing unnecessary force or violence and never accepting gratuities.

I recognize the badge of my office as a symbol of public faith, and I accept it as a public trust to be held so long as I am true to the ethics of police service. I will never engage in acts of corruption or bribery, nor will I condone such acts by other police officers. I will cooperate with all legally authorized agencies and their representatives in the pursuit of justice. I know that I alone am responsible for my own standard of professional performance and will take every reasonable opportunity to enhance and improve my level of knowledge and competence.

I will constantly strive to achieve these objectives and ideals, dedicating myself before God to my chosen profession . . . law enforcement.

Figure 2-1   Law Enforcement Code of Ethics

TYPES OF ETHICS

There are three general categories of ethics: meta-ethics, normative ethics, and applied ethics.

Meta-Ethics

Meta-ethics asks the bigger questions; it evaluates specific claims and arguments made by the other forms of ethics. Philosophers theorize with the focus not on what we should do but on the status of ethical theories (Attfield, 1995; Warburton, 1999; Williams & Aggrio, 2008). Meta-ethics asks questions such as:

- How do we develop our moral principles?
- What is the scope of morality?
- Do we have a choice in our actions and decisions, or are they beyond our control?

meta-ethics

a branch of ethics that asks the bigger questions; it is seen as evaluating specific claims and arguments made by the other forms of ethics. Philosophers theorize with a focus not on what we should do but on the status of ethical theories.

Normative Ethics

Normative ethics attempts to arrive at conclusions regarding moral standards or, in essence, what is right and wrong. Kagan (1998) offers that normative ethics asks a number of questions that begin with: How? Such assessments, however, are greatly influenced by a host of other value systems, including those related to culture, ethnicity, gender, religion, community standards, and professions. One example is the difference between American and Muslim cultures in regard to violence against women.

- *Muslim culture:* One crime that has recently come to the forefront is known as *honor killing*. **Honor killing** is an act of murder, usually by the father, where he kills his daughter to defend the honor of his family. In Muslim culture, infringement of a daughter's honor is the greatest humiliation. Such acts include failure to wear a headscarf, having non-Muslim boyfriends, refusing to marry those who have been selected by the family in an arranged marriage, and infidelity (Goodwin, 2003; Mayell, 2002; Stillwell, 2008).

- *American culture:* In American culture, there is no correlation. Although American culture honors children and family disagreements arise regarding dating, premarital sex, teen pregnancy, whom one might marry, and divorce, rarely do these disagreements end in murder. However, in America, there is one act of violence against women that has reached epidemic proportions over the years, domestic violence. Keep in mind that American laws have evolved over the years. From the 1950s through the mid-1980s, **domestic violence** was considered a personal issue or family matter. Officers could not make an arrest because it was deemed a simple misdemeanor and the offense did not occur in the officer's presence. Cavanaugh, Gladstone, and Teasley (2002) report that nearly two million women are assaulted annually by a current or former male partner (p. 7).

The primary difference between the two cultures is religion. From an outsider's point of view, who or which is correct? For police, their actions are influenced by the same variables as those found in normative ethics, with the questions being: How should I handle a call for service? What should I do? In the search for answers, we have to examine the category of applied ethics.

Applied Ethics

Applied ethics attempts to answer practical ethical questions, meaning issues to which the answer is an action (Almond, 1999; Spurgeon Hall,

---

normative ethics

a branch of ethics that attempts to arrive at conclusions regarding moral standards or, in essence, what is right and wrong.

honor killing

in Muslim culture, an act of murder to defend the honor of the family, usually by a father who kills his daughter because her honor has been infringed upon.

domestic violence

in American culture, violence in the home that, until the mid-1980s, was considered a personal issue and a misdemeanor.

applied ethics

a branch of ethics that attempts to answer practical ethical questions, meaning issues to which the answer is an action. The common professional fields that are most often researched are: business, education, the media, science and technology, human genome projects, medicine, police, the law, and the environment.

Dennis, & Chipman, 2000). The common professional fields that are most often researched are: business, education, the media, science and technology, human genome projects, medicine, police, the law, and the environment. These topics have been hotly debated in American society. Much of the debate has centered on personal beliefs of what is right or wrong. Like normative ethics, belief systems in applied ethics are influenced by one's religion, peers, profession, ethnicity, race, gender, community standards, and profession. It is important to understand that we do not live in a vacuum; each of these influences has a great impact on how we as individuals view the world. For example, one of the greatest debates in the United States is about abortion. Before moving on, take a moment and reflect on these questions: What are your personal views on abortion? Why do you hold these views?

For police, answers to questions about duty and the discretionary decisions they make can be found in applied ethics. As a profession, law enforcement has a code of ethics (see Figure 2-1); however, these standards are philosophical at best. The concept of policing is that officers should do what is best for society by performing their duties void of bias. This argument, supported by Almond (1999), is based on the idea that applied ethics is closely associated with utilitarianism; that is, actions based on such ethics go beyond self-interest and are considered doing what is good for most of society (p. 7).

Situations that raise questions regarding police conduct and abuse include: high-speed pursuits where innocent bystanders are killed; the shooting of unarmed suspects; the death of a suspect that occurs while the suspect is in custody or during the arrest process; and arrests that the public may view as questionable. It is important to note: "In policing it is not the end result. It is the road that an officer takes to get the end result that he/she will be judged by. Scrutiny begins with your peers; your agency's chain of command; the prosecutor's office; the courts; and finally a jury which makes the final decision regarding your case" (Thomas, 2003).

From a moral standpoint, we believe that certain things are morally and ethically wrong, such as lying and taking the life of another human being. Yet, these are situations that officers may face during the course of their career. From a practical standpoint, do you believe that it is acceptable to lie to a suspect to get a confession? Under what circumstances would you lie to get a confession? In such a case, does the end justify the means? Although many of us believe that lying to anyone is wrong, you may find that it is a necessary evil in policing. In fact, such actions were supported by the U.S. Supreme Court in *Frazier v. Cupp*, 394 U.S. 731 (1969). In this case, the court ruled that police could use deception to obtain a confession and its use was not considered coercive or illegal (394 U.S. 731, 739–740).

The dilemma that you may face after taking such an action, especially if you find that such behavior is acceptable, is this: What other questionable actions will you deem acceptable? What is to keep you from striking a suspect during questioning, or from beating a suspect who flees from you? As you attempt to answer these questions, consider the concept of the slippery slope.

Almond (1999) offers the concept of the slippery slope, meaning that once you begin down the slope of violating your ethical principles, you will not stop until you reach the bottom, which is impossible to define. The concept of deterrence is used in relationship to those who choose not to commit crimes. In the case of police who have violated every ethical standard of the profession, what happened to that sense of right and wrong, or what happened to their personal form of deterrence that made such behavior acceptable?

All of our lives we are told that it is wrong to kill another human being. In fact, this rule is the very fabric of America's Judeo-Christian background and can be found in the Ten Commandments. However, an American police officer may be faced with taking another's life if the situation dictates the use of deadly force. Prior to the landmark deadly force decision (*Tennessee v. Garner*, 1985), in most states the law of the land in regard to the use of deadly force was that an officer could shoot and kill a fleeing felon. The law did not differentiate between those who had committed violent felonies, such as robbery or murder, and those who had committed property crimes such as burglary or felony theft. Today, as was the case prior to 1985, the decision to use deadly force is one that is highly personal and discretionary, but now must be limited to self-defense or defense of others.

ETHICS VERSUS LAW

At times, the law and ethics are in conflict, as illustrated in Scenario 2-1. It is not safe to assume that laws are ethically and/or morally just. Spurgeon Hall, Dennis, and Chipman (2000) note that there are three differences in the moral institution and the legal institution of law: (1) Moral laws are thought to be universal, for example, those that proscribe murder; however, other laws, such as speed limit laws, vary from

SCENARIO 2-1: THE DISTURBANCE

You are on patrol and receive a call of a disturbance. Upon your arrival, the suspect is still there; in fact, he is standing over the victim with a knife drawn back over his head, preparing to stab the victim. It is clear that the victim was stabbed prior to your arrival as he is lying in a pool of blood and begging for his life. You order the suspect to drop the knife. Instead, he stops for a moment, looks at you in the eyes, and makes the following statement: "You will have to kill me before I stop. I caught this bastard in the bed with my 2-year-old and chased him. He has to die." Before you can say another word, the suspect turns to the victim, draws the knife back over his head, and starts a downward strike with the knife, attempting to stab the victim again. You shoot and kill the knife-wielding suspect to stop the attack.

Analysis and Reflection

From the standpoint of ethics and morals, several value systems are in conflict.

1. In our society, which is based on Judeo-Christian values and morals, it is considered immoral to kill another human being. For police, this conflict is often a point of contention, even in justifiable shootings.

2. Ethically you have taken a sworn oath to protect citizens within your jurisdiction, which when examined thoroughly means that you may have to take the life of another human being.

3. The suspect stated that the victim had just raped his 2-year-old daughter. If this is true, then how does this impact you morally and ethically? This is a true contradiction in that you had to kill a father who was protecting his child.

4. Were your actions ethical and moral? They are more ethical than moral because the law and your oath of office demand that you do the right thing, although therein lies the conflict.

After the scene is secure, you find the mother and she states that the victim was in the bed with their 2-year-old daughter. In fact, they had a party and the victim stated he was leaving. He then slipped into the children's bedroom and was raping the 2-year-old. Their 5-year-old son came and told both dad and mom what was going on; as a result, the suspect that you killed was protecting his family. Dad had caught the victim in the bed with his 2-year-old daughter.

state to state; (2) moral laws apply to more than our overt actions; they apply also to our inner dispositions and motives (p. 9); and (3) moral laws may be in conflict with civil law. Examples of this latter element in American history include:

- The *Dred Scott* (1856) decision determined that African Americans were not citizens of the United States, that a slave was personal property and should not be free, and that Congress was forbidden from outlawing slavery.

- The *Civil Rights Act of 1964* abolished discrimination and made the playing field level no matter who you were. African Americans no longer had to ride in the back of the bus, nor could they be denied service at a restaurant; they could use the same bathroom facilities and drinking fountains as their white counterparts.

- The *Voting Rights Act of 1965* forced southern states to abolish the laws that had been established to keep African Americans from voting, such as the poll tax, passing a written examination, and the use of trickery by having two distinct ballot boxes so that the votes could be discounted.

Each of these laws was enforced by law enforcement officers. In the 1800s, there were slave patrols in which local southern sheriffs were actively involved. Prior to the passage of the Civil Rights Act and the Voting Rights Act, police beat African Americans who engaged in nonviolent protests in the south because they wanted to be treated as equals. The question here is: Were these laws ethical or moral?

From a law enforcement officer's view, officers are doing the right thing by following the law even when it is unpopular. With this in mind, you can understand that what is considered an ethical action may be in conflict with one's moral values or loyalty.

QUALITIES OF POLICING VERSUS LEADERSHIP

The ideal personal qualities of a police officer are specified in the *Law Enforcement Code of Ethics* (see Figure 2-1). The Code of Ethics uses descriptive phrases such as: an unsullied personal life; honesty; courageousness; obeying the law; be void of personal feelings in an official capacity; courteous; trustworthiness; and protector. In reviewing several police Web pages, you can see that people with these personal characteristics are actively recruited. In fact, these qualities of an ideal officer are perhaps the qualities of an ideal actor in any profession.

Bennis (1989) describes the qualities of a leader, and there is little difference between those qualities and the qualities described in the Code of Ethics. In his discussion, Bennis defines **integrity** as the basis of trust, which is the foundation of policing and goes hand-in-hand with ethics (p. 41).

integrity

the basis of trust; the one quality that cannot be acquired, but must be earned.

Integrity is a necessary component in an officer's ethical arsenal, and it is the quality that is most often challenged when responding to calls for service. The challenges come in many forms: bribes; gratuities; sex; drugs; lack of control during an arrest; turning one's head while others abuse their authority; the temptation to plant evidence; falsifying of police reports; and scrutiny of the courts, internal affairs, peers, and media. In fact, integrity is all that officers may have when it comes to defending their actions. (See Scenario 2-2.)

SCENARIO 2-2: BURGLARY OF A DEPARTMENT STORE

You respond as backup to a burglary of a local department store. On your arrival, you find the first officer on the scene removing jeans and polo shirts and placing them in the trunk of his patrol car. He states: "They will never know; they will think that they were taken in the burglary. The insurance will pay for the loss. Come on, get some."

Analysis and Reflection

1. Can you honestly let this happen and do nothing?

2. What will happen if he is seen on the security tape taking the items and you do nothing?

3. More importantly, given his actions and your failure to act to his violations of the law and policy, how are you and he any different from the suspects you encounter daily?

4. If you turn the officer in, how will your peers respond? Will they embrace you as having done the right thing? Or will you be considered a "rat" and ostracized?

5. In this situation, you have two options: (a) turn in the suspect officer by contacting a supervisor and documenting your observations in a report; or (b) decide that you will be loyal to the suspect officer and not turn him in. Which will you choose, and why?

If you choose the second option, the suspect officer will trust you to support him in all his future decisions, no matter what. He will have your loyalty because your lack of action will create a criminal bond. By not acting, you will be guilty of violating the public trust, state law, department policy, and, more importantly, your principles.

ORGANIZATIONAL ETHICS

Many of you who are reading this text want to become a law enforcement officer. You will eventually choose an agency because of pay and benefits, and because of the opportunities the agency offers, or you will make a decision based on an agency's public persona or reputation. As you read this section, take a moment and reflect on the reputation of the agency that serves the community in which you live. It is important to understand that the public's perception is the reality in which that organization operates. Ethical problems in policing occur because they are supported by an organization that has chosen to look the other way or is tolerant of such actions (Kultgen, 1988; O'Hara, 2005).

Organizational ethics, the principles and value systems that are established by an agency's administration and to which agency employees are expected to strictly adhere, starts with the chief/sheriff and the message he or she sends to the troops of what will and will not be tolerated.

organizational ethics

those principles and value systems that have been established by an agency's administration and to which agency employees are expected to strictly adhere.

Braunstein (1998) argues that organizational culture encompasses the history of the organization, which has a direct influence on the future and the belief system of its members (p. 124).

After the Rodney King incident, the Christopher Commission was impaneled in 1991 to examine the practices of the Los Angeles Police Department (LAPD). The commission noted that former Assistant Chief Jesse Brewer blamed the excessive force problem in the LAPD on management's lack of attention to detail and accountability, beginning with the first-line supervisors and going up to the captains, and ultimately to the chief of police (City of Los Angeles, 1991, p. 9).

To understand how any police organization develops a culture that is unethical and/or permissive of questionable conduct, we must examine an agency's role players and their levels of responsibility. In addition, we also must examine the impact their decision making has on the agency's culture.

The *chief/sheriff* is the top administrator of a law enforcement organization. The people in this role are responsible for overseeing the daily operations of their organizations. They ensure that policies are followed and that their agency's actions are in concert with the needs of their community. Each community has different needs, so it is important for an administrator to identify these needs before taking an oath of office. The primary objective of any top administrator is consistency.

Top administrators are also responsible for any failure of policy that may occur. The public understands that sometimes officers will make mistakes and that occasionally an agency will hire a *rotten apple*. This is known as *public trust*. It is interesting to note that public trust will be defined differently by various segments of a community. In a community that is mostly minority and poor, there may be *public mistrust* because of the many abuses the community has experienced over the years.

Holmes (2000) argues that it is hardly surprising that many minority citizens distrust the justice system, just as many criminal justice agents distrust them (p. 343). The conflict theory of law maintains that crime control is an instrument used by powerful groups to regulate threats to their interests. Ultimately, the police function is to control the dangerous classes of immigrants, racial minorities, and the poor (Jackson, 1985; Liska, Chamlin, & Reed, 1985; Turk, 1969). This theory is supported by a host of issues and actions within the criminal justice system.

One issue that is presented as evidence of the conflict theory of law is the harsher penalties that are involved for the possession and use of crack cocaine as compared to powder cocaine. African Americans are more affected by these penalties than other groups, since crack has been the drug of choice within their communities. Possession of five grams of crack is a minimum five-year mandatory sentence, whereas for the same amount of powder cocaine, the mandatory sentence is one year (U.S. Department of Justice, 2002; Walker, 2006). The *U.S. Sentencing Commission's Sourcebook of Federal Sentencing Statistics* (U.S. Sentencing Commission, 2008) states that in 2007, 82% of the arrests for crack cocaine were African American and that the average length of imprisonment for crack cocaine was 121.5 months, in contrast to 84.7 months for powder cocaine. Minority communities look at these penalties as a form of racism within the system.

Harrison and Beck (2005) provide a startling view of racial disparity in their research findings. In 2004, 1.5 million people were incarcerated in local and state prisons. Of those incarcerated, 41% were African American, and yet African Americans comprise only 13% of the U.S. population (p. 8).

Racially biased policing is the term chosen by researchers Fridell et al. (2001), instead of *profiling*, as it is a comprehensive term that envelops all aspects of race and policing. **Racially biased policing** occurs when law enforcement inappropriately considers race or ethnicity in deciding with whom and how to intervene in an enforcement capacity. The research by Fridell et al. shows a disconnection between law enforcement officials' perception of the problem and the public's perception of the problem. Law enforcement executives believe that the issue is minor at best, while the minority community perceives the problem to be much worse (pp. 35–40).

To limit negative publicity and have a positive impact within the minority community, a successful administrator is expected to: maintain an open line of communication with the community; release all the facts upon completion of an investigation; if there is a finding of wrongdoing, acknowledge the action and apologize; prosecute officers who are found criminally liable; and terminate officers who are not found criminally liable for their actions but who have seriously violated departmental policy. These concepts are supported in a 2001 report published by the Rhode Island Select Commission on Race and Police-Community Relations, which addresses the need for partnerships and open doors for an exchange of dialogue. The commission was formed as a result of a friendly-fire incident where an off-duty officer of color was shot and killed by on-duty responding officers.

The *deputy chief/colonel/major* position is usually second in command of the organization. The role of people in this position is unique in that they support the agenda of their chief administrators and are really responsible for the day-to-day operations of an organization. This person is rarely seen publicly but is often described as the most important

racially biased policing

occurs when law enforcement inappropriately considers race or ethnicity in deciding with whom and how to intervene in an enforcement capacity.

individual in the administration because of the responsibilities of this position and the fact that this person is the chief/sheriff's most trusted advisor. Although the deputy chief/colonel/major has this responsibility, the chief/sheriff is the final decision maker and can interject himself or herself at any time.

At the *captain/lieutenant* level of supervision, the people in these positions are in direct contact with the personnel. In fact, they are responsible for all operations and support services. They may be in charge of patrol, detectives, narcotics, and neighborhood services; and they report directly to the deputy chief/colonel/major. In large agencies, a captain/lieutenant may be responsible for a precinct or district.

The captain/lieutenant is an interesting position because the officers look to this group of managers for support for their decisions. Often the position that a captain/lieutenant takes in regard to an officer's actions determines whether the administration is one that is for or against the officers. If the captain/lieutenant's decisions seem to be against the officers, the officers can develop an us-versus-them attitude toward the administration. Nevertheless, it is a problem when these administrators cannot separate themselves from the role of the street officer, since in fact they should be holding the officers accountable for their actions.

This position is uniquely autonomous and powerful in that many of the disciplinary matters are handled at this level and never make it to Internal Affairs or the chief's office (Brown, 1988). In fact, much of what happens in an organization, be it good or bad, never makes it to the chief's office. If a commander is a decision maker, the chief never hears about many issues, since law enforcement agencies are paramilitary and enforce a strict *chain of command.* Violating the "chain" can lead to disciplinary action. To be successful, however, a commander must be fair and equitable.

Sergeants are the first-line supervisor in all functions of an agency; however, they are most often associated with patrol and supervising patrol officers. The sergeant checks all the paperwork, handles simple citizen complaints, and evaluates officers' performances, but their most important task is to arrive at crime scenes and offer advice and support. They often assist in decision making. In this role, it is very difficult to differentiate the first-line supervisor from the role of an officer. This role is very similar to that of a captain/lieutenant, but with one major difference: the sergeant is much closer to the daily operation of the officers he or she supervises. This closeness fosters friendships, which often hinder the sergeant's ability to discipline the officers.

The *officer/deputy* is the final piece in the sworn organization. The group of officers is what the public sees on a daily basis. In fact, the officers are the only form of visible government after 5:00 P.M. (Crawford, 2008; Valverde, 2006). The public develops their opinion of the agency based on these officers' actions. In essence, the community's reality—their trust or mistrust—is a direct result of the police-citizen contacts made at this level.

Figure 2-2 shows the roles the various levels of leadership may play in promoting unethical behavior.

If we examine Scenarios 2-1 and 2-2 again, it is clear that the decisions made have an impact on the organization. If an agency has a permissive or forgiving policy, then officers will push the limits just to see what they can get away with. When an administrator fails to supervise and follow the prescribed disciplinary directives, he or she sets a precedent by which every other disciplinary decision will be judged. This lack of action or air of permissibility begs officers to question: How far can I travel down the slippery slope before I get caught? With that question in mind, review Scenario 2-3, see p. 40.

Many components comprise an agency's ethical culture. However, Paine (1994) asserts that ethics has everything to do with management; unethical practices require the cooperation of others and are the result of an agency's values and beliefs (p. 106).

PERSONAL ETHICS

Ethics is an intangible item that each one of us possesses and is intertwined with our other belief systems such as morals and values. Kohlberg

Leadership
- The organization is at odds with the community regarding officer misconduct.
- The leadership and organization lack integrity.
- The leadership has adopted a policy of refusing to discipline officers by minimizing their actions or defending them publicly.

+

First-line supervisors
- Not supported by command staff.
- Turn a blind eye to unethical behavior.
- Supervisors may participate, look to profit from the subordinates' actions, and will protect officers from citizens' complaints as well as run interference with the administrative inquiries.

Line officers
- There is no discipline by command staff for unethical behavior.
- Officers test waters by violating small policies.
- Once officers are sure that atmosphere is tolerant of unethical behavior, they move from small violations such as gratuities to accepting bribes, robbery, and extortion.

Figure 2-2   Formula for Unethical Behavior

SCENARIO 2-3: TRAFFIC STOP

You are on patrol and make a traffic stop on an out-of-town violator. As you approach the car, you ask for the driver's license, registration, and proof of insurance. You wait a moment, and the driver hands you all the correct paperwork. As you return to your patrol vehicle to write the citation, you discover a $50 bill between the license and registration. You believe the driver made a mistake, so once you are back at his vehicle, you ask him if the $50 bill is his, and he replies "No." You have a conversation about the $50, and he continues to deny that the $50 is his; in fact, he suggests that you keep it.

Because the driver denies any knowledge of the money, you believe that he is attempting to bribe you with the $50. You advise the driver that he can be arrested for bribery of a public official, which is a felony in your state. He continues to deny knowledge of the money. To resolve the matter, you tear the $50 bill into tiny pieces. You can see that the driver is very irate, but he cannot say anything because he has denied ownership of the $50. To complete the transaction, you throw the money into a public trash can that just happens to be where you are stopped. You then issue the driver the citation.

Analysis and Reflection (Part 1)

1. What do you believe the driver is attempting to do here?

2. Do you believe that he has done this in the past and walked away without receiving a citation?

3. What are the ramifications if you accept the $50?

4. What could possibly happen to you if he drives to the department to complain that you took the money?

Analysis and Reflection (Part 2)

1. What message were you trying to send to the driver?

2. Does he have any legal recourse against you at this time?

3. Did you handle this matter properly?

4. Did you become angry because the driver tried to bribe you?

5. Were your actions ethical?

6. Would it have been better to arrest the driver?

7. Will your actions be supported by the chief?

(1981) found that a person's ability to deal with moral issues is not formed all at once. Just as there are stages of growth in physical development, the ability to think morally also develops in stages. *Kohlberg's theory of moral development* has three stages: *preconventional,* which is often associated with a young child who learns the difference between right and wrong; *conventional,* when the child has reached the age of reasoning; and *post-conventional,* when the adult develops principles that define right/wrong and reward/punishment from a universal point of view (Kohlberg, 1981, pp. 17–22).

The analysis in Kohlberg's theory would lead one to believe that moral development and ethics stem from a process of maturation. So how does Kohlberg's theory apply to unethical police? If ethics is a process of maturation and learning, it would seem that police would be ethical, since they are bombarded with ethical principles from the time they enter the academy. In fact, during the interview process, a standard question is: Why do you want to be a police officer? The most common answers are:

1. I want to help people.
2. I see police as making a difference and I want to do that.
3. I want my family to be proud of me.
4. I believe in my community and want to contribute to it; what better way than by becoming a police officer?

When examining such responses from initial interviews, it is clear that at some point in some police officers' careers, there is a transition from the initial concept of helping and changing the world for the better to disillusionment and seeing their role as not having a positive impact, which opens up the thought processes to a host of possibilities: lack of experience, cynicism, disenchantment, change in career goals, apathy, and the unethical behavior in which some police become involved. Stevens (1999) concluded that an officer's value system or ethics appears to change over time (p. 7).

UNDERSTANDING BRUTALITY

In examining unethical behavior, there is no real profile for unethical police officers. In a survey of sixty-five police departments, Scrivner (1994) was able to categorize officers who are involved in brutality as: those at chronic risk; those who suffer from job-related tendencies; those who exhibit early career problems; those who are defined by a particular patrol style; and those who are plagued with a series of personal problems (pp. 11–14). In an analysis of these categories, it is clear that they may occur during different stages of an officer's career.

Since the problems may occur at any stage in an officer's career, police departments have developed what are known as early warning systems. **Early warning systems** are a data-based management tool used to identify problem officers before their conduct gets out of control (Rahtz, 2003; Walker, Alpert, & Kenney, 2001). Walker et al. note that this is a trend found in larger agencies servicing populations of 50,000 or more, and less prevalent in smaller agencies (pp. 1–2). The early warning system is but one tool of many and requires that management monitor and intervene with problem employees.

early warning systems

a data-based management tool used to identify problem officers before their conduct gets out of control.

Tools such as the early warning system and the results of Scrivner's survey are far from complete and are limited in their scope. However, if we think of human nature, given the right set of circumstances, any officer is capable of excessive force, taking a bribe, or even committing murder. The reality remains twofold when discussing unethical behavior by officers:

1. We are unable to predict future behavior.
2. There is no way of understanding the impact that policing has on an officer's personality that would lead that officer to such acts.

INTERNAL AFFAIRS AND THE COMPLAINT PROCESS

Internal Affairs is often viewed with skepticism by those outside an organization: "Police investigating the police—how can we trust them? And who investigates the internal police?" To police, those in Internal Affairs are seen as headhunters; the most common perception is that those who work in the division are looking to be promoted or get personal satisfaction in the termination of their fellow officers. The Alachua County Sheriff's Office located in Gainesville, Florida, Directive 122 establishes the role and responsibilities of the *Office of Professional Standards (Internal Affairs):*

A. The *Chief Inspector* is in charge of the Office of Professional Standards and has the responsibility, among other duties, for conducting internal investigations, and reports directly to the Sheriff. One function of this Office is to provide fact-finding assistance to the Sheriff and his staff by providing a systematic, objective and impartial method of investigating citizen complaints of employee misconduct.

B. *Inspectors* assigned to the Office of Professional Standards will be responsible for:

1. Conducting Administrative Inquiries arising from employee misconduct or lack of performance and have full authority to discharge this responsibility.
2. On occasion, conducting criminal investigations prior to commencement of the administrative inquiry.
3. Investigating Category One Use of Deadly Force incidents.
4. Investigating any matter as directed by the Sheriff.

C. An employee who is the subject of an administrative inquiry will cooperate with and assist Inspectors, recognizing that internal investigations are conducted under the immediate authority of the Sheriff.

In any internal investigation, complaints can come from five sources: citizens, civilian employees, sworn employees, supervisors, and suspects. Often citizens call to complain regarding an officer's conduct or to determine if what they observed was proper police procedure, their inquiry is answered, and a complaint is never filed.

Complaints that are filed can be addressed in one of two formats. If the conduct is criminal, an agency must perform two separate investigations, one administrative and one criminal.

1. *Administrative investigations.* Administrative investigations are performed by Internal Affairs with recommendations for discipline. Internal investigations are unique in that an officer is *compelled* to cooperate with the investigator. Since it is an administrative investigation and no criminal charges can be filed as a result of the investigation, then *Miranda* does not apply. This is supported by the U.S. Supreme Court decision in **Garrity v. New Jersey**, 385 U.S. 493 (1967). *Garrity* provides that an officer must cooperate. However, the information that is provided to Internal Affairs during the administrative investigation cannot be used against the officer in a criminal investigation (see Figure 2-3, *Garrity* Rights, as provided by the Virginia Troopers Alliance).

Garrity v. New Jersey

1967 legal case (385 U.S. 493) providing that an officer must cooperate with an administrative investigation; however, information provided to Internal Affairs during the investigation cannot be used against the officer in a criminal investigation.

Garrity Rights

On (date & time) at (place) I was ordered to submit this statement by (name & rank). I give this statement at his/her order as a condition of employment. I have no alternative but to abide by this order or face job forfeiture or discipline.

It is my belief and understanding that the Department requires this statement solely and exclusively for internal purposes and will not release it to any other agency. It is my further belief that this statement will not and cannot be used against me in any subsequent proceedings. I authorize release of this report to my attorney or designated union representative. I retain the right to amend or change this statement upon reflection to correct any unintended mistakes without subjecting myself to a charge of untruthfulness.

For any and all purposes, I hereby reserve my Constitutional right to remain silent under the Fifth and Fourteenth Amendments to the United States Constitution and any other rights prescribed by law. I rely specifically upon the protection afforded me under the doctrines set forth in *Garrity* and *Spevack* should this statement be used for any other purpose of whatsoever kind or description.

Figure 2-3   *Garrity* Rights

Source: Retrieved September 15, 2007, from http://www.virginiatroopersalliance.com/.

2. *Criminal investigations.* If there is a possibility that criminal charges can be filed against an officer as a result of the same incident, the agency *must initiate a separate criminal investigation, and the information cannot be shared between investigators.* For an agency to avoid allegations of impropriety, an outside agency should conduct the criminal investigation. However, in larger agencies this is rarely done.

Outcomes for administrative complaints include the following:

- Unfounded: The act or acts complained of did not occur or did not involve agency personnel.
- Not sustained: Insufficient evidence to clearly prove or disprove the allegation/complaint.
- Sustained: The preponderance of evidence clearly proves the allegation/complaint.
- Exonerated: The act or acts did occur, but were justified, lawful, and proper.
- Exonerated due to policy failure: A finding or conclusion that the policy, procedure, rule, or regulation covering the situation was nonexistent or inadequate.

Outcomes of the criminal complaint process include the following:

- Prosecutor can dismiss the charges because (a) he or she thinks the department sanctions are enough, or (b) there is insufficient evidence to support the criminal complaint.
- Prosecutor can file formal criminal charges against the officer.
- In either case, the agency will probably terminate the officer because he or she has violated department policy.

The purpose of internal investigations is to protect the public and the agency. Law enforcement officers have a difficult job, and it is compounded when officers are accused of violating the public trust. The issues in this category are many, with some of the most common being: conduct unbecoming an officer; dereliction of duty/failure to perform; accepting gifts, gratuities, or privileges; conducting personal business on duty; profiting from employment; verbal abuse/harassment; use of alcohol/illegal drugs on duty; sleeping on duty; and association with known felons. Unlike other professions, a law enforcement officer is on duty 24 hours a day (Ruiz & Morrow, 2007), meaning that an off-duty officer can still be charged with and investigated for a violation of law or department policy.

Table 2-1 Progressive Discipline: Sleeping on Duty				
Offense	**1st Offense**	**2nd Offense**	**3rd Offense**	**4th Offense**
Sleeping on duty	Written instruction and cautioning	Instruction and 3-day suspension	Instruction and 5-day suspension or dismissal	Dismissal

The purpose of any disciplinary action in policing is to correct behavior. Officers who violate a department policy are not necessarily automatically suspended or terminated. Most agencies utilize what is known as **progressive discipline,** which means that officers may be counseled for first violations, and then receive progressively strict discipline if violations persist, until possible termination (see example in Table 2-1).

progressive discipline

officers who violate a department policy may be counseled for first violations, and then receive progressively strict discipline if violations persist, until possible termination.

CONCLUSION

Ethical principles are the foundation of all policing. However, in the course of doing routine police business, a small percentage of officers are lured to the dark side. From an administrator's standpoint, it is difficult to determine who will become unethical and who will not. Some may be identified before they ever hit the streets based on the research provided by Scrivner, but it is impossible to tell how the job will impact the psyche of each individual officer. We do know from research, however, that an administration that is tolerant of unethical behavior is one that encourages officers to begin the slide down the slippery slope.

 DISCUSSION QUESTIONS

1. How does police discretion play a role in police misconduct?
2. Which one of the three types of ethics most applies to law enforcement and why?
3. Describe the concept of the slippery slope as it applies to ethics in law enforcement. Does this concept apply to lying during an interrogation? Why or why not?

4. There is a perception problem that exists between police administrators and minority communities. Discuss the problem and explain why minority communities have a bias against police.

5. What role do organizational ethics play in an officer's decision to remain ethical or become unethical?

RESEARCH TOPICS

Following are two topics that are central to this chapter. Choose one, and research the topic based on the instructions of your professor.

- *The conflict between ethics and law.* This chapter discussed the conflict between ethics and law. Simply put, ethics is a study of what is morally right, wrong, good, bad, obligatory, and permissible. If you were a police officer in the 1950s and did not believe in segregation, how would you reconcile the differences in the law and your personal belief system? Defend your answer with research.

- *Choosing the right police candidate.* Scrivner (1994) provides a number of profiles of officers who are prone to brutality and misconduct. Since we are incapable of predicting future behavior, what tools would you use to track an officer's conduct and intervene before the officer destroyed his or her career? Defend your answer with research.

BIBLIOGRAPHY

Alachua County Sheriff's Office. (2005). *Alachua County Sheriff's Office directives.* Gainesville, FL: Author.

Almond, B. (1999). Introduction: Ethical theory and ethical practice. In B. Almond (Ed.), *Introducing applied ethics* (pp. 1–14). Oxford, UK: Blackwell.

Attfield, R. (1995). *Value, obligation, and meta-ethics.* The Netherlands: Rodopi B.V.

Bennis, W. (1989). *On becoming a leader.* Reading, MA: Addison-Wesley.

Boehm, R., Hall. K., & Walker, S. (1997). *Part 1: Records of the committee on official lawlessness.* Bethesda, MD: University Publications of America.

Bradley, R. (1998). *Public expectations and police perception.* London, England: Research, Development and Statistics Directorate.

Braunstein, S. (1998). Are ethical problems in policing a function of poor organizational communications? In J. D. Sewell (Ed.), *Controversial issues in policing* (pp. 123–131). Boston: Allyn & Bacon.

Broder, J. (2005, April 1). Los Angeles paying victims $70 million for police graft. *New York Times,* archives.

Brown, M. K. (1988). *Working the street: Police discretion and the dilemmas of reform.* New York: Russell Sage Foundation.

Cavanaugh, S., Gladstone, L., & Teasley, D. (2002). Violence against women: An overview. In J. P. Gordon (Ed.), *Violence against women* (pp. 1–22). Bel Air, CA: Novinka Books.

Champion, D. J. (2001). *Police misconduct in America: A reference handbook.* Santa Barbara, CA: ABC-CLIO.

City of Los Angeles. (1991). *Independent commission on the Los Angeles police department.* Los Angeles: Author.

Cooper, C., & Philbin, W. (1995, May 7). NOPD didn't see the red flags, records say. *Times-Picayune,* archives.

Corruption in uniform; Excerpts of what the commission found: Loyalty over integrity. (1994, July 7). *New York Times,* archives.

Crawford, A. (2008). Plural policing in the U.K.: Policing beyond the police. In T. Newburn (Ed.), *Handbook of policing* (2nd ed., pp. 147–181). Portland, OR: Willan.

Frazier v. Cupp, 394 U.S. 731 (1969).

Fridell, L., Lunney, R., Diamond, D., Kubu, B., Scott, M., & Laing, C. (2001). *Racially biased policing: A principled response.* Washington, DC: Police Executive Research Forum.

Fried, J. P., & Harden, B. (1999, June 9). The *Louima* case: The overview; Officer is guilty in torture of Louima. *New York Times,* archives.

Garrity v. New Jersey, 385 U.S. 493 (1967).

Gibbs, J. C. (2003). *Moral development & reality: Beyond the theories of Kohlberg and Hoffman.* Thousand Oaks, CA: Sage.

Goldstein, H. (1977). *Policing a free society.* Cambridge, MA: Ballinger.

Goodwin, J. (2003). *Price of honor: Muslim women lift the veil of silence on the Islamic world.* Boston: Plume Group.

Harrison, P. M., & Beck, A. J. (2005, October). Prisoners in 2004. *Bureau of Justice Statistics Bulletin,* NCJ 210677.

Herszenhorn, D. B. (2002, March 1). The *Louima* ruling; Chronology of the case. *New York Times,* archives.

Holmes, M. D. (2000). Minority threat and police brutality: Determinants of civil rights criminal complaints in U.S. municipalities. *Criminology, 38*(2), 343–368.

International Association of Chiefs of Police (IACP). (1989). *The law enforcement code of ethics revised.* Washington, DC: Author.

Jackson, P. I. (1985). Ethnicity, region, and public fiscal commitment. *Justice Quarterly, 2,* 167–195.

Kagan, S, (1998). *Normative ethics.* Boulder, CO: Westview Press.

Kappeler, V. E., Sluder, R. D., & Alpert, G. P. (1994). *Forces of deviance: Understanding the dark side of policing.* Prospect Heights, IL: Waveland Press.

Keeling, G. L. (1999). *Broken windows and police discretion.* Washington, DC: National Institute of Justice.

Kleinig, J. (1996). *The ethics of policing.* New York: Cambridge University Press.

Klingaman, S. (2007). In law enforcement we trust: Ethical attitudes and behaviors of law enforcement officers and supervisors. *Law Enforcement Executive Forum, 7*(4), 51–71.

Klockars, C. B., Ivkovich, S. K., Harber, W. E., & Haberfeld, M. R. (2000). *The measure of police integrity.* Washington, DC: National Institute of Justice.

Kohlberg, L. (1981). *The philosophy of moral development: Moral stages and the idea of justice: Vol. 1. Essays on moral development.* New York: Harper & Row.

Kocieniewski, D. (1997, August 13). Injured man says Brooklyn officers tortured him in custody. *New York Times,* archives.

Kultgen, J. (1988). *Ethics and professionalism.* Philadelphia: University of Pennsylvania Press.

Liska, A. E., Chamlin, M. B., & Reed, M. D. (1985). Testing the economic production and conflict models of crime control. *Social Forces, 64,* 119–138.

Los Angeles Police Department (LAPD). (1991). *Report of the independent commission on the Los Angeles Police Department.* Los Angeles: Author.

Mayell, H. (2002, February 12). Thousands of women killed for family honor. *National Geographic News,* archives.

O'Hara, P. (2005). *Why law enforcement organizations fail: Mapping the organizational fault lines in policing.* Durham, NC: Carolina Academic Press.

Paine, L. S. (1994). Managing for organizational integrity. *Harvard Business Review* (March–April), 106–117.

Palmiotto, M. J. (2001). Police misconduct and minority citizens: Exploring key issues. In M. J. Palmiotto (Ed.), *Police misconduct: A reader for the 21st century* (pp. 580–571). Upper Saddle River, NJ: Prentice Hall.

Rahtz, H. (2003). *Understanding police use of force.* Monsey, NY: Criminal Justice Press.

Ramirez, A. (2007, February 4). Officer in *Louima* case returns to state to finish sentence. *New York Times,* archives.

Reisig, M. D. (2002). *Satisfaction with police: What really matters.* Washington, DC: National Institute of Justice.

Rhode Island Select Commission on Race and Police-Community Relations. (2001). *Rhode Island select commission on race and police-community relations.* Providence, RI: Author.

Ruiz, J., & Morrow, E. (2007). Retiring the old centurion: Life after a career in policing—An exploratory study. In J. Ruiz & D. C. Hummer (Eds.),

Handbook of police administration (pp. 305–334). Boca Raton, FL: CRC Press.

Schmalleger, F. (2005). *Criminal justice today: An introductory text for the 21st century* (8th ed.). Upper Saddle River, NJ: Pearson/Prentice Hall.

Schoettler, J. (2000, December 15). Police accused of slaying, theft. *Florida Times-Union,* archives.

Scott v. Sandford, 60 U.S. 19, How. 393 (1856).

Scrivner, E. (1994). *The role of police psychology in controlling excessive force.* Washington, DC: National Institute of Justice.

Spurgeon Hall, R. A., Dennis, C. B., & Chipman, T. L. (2000). *The ethical foundations of criminal justice.* Boca Raton, FL: CRC Press.

Stambaugh, J. J. (2007, December 5). Competition, longtime mistrust hinder efforts to diversify police force. *Knoxville-News Sentinel,* archives.

Stevens, D. J. (1999). Corruption among narcotics officers: A study of innocence and integrity. *Journal of Police and Criminal Psychology, 14*(2), 1–11.

Stillwell, C. (2008, January 23). Honor killings: When ancient and modern collide. *San Francisco Chronicle,* archives.

Tennesse v. Garner, 471 U.S. 1 (1985).

Thomas, D. J. (2003). Graduation speech: Law enforcement recruit class BLE 01-003. St. Johns River Community College, Palatka, FL.

Turk, A. (1969). *Criminality and the legal order.* Chicago: Rand McNally.

U.S. Department of Justice. (2002). *Federal cocaine offenses: An analysis of crack and powder penalties.* Washington, DC: Author.

U.S. Sentencing Commission. (2008). *U.S. sentencing commission's source book of federal sentencing statistics.* Washington, DC: Author.

Valverde, M. (2006). *Law and order: Images, meanings, and myths.* New Brunswick, NJ: Rutgers University Press.

Virginia Troopers Alliance. (2007). *Garrity rights.* Online. Retrieved September 15, 2007, from http://www.virginiatroopersalliance.com/.

Walker, S. (2006). *Sense and non-sense about crime and drugs: A policy guide* (6th ed.). Belmont, CA: Thomson/Wadsworth.

Walker, S., Alpert, G. P., & Kenney, D. J. (2001). *Early warning systems: Responding to the problem officer.* Washington, DC: National Institute of Justice.

Walker, S., Spohn, C., & DeLone, M. (2007). *The color of justice: Race, ethnicity, and crime in America.* Belmont, CA: Thomson Higher Education.

Warburton, N. (1999). *Philosophy: The basics.* New York: Routledge.

Williams, C. R., & Arrigo, B. A. (2008). *Ethics, crime and criminal justice.* Upper Saddle River, NJ: Pearson/Prentice Hall.

Wilson, J. Q. (1968). *Varieties of police behavior.* Cambridge, MA: Harvard University Press.

CHAPTER 3

CRIMINAL LAW

OBJECTIVES

After completing this chapter, the student will be able to:

- Discuss the history of U.S. law.
- Describe the Fourth, Fifth, Sixth, Tenth, and Fourteenth Amendments and their impact on policing in the United States.
- Discuss the three types of citizen contacts: consensual, reasonable suspicion, and probable cause.
- Describe the differences in *detain* versus *custody*.
- Describe the differences in *pat down* versus *search*.
- Explain the significance of *Terry v. Ohio*.
- Describe the plain-feel/plain-touch doctrine.
- Discuss *exigent circumstances* as the concept applies to police procedure.
- Discuss the classifications and categories of crimes.
- Describe public policy and its impact on law enforcement.
- Discuss the history of the *Miranda* decision and when *Miranda* applies in criminal cases.
- Discuss the rules of evidence as they apply to law enforcement.

KEY TERMS

arrest – subjecting a person to physical control based on a violation of the law; based on the fact the officer has probable cause to believe that a crime was committed and that the person in question committed that crime based on facts.

Bill of Rights – first ten amendments of the U.S. Constitution.

Carroll **doctrine** – an automobile exception; in order for the warrantless search and seizure of contraband to be valid, an officer must meet the burden of probable cause.

case law – provides the fundamental guidelines from which police operate.

civil infractions – traffic violations that are not arrestable (e.g., speeding, running a red light/stop sign, improper lane change, etc.); penalties are usually fines and points on one's driving record.

consensual citizen contact – contact with a citizen where there is no obligation for the citizen to engage in conversation with the police.

detain – an officer may stop an individual while in the process of an investigation, but this is not an indefinite stop; each case is based on its merits, and the test for such a stop is reasonableness.

felony – the most serious crime; punishable by no less than 366 days in prison and a fine, which is stipulated by the statute.

hate crime – a crime in which the defendant's conduct was motivated by hatred, bias, or prejudice, based on the actual or perceived race, color, religion, national origin, ethnicity, gender, sexual orientation, or gender identity of another individual or group of individuals.

Miranda warning – to be read when a subject is in custody and not free to leave at any time during the interrogation.

misdemeanor – a violation of the law where if convicted the suspect will spend up to one year in jail and/or can be fined; in most states, an officer must witness the crime before an arrest can be made.

misdemeanor exceptions – misdemeanor crimes that the legislature has deemed arrestable without a warrant based on an officer developing sufficient probable cause.

ordinance violation – a violation of law that is unique to a municipality or county government and can be enforced only by that body's law enforcement agency; such violations are misdemeanors and carry the possibility of both jail time and a fine.

pat down – the patting of exterior clothing for weapons and in some cases contraband.

plain-view doctrine – the seizure of property in plain view involves no invasion of privacy and is presumptively reasonable, assuming there is probable cause to associate the property with criminal activity.

probable cause – an investigation or action that provides an officer with a series of articulable facts that meet the criteria for an arrest; such facts must be those that would lead a reasonable person to believe that a crime was committed and that the person in question committed the crime.

reasonable suspicion – best described as a hunch; could be based on a call for service, but an officer may not have enough articulable facts to move to next level; officer can stop, inquire, and investigate, but cannot make an arrest without probable cause.

search – in all cases, a warrantless search of a person is allowed incident to arrest. The search is much more intrusive than a pat down, and allows an officer to enter a subject's pockets, shoes, jackets, and so on.

social contract – in order for the group to receive protection from society, we informally agree to a social contract, which means that we will give up our free will.

traffic violation – a violation of a traffic law; there are three categories: civil infractions, misdemeanor traffic offenses, and felony traffic offenses.

Doc's Words of Wisdom

The greatest tool that officers have at their disposal is their knowledge of the law.

INTRODUCTION

An officer learns many things in the academy: firearms, defensive tactics, driving, investigations, and patrol. However, the one subject that is scrutinized more than any other is knowledge and application of the law. The challenges come from supervisors who review the reports at the end of every shift; the prosecutor's office, which makes the decision to file charges and prosecute the case; the defense attorneys who are looking for procedural errors as they relate to *Miranda*, search and seizure, or rules of evidence; the judges who must rule on the challenges; a jury who must hear the case and examine the evidence; and any number of courts that may review the case if it is appealed.

The concept relating to the body of knowledge is best summed up in the following statement: "In most professions it is not the journey that one takes to get to the end, it is the end result. However, when it comes to policing the journey is more important than the end result" (Thomas, 2003). For a law enforcement officer, the law should be viewed as having three distinct components that are intricately woven and interdependent upon each other: (1) constitutional law—the foundation; (2) case law—the guidelines; and (3) state statutes—to protect society.

HISTORY OF LAW

The design of our legal system is based on history in that the founding fathers chose what they believed to be the best principles in developing what we know as the Constitution of the United States. From a historical perspective, our law finds its modest beginnings in the *Code of Hammurabi,* which was developed in 1780 B.C.E. The *Code of Hammurabi* consisted of 282 laws and prescribed punishment for violations of each, with the most famous being "an eye for an eye" (King, 2004).

Other forms of law that have influenced the U.S. system are: the Judeo-Christian values, more specifically the Ten Commandments, and the British common law system, which is ever apparent in reviewing the U.S. Constitution (Federer, 2003; Holmes, 1909). Keep in mind that the main purpose of the Constitution is to limit the government's powers and provide protections to the citizens of the United States. Dahl (2003) supports this assertion in his description of the Constitution, noting that an important provision of these rights is that they are guaranteed by imposing constitutional limits on the government (p. 144).

The U.S. criminal justice system is a combination of many things. However, when you examine the Fourth, Fifth, Sixth, and Fourteenth Amendments, you can see the influence of Italian philosopher Cesare Beccaria who published his thoughts on criminal justice in the text *An Essay on Crime and Punishment 1764,* twenty-four years before the U.S. Constitution. Beccaria (1983/1764) provides forty-seven principles that were designed to do away with the indiscriminate abuses by the government in criminal cases when it came to common people. The most notable of the principles are: the right to punish; the interpretation of laws; the proportion between crimes and punishment; the degree of crimes; the division of crimes; evidence; torture; secret accusations; the death penalty; and crimes difficult to prove, to name a few. Most notable in his debate is that we as free people give up certain freedoms or acquiesce to a social contract so that we can rest in peace and security, with the idea that we will be treated fairly and justly (pp. 14–74).

CONSTITUTIONAL LAW

In discussing the Constitution, one must be mindful of its historical significance. Our forefathers came to this country to escape what they saw as government intrusion into their private lives, and in fleeing they were determined that this new government would not be given the power to do the same. Although the first ten amendments of the Constitution are known as the **Bill of Rights**, the amendments that govern police action are the Fourth, Fifth, Sixth, and Fourteenth Amendments (see Figure 3-1 for these and others that limit police authority) (Champion, 2002; Feinman, 2006; Isarel and Lafave, 2001).

Bill of Rights

first ten amendments of the U.S. Constitution.

As you read the remainder of this chapter, refer to the amendments in Figure 3-1, and apply their principles to the laws and actions presented in the text. Many times a law enforcement officer's role is not clearly defined in our society. With that said, police have two primary roles: protectors of our rights, and protectors of society (Gunderson & Hopper, 1988; Stanko, 1989).

CASE LAW

Case law is the cornerstone of policing. In essence, **case law** provides the fundamental guidelines from which police operate. The Bill of Rights provides the framework, and the Supreme Court has filled in the missing links with such cases as *Miranda, Terry, Escobedo,* and *Mapp.* The issue that you may find compelling in regard to police practices and these decisions is that officers are still making the same mistakes. As a student, pay particular attention to the date of each case decision, look at the circumstances surrounding the police action, and then attempt to figure out: why do the police continue to make the same mistakes over and over?

case law

provides the fundamental guidelines from which police operate.

Before we can examine the cases, we must first define lawful police conduct in police-citizen contacts. A police officer is naturally suspicious or curious of behavior. Skolnick (2004) argues that a police officer's personality is comprised of two elements: danger and authority. Danger makes police officers attentive to violations of the law and acts of violence; by the very nature of the job, officers are suspicious (p. 101). Their role is

Amendment I
Congress shall make no law respecting an establishment of religion, or prohibiting the free exercise thereof; or abridging the freedom of speech, or of the press; or the right of the people peaceably to assemble, and to petition the government for a redress of grievances.

Amendment II
A well regulated militia, being necessary to the security of a free state, the right of the people to keep and bear arms, shall not be infringed.

Amendment IV
The right of the people to be secure in their persons, houses, papers, and effects, against unreasonable searches and seizures, shall not be violated, and no warrants shall issue, but upon probable cause, supported by oath or affirmation, and particularly describing the place to be searched, and the persons or things to be seized.

Amendment V
No person shall be held to answer for a capital, or otherwise infamous crime, unless on a presentment or indictment of a grand jury, except in cases arising in the land or naval forces, or in the militia, when in actual service in time of war or public danger; nor shall any person be subject for the same offense to be twice put in jeopardy of life or limb; nor shall be compelled in any criminal case to be a witness against himself, nor be deprived of life, liberty, or property, without due process of law; nor shall private property be taken for public use, without just compensation.

Amendment VI
In all criminal prosecutions, the accused shall enjoy the right to a speedy and public trial, by an impartial jury of the state and district wherein the crime shall have been committed, which district shall have been previously ascertained by law, and to be informed of the nature and cause of the accusation; to be confronted with the witnesses against him; to have compulsory process for obtaining witnesses in his favor, and to have the assistance of counsel for his defense.

Amendment X
The powers not delegated to the United States by the Constitution, nor prohibited by it to the states, are reserved to the states respectively, or to the people.

Amendment XIV
Section. 1. All persons born or naturalized in the United States and subject to the jurisdiction thereof, are citizens of the United States and of the State wherein they reside. No State shall make or enforce any law which shall abridge the privileges or immunities of citizens of the United States; nor shall any State deprive any person of life, liberty, or property, without due process of law; nor deny to any person within its jurisdiction the equal protection of the laws.

Figure 3-1   Bill of Rights Amendments That Limit Police Authority (Amendments I, II, IV, V, VI, X, & XIV)

to ask questions in an attempt to dispel any fears when something is out of the ordinary. However, this should not be considered a license to stop someone just because he or she is riding a bicycle at night or because the officer feels that the person in question does not belong in a particular neighborhood. There is a delicate balance between officer curiosity/crime prevention and the freedoms that we cherish as Americans.

Police and citizens have contact on three occasions (Florida Department of Law Enforcement, 2008; Michigan State Police Training Academy, 2004):

1. **Consensual citizen contact:** This is considered a common ground. These contacts may occur at crime watch meetings or when the police see people walking down the street and would like to speak to them. During this type of encounter, citizens are *not* required to engage in conversation with the police and are free to walk away.

2. **Reasonable suspicion:** This is best described as a hunch. It could be a hunch based on a call for service, but an officer may not have acquired enough articulable facts to move this to the next level. However, the officer can stop to investigate. Officers are limited in their abilities; they can stop, inquire, and investigate but cannot make an arrest unless they develop probable cause. Reasonable suspicion does not rise to the level of probable cause (Missouri State Statutes, 2008; Nebraska State Statutes, 2008; New York State Statutes, 2008).

3. **Probable cause:** This is an investigation or action that provides an officer with a series of articulable facts that meet the criteria for an arrest. These must be facts that would lead a reasonable person to believe that a crime was committed and that the person in question committed the crime (California Penal Code, 2008; Michigan State Statutes, 2008; New York State Statutes, 2008). (See Figure 3-2.)

Figure 3-2 is a visual representation of the investigative process where each bar represents the collection of facts moving from reasonable suspicion to probable cause to making an arrest. The process is as follows:

1. *Call for service:* Understand that every arrest begins with a citizen contact, call for service, or something that an officer observed while driving that looked suspicious. This requires an investigation. This is an officer's legal justification for being at the location in question.

2. *Reasonable suspicion begins:* After an officer makes contact with the subjects in question and establishes their reason for being at that location, the investigation begins. After a short period of time, an investigating officer will know if a crime has been committed, or is about to be, and will either continue to investigate to establish probable cause or clear the call with no action taken.

3. *Developing probable cause:* If a crime has occurred, the investigating officer will have to articulate all the facts, with the most important being the elements of the crime and establishing the victim and witnesses if there are any.

4. *Probable cause:* Once an officer's investigation has met the criteria for an arrest based on probable cause, then an arrest can be effected.

consensual citizen contact

contact with a citizen where there is no obligation for the citizen to engage in conversation with the police.

reasonable suspicion

best described as a hunch; could be based on a call for service, but an officer may not have enough articulable facts to move to next level; officer can stop, inquire, and investigate, but cannot make an arrest without probable cause.

probable cause

an investigation or action that provides an officer with a series of articulable facts that meet the criteria for an arrest; such facts must be those that would lead a reasonable person to believe that a crime was committed and that the person in question committed the crime.

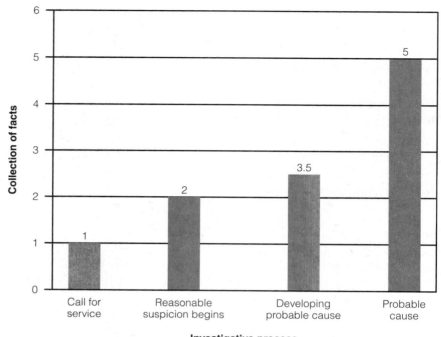

Figure 3-2   Probable Cause

Most state statutes provide an *authority to arrest* clause in regard to an arrest:

A law enforcement officer may arrest a person when:

a. He has a warrant commanding that such person be arrested; or

b. Any crime has been or is being committed in the presence of the officer;

c. Or he has probable cause to believe that an offense was committed and has probable cause to believe that the offense was committed by the person to be arrested. (Florida State Statutes, 2008; Georgia State Statutes, 2008; Massachusetts State Statutes, 2008; New York State Statutes, 2008; Ohio State Statutes, 2008)

DETAIN, ARREST, PAT DOWN, AND SEARCH INCIDENT TO ARREST

The issue of citizen contact is very important in determining or guiding an officer in his or her duties. The issue of citizen contact does not exist in a void or vacuum. In order to understand how an officer proceeds without violating a citizen's rights, four terms must be discussed. Remember that the definitions of these terms are imperative when it comes to articulating an officer's actions. The ability to define these terms in police reports and arrest affidavits may mean the difference between dismissal of a case or prosecution. To the casual reader, this may seem like a game of semantics, but in a court of law, an officer's attention to detail can be the difference between winning and losing.

The terms and specific police actions are: *detain* versus *arrest*, and *pat down* versus *search*. Often the terms in each pair are used interchangeably; but make no mistake, in a court of law, each term has its own unique meaning.

Detain Versus Arrest

Detain: This allows an officer to stop an individual while in the process of an investigation, but this is not an indefinite stop. Each case is based on its merits. The test for such a stop is reasonableness. An officer cannot arbitrarily pick someone out of a crowd and detain that person for no reason. To stop and detain someone, the officer must base the decision on a series of articulable facts. The facts needed are less than those needed to make an arrest and meet the test of reasonable suspicion (Greene, 2006; Lyman & Geberth, 2001).

Arrest: This is based on the fact the officer has probable cause to believe that a crime was committed and that the person in question committed that crime based on facts. Marderosian and Weiner (1980) define an arrest as subjecting a person to physical control based on a violation of the law. For an arrest to be valid, each of these elements must be present: authority, intent, custody, force, and submission (Greene, 2006; Lyman & Geberth, 2001).

Pat Down Versus Search

Pat down: This is the patting of exterior clothing for weapons and in some cases contraband. Although some court opinions have called a *pat down* a *search*, the two actions are not the same. There are limits to a pat down. It should *not* be viewed as a search and should be identified only as a *pat down* in police reports and arrest affidavits (Dorf, 2006; Yarbrough, 2000).

Search: In all cases, a warrantless search of a person is allowed incident to arrest. The search is much more intrusive than a pat down, and allows an officer to enter a subject's pockets, shoes, jackets, and so on (Dorf, 2006; Yarbrough, 2000).

detain

an officer may stop an individual while in the process of an investigation, but this is not an indefinite stop; each case is based on its merits, and the test for such a stop is reasonableness.

arrest

subjecting a person to physical control based on a violation of the law; based on the fact the officer has probable cause to believe that a crime was committed and that the person in question committed that crime based on facts.

pat down

the patting of exterior clothing for weapons and in some cases contraband.

search

in all cases, a warrantless search of a person is allowed incident to arrest. The search is much more intrusive than a pat down, and allows an officer to enter a subject's pockets, shoes, jackets, and so on.

Stop and Frisk

The issue of stop and frisk is associated with one of the most celebrated cases in policing, *Terry v. Ohio*, 392 U.S. 1 (1968). The *Terry* case is commonly known in police circles as a *Terry stop* or *Terry*. The case of *Terry* was the first time police were afforded the right to "pat down" the exterior clothing of a suspect based on reasonable suspicion; and it is limited to just that—no intrusion into the pockets is allowed unless weapons are found. What makes the case celebrated is that it allows officers to seize a person and be minimally intrusive without arresting the individual. However, this intrusion is based on a series of facts and not a hunch, and at a minimum the officer must meet the standard of reasonable suspicion.

Most officers apply *Terry* to every encounter because it is an issue of officer safety. Simply stated, during any encounter, an officer should be prepared to go further in regard to the use of force and to possibly arrest the subject based on the facts that have been gathered before and during the police-subject contact. *Terry* is very clear on this matter. In essence, officers must be able to justify their actions (see Scenario 3-1).

SCENARIO 3-1: STOP AND FRISK

You are on patrol and receive the following call: Echo 169, 10-65; There is a B/M standing at the corner of N.E. 11th Ave. and 10th St. The complainant advises that the suspect is on the corner selling drugs. In fact, the complainant has observed the subject make three drug deals within the last ½ hour. The suspect's description is as follows: B/M, 5'10–6'0, wearing blue jean knee-length shorts, and a black Nike T-shirt. The suspect is medium complexion, has a mustache and short hair. The complainant wants to remain anonymous and refuses to give her name or address.

As you make contact with the subject his hands are in plain view and there are no apparent bulges that suggest that he is armed. As you begin dialogue the subject states that he heard a woman screaming behind a house and that you should go investigate.

You ask the subject for identification and he says that he has none. However, he does give you his correct name and date of birth. Your backup arrives and immediately the subject puts his hands in his pockets. At this point there are no indicators that anything is suspicious or wrong. The backup officer orders the subject to remove his hands and he complies. You run the subject in the computer and find that he is wanted on a warrant for *fishing w/o a license*. The issuing agency will only pick up the subject if the location is within twenty-five miles of their office; you are two hundred miles away. As you step aside to run the subject you hear your partner order the subject to remove his hands from his pockets a second time. The subject's body language changes and now he displays a nervous stutter and is jittery.

Analysis and Reflection (Part 1)

1. The question here is: do you have enough to apply *Terry* and pat the subject down for weapons? Yes, you can pat the subject down, because his actions, and your observations, rise to the level of *Terry*. This is an officer safety issue.

2. What should make you suspicious is that the subject advised that he heard a lady screaming. *Articulable fact number one: the subject stated he heard a woman screaming.*

The suspect has no identification but gives you his correct name and date of birth. Your backup arrives and the suspect places his hands in his jacket pockets twice. He is ordered to remove them both times and complies. He also becomes nervous. This occurs when the suspect gives you his name. Officers often say that the hair stands up on the back of their neck in situations like this. Other terms that describe the officer's feelings are *hunch* and *gut feeling*. The key here is to articulate each of the things you have observed—in this case, the hands and the change in body language once you received the subject's personal information. There is a warrant for the suspect, but it is invalid because of the pickup radius.

Analysis and Reflection (Part 2)

1. The question at this time is: do you have the right to search the suspect because of the warrant? No, the warrant is invalid because of the limitations.

2. Can you pat him down because he put his hands in his jacket pocket? *Terry* applies here because of the body language, change in speech pattern, and the subject's placing his hands in his pockets after being told not to do so. *Articulable fact number two: Terry applies.*

The suspect hears the radio transmission, reaches into his pockets, throws something to the left and right, and begins to run. You tackle him.

Analysis and Reflection (Part 3)

1. Do you have a right to detain the suspect with force? Yes, you can use force to stop the suspect, so to tackle him is absolutely acceptable because he chose to run.

2. Can you handcuff the suspect? Yes, you can handcuff the suspect. He has already shown a propensity to run, so you can apply the handcuffs, but you must advise the suspect that he is being *detained* until you complete your investigation. This is important because you do not have probable cause or a charge, but you are in the process of completing an investigation.

3. What are you investigating? The scope of the investigation changed where he could have walked away before throwing the items but instead he threw them; his actions changed the focus of the detainment.

4. Can you collect and examine what the suspect discarded? Yes, because based on your experience and training, the items appear to be drugs. More importantly, once the suspect discarded the items, they were in plain view and therefore meet the criteria of the *plain-view doctrine*. They were discarded on the street for anyone to handle.

5. Can you field-test the substance found in the plastic bag? Yes, because based on your experience and training, it appears to be crack cocaine, a crack pipe, and stem. Not to mention the items had been discarded.

6. Once the substance is field-tested and is positive, then you can arrest the suspect for *possession of crack cocaine* and *possession of drug paraphernalia*. You can also move to the next level, which is search incident to arrest.

PLAIN-TOUCH/PLAIN-FEEL DOCTRINE: AN EXCEPTION TO *TERRY*

Terry was limited to weapons and did not include contraband until the case of *Minnesota v. Dickerson,* 508 U.S. 366 (1993), when the U.S. Supreme Court created the *plain-feel exception.* Under this rule, a police officer who pats down a suspect for weapons may proceed to a seizure of other property (contraband) *only* if the pat down is lawful and meets the initial criteria for *Terry.* The contraband *must* be identifiable as contraband by its contour and mass, and the contraband *must* be identified without manipulation.

The aforementioned requirements do *not* mean that upon touch an officer must be able to identify the item specifically as, for example, a piece of crack cocaine or heroin. What it does mean is that without manipulation an officer must identify the item as contraband. The officer's expertise is gained through training and experience.

SEARCH INCIDENT TO ARREST

In any discussion of criminal law and/or search and seizure, it should be noted that there are many different categories of a search. There are searches of persons, automobiles, and houses; warrantless searches; searches conducted with exigent circumstances; and searches conducted with a warrant, to name a few. However, there is only one category for a warrantless search of a person: search incident to arrest.

An officer is allowed to search anyone who is under arrest. The only limitation is that the subject cannot be strip-searched. A strip search is the removal of clothing exposing underclothing, breasts, buttocks, or genitalia of another person, and the statute provides very strict guidelines that include privacy, conducted by an officer of the same sex, a detailed report, and a copy of the written authorization allowing the search (*Tinetti v. Wittke,* 479 F. Supp. 486, 491 [E.D. Wis. 1979]; *Delaware v. Prouse,* 440 U.S. 648, 99 S. Ct. 1391, 1396 [1979]).

Search incident to arrest is done prior to transporting a subject to jail. A search may *not* be conducted to establish evidence for the arrest. As noted in *Sibron v. New York,* 392 U.S. 40 (1968), a search cannot be justified as incident to a lawful arrest if there was no probable cause before the search (p. 392). However, any contraband, weapons, or fruits of a crime found on the subject during the search can lead to additional charges (*United States v. Robinson,* 414 U.S. 218 [1973]). The subject will be searched again by correctional officers once he or she arrives at the jail.

The additional search is conducted as a precaution to keep the subject from introducing weapons/contraband or destroying evidence that the arresting officer may have missed during the initial search.

Although an officer has a right to search a subject who is under arrest, this should not be done without understanding the precautions that need to be taken. From an officer safety standpoint, an officer needs to be mindful of the fact that subjects may have drug paraphernalia in their possession. What makes this so dangerous is that abusers of crack, methamphetamines, or heroin may have in their possession, or taped to their bodies, dirty needles and razor blades, which are associated with HIV/AIDS, hepatitis, and tuberculosis.

A final note regarding a search conducted incident to arrest. Officers must be mindful of searching subjects of the opposite sex. It is not illegal for a male officer to search a female arrestee (Minneapolis Police Department Policy 9-202; Stering, 2004), but the male must be mindful of the claim that the female can make regarding the male officer touching her breasts, buttocks, and crotch. The officer is looking for weapons and contraband. The woman can claim that the officer's actions were sexual. To avoid such allegations, most agencies have a policy that requires officers to call an officer of the same sex as the offender to conduct the search when practical.

SEARCH AND SEIZURE

The one area of policing that is under continual scrutiny and change is that of search and seizure. The most common questions associated with searches are: When can an officer search a home, a vehicle, or luggage? What are the limitations and exceptions? and When does the officer need a search warrant?

In the United States, an individual's home is his or her castle. In fact, our homes are protected from unreasonable searches and seizures. The Fourth Amendment of the U.S. Constitution states the following: "The right of the people to be secure in their persons, houses, papers, and effects, against unreasonable searches and seizures, shall not be violated, and no warrants shall issue, but upon probable cause, supported by oath or affirmation, and particularly describing the place to be searched, and the persons or things to be seized."

Plain-View Doctrine

In *Texas v. Brown*, 460 U.S. 730 (1983), the court established the following definition in regard to the **plain-view doctrine:** "The seizure of

plain-view doctrine

the seizure of property in plain view involves no invasion of privacy and is presumptively reasonable, assuming there is probable cause to associate the property with criminal activity.

property in plain view involves no invasion of privacy and is presumptively reasonable, assuming that there is probable cause to associate the property with criminal activity."

Search of a Residence

The landmark case that specifically defined police actions in regard to entering a residence and seizing property is *Mapp v. Ohio,* 376 U.S. 643 (1961). In the *Mapp* case police forcibly entered the residence of Ms. Dollree Mapp after Ms. Mapp denied them access on two separate occasions. The police kicked in the door and entered the house without an arrest or search warrant. They were looking for a suspect wanted in an alleged bombing. Once inside the house, the police searched the residence and did not find the suspect in question. However, they did discover obscene material in a closed trunk in the basement of Ms. Mapp's residence. Ms. Mapp was found guilty of *possession of pornographic material.* The U.S. Supreme Court overturned the conviction, stating the following:

> Seventy-five years ago, in *Boyd v. United States,* 116 U.S. 616, 630 (1886), considering the Fourth and Fifth Amendments as running "almost into each other" on the facts before it, this Court held that the doctrines of those Amendments apply to all invasions on the part of the government and its employees of the sanctity of a man's home and the privacies of life. It is not the breaking of his doors, and the rummaging of his drawers, that constitutes the essence of the offence; but it is the invasion of his indefeasible right of personal security, personal liberty and private property. . . . Breaking into a house and opening boxes and drawers are circumstances of aggravation; but any forcible and compulsory extortion of a man's own testimony or of his private papers to be used as evidence to convict him of crime or to forfeit his goods, is within the condemnation [of those Amendments]. (p. 635)

Vehicle Searches

A vehicle has the same protection as a home, which is provided by the Fourth Amendment to the Constitution. A vehicle creates unique challenges, the most obvious being that of mobility. In regard to vehicles, the U.S. Supreme Court recognized that uniqueness in the landmark case *Carroll v. United States,* 267 U.S. 132 (1925). As a result of this case, police abide by what is known as the ***Carroll* doctrine** and can best be defined as an *automobile exception.* In order for the warrantless search of a vehicle and seizure of contraband to be valid, an officer *must* meet the burden of probable cause.

Carroll **doctrine**

an automobile exception; in order for the warrantless search and seizure of contraband to be valid, an officer must meet the burden of probable cause.

The motor vehicle exception was further refined in *United States v. Ross*, 456 U.S. 798 (1982). The *Ross* decision stated the following:

> Where police officers have probable cause to search an entire vehicle, they may conduct a warrantless search of every part of the vehicle and its contents, including all containers and packages, that may conceal the object of the search. The scope of the search is not defined by the nature of the container in which the contraband is secreted. Rather, it is defined by the object of the search and the places in which there is probable cause to believe that it may be found. For example, probable cause to believe that undocumented aliens are being transported in a van will not justify a warrantless search of a suitcase. (pp. 817–824)

The key to a warrantless search as provided in *Carroll* and *Ross* is probable cause. The question here is: How does an officer develop probable cause in regard to a motor vehicle? Probable cause can be developed through a number of sources: the officer being an eyewitness to the crime in question; through investigation of a crime and developing a suspect; use of a police dog to track or detect narcotics; and through the use of a reliable informant. (See Scenario 3-2.)

SCENARIO 3-2: TRAFFIC STOP

You are on patrol and driving on the interstate checking for stranded motorists. You observe a 2005 Black Yukon, bearing TX license plate 385-HDM pass you doing the following: the vehicle changes lanes twice without signaling; and during the second lane change, it almost strikes another vehicle, forcing that driver to slam on his brakes to avoid a collision with the rear of the Yukon. You stop the Yukon and the driver states he is in a hurry to get to the local hospital because his wife was just transported by ambulance. When you ask what hospital, the driver is unable to advise you of any hospitals in your city. You advise the driver why you stopped him and request his driver's license and registration. The driver is from Florida and the vehicle is a rental with a Texas registration. The driver appears to be nervous and jittery.

To check the driver's story, you have dispatch check to see if there were any ambulance runs in the last ½ hour and they advise that there were none. There are no indications of impairment such as: a strong odor of an alcoholic beverage on the driver's breath; eyes bloodshot and watery; pupils dilated; and/or slurred incoherent speech. The driver does make the following statement: "The only reason you stopped me is because I'm black. This shit happens all the time! A brother can't come to town without being harassed. Man this is profiling!"

You advise the driver that you are going to write several citations and to stay seated in his vehicle. You notice that the driver becomes more agitated while you are in your car writing the citations. Since the driver has told you several lies and has become more agitated, you ask for consent to search the vehicle. The driver declines the request.

(continued)

(continued)

With everything that has occurred during your encounter with the driver, you feel that he is probably transporting some form of contraband in the car. You request a canine unit to sniff the exterior of the Yukon. As the dog checks the exterior of the vehicle, it alerts on the engine compartment, gas tank, and the rear cargo area. The suspect and passenger are placed under arrest. You search the rear cargo area and recover a half kilo of marijuana. The vehicle is secured and towed to the police station, and the search is continued. More marijuana is located in the engine compartments and in a false gas tank. The sum total of the narcotics seized is two kilograms.

Analysis and Reflection

1. Did you have probable cause to make the traffic stop? Yes, the driver's erratic driving pattern.

2. Based on the initial observations of the driving pattern, what would be your first suspicions?

   • That the driver is possibly driving impaired. However, upon approaching the vehicle, the driver did not display any signs of impairment: slurred speech, strong odor of an alcoholic beverage, or bloodshot, watery eyes.

   • The driver was also void of other signs of drug impairment such as: cognitive impairment, pinpoint pupils, or the odor of an illegal drug such as marijuana, crack cocaine, or methamphetamine.

3. Did the driver raise your suspicions that something was wrong during the stop? Yes.

   • He was extremely nervous when you approached the vehicle.

   • He lied about his wife being transported to the hospital.

   • He became more agitated when he was found to be lying.

4. Based on his actions, do you have probable cause to believe that the suspect is involved in a crime? No, but you do have reasonable suspicion.

5. Did you have the right to call for a canine unit? Yes. Keep in mind, however, that there are limitations to the use of the canine unit. It is time-sensitive and is governed by the Fourth Amendment. Time-sensitive means that your stop must be reasonable, and the litmus test is how long it will take you to write the citation(s). So if you are at the end of the stop and the driver is ready to be released, you have probably waited too long. The canine unit should be called as soon as an officer returns to his or her vehicle to write the citation(s). Reasonableness is determined based on the totality of the circumstances. The writing of a citation is just a rule of thumb.

6. When the dog alerted on the different compartments of the vehicle, did you have probable cause to make an arrest and search the vehicle? Yes. The dog can be used to sniff the exterior of the vehicle. In the case *United States v. Place*, 462 U.S. 696 (1983), the Court determined the following regarding the use of canines: "A 'canine sniff' by a well-trained narcotics detection dog, however, does not require opening the luggage. It does not expose non-contraband items that otherwise would remain hidden from public view, as does, for example, an officer's rummaging through the contents of the luggage." It is not an intrusive search and can be equivocated to *Terry* (pp. 706–707). Other case law that supports the use of a canine unit includes: *United States v. Perez*, 440 F.3d 363 (2006), Sixth Circuit; *United States v. Eura*, 440 F.3d 625 (2006), Fourth Circuit; *United States v. Alexander*, 448 F.3d 1014 (2006), Eighth Circuit; and *United States v. Valle Cruz*, 452 F.3d 698 (2006), Eighth Circuit.

7. Although you made an arrest for the marijuana, do you need to write the citations? Yes, because the citations establish that you had a lawful reason to stop the vehicle. Without the citations your stop would be considered an unlawful detention or seizure under the Fourth Amendment.

The use of an informant poses a problem because of the informant's character. Often informants are involved in criminal activity, so their motivation for acting as an informant and their reliability can come into question. Holtz (2001) provides the following guidelines for the use of informants as tests of their reliability: prior participation, prior investigations, quality of prior information, and whether information source had an arrest and/or conviction (pp. 101–102). In *Illinois v. Gates*, 462 U.S. 213 (1983), the Court abolished the two-pronged test and established that all warrants should be issued based on the totality of the circumstances and that the informant's veracity, reliability, and basis of knowledge should be considered as elements of the probable cause (pp. 230–241).

Exigent Circumstances

Exigent circumstances can best be described as follows: without immediate police action, there will be destruction or loss of the evidence; police in hot pursuit; safety of a law enforcement officer; or the safety of the public is in jeopardy (Bergman & Bergman-Barrett, 2007; Holtz, 2004; Scott, 2004). Vehicles pose a particular problem because they are mobile; however, an officer must meet the standard of probable cause to search them. It is easy to understand the circumstances surrounding a vehicle, but what about a house? Let's examine Scenario 3-3 to see how exigent circumstances may apply to a house.

SCENARIO 3-3: EXIGENT CIRCUMSTANCES

You are on patrol and receive the following call: David 145, 10-65: See the victim at 1425 N.E. Michigan Ave. He states that he was walking southbound on Mecca passing the Smith Housing Project, when he was approached by two B/M suspects. One was armed with a handgun. The suspects robbed the victim at gunpoint, taking his Air Jordan basketball shoes and his Jordan black leather jacket. The victim knows both suspects from school, can identify them, and can identify the apartment they ran to. The robbery occurred 10 minutes ago.

You meet with the victim approximately 15 minutes after the robbery occurred. The victim confirms the information provided by dispatch. He also tells you that he knows the suspects by name because he goes to school with both of them and that they are in some of his classes at the local high school. Their physical descriptions are as follows:

Suspect 1: Daron Mitchell, B/M, 16/17 yrs old, 5'11, 190 lbs, short brown hair, brown eyes. He was wearing a black hooded ski parka, blue jeans, and wheat-colored Timberland boots.

(continued)

(continued)

Mitchell was armed with a semi-auto pistol believed to be a Glock. Mitchell pointed the gun at the victim's head and stated: "I want the coat and the shoes. If you don't give them to me I will kill you. If you call the police I will kill you. I never liked you anyway."

Suspect 2: Michael Smart, B/M, 16/17 yrs old, 6'2, 200 lbs, brown hair worn in a large afro, and brown eyes. He was wearing a Chicago Bulls jacket, blue jeans, and black Timberland boots. Michael took the items as the victim removed them. Mike stated: "If you call the police, you and your family are dead."

Description of Stolen Property:

1. Pair of Air Jordan 21 basketball shoes, size 13, black in color. Value $140.00.
2. One Jordan leather jacket, size XL, black in color. Value $400.00.

Once the suspects took the property, they ran upstairs to apartment 3B of the Smith Housing Project. It is adjacent to Mecca Street.

You arrive at apartment 3B. When you knock on the door, you hear the voices of two male subjects. A suspect fitting the description of Daron Mitchell answers the door. In fact, he is wearing the same clothing that the victim described. Standing behind Mitchell is the second suspect fitting the description of Michael Smart. As you look into the living room through the open door, you see the Jordan leather jacket on the floor. The suspect immediately screams "Oh shit, it's the police!" and attempts to slam the door in your face.

You force the door open and both suspects run. Suspect Mitchell flees to the back of the house and you give chase, tackling him as he grabs for a jacket on the floor. You handcuff Mitchell and check the jacket only to find the Glock pistol that the victim described. Your partner tackles Smart in the living room and handcuffs him.

Analysis and Reflection

1. Did you have a legal reason to go to apartment 3B? Yes. You were there to do a follow-up investigation regarding an alleged robbery. You had credible information, given the fact that the victim personally knew both suspects and was able to describe them and their clothing in detail.

2. Once the occupant of the house opened the door and you saw that it was the suspects as described, did you have a right to enter the house and in this case force the door open? Yes. Not only did the occupants match the victim's description, but you also observed the stolen jacket in plain view. Once the suspects saw that the police were at the door, they attempted to close the door. If the door had been closed, then the suspects could have possibly destroyed the evidence before you could get a search warrant.

3. Did you have a right to chase Mitchell to the back of the house and search the jacket once you placed him under arrest? Yes. Mitchell and Smart attempted to flee in the house and you were in *hot pursuit*. When you arrest someone in his or her house, you do not have a right to search the entire house—just the area where he or she has immediate control. A good rule of thumb is within arm's reach of the arrest.

4. Did you meet the criteria for probable cause in making the entry and the arrest? Yes, based on the information that the victim gave you beginning with the suspects' identities, physical description of the clothing and hair styles, type of weapon, the items stolen, and apartment number. This information was verified once the door was opened; both suspects fit the physical description, they reacted by trying to lock you out of the apartment, and the stolen jacket was lying on the floor.

CRIMINAL LAW

All forms of law and public policy are designed to protect the public. They also serve another function, which is to provide order in our daily lives. Other components of our society that assist in this arena are value systems, morals, and beliefs. This concept is best described by moral philosopher Thomas Hobbes in his discussion of the *social contract*. Hobbes (as cited in Spurgeon Hall, Dennis, & Chipman, 2000) theorizes that without government we would exist in a state of nature, which would consist of a life that was solitary, poor, nasty, brutish, and short. Hobbes further theorizes that we are social creatures who need protection and seek to protect our property as well as our lives. In order for the group to receive protection, we informally agree to a **social contract,** which means that we will give up our free will (pp. 111–115).

The problem with value systems or one's perception of the social contract is that they may be tainted. A short list of those who have a value system that is contrary to America's social contract are groups who espouse such values as racism, child pornography, rape, murder, robbery, or identity theft. It is because of such deviant belief systems that we seek the protection Hobbes describes in the social contract.

As we discuss the legislation of deviant behavior, we must recognize that we all possess the potential to be deviant. In fact, in our lifetime we have all violated a few of the very laws that are designed to protect us. The most often violated laws are traffic laws, with speeding being number one, and the primary reason being that we are in a hurry.

The laws of the United States are governed by the U.S. Constitution. A unique amendment in the Constitution is Amendment X, which allows states to govern themselves and states the following: "The powers not delegated to the United States by the Constitution, nor prohibited by it to the states, are reserved to the states respectively, or to the people."

It is because of states' rights that each state's laws are different. The difference lies in the penalties associated with particular criminal acts, and often in the names of the acts as well. In some states, rape is not called rape but is called sexual battery, criminal sexual conduct, or something else. However, when you examine the definitions, they are similar, as are the penalties.

Along with the differences in the names of laws, some state statutes provide a series of penalty enhancements for certain crimes. The classifications of penalties are fourth degree, third degree, second degree, and first degree, with first degree providing the harshest penalty in such states as Colorado and Florida. Other states may classify penalties with letters and numbers, and some states (e.g., Michigan) do not use either except in rare cases.

social contract

in order for the group to receive protection from society, we informally agree to a social contract, which means that we will give up our free will.

Classifications/Categories of Crimes

Misdemeanors pose a unique problem for police in that they are divided into two categories: *misdemeanors* and *misdemeanor exceptions.* Unlike a felony, an officer *cannot* make an arrest without a warrant for a simple misdemeanor, depending on the state (Bacigal, 2001; Kansas State Statutes, 2008; Scheb & Scheb II, 1998). In order to make a warrantless arrest for a crime in the classification of misdemeanor, the officer must personally witness the crime unless it falls into the category of a *misdemeanor exception.*

A traditional misdemeanor requires an officer to complete an investigation and forward the investigation to the *prosecutor or state attorney's office* where there will be a determination if there is sufficient probable cause to issue a warrant. Examples of crimes that might fall into this category are: *assault* and/or *battery, theft/larceny,* and *criminal mischief/property destruction.* Theft and criminal mischief can either be a felony or a misdemeanor, which is determined by the dollar value assigned by the legislature.

Misdemeanor exceptions are misdemeanor crimes that the legislature has deemed arrestable without a warrant based on an officer developing sufficient probable cause. If a misdemeanor is classified as an exception, an officer can make a warrantless arrest if the officer is an eyewitness to the crime, or if during an investigation the officer develops probable cause to believe that a crime was committed and that the person in question committed the crime. Examples of such offenses are *domestic violence, battery* (depending on the state), and *shoplifting* (Colorado State Statutes, 2008; Florida State Statutes, 2008; Michigan State Statutes, 2008).

A police officer, irrespective of his or her jurisdiction, must know two things during any investigation: categories/classifications of crimes and the elements of the crime in question. The four categories/classifications of crimes or violations are:

1. **Felony:** the most serious crime. It is punishable by no less than 366 days in prison and a fine, which is stipulated by the statute (Bacigal, 2001; Kansas State Statutes, 2008; Scheb & Scheb II, 1998).

2. **Misdemeanor:** the least serious criminal category. It is punishable by a maximum of 365 days in the county jail and a fine, which is defined by statute (Bacigal, 2001; Kansas State Statutes, 2008; Scheb & Scheb II, 1998).

3. **Ordinance violation:** a violation of law that is unique to a municipality or county government and can be enforced only by that body's law enforcement agency. These violations are misdemeanors and carry the possibility of both jail time and a fine (Alaska State Statutes, 2008; Dillon, 1911; West Virginia Code, 2008).

misdemeanor exceptions

misdemeanor crimes that the legislature has deemed arrestable without a warrant based on an officer developing sufficient probable cause.

felony

the most serious crime; punishable by no less than 366 days in prison and a fine, which is stipulated by the statute.

misdemeanor

a violation of the law where if convicted the suspect will spend up to one year in jail and/or can be fined; in most states, an officer must witness the crime before an arrest can be made.

ordinance violation

a violation of law that is unique to a municipality or county government and can be enforced only by that body's law enforcement agency; such violations are misdemeanors and carry the possibility of both jail time and a fine.

4. **Traffic violation** has three categories of violations:

   a. **Civil infractions** are traffic violations that are not arrestable. The penalties are usually fines and points on one's driving record. Violations that fit into this category are: *speeding, running a red light/stop sign, improper lane change,* and so on (California Penal Code, 2008; Florida State Statutes, 2008; Michigan State Statutes, 2008).

   b. **Misdemeanor traffic offenses** are the same as misdemeanors and are punishable by up to one year in jail and a fine. Violations that fit this category are: *fleeing and attempting to elude a police officer, driving under the influence, driving on a suspended driver's license,* and so on.

   c. **Felony traffic offenses** offer the same penalty as a traditional felony. Most of these deal with traffic crashes; examples are: *vehicular homicide* and, depending on the state, *fleeing and attempting to elude a police officer.*

traffic violation

a violation of a traffic law; there are three categories: civil infractions, misdemeanor traffic offenses, and felony traffic offenses.

civil infractions

traffic violations that are not arrestable (e.g., speeding, running a red light/stop sign, improper lane change, etc.); penalties are usually fines and points on one's driving record.

Elements of a Crime

Elements of a crime are paramount in determining probable cause and the development of articulable facts. When an officer is interviewing a complainant/victim, the first thing that needs to be determined is whether a crime has been committed. Intimate knowledge of the most common state statutes, ordinances, and traffic violations is essential. Reexamine the definition of *probable cause* provided earlier: an investigation or action that provides an officer with a series of articulable facts that meet the criteria for an arrest. These facts would lead a reasonable person to believe that a crime was committed and that the person in question committed the crime (California Penal Code, 2008; Michigan State Statutes, 2008; New York State Statutes, 2008).

Since each state has its own set of laws, it would be impossible to address or examine each. However, examining one standard that is used in the development of statistics for the FBI's *Uniform Crime Reports* (UCR) will be helpful. We will examine *part one* and *part two* crimes, offering their definitions and elements as provided by the UCR. Part one crimes are crimes of violence, and part two crimes are property crimes.

Part One Crimes/Crimes of Violence

There are four part one crimes, and the necessary elements in each of these crimes involve *force or the threat of force.* Part one crimes include: *murder, forcible rape, robbery,* and *aggravated assault.*

Murder and *nonnegligent manslaughter* are defined by the UCR as the willful (nonnegligent) killing of one human being by another. There are two ways one can be convicted of first-degree murder: in the first, there must be intent, meaning that the suspect has malice aforethought prior to killing the victim; the other is known as felony murder, where there is no intent, and it is the easier of the two for the state to prove. When discussing intent, the state must know the motive, or why the suspect killed the victim. Depending on the nature of the case, intent is difficult to prove. The best indicator of premeditation is the understanding of why one would kill another human being. The most common motives for murder are: revenge, jealousy, money/greed, and lust.

Examine the elements of *premeditated murder;* these must be present for an officer to have probable cause at the time of an arrest and are the same elements that the state must prove in court (Brody, Acker, & Logan, 2001; Gould Publications, 2005a):

1. The victim is dead.
2. The death was caused by a criminal act.
3. There was premeditated killing of the victim.

Now examine the elements of *nonnegligent manslaughter;* these must be present for an officer to have probable cause at the time of arrest, and these are the same elements that the state must prove in court (Gould Publications, 2005a; Lynch & Addington, 2007):

1. The victim is dead.
2. The suspect intentionally caused the death, or the suspect procured the death of the victim; or the death of the victim was caused by culpable negligence of the suspect.

Forcible rape, as defined by the UCR, is the carnal knowledge of a female forcibly and against her will. Assaults and attempts to commit rape by force or threat of force are also included; however, statutory rape (without force) and other sex offenses are excluded. In some states, it is penetration digitally, with a sexual organ or object, or the mere touching of sexual organs (Carney, 2004; Groth & Birnbaum, 2001).

The context of rape has changed over the years. In the 1950s and 1960s, the victim's motives were often suspect, and at times it was stated that the victim brought it on herself. In fact, if there was no evidence of a physical assault or that the victim fought back, often the complaint was not taken seriously. It was not enough that the victim feared for her life. Today, the mere fact that the victim says "No" and the suspect continues is rape. Note that forcible rape also can occur when the victim and perpetrator are the same sex (Cuklanz, 1999; McGregor, 2005).

Examine the elements of *rape;* these must be present for an officer to have probable cause at the time of arrest, and these are the same elements that the state must prove in court (Flora, 2001; New Hampshire State Statutes, 2008; Nussbaum, 1999):

1. The victim was 12 years old or older.
2. The suspect committed an act in which the sexual organ penetrated or had union with the victim's anus, vagina, and /or mouth. Or the suspect committed an act in which the victim's anus, vagina, or mouth was penetrated with an object.
3. The act was committed without consent.

Robbery as defined by the UCR is the taking or attempting to take anything of value from the care, custody, or control of a person or persons by force or threat of force or violence and/or by putting the victim in fear. Robbery can be either armed or unarmed. Examine the elements of *robbery;* these must be present for an officer to have probable cause at the time of arrest and are the same elements that the state must prove in court (Bergman & Bergman-Barrett, 2007; Brody et al., 2001; Gould Publicatons, 2005a):

1. The suspect took the item, be it money or property, that the victim had in his or her possession.
2. Force, violence, or threats were used to place one in fear of harm.
3. The property taken was of some value.
4. The intent was to permanently or temporarily deprive the victim of the property.

Aggravated assault is defined by the UCR as an unlawful attack by one person upon another for the purpose of inflicting severe or aggravated bodily injury. The UCR further specifies that this type of assault is usually accompanied by the use of a weapon or by other means likely to produce death or great bodily harm. In addition, the UCR also defines *attempted aggravated assault* that involves the display of—or threat to use—a gun, knife, or other weapon as included in this crime category because serious personal injury would likely result if the assault were completed.

The definitions provided by the UCR in regard to *aggravated assault* and *attempted aggravated assault* differ from those in some states. Some states use the terms *aggravated battery* and *aggravated assault,* which have alternate definitions that are provided here as another point of reference.

Aggravated assault is the threat of violence, which is directed at a person(s), with the apparent means to act on the threat. The suspect is usually armed with a knife, a bludgeon, or a gun. This is a threat only by gesture and mouth; there is no touching of the victim. Examine the elements of *aggravated assault* (non-UCR); these must be present for an officer to have probable cause at the time of arrest, and these are the same elements that the state must prove in court (Florida State Statute 784.021; Michigan State Statute 750.81a):

1. The suspect intentionally and unlawfully threatened by word or act to do violence to the victim.
2. At the time the suspect appeared to have the ability to carry out the threat.
3. The act of the suspect created a well-founded fear in the victim that the violence was imminent.
4. The assault was made with a deadly weapon.

Aggravated battery is an unlawful attack on another with a weapon causing great bodily harm, a permanent disability, or permanent disfigurement. In most cases the suspect is armed with a weapon such as a knife, bludgeon, or gun, although it is possible for the injuries sustained in a fistfight to be so severe that they rise to the level of aggravated battery. Examine the elements of *aggravated battery* (non-UCR); these must be present for an officer to have probable cause at the time of arrest, and these are the same elements that the state must prove in court (Florida State Statute 784.045; Georgia State Statute 16-5-24):

1. The suspect intentionally touched or struck the victim.
2. In committing the battery the suspect intentionally or knowingly caused: great bodily harm, or permanent disability, or permanent disfigurement to the victim.
3. The suspect used a deadly weapon in the commission of the battery.

Common Violent Crimes Not Defined by the UCR

Assault is the mere threat of violence, having the apparent ability to carry out the threat, and fear or belief that the suspect will injure the victim. There is no weapon involved in an assault. Examine the elements of *assault* (non-UCR); these must be present for an officer to have probable cause at the time of arrest, and these are the same elements that the state must prove in court (California Penal Code 240; Michigan State Statute 750.81; Virginia State Statute 18.2-57):

1. The suspect intentionally and unlawfully threatened by word or act to do violence to the victim.

2. At the time the suspect appeared to have the ability to carry out the threat.

3. The act of the suspect created a well-founded fear in the victim that the violence was imminent.

Battery is the unlawful touching or striking of another human being. If injury is sustained, the injury is less than great bodily harm. In most cases it is bruising or a bloody lip. Examine the elements of *battery* (non-UCR); these must be present for an officer to have probable cause at the time of arrest, and these are the same elements that the state must prove in court (California Penal Code 242; Florida State Statute 784.03):

1. The suspect intentionally touched or struck the victim.

2. In committing the battery the suspect intentionally or knowingly caused bodily harm to the victim.

Part Two Crimes/Property Crimes

There are four part two crimes, which are: *burglary, larceny/theft, motor vehicle theft,* and *arson.*

Burglary is defined by the UCR as the unlawful entry of a structure to commit a felony or theft. The use of force to gain entry is not required to classify an offense as a burglary. Burglary in the UCR is categorized into three subclassifications: forcible entry, unlawful entry where no force is used, and attempted forcible entry. Examine the elements of *burglary;* these must be present for an officer to have probable cause at the time of arrest, and these are the same elements that the state must prove in court (Illinois State Statute 720-5/19.1; South Carolina Code of Laws 16-11-312.):

1. The suspect entered and remained in a structure or conveyance owned by or in the possession of the victim.

2. The suspect did so without permission of the victim.

3. At the time of entering the suspect did so with the intent to commit a crime therein.

Larceny/theft is defined by the UCR as the unlawful taking, carrying, leading, or riding away of property from the possession or constructive possession of another; attempts to do these acts are included in the definition. This crime category includes shoplifting, pocket-picking, purse-snatching, thefts from motor vehicles, thefts of motor vehicle parts and accessories, bicycle thefts, and so forth, in which no use of force, violence, or fraud occurs.

In theft cases, the dollar value of the property determines whether the theft can be classified as a felony or misdemeanor. Some states place a value on items that are unique to the particular state. The classic example is Florida State Statute 812.014, which classifies the theft of 2,000 or more pieces of *citrus fruit* as a third-degree felony. Examine the elements of *larceny/theft;* these must be present for an officer to have probable cause at the time of arrest, and these are the same elements that the state must prove in court (Florida State Statute 812.014; Illinois State Statute 720-5/16-1):

1. The suspect knowingly and unlawfully took the property of another.
2. In doing so the suspect had the intent to temporarily or permanently deprive the victim of his or her right to the property.

Motor vehicle theft is defined by the UCR as the theft or attempted theft of a motor vehicle. The offense includes the stealing of automobiles, trucks, buses, motorcycles, snowmobiles, and so on. The taking of a motor vehicle for temporary use by persons having lawful access is excluded from this definition. This definition excludes the crime of carjacking, which possesses the same elements as robbery. Examine the elements of *motor vehicle theft;* these must be present for an officer to have probable cause at the time of arrest, and these are the same elements that the state must prove in court (California Penal Code 487; Indiana State Statute 35-43-4-2.5):

1. The suspect knowingly and unlawfully took a motor vehicle of another.
2. In doing so the suspect had the intent to temporarily or permanently deprive the victim of his or her right to the vehicle.

Arson is defined by the UCR as any willful or malicious burning or attempting to burn, with or without intent to defraud, a dwelling house, public building, motor vehicle or aircraft, personal property of another, and so on. Examine the elements of *arson;* these must be present for an officer to have probable cause at the time of arrest, and these are the same elements that the state must prove in court (Utah Criminal Code 76-6-102; Revised Code of Washington Crimes and Punishment 9A.48.020):

1. The suspect caused to be damaged structure or contents by fire or explosion.

2. The suspect did so willfully and unlawfully; or the damage was caused while the suspect was engaged in the commission of a crime.

3. The structure was a dwelling, or an institution in which the damage occurred during normal hours of occupancy, or a structure.

Common Crimes Not Defined by the UCR

There are a host of crimes that are not defined by the UCR. Following you will find definitions of some these: *criminal trespass, property destruction,* and *carrying a concealed weapon*. These are common offenses. Note that *trespass* is similar to *burglary* with a minor twist.

Criminal trespass is defined as the unlawful entry in a dwelling, conveyance, or structure or onto property where they are not authorized and refuse to leave after they have been warned to do so. Examine the elements of *trespass;* these must be present for an officer to have probable cause at the time of arrest, and these are the same elements that the state must prove in court (Code of Alabama 13-A-7-2; Arizona Criminal Code 13-1502):

1. The suspect willfully and illegally entered and remained in a structure or on property or conveyance, refusing to leave after being warned by the owner or his or her representative.

2. The structure or property was in lawful possession of the owner or representative.

3. After the suspect entered the property, he or she remained without permission of the owner or his or her representative.

Take a moment and examine the differences between *criminal trespass* and *burglary*. The elements are similar except that in burglary the suspect enters the property with the intent to commit a crime therein and in trespass the offender refuses to leave the property.

Criminal mischief/property destruction is defined as the willful malicious injury or damage by any means to any real or personal property belonging to another. Criminal mischief is similar to theft in that its classification of being a felony or misdemeanor is determined by a dollar value. Examine the elements of *criminal mischief;* these must be present for an officer to have probable cause at the time of arrest, and these are the same elements that the state must prove in court (Georgia State Statute 16-7-23; Indiana State Statute 35-43-1-2):

1. The suspect injured or damaged property.

2. The property injured or damaged belonged to another.

3. The injury or damage was done willfully and maliciously.

Carrying a concealed weapon is carrying any dirk, metallic knuckles, slingshot, billie, tear gas gun, chemical weapon or device, or other deadly weapon on or about a person in such manner as to conceal the weapon from ordinary sight of another person (Florida State Statutes 790.01–790.33; Michigan State Statutes 750.222–750.237a). This definition does not necessarily include firearms, although it could, depending on the state. Examine the elements of *carrying a concealed weapon;* these must be present for an officer to have probable cause at the time of arrest, and these are the same elements that the state must prove in court (Florida State Statutes 790.01–790.33; Michigan State Statutes 750.222–750.237a):

1. The suspect knowingly carried a weapon on or about his or her person.
2. The weapon was concealed from ordinary sight of another.

PUBLIC POLICY AND LAW

Historically we like to think that the enforcement of the law has been fair, unbiased, and for the good of all people. However, there have been instances where law enforcement has failed to enforce the law adequately or their hands have been tied because the laws were not adequate. The lack of attention and/or failed laws have created a public outcry, forcing legislators to change ineffective laws and in other cases challenging police to reexamine their mission and policies. White (2004) argues that police in America have no real identity or mission and that they respond to whatever society demands or needs at a given time (p. 53).

If you think of policing as an instrument of the people, then it is incumbent upon the profession to have flexible policies to meet the needs of the public that they serve. With that said, let's examine four bodies of legislation where public outcry has forced change: domestic violence, drunk driving, hate crimes, and sex offenders.

Domestic Violence

Historically, matters of the home were considered private issues between a man and a woman. The laws were designed to keep it that way. From the 1950s until the mid-1970s, there was no such thing as arresting someone for the act of domestic violence, because it was considered a misdemeanor and not a misdemeanor exception (see the earlier discussion of misdemeanors). Gelles (1997) states that it was not until the mid-1970s that women's groups began demanding that their significant others be arrested for acts of domestic violence. In 1974, a class action law suit was filed in Cleveland, and in 1976 another was filed in New York City, with both suits demanding that women be protected against abusive spouses (p. 146).

Durose, Harlow, Langan, Montivans, Rantala, and Smith (2005) provide data that puts the issue of family violence in perspective. Durose et al. argue that family violence accounted for 11% of all the violence in America between the years 1998 and 2002, which translates to approximately 3.5 million members being the victims of violent crimes (p. 1).

A landmark case that was responsible for changing how police and the criminal justice system respond to domestic violence is *Thurman v. City of Torrington, Connecticut,* 595 F. Supp. 1521 (1984 U.S. Dist. Ct.). This case epitomized the failure of the system as a whole and, more specifically, of the police (see Case Study 3-1 on p. 80).

After reviewing Case Study 3-1, we would like to believe that a mandatory arrest policy will help resolve most of the problems associated with domestic violence. The concept of mandatory arrest is supported by Maxwell, Garner, and Faggan's (2001) research where they observed that arrests reduced the probability of future acts of domestic violence and that there was not an increased risk of future aggression if an arrest was made (pp. 1–2). The problem is the role of the victim in the prosecution of the offender. Many refuse to participate because they fear for their personal safety, are still in love with the offender, experience a loss of security, or experience feelings of guilt (Gamache & Asmus, 1999; Lockton & Ward, 1997).

Examine the elements of domestic violence; these must be present for an officer to have probable cause at the time of arrest, and these are the same elements that the state must prove in court (Florida State Statute 741.28; South Carolina Code of Laws 16-25-10):

1. It is unlawful to cause physical harm or injury to a person's own household member; or

2. Offer or attempt to cause physical harm or injury to a person's own household member with apparent present ability under circumstances reasonably creating fear of imminent peril.

At issue in domestic violence is the definition of a *household member,* which is dependent upon the state. Some states allow for same-sex relationships as being family members; some include a spouse, a former spouse, persons who have a child in common, a male and female who are cohabiting or formerly have cohabited, persons related by blood or marriage, and/or persons who are presently residing together as if a family or who have resided together in the past as if a family.

Drunk Driving

Another law that did not receive much attention until the early 1980s is drunk driving. Voas and Lacey (1989) state that in the 1970s about

CASE STUDY 3-1: DOMESTIC VIOLENCE

On June 10, 1983, Charles Thurman appeared at the Bentley-St. Hilaire residence in the early afternoon and demanded to speak to Tracey. Tracey, remaining indoors, called the defendant police department asking that Charles be picked up for violation of his probation. After about 15 minutes, Tracey went outside to speak to her husband in an effort to persuade him not to take or hurt Charles Jr. Soon thereafter, Charles began to stab Tracey repeatedly in the chest, neck, and throat.

Approximately 25 minutes after Tracey's call to the Torrington Police Department and after her stabbing, a single police officer, the defendant Petrovits, arrived on the scene. Upon the arrival of Officer Petrovits at the scene of the stabbing, Charles Thurman was holding a bloody knife. Charles then dropped the knife and, in the presence of Petrovits, kicked the plaintiff Tracey Thurman in the head and ran into the Bentley-St. Hilaire residence. Charles returned from within the residence holding the plaintiff Charles Thurman, Jr., and dropped the child on his wounded mother. Charles then kicked Tracey in the head a second time.

Soon thereafter, defendants DeAngelo, Nukirk, and Columbia arrived on scene but still permitted Charles Thurman to wander about the crowd and to continue to threaten Tracey. Finally, upon approaching Tracey once again, this time while she was lying on a stretcher, Charles Thurman was arrested and taken into custody (pp. 153–155).

Analysis and Reflection

1. Did the system fail Ms. Thurman prior to the final assault? Yes, she had requested police assistance many times and they had done nothing.

2. What should have been the police response during the final assault? The first officer on the scene should have ordered the suspect to stop the attack. If he refused, the officer should have shot the suspect in defense of Ms. Thurman.

3. What were the limitations of the police before the mandatory arrest policy was enacted?
   - Counsel and leave the parties in the house, or
   - Counsel and ask one party to leave for the night.
   - In either case, the limitations were due to the classification in the law of domestic violence as a misdemeanor. However, in this final attack, there were no limitations placed on the police.

one-half of 1% of licensed drivers were arrested for driving while impaired and that the number had increased to 1% or 1.9 million in 1983 (p. 136). Mothers Against Drunk Driving (MADD) is responsible for bringing the issue to the forefront, and it is because of the loss of so many children.

One of the major problems with alcohol is perception. Prior to 1980 our society, as well as police, did not view alcohol as dangerous because it was legal. Clark and Hilton (1991) argue that it was not until the mid-1980s that this perception began to change (p. 149). The danger of alcohol was first noted in newspaper articles and magazines such as *Newsweek*. The focus of alcohol consumption changed from a good time to public health and abuse. Although Americans have become aware of the public health risks associated with alcohol, such as drunk driving, the practice of social drinking varies from year to year. Research conducted by Qiunlan, Brewer, Siegel, Sleet, Mokdad, Shults, and Flowers (2005) support the concept that the perception of acceptable drinking changes from year to year, noting that impaired driving declined from 123 million in 1993 to 116 million in 1997, but then the trend increased to 159 million in 1999 and 2002 (p. 346).

The term *drunk driving* has many monikers: in Michigan, *operating while impaired* (OUI); in Colorado and Florida, *driving under the influence* (DUI); and in New York and Texas, *driving while intoxicated* (DWI). However, the penalties are similar. Drunk driving is unique because it is the only crime that allows an officer to develop probable cause with suspects incriminating themselves by participating in field sobriety exercises. In fact, the field sobriety exercises may be the only opportunity for drivers to display that they are not impaired.

For an officer to make an arrest for *driving under the influence,* these elements must be present and are the same elements that the state must prove in court (Code of Alabama 352-5A-191; Kansas State Statute 8-1001):

1. The suspect drove or was in physical control of a vehicle.
2. While driving or in actual physical control of the vehicle,
   a. the suspect was under the influence of an alcoholic beverage or a chemical substance or a controlled substance to the extent that his or her normal faculties were impaired and/or
   b. had a blood alcohol level of 0.08 or more grams of alcohol per 100 milliliters of blood or breath alcohol level of 0.08 or more grams of alcohol per 210 liters of breath.

Hate Crimes

From a historical perspective, hate crimes are relatively new, and no statistical data were kept until mandated by Congress with the Hate Crimes Statistics Act of 1990. The Hate Crimes Sentencing Enhancement Act of 1992 defines a **hate crime** as: "a crime in which the defendant's conduct was motivated by hatred, bias, or prejudice, based on the actual or perceived race, color, religion, national origin, ethnicity, gender, sexual orientation or gender identity of another individual or group of individuals."

Although data was not kept until 1990, the criminal acts are nothing new and date back to the days of slavery. Today hate crimes include anti-Semitism, homophobia, xenophobia, racism, and misogyny. As with domestic violence, hate crimes were brought to the forefront because civil rights organizations demanded change (Jacobs & Potter, 2001; Wolitski,

hate crime

a crime in which the defendant's conduct was motivated by hatred, bias, or prejudice, based on the actual or perceived race, color, religion, national origin, ethnicity, gender, sexual orientation, or gender identity of another individual or group of individuals.

Stall, & Valdiserri, 2007). Since the FBI began collecting data, there have been approximately 7,000 incidents annually. The categories of hate crimes are: crimes against persons, property, or society at large.

In most states there is no formal charge of a hate crime. As with domestic violence, the criminal charge is primary, and then hate crime is added to that charge. For example: A suspect is arrested and charged with *aggravated battery*. During the course of the investigation, police determine that the crime met the criteria to be classified as a *hate crime*. Then the charge will read: *aggravated battery (hate crime)*. The addendum of hate crime to the charge enhances the penalty if the suspect is convicted in court (Vermont State Statute 31: 1455; Wisconsin State Statute 939.645).

How do police determine that they are investigating a hate crime? Is it because the suspect is straight and the victim is gay, or the suspect is white and the victim is black? What evidence would have to be present if damage was done to property, such as a Jewish synagogue? Such cases are very difficult because the investigator is attempting to determine what the suspect's motives were during the commission of the crime.

During the course of an assault, the suspect may use racial epithets in relationship to the victim's race, ethnicity, sexual orientation, or religious beliefs. Short of that, an officer and the victim may never know the reason for the attack. During an investigation such as this, it is important to ask the victim and witnesses: Did the suspect make any statements before, during, or after the attack? In regard to property crime offenses, often the suspect will leave graffiti that clearly articulates the suspect's intentions.

Sex Offender Laws

Until recently the issue of sex offenders and their threat had not made it to the forefront of policing. It is not that they were not a threat to society; in fact, Brown (2005) states that the legislation to control sex offenders dates back to the 1930s with sexual psychopath legislation (pp. 17–18). But the crimes that were perpetrated against children in recent decades made the public demand comprehensive legislative changes to protect children.

Some of the celebrated cases that brought attention to this subject include: the disappearance and murder of 6-year-old Adam Walsh, July 27, 1981; the disappearance of 12-year-old Jacob Wetterling, October 22, 1989; the disappearance and murder of 12-year-old Polly Klaas, October 1, 1993; the disappearance, rape, and murder of 7-year-old Megan Kanka, July 29, 1994; and the abduction, rape, and murder of 9-year-old Jessica Lunsford, February 24, 2005. As a result of these acts, two pieces of national legislation were enacted in an attempt to ensure public safety and the safety of children:

- As a result of Jacob Wetterling's abduction, Congress enacted *The Jacob Wetterling Act,* which requires states to register all sexually violent predators. As of January 2009, Jacob still had not been found.

- As a result of the disappearance, rape, and murder of Megan Kanka, Congress enacted a law known as *Megan's Law,* which gave states the right to publish the names, pictures, and addresses of sex offenders.

- As a result of the abduction, rape, and murder of Jessica Lunsford, the state of Florida enacted a law entitled *The Jessica Lunsford Act* that requires school districts to complete a background screening of noninstructional or contract employees.

MIRANDA

Today the two words *Miranda warning* are two of the most famous words in the U.S. justice system. They have been publicized in every police show since *Adam 12,* which dates back to 1968. Even a first grader can tell you what they are. However, there seems to be confusion by the public and the police as to when the Miranda warning is supposed to be read. The **Miranda warning** is only required to be read when a suspect is in custody and not free to leave at any time, and the police plan to question the suspect in relationship to a crime (Garrow & Deer, 2004; Granno, 1996).

Miranda warning
to be read when a subject is in custody and not free to leave at any time during the interrogation.

The foundation of the *Miranda* decision can be found in the Fifth, Sixth, and Fourteenth Amendments to the U.S. Constitution, along with a host of court cases prior to the 1966 *Miranda* decision. Following is the chronology of cases that led to the *Miranda* decision:

- *Brown v. Mississippi,* 297 U.S. 278 (1936): Brown and two other defendants were arrested and charged with murder. The defendants were black, and in order to obtain confessions, the deputy ruthlessly beat the defendants. There was no physical evidence, nor were there any eyewitnesses to the crime. The only evidence presented at trial was the confessions, which were obtained through the use of torture.

  The question before the Court was: Was the method in which the confessions were obtained consistent with the due process clause of the Fourteenth Amendment of the U.S. Constitution? The U.S. Supreme Court reversed the state court's decision, and in doing so made the following observation: "It would be difficult to conceive of methods more revolting to the sense of justice than those taken to procure the confessions of these petitioners, and the use of the confessions thus obtained as the basis for conviction and sentence was a clear denial of due process."

- *Betts v. Brady,* 316 U.S. 455 (1942): Betts was charged with robbery in the state of Maryland. He was unable to afford an attorney because he was indigent. The court advised that it only provided attorneys in cases of murder and rape, but for no other cases for indigent defendants.

  The question before the Court was: Do defendants have a right to counsel in state courts? The U.S. Supreme Court upheld the decision of the lower court in the majority opinion, stating that the right to counsel only applied in federal cases.

- *Gideon v. Wainwright,* 372 U.S. 335 (1963): Gideon was charged with a noncapital felony in the state of Florida. He requested an attorney because he was indigent. The state refused because they only provided an attorney in capital cases for indigent defendants. The U.S. Supreme Court overturned the *Betts* case and, in their decision, advised that it is a fundamental right essential to a fair trial.

- *Escobedo v. Illinois,* 378 U.S. 478 (1964): Escobedo was arrested for an alleged murder. While being transported to the police station, with his hands cuffed behind his back, he made the following statement: "I am sorry, but I would like to have advice from my lawyer." Once at the station, his attorney arrived and made several attempts to meet with Escobedo and was denied access.

  The question before the Court was: Is this a denial of his Sixth Amendment rights guaranteeing the assistance of an attorney and the Fourteenth Amendment rights guaranteeing due process? The Illinois decision was reversed by the U.S. Supreme Court, and they made the following observation: "We hold only that when the process shifts from investigatory to accusatory—when its focus is on the accused and its purpose is to elicit a confession—our adversary system begins to operate, and, under the circumstances here, the accused must be permitted to consult with his lawyer." *Escobedo* was a landmark case; however, it did not go far enough in that it did not provide police with guidelines as to what should be said, when a suspect is in custody, and before an interrogation can begin.

Although *Miranda v. Arizona,* 384 U.S. 436 (1966), is the most famous case, it actually was consolidated with four other cases, with similar police conduct in all. Miranda was arrested and charged with robbery, kidnapping, and rape. He was interrogated by police for two hours and was never informed of his rights. Although he was never formally advised of his rights, Miranda provided a written confession. At the top of each page of his written confession appeared a statement that advised that Miranda was making the statement voluntarily and that he knew the statement could be used against him. The Court held that an individual must be advised of his or her rights when in police custody and being interrogated. The Court did not provide verbiage but advised that the police are compelled to offer individuals the following prior to custodial interrogation: the right to an attorney, the right to remain silent, and that anything said can and will be used against them in a court of law.

Most police departments have adopted warnings that are almost identical to the Supreme Court's citation and read similar to this:

1. You have the right to remain silent.
2. Anything you say can and will be used against you in a court of law.
3. You have the right to an attorney and to have him present before and during any questioning.
4. If you cannot afford an attorney, one will be provided for you.

Although the Court was very specific regarding what the warnings should include, some states have taken the matter a step further to ensure that there is no misunderstanding and provide the following waiver:

1. Do you understand each of these rights that I have read to you?
2. Taking this into account, do you wish to talk to me?

When Are Police Required to Read Miranda?

In reviewing the *Miranda* decision, the Court repeated one phrase consistently: *custodial interrogation. Custody* defined in terms of police interrogation means the subject is *not* free to leave at any time during the interrogation (Brooks, 2001; Gould, 2008; Grano, 1996). The issue may be best explained in the case of *Oregon v. Mathiason,* 429 U.S. 492 (1977):

> Mathiason responded to a police officer's request to voluntarily come to a police station regarding a burglary. He was immediately informed that he was not under arrest, during the half-hour interview, yet he confessed to the burglary. However, at the conclusion of the interview he was allowed to leave the station. The question before the court was: Was Mathiason in custody at the time of his interrogation?
>
> The Oregon Supreme Court stated that he was and threw out the confession. However, the U.S. Supreme Court made the following observation: "Such a non-custodial situation is not converted to one in which *Miranda* applies simply because a reviewing court concludes that, even in the absence of any formal arrest or restraint on freedom of movement, the questioning took place in a coercive environment. . . . Police officers are not required to administer Miranda warnings to everyone whom they question. Nor is

Figure 3-3   Formula for Miranda Warning

the requirement of warnings to be imposed simply because the questioning takes place in the station house, or because the questioned person is one whom the police suspect. Miranda warnings are required only where there has been such a restriction on a person's freedom as to render him "in custody." It was that sort of coercive environment to which *Miranda* by its terms was made applicable, and to which it is limited. (p. 429)

A simple formula to remember regarding the reading of the Miranda warning is shown in Figure 3-3.

You have had an opportunity to review the most prominent cases associated with Miranda—a history, if you will. Knowing the rules as you now know them, why do you think that police continue to violate the very precedent that has been a standard police practice since 1966?

An example of such a case is the interrogation of John Couey, who was arrested for the 2005 rape and murder of 9-year-old Jessica Lunsford. Couey was convicted in 2007 of the following charges: burglary, kidnapping, rape, and murder. However, the police could not use the confession because Couey requested an attorney on five separate occasions and his requests were ignored. The confession was thrown out by Florida Circuit Court Judge Richard Howard on the grounds that the police violated Couey's right to counsel (Aguayo, 2006; Frank, 2006).

CONCLUSION

Knowledge of the law is the most powerful tool that law enforcement officers have in their arsenal. In this analysis, consider that a firearm is rarely used, but the law is used on every call. The law also provides officers with the ability to deny citizens of their most coveted constitutional guarantee, "freedom." It is because of this that police are tasked with knowing the issues of search and seizure, laws of arrests, statutes, and local ordinances with the idea that police will provide a fair and unbiased service to their respective communities.

When you hear that a suspect got off on a technicality, it is important to examine the case to determine where the mistakes were made to avoid the same mishaps in the future. Take a moment and reflect on the John

Couey case where he asked for an attorney several times during questioning and the police ignored his request. What would have happened if the confession was the only evidence the state had and Couey had walked?

The law and its rules are the only thing that separates policing in a civilized society from a tyrannical government. It is important to remember: when it comes to criminal law, it is not the end that is important, but the journey that one takes, because that is what will be scrutinized by the courts and ultimately the public.

DISCUSSION QUESTIONS

1. Discuss the impact of the Bill of Rights on the institution of policing. In your discussion, explain what differentiates a communist country that does not subscribe to the concepts associated with the U.S. and state constitutions from countries like the United States.

2. The author makes the argument that when it comes to policing and the interpretation of the law, simple semantics in report writing and testifying in court can make a difference. Explain how this is possible; give examples. Can a criminal case be lost or evidence excluded because an officer has used the wrong terminology in court or in the police report? Why or why not? Defend your answer.

3. The public has demanded change in our legislative process, bringing to the forefront such issues as domestic violence, strengthening drunk driving laws, and enhancing the penalties for hate crimes. When you examine these changes, do you believe that they are necessary, or do you believe that the laws were strong enough prior to their modern-day amendments? Many public interest groups seek some form of protection under the law and seek policy changes. Will policing as we know it be able to keep up with the demands; or as new legislation is enacted, will the enforcement of other laws receive less attention? Defend your answer.

4. Examine the history of the *Miranda* decision, and explain why the police in the John Couey case denied his request for an attorney. Can you see any reason why the officers would ignore the law? What are the possible ramifications of such behavior when police ignore the Constitution? Defend your answer.

5. This chapter is an examination of criminal law and procedure as it relates to police in the United States. Describe the process of arrest by examining the concept of articulable facts, detailing the

relationship between probable cause and the elements of a crime, using the crime of murder for your explanation.

RESEARCH TOPICS

Following are two topics that are central to this chapter. Choose one, and research the topic based on the instructions of your professor.

- *The evolution of law.* Laws have been implemented to protect society and have evolved over the years to meet society's ever-changing demands. Examine this statement: The problem today is that we have too many laws, especially since we subscribe to a social contract. Do you agree or disagree? Defend your position.

- *Limitations of research.* In this chapter you were presented with a discussion of one database, the *Uniform Crime Reports* (UCR), which is maintained by the FBI. Along with the UCR, there are a number of other databases, including the *National Crime Victimization Survey* (NCVS). Research the limitations of the UCR and NCVS, and describe your responsibilities when using data from such sources as a part of your research.

BIBLIOGRAPHY

Aguayo, T. (2006, July 1). Confession barred because of request for lawyer. *New York Times,* archives.

Alabama State Legislature. (2008). *The code of Alabama 1975.* Montgomery: Author.

Alaska State Legislatture. (2008). *Alaska state statutes.* Juneau: Author.

Arizona State Legislature. (2008). *Arizona criminal code title 13.* Phoenix: Author.

Bacigal, R. J. (2001). *Criminal law and procedure: An introduction* (2nd ed.). New York: Delmar Cengage Learning.

Beccaria, C. (1983). *An essay on crime and punishment* (A. Caso, Trans.). Boston: International Pocket Library. (Original work published 1764).

Bergman, P., & Bergman-Barrett, S. (2007). *The criminal law handbook: Know your rights, survive the system.* Berkley: Nolo Publishing.

Betts v. Brady, 316 U.S. 455 (1942).

Boyd v. United States, 116 U.S. 616, 630 (1886).

Brody, D. C., Acker, J. R., & Logan, W. A. (2001). *Criminal law.* Boston: Jones & Bartlett.

Brooke , J. (1998, October 13). Gay man dies from attack, fanning outrage and debate. *New York Times,* p. 1.

Brooks, P. (2001). *Troubling confessions.* Chicago: University of Chicago Press.

Brown v. Mississippi, 297 U.S. 278 (1936).

Brown, S. (2005). *Treating sex offenders: An introduction to sex offender treatment programmes.* Portland, OR: Willian.

California Department of Justice. (2006). *California firearms laws 2006.* Sacramento: Office of the Attorney General of California.

California State Legislature. (2008). *California penal code.* Sacramento: Author.

Carney, T. P. (2004). *Practical investigation of sex crimes.* Boca Raton, FL: CRC Press.

Carroll v. United States, 267 U.S. 132 (1925).

Champion, D. J. (2002). *Police misconduct in America: A reference handbook.* Santa Barbara, CA: ABC-ClIO.

Clark, W. B., & Hilton, M. E. (1991). *Alcohol in America.* Albany, NY: SUNY Press.

Colorado State Legislature. (2008). *Colorado state statutes.* Denver: Author.

Cuklanz, L. M. (1999). *Rape on prime time.* Philadelphia: University of Pennsylvania Press.

Dahl, R. A. (2003). *How democratic is the American Constitution?* New Haven, CT: Yale University Press.

Delaware v. Prouse, 440 U.S. 648, 99 S. Ct. 1391, 1396 (1979).

Dillon, J. F. (1911). *Commentaries on the law of municipal corporations.* Boston: Little Brown.

Dorf, M. C. (2006). *No litmus test.* Lanham, MD: Rowman & Littlefield.

Durose, M. R., Harlow, C. W., Langan, P. A., Montivans, M., Rantala, R. R., & Smith, E. L. (2005). *Family violence statistics including statistics on strangers and acquaintances* (NCJ 207846). Washington, DC: U.S. Department of Justice.

Escobedo v. Illinois, 378 U.S. 478 (1964).

Federer, W. J. (2003). *The ten commandments and their influence on American law: A study in history.* St. Louis, MO: Amerisearch, Inc.

Feinman, J. M. (2006). *Law 101: Everything you need to know about the American legal system.* New York: Oxford University Press.

Flora, R. (2001). *How to work with sex offenders: A handbook for criminal justice, human service, and mental health professionals.* Philadelphia, PA: Haworth Press.

Florida Department of Law Enforcement. (2008). *Florida basic recruit training program: Law enforcement* (Vol. 1/2008.4). Tallahassee, FL: Author.

Florida State Legislature. (2008). *Florida state statutes.* Tallahassee: Author.

Frank, J. (2006, July 1). Couey's confession won't get to jurors. *St. Petersburg Times*, archives.

Gamache, D., & Asmus, M. (1999). Enhancing networking among service providers: Elements of successful coordination strategies. In M. Shepard & E. Pence (Eds.), *Coordinating community responses to domestic violence: Lessons from Duluth and beyond* (pp. 65–88). Thousand Oaks, CA: Sage.

Garrow, C. E., & Deer, S. (2004). *Tribal criminal law and procedure.* Lanham, MD: Rowman Altamira.

Gelles, R. J. (1997). *Intimate violence in families.* Thousand Oaks, CA: Sage.

Georgia State Legislature. (2008). *Georgia state statutes.* Atlanta: Author.

Gideon v. Wainwright, 372 U.S. 335 (1963).

Gould, J. B. (2008). *The innocence commission.* New York: New York University Press.

Gould Publications. (2005a). *Florida crimes, motor vehicles, and related laws with criminal jury instructions* (2005 ed.). Longwood, FL: Author.

Gould Publications. (2005b). *Texas criminal and traffic code.* Longwood, FL: Author.

Gould Publications. (2006). *Colorado peace officer's handbook.* Longwood, FL: Author.

Grano, J. D. (1996). *Confessions, truth, and the law.* Ann Arbor: University of Michigan Press.

Greene, J. R. (2006). *The encyclopedia of police science* (3rd ed.). Boca Raton, FL: CRC Press.

Groth, A. N., & Birnbaum, H. J. (2001). *Men who rape.* Cambridge, MA: Da Capo Press.

Gunderson, D. F., & Hopper, R. (1988). *Communication and law enforcement.* Lanham, MD: University Press of America.

Hate Crimes Sentencing Enhancement Act of 1992, 102nd U.S. Congress. Washington, DC: U.S. House of Representatives.

Hennessey, R. (1994, July 31). Neighbor girl found: Neighbor arrested. *Princeton-Times,* pp. A1, A14.

Holmes, O. W. (1909). *The common law.* Boston: Little, Brown.

Holtz, L. (2001). *Contemporary criminal procedure: Court decisions for law enforcement* (7th ed.). Longwood, FL: Gould.

Holtz, L. (2004). *Contemporary criminal procedure court decisions for law enforcement* (8th ed.). Longwood, FL: Gould.

Illinois v. Gates, 462 U.S. 213 (1983).

Illinois State Legislature. (2008). *Illinois state criminal code of 1961.* Springfield: Author.

Indiana State Legislature. (2008). *Indiana state statutes.* Indianapolis: Author.

Israel, J. H., & Lafave, W. R. (2001). *Criminal procedure: Constitutional limitations in a nutshell* (Nutshell Series). St. Paul, MN: West Group.

Jacobs, J. B., & Potter, K. (2001). *Hate crimes: Criminal law and identity politics.* New York: Oxford University Press.

Kansas State Legislature. (2008). *Kansas state statutes.* Topeka: Author.

King, L. W. (2004). *The code of Hammurabi.* Whitefish, MT: Kessinger.

Lockton, D., & Ward, R. (1997). *Domestic violence.* New York: Routledge.

Lyman, M. D., & Geberth, V. J. (2001). *Practical drug enforcement* (2nd ed.). Boca Raton, FL: CRC Press.

Lynch, J. P., & Addington, L. A. (2007). *Understanding crime statistics: Revisiting the divergence of the NCVS and UCR.* New York: Cambridge University Press.

Mapp v. Ohio, 376 U.S. 643 (1961).

Marderosian, H. C., & Weiner, W. P. (1980). *Handbook of Michigan criminal law and procedure.* Lansing, MI: Mid-Michigan Law Enforcement Center.

Massachusetts State Legislature. (2008). *Massachusetts state statutes.* Boston: Author.

Maxwell, C., Garner, J., & Faggan, J. (2001). *The effects of arrest on intimate partner violence: New evidence from the spouse assault replication program.* Washington, DC: National Institute of Justice.

McGregor, J. (2005). *Is it rape?* United Kingdom: Ashgate Publishing.

Michigan State Legislature. (1999). *Strip search* (MCL 764.25a). Lansing: Author.

Michigan State Legislature. (2008). *Michigan state statutes.* Lansing: Author.

Michigan State Police Training Academy. (2004). *Criminal law and procedure: A manual for Michigan police officers.* Lansing: Author.

Minneapolis Police Department. (2002, May 31). *Searching arrestees of the opposite sex* (9-202). Minneapolis: Author.

Minnesota v. Dickerson, 508 U.S. 366 (1993).

Miranda v. Arizona, 384 U.S. 436 (1966).

Missouri State Legislature. (2008). *Missouri state statutes.* Jefferson City: Author.

Nebraska State Legislature. (2008). *Nebraska state statutes.* Lincoln: Author.

Nevada State Legislature. (2008). *Nevada state statutes: Domestic violence* (NRS 33.018/171.137). Carson City: Author.

New Hampshire State Legislature. (2008). *New Hampshire state statutes.* Concord: Author.

New York State Legislature. (2008). *New York state statutes.* Albany: Author.

Nussbaum, M. C. (1999). *Sex and social justice.* New York: Oxford University Press.

Ohio State Legislature. (2008). *Ohio state statutes.* Columbus: Author.

Oregon v. Mathiason, 429 U.S. 492 (1977).

People v. Defore, 242 N.Y. 13, 21, 150 N.E. 585, 587 (1926).

Pieklik, D. (2005, April 21). Documents shed light on Jessica's death. *Citrus County Chronicle.*

Pollack, D. (2003). *Social work and the courts: A casebook.* New York: Routledge.

Qiunlan, K. P., Brewer, R. D., Siegel, P., Sleet, D. A., Mokdad, A. H., Shults, R. A., & Flowers, N. (2005). Alcohol-impaired driving among U.S. adults, 1993–2002. *American Journal of Preventive Medicine, 28*(4), 346–350.

Scheb, J. M., & Scheb II, J. M. (1998). *Criminal law and procedure.* New York: Thomson/Brooks Cole.

Scott, A. H. (2004). *Computer and intellectual property.* Arlington, VA: BNA Books.

Sibron v. New York, 392 U.S. 40 (1968).

Skolnick, J. (2004). A sketch of a police officer's "working personality." In B. W. Hancock & P. M. Sharp (Eds.), *Criminal justice in America: Theory, practice, and policy.* Upper Saddle River, NJ: Prentice Hall.

South Carolina State Legislature. (2008). *South Carolina code of laws.* Columbia: Author.

Spurgeon Hall, R. A., Dennis, C. B., & Chipman, T. L. (2000). *The ethical foundations of criminal justice.* Boca Raton, FL: CRC Press.

Stanko, E. A. (1989). Missing the mark? Police battering. In J. Hanmer, J. Radford, & E.A. Stanko (Eds.), *Women, policing, and male violence: International perspectives* (pp. 46–69). New York: Routledge.

Stering, R. (2004). *Police officer's handbook: An introductory guide.* Sudbury, MA: Jones & Bartlett.

Terry v. Ohio, 392 U.S. 1 (1968).

Texas v. Brown, 460 U.S. 730 (1983).

Thomas, D. (2002). *The role of police in American society.* (Speech). St. Johns River Community College, delivered June 1, 2003, St. Augustine, FL.

Thurman v. City of Torrington, Connecticut, 595 F. Supp. 1521 (1984 U.S. Dist. Ct.).

Tinetti v. Wittke, 479 F. Supp. 486, 491 (E.D. Wis. 1979).

Tromanhauser, E. (2003). Comments and reflections on forty years in the American criminal justice system. In J. I. Ross & S. C. Richards (Eds.), *Convict criminology* (pp. 81–94). Belmont, CA: Wadsworth/Thomson Learning.

United States v. Leon, 468 U.S. 897 (1984).

United States v. Place, 462 U.S. 696 (1983).

United States v. Robinson, 414 U.S. 218 (1973).

United States v. Ross, 456 U.S. 798 (1982).

U.S. Department of Justice. (2004). *Crime in the United States 2004: Uniform crime reports.* Washington, DC: U.S. Government Printing Office.

U.S. Department of Transportation. (2001). *Development of a standardized field sobriety test (SFST): Training management system* (DOT HS 809400). Washington, DC: National Highway and Traffic Administration.

Utah State Legislature. (2008). *Utah criminal code.* Salt Lake City: Author.

Vermont State Legislature. (2008). *Vermont state statutes* (Chapter 31: Discrimination: Hate motivated crimes, 13 V.S.A. 1455). Montpelier: Author.

Virginia State Legislature. (2008). *Virginia state statutes.* Richmond: Author.

Voas, R. B., & Lacey, J. H. (1989). Issues in the enforcement of impaired driving laws in the United States. In *Surgeon General's workshop on drunk driving: Background papers* (pp. 136–156). Rockville, MD: Office of the Surgeon General.

Washington State Legislature. (2008). *Revised code of Washington crimes and punishments.* Olympia: Author.

West Virginia Legislature. (2008). *West Virginia code.* Charleston: Author.

White, J. R. (2004). *Defending the homeland: Domestic intelligence, law enforcement, and security.* Belmont, CA: Wadsworth/Thomson Learning.

Wisconsin State Legislature. (2008). *Wisconsin state statutes.* Madison: Author.

Wolitski, R. J., Stall, R., & Valdiserri, R. O. (2007). *Unequal opportunity: Health disparities affecting gay and bisexual men in the United States.* New York: Oxford University Press.

Yarbrough, T. E. (2000). *The Rehnquist Court and the Constitution.* New York: Oxford University Press.

CHAPTER 4

POLICE SOCIALIZATION

OBJECTIVES

After completing this chapter, the student will be able to:

- Discuss the impact that entering policing has on one's personal life.
- Explain the preemployment screening process.
- Describe the differences in police and firefighter fitness needs.
- Discuss the role of fitness in policing and its relationship to longevity.
- Describe the role of the police academy in socializing a new officer.
- Explain the differences between an agency-run police academy and a college/university academy.
- Discuss the field training program and its impact on a new officer.
- Discuss the stages of a career.
- Describe the impact that politics has on policing.
- Discuss the role of police psychology in law enforcement.

KEY TERMS

acceptable criminal histories – minor law violations that do not disqualify police applicants who enter the preemployment process.

certifiable candidate – one who has completed the academy and is eligible to take the state examination to become certified, and who will then be able to be hired by an agency.

certified candidate – one who has completed the academy and can get a job immediately without taking a state examination.

95

daily observation report (DOR) – designed to assess a candidate's daily performance under normal conditions and stressful conditions in the field training program.

field training officer (FTO) – an experienced officer who has completed specialized training and is assigned to train new officers upon successful completion of the police academy.

field training program – on-the-job training; occurs after a candidate has completed the police academy. It is usually fourteen weeks and is considered an evaluation period.

general adaptation syndrome (GAS) – the body's physiological response to stressors consisting of three stages: alarm, resistance, and exhaustion.

police psychology – specialized to meet the needs of police officers. It can be and is used in the preemployment process; is utilized in hostage negotiations; determines if an officer is fit for duty; and is used in critical incident debriefings to debrief and counsel officers who have been involved in traumatic events and their aftermath.

total institution – an institution in which all aspects are under the control of a single authority, and all daily activities are designed to meet the needs and goals of the organization; policing is considered to be a total institution.

DOC'S WORDS OF WISDOM

There are two types of people who enter law enforcement, those who have a desire to help their community and those who are adrenaline junkies. The ones who will do the most damage to the profession are those who sign on for the sole purpose of excitement.

INTRODUCTION

The decision to be a police officer is something that one should not take lightly. The most profound question that an individual should ask is: Why do I want to be a police officer? In informal surveys with recruit classes, the most common answer is: "I want to help people." However, the reasons people decide to enter policing are numerous. Some choose policing because it is family tradition, while others are seeking job security, employee benefits, and/or excitement (Miller, 2007; Rafilson, 2003).

This chapter will allow you to explore the process of becoming a police officer and address the personal sacrifices that one makes as a result of the profession. You will learn about the preemployment process that qualifies and disqualifies a candidate; the academy and the different avenues to police certification; the field training program, where the books meet the streets; life beyond the first year to the twenty-year career and retirement; and the pitfalls of policing, including the personal toll it takes on one's psyche and police psychology.

THE DECISION

The opening quotation describes why the public is so intrigued with law enforcement. Television portrays it as a demanding profession full of challenges, adversity, and conflict. The media also describes the profession as a rewarding one, and that is what draws people to it. Some people come to policing from other professions, such as stockbrokers, pharmacists, educators, attorneys, and even nurses, to name a few. Discussions this author has had while training police recruits over the last thirty years have often included the question: Why do you want to be a police officer? Individuals coming from other professions have all had a similar response: "The job I had was boring" or "I did not get any satisfaction from what I was doing."

A personal decision to become a police officer is often met with fear by family members. Mothers and wives fear that their loved one will be killed. They all remember the last officer in the community who was killed, and in an attempt to have an impact on their loved one's decision, they will remind one of that: "Officer Smith was killed, and now his wife is a widow with three children." But just as some families fear the decision, others find that there is a sense of pride in the decision.

In stark contrast, minority and immigrant families may be very fearful of the decision that their child has made. In the case of the African American community, their relationship with the law enforcement community is one that has been tenuous at best. In the United States, this apprehension dates back to the slave patrols of the 1800s, and more recently the African American community has been a victim of racial profiling (Cooper, 2006; Hadden, 2001; Kops, 2007; Wilson, 1996). Other constant reminders are such cases as Rodney King, Abner Louima, and the 2006 shooting of Sean Bell who was leaving his bachelor party in Queens, New York (Browne-Marshall, 2007; Skolnick & Fyfe, 1993).

Those of Latin American descent have memories of police, secret police, national police, or a combination of military and police who were responsible for death squads, killing innocent bystanders with impunity, or were ethically and morally challenged while their governments looked the other way. In these circumstances, the police in some countries are considered evil, as opposed to being protectors. Such activities have been especially common in Chile, Argentina, Brazil, and Uruguay (Fagen, 1992; Heinz & Fruling, 1999).

Minorities who choose law enforcement as a career in the United States are often seen as traitors to their race because they have chosen to become a part of the system. Smith and Natalier (2005) argue that minority officers experience hostility from members of their own community and are seen as traitors; in such cases, this creates a stressful situation, with minority officers being torn between their communities and their profession (p. 90).

Law enforcement does have a negative impact on one's personal life. Officers have few friends outside of police work. Russell and Beigel (1990) describe the impact on an officer's personal life as an overinvestment in the profession—meaning that officers and eventually their families invest too much of their personal lives in the profession, often forsaking personal relationships outside of the profession (pp. 405–408). Skolnick (2004) describes policing as a form of social isolation and loneliness (p. 106).

PREEMPLOYMENT SCREENING

The employment process with a law enforcement agency is unlike any other except for those in organizations that deal with sensitive or dangerous material. The minimum qualifications for most states are: at least 18 years of age; a U.S. citizen; high school diploma or GED; no felony convictions; weight in proportion to height; good physical condition; and a valid driver's license.

Age Requirement

The state requirements are very simple; however, agency requirements are much more demanding, and the preemployment process is designed to weed out undesirable applicants. Although most states have a minimum age of 18, most agencies will not consider applicants until they are at least 21 years of age. The logic here is that with maturity and some life experience, a candidate will be more likely to make sound decisions.

Physical Fitness Requirement

Some states, such as Michigan, have mandatory physical fitness tests. Many states leave such tests to the agency. The issue of fitness has been debated for years. The only requirement in most states in regard to fitness is that a candidate must pass a physical examination by a licensed physician. The problem is that there is no clearly identifiable fitness level for a police officer. In fact, policing is considered a sedentary profession that may, at times, require strenuous activity (Charles, 1982; Thomas & Barringer, 2008).

Firefighter Standards Versus Police Standards

Firefighters have a definitive task every time they arrive at a fire or rescue. Their job requires pulling hoses, swinging an axe, climbing stairs or ladders, handling a charged hose, handling heavy equipment, and removing victims from buildings or automobiles. The firefighter must complete these tasks wearing bunker gear, air tanks, and face masks. A firefighter's physical requirements are much easier to quantify than those of a law enforcement officer. Fahy (2005) noted that during a ten-year period from 1995 to 2004, nearly half of the firefighter deaths were due to sudden cardiac arrest (p. 1).

Because of the physical demands and the specific job tasks, fitness requirements for firefighters have been identified through the development of a "Firefighter Combat Fitness Model," of which there are various versions. One version consists of a stair climb, hose hoist, forcible entry, hose advance, and victim rescue. This exercise is completed wearing full fire gear and is timed. The St. Petersburg College Fire Academy in St. Petersburg, Florida, requires that the tasks must be completed in less than seven minutes.

Police Fitness

It is impossible to define police officers' responsibilities and know how often they will be challenged physically. Lee (2007) argues that police achieve a certain level of fitness while attending the police academy. However, once employed by an agency, there are very few agencies that have maintenance standards with annual or biannual testing. Quire and Blount (1990) state that in American law enforcement agencies, heart disease is the single greatest cause of early retirement and the second greatest cause of limited-duty assignments.

It is a given that at some point during an officer's career, he or she will have to arrest a combative subject. To further support the notion of police fitness and readiness, the periodical *Officers Killed or Assaulted* (FBI, 2002) offers that officers are physically assaulted with hands, fists, or feet on an average of 58,000 times per year. The amount of force that an officer utilizes during a physical encounter is determined by the amount of resistance the officer encounters. Truncale and Smith (1994) assert that a number of elements should be taken into account during the altercation; these are entitled *officer/subject factors* and include: age, size, sex, skill levels, and number of officers/subjects involved. In addition to the officer/subject factors identified by Truncale and Smith, the Florida Department of Law Enforcement (2000) identified additional factors to include: the suspect's demeanor and actions; the nature of the crime or incident; weapons involved; number of suspects involved; potential danger to the officer and others; and the concept of last resort.

Downey and Roth (1981) identify the profile of a suspect as a constant: male, 24 years of age, weight 170 pounds, and waist 31 inches. They also describe a typical male officer's physical decline over a twenty-five-year period: an officer who starts the career at age 22 with a 31-inch waist and weighing 170 pounds will, twenty-five years later, at age 47, have a 38-inch waist and weigh 228 pounds (pp. 4–5). (See Figure 4-1.)

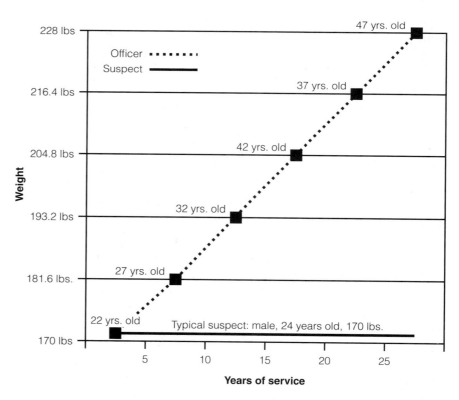

Figure 4-1   Police Fitness Versus Suspect Fitness

Brooks (2001) provides an analysis of *Lanning v. Southeastern Pennsylvania Transportation Authority (SEPTA)*, which states that agency-specific requirements that are researched and validated are defensible. In the case of SEPTA, it was the inclusion of a 1.5-mile run in 12 minutes. Unlike a patrol officer in a marked car, transit officers are on foot and are required to run from one station to the next to back up fellow officers. If an officer is incapable of running that distance and upon arrival lacks the stamina to assist in the apprehension and arrest of a subject, then the issue becomes a matter of public safety. In regard to SEPTA, the court ruled that the aerobic standard is unique to SEPTA, making it the responsibility of each agency to develop individual standards that are unique to that agency (pp. 26–28).

Written Examination

The written examination comes in many forms. It may be as simple as what is known as the Tests of Adult Basic Education (TABE), which is a test containing sections on English, math, and reading assessment with a particular grade cutoff. Other exams look to address such issues as reasoning, judgment, inferential thinking, and memory.

Some exams may require a candidate to write a basic police report or a writing sample. This provides an agency with two assessment tools: the first is to identify if an applicant can write using proper noun/verb agreement as well as organize the report. Second, writing a police report provides an assessment of listening skills; ability to identify pertinent information; and ability to answer the six most relevant questions in report writing: who, what, where, when, how, and why. If you are required to take such an exam, don't panic; the assessors know whether you have had police experience or not and will look for the basic elements (LeQuang, 2005; Schroeder & Lombardo, 2001).

Oral Board/Interview

The oral board is designed to see how candidates present themselves to the public, handle stress, and think on their feet. The makeup of an oral board is usually a minimum of three members. Some agencies use just agency personnel, so this board may consist of officers or a mix of officers and administrative personnel. Other agencies believe it is important to provide a mix of community leaders and police on the oral board. Just like the written portions, the oral board is graded. The questions are the same for every candidate, with standardized responses and scoring.

The most difficult aspect of the oral board is answering each question correctly. The dilemma that a candidate often faces is: "Do I say what is correct, or do I say what I think they want to hear?" A candidate who has had prior police experience has a knowledge base that consists of law, previous experience, and departmental policies. Candidates who have had no prior experience must draw from personal experience with the idea that common sense and logic will guide them.

The written exam, writing sample, fitness test, and oral board are usually completed before a candidate moves on in the process. The idea here is to weed out the candidates who are not suitable for employment with that particular agency with a minimum investment of agency money and time.

Background Investigation

The background investigation is an exhaustive examination of a candidate's background. The agency addresses criminal history, driving record, substance abuse/use of illegal substances, credit history, current and past relationships, neighborhood canvas, high school and college transcripts and discipline records, medical records, friends and associates, and family. The two most common disqualifiers for a candidate are a poor driving record and substance abuse.

Stevens (2008) notes that for a number of years, there has been a lack of qualified applicants; agencies have been competing for those who are qualified (p. 256). Since this has become a trend, some agencies have lowered their hiring standards and are hiring candidates with what is described as **acceptable criminal histories.** So, for example, some agencies will overlook drug abuse if the candidate has not used an illegal substance six months prior to applying (this is usually limited to marijuana use). Other law violations in an acceptable criminal history might include fighting or misdemeanor theft/shoplifting.

acceptable criminal histories

minor law violations that do not disqualify police applicants who enter the preemployment process.

Medical Examination

Candidates are sent for routine physical examinations as a part of the complete examination process. They are given a stress test to determine if they are heart-healthy, and they are required to provide a urine sample to test for drug abuse. The urine test is not designed to disqualify a candidate who takes prescribed medication for an ailment such as asthma.

Polygraph

The polygraph is usually administered after a candidate has completed each of the other tests. The polygraph is not administered in all states, so it is an instrument that may be unique to a particular state or agency.

The most interesting aspect of the polygraph is that a candidate gets to see and answer the questions before he or she is given the test. Some agencies use what is known as a polygraph packet with very specific answers to questions. Other agencies use a candidate's background packet, application, and medical history as a source of truthfulness. During this process, the polygrapher will establish a baseline for truthfulness through a series of questions in which the candidate is instructed to be untruthful.

Psychological Evaluations

The final phase of preemployment screening is the psychological evaluation and interview. The objective here is to determine if a candidate suffers from mental illness or a psychological disorder. The two most commonly used psychological instruments are the *Minnesota Multiphasic Personality Inventory—2 (MMPI-2)*, which consists of 567 true-false items, and the *California Psychological Inventory—Revised (CPI-R)*, which consists of 434 true-false items. Upon completion and scoring of the instrument, the department psychologist will meet with the candidate and address the items that appear to be unusual. This interview is usually the final step in the hiring process and is applied to candidates with prior experience as well as new hires. Employers would like to use these tests as a predictor of which candidates will be good police officers; however, research has shown that the instruments are limited in their ability, and researchers caution employers against using them as such (Aylward, 1985; Burbeck & Furnham, 1985; Dwyer, Prien, & Bernard, 1990).

THE ACADEMY

The academy is where the real socialization begins. For municipal and county law enforcement officers, generally there are two types of academies: those affiliated with the local community college or a college and those that are agency-run. Most of the instructors are sworn law enforcement officers or practicing attorneys from multiple jurisdictions within the area who have been certified by a state credentialing body. In California, this body is known as the Commission on Peace Officer Standards and Training (POST); in Texas, it is called the Texas Commission on Law Enforcement Officer Standards and Education (TCLEOSE); in Michigan, it is known as the Michigan Commission on Law Enforcement Standards (MCOLES); and in Florida, it is titled the Criminal Justice Standards and Training Commission (CJSTC). Although the names are different, these credentialing agencies share the same responsibility:

mandating and establishing training standards, and overseeing the quality of all law enforcement training offered within their respective states.

The college-affiliated academies often are run by local community colleges and in some cases universities. Most candidates who attend these academies pay for their training and are not sponsored by an agency. Law enforcement agencies like this approach because it saves them tremendous amounts of money. Since these academies are not affiliated with an agency, some run as an assessment center, which means that the college provides the preemployment screening services prior to the candidate entering the academy. The models vary from state to state. Some have developed a curriculum that meets two educational goals: first, upon completion of the two-year program, the candidates will graduate with an *associate's degree;* and second, the candidates will have completed the police academy and be *certifiable or certified,* depending on the state (Holden, 2006).

certifiable candidate

one who has completed the academy and is eligible to take the state examination to become certified, and who will then be able to be hired by an agency.

certified candidate

one who has completed the academy and can get a job immediately without taking a state examination.

- **Certifiable candidate:** one who has completed the academy and is eligible to take the state examination to become certified, and who will then be able to be hired by an agency.
- **Certified candidate:** one who has completed the academy and can get a job immediately without taking a state examination.

The biggest complaint that agencies have with the college model is that they have no control over the training. Although the state standard is universal, there is no specificity to a particular organization—meaning that once candidates graduate, they need a lot of additional training to meet agency needs.

The agency model is the most desirable because the agency is hiring and training their personnel in a manner that is tailor-made for the organization. However, this model is also the most expensive. Upon successful completion of preemployment screening, a candidate is hired and enters the agency academy. All the instructors are agency instructors. One organization throughout the United States that runs its own academies are the forty-nine State Police and Highway Patrol agencies (Bailey, 1995).

The benefit of an agency academy is that candidates meet all of the mandatory state requirements and in addition they are introduced to the agency policies, local ordinances, and agency philosophy. This type of academy also gives the agency and the candidate an opportunity to see if they are compatible. Since each agency is unique with unique philosophies, this is a very important stage in the socialization of an officer. The candidate may not be the right candidate for that agency, and yet he or she may find that an adjoining jurisdiction is compatible with his or her personality and philosophy.

The concept of compatibility is demonstrated in a study completed by Yearwood (2003), which states that the average length of stay by a newly hired candidate is thirty-four months. Yearwood's study noted that 30% of the officers transferred to larger agencies, 26% to agencies of the same size, 30% to state agencies, and less than 10% went to smaller agencies. There was no common denominator; at best what we find is a lack of compatibility with the agency, greater opportunities, or an agency culture that is similar to the philosophy of those who transferred (p. 23).

Curriculum in each academy is much the same. In fact, from one state to the next, academies have similar course content and titles. What does vary drastically from state to state is the actual number of training hours that the state mandates. An example of an academy curriculum is that developed for the Florida Gulf Coast University Criminal Justice students who are allowed to attend the local police academy and receive fifteen undergraduate college credits for completion of the academy. Following are course descriptions detailing the content of an academy curriculum:

- *Medical First Responder:* This course is based on Department of Transportation (DOT) techniques for handling medical emergencies. The course includes injury assessment; types of resuscitation; and signs, symptoms, and methods of transmission of communicable diseases.

- *Police Communications:* This course is an examination of the police report writing process. The student will be introduced to report writing, interviewing, taking statements, the use of telecommunications, crisis intervention, community-oriented policing, and officer survival.

- *Firearms:* This course includes the use of officer firearms including the semi-automatic pistol, revolver, rifle/carbine, and shotgun. Instruction includes firearms safety, ammunition use, discretionary shooting, day and night courses of fire, and survival firearms training.

- *Defensive Tactics:* This course is an examination of police defensive tactics. The student will be introduced to the techniques used for an officer's personal safety; and the use of dialogue, empty hand control techniques, impact weapons, chemical agents, and restraining devices are covered.

- *Vehicle Operations/Driving:* This course examines the components of police driving, including the physiological and psychological factors that impact the operation of a vehicle. The student will be introduced to vehicle maintenance, vehicle dynamics, environmental conditions, skids and their causes, and practical driving exercises, which are conducted on the driving range.

- *Human Services:* This course is an examination of the many services that a police officer has to provide to the public. The student will be introduced to the following special populations: the mentally retarded, mentally ill, substance abusers, physically disabled, and the elderly.

- *Patrol Operations:* This course addresses the daily skills and techniques needed by officers to perform patrol tactics and respond to various types of calls. Students will be introduced to community-oriented policing (COP), patrol procedures, arrest and custody, and responding to alarms.

- *Special Topics:* This course is an examination of the court process, rescue, bombs and explosives, terrorism, street gangs, extremist groups, and crowd control.

- *Fitness:* This course is an examination of wellness as it relates to the police officer. The student will examine stress, nutrition, stretching, strength, and aerobic conditioning as it relates to an officer's survival and daily living.

- *Investigations:* This course is an examination of the criminal investigation process. The student will be introduced to the investigation of various crimes, including property crimes, persons crimes, narcotics offenses, vice, organized crime, and death investigations. Techniques are developed from the initial observation methods through the processing of the crime scene and case preparation. The state's computer network is studied as an information source.

- *Traffic:* This course includes traffic enforcement and control, with the inclusion of DUI offenses and enforcement. The student will also be introduced to traffic crash investigation, scene management, reporting procedures, and the court process.

- *Constitutional Law:* This course is an examination of and an introduction to policing. The student will be introduced to the criminal justice system, constitutional law, state statutes, court procedures, rules of evidence, search and seizure, and ethics.

The academy structure is like military boot camp. If the academy is an overnight academy, like the state police facilities, then it is just like boot camp. The only difference is that candidates get to go home on the weekends. A traditional academy can last anywhere from eight weeks to six months, depending on the requirements (Klockars, Ivković, & Haberfeld, 2006).

The academy and the training process are designed to weed out those who are unwilling to conform socially and those who cannot meet the minimum academic standard, which can be 70% or 80% per examination depending on the state (Barker, 1999; Kessler, 1993; Klinger, 2004). The third category of unsuccessful candidates is those who are injured in training and released, although this group is usually allowed to attend another class once the injury has healed.

Policing is not a profession for everyone. For those who are successful in the academy and complete the **field training program,** the profession produces a number of bonds that begin with an officer's first assignment. These relationships are fostered between officers who ride as partners and respond to calls together, and they become lifelong bonds that follow officers throughout their tenure (Reuss-Ianni, 1993). The scenarios that you have read and will continue to read in this text are a testament to that. (See Figure 4-2.)

field training program

on-the-job training; occurs after a candidate has completed the police academy. It is usually fourteen weeks and is considered an evaluation period.

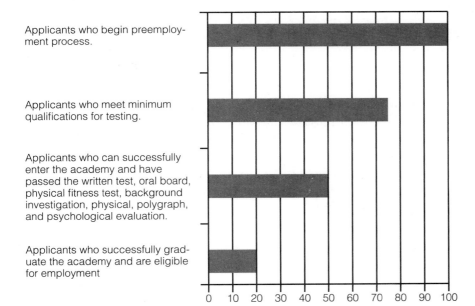

Figure 4-2   Preemployment Hiring Process

This graph depicts the outcome of every 100 applicants who apply with police departments. The data supports that each phase of the hiring process is a process of elimination. The outcomes presented are based on the experiences of several large agencies in the Southeastern United States and are averages.

With that said, there is an attrition rate in every academy, which is dependent upon the style of the training philosophy to which the academy director subscribes. If it is demanding with a military structure, a class may start with one hundred candidates and graduate fifty at the end of sixteen weeks (Latting & Deshazo, 2005). If the academy does not adhere to strict military discipline, then the average attrition rate is between 10% and 15% (Greene, 2006).

FIELD TRAINING OFFICER PROGRAM

The field training officer (FTO) program is the next step in the evaluation process. It can and should be considered a phase in training where academics meets application. It is understood, depending on the agency, that there will be an attrition rate of between 20% and 50% of those who enter the program. The Florida Department of Law Enforcement (FDLE, 2003) states that the goal of the FTO program is to produce a probationary officer who has satisfactorily demonstrated the basic job skill, knowledge, and ability/attitude competencies as required by the agency (p. 8).

The FTO program was born out of two tragic incidents that occurred at the San Jose Police Department. The first involved an officer who was in a fatal accident. Everyone at the agency knew that he was having problems, but supervisors gave the officer satisfactory evaluations. The second incident was a fatal shooting of an unarmed motorist (FDLE, 2003). The San Jose Police Department and supervisory staff were held responsible under three standard tenets of negligence: failure to supervise, failure to train, and negligent retention. In response to the claims of negligence, the San Jose Police Department developed the current program known as the *San Jose model*. This program was developed in the 1970s and has remained the standard, because it provides two critical components in the assessment and evaluation of probationary officers: training in the critical areas and, most important, evaluation.

The FTO program is stressful for probationary officers because they are being evaluated daily by their **field training officer (FTO)** with an instrument known as a **daily observation report (DOR).** The DOR is designed to assess performance under normal conditions and stressful conditions in these disciplines or skills sets: Driving, Orientation, Field Performance, Officer Safety, Control of Conflict, Physical Skill, Problem Solving and Decision Making, Self-Initiated Activity, Patrol Procedures, Investigative Procedures, Interview and Interrogation Skills, Technology, Report Writing, and Radio. Although more than twenty items are being assessed daily, it is unreasonable to think that anyone could possibly be

field training officer (FTO)

an experienced officer who has completed specialized training and is assigned to train new officers upon successful completion of the police academy.

daily observation report (DOR)

designed to assess a candidate's daily performance under normal conditions and stressful conditions in the field training program.

exposed to each of these conditions every day they are on patrol. Scoring of the DOR is on a scale from 1 to 7, as follows:

1–3	Unsatisfactory
4–6	Minimum Acceptable
7	Exceeds Minimum Acceptable

The FTO program is designed to be an average of fourteen weeks, exposing the probationary officer to each shift and a new FTO every four weeks:

- *Phase one:* This phase is a probationary officer's first shift assignment in patrol, first four weeks of training, and first field training officer (FTO). The first two weeks are known as the *limbo stage* and afford the probationary officer an opportunity to become acclimated to radio procedures, geography, calls for service, and report forms. The first two weeks are an observation period. As the new officer becomes comfortable, he or she will begin using the radio, writing simple reports, and driving.

- *Phase two:* The probationary officer is assigned to a new shift and a new FTO. There is an expectation that the probationary officer will take on more of the complex tasks: investigate the more serious offenses, and write the more complex reports with the assistance of the FTO. At this point, the probationary officer should have a much better understanding of the geography as well as the radio procedures. It is expected during this phase that the probationary officer is capable of completing 50% of the job tasks on a daily basis without much direction.

- *Phase three:* The probationary officer is assigned to a new shift and a new FTO. In this phase the probationary officer is expected to complete 75% to 100% of the tasks with some guidance. At the completion of phase three, officers are expected to move to the final phase of training where they will be responsible for 100% of the workload.

- *Final phase:* This phase is unique in that the probationary officer is assigned to his or her phase-one FTO for final evaluation. It is also unique because it is two weeks in duration rather than four, and the FTO is an observer who wears plain clothes (Dantzker, 2005; FDLE, 2003; Klockars et al., 2006; Walker & Katz, 2005).

Probationary officers who successfully complete all four phases of training will be assigned to a shift and begin work. (See Figure 4-3.)

The probationary officer is usually on probation for one year from the date of employment. Officers who complete the year without any major

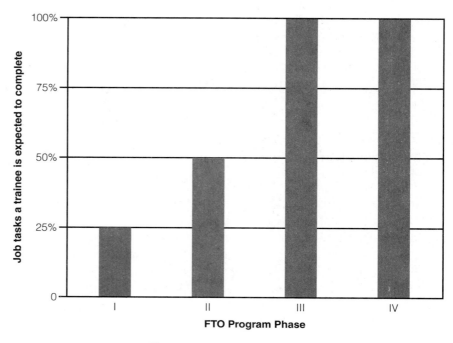

Figure 4-3   Trainee Job Tasks

This chart depicts the percentage of job tasks that a trainee is expected to complete without
assistance by the end of each phase. The trainee's successes and/or failures
are noted on the daily observation report.

problems will be retained and off probation. Probationary employees can
be terminated for any reason.

If there is a problem in field training, an agency has two options: terminate the probationary officer or provide remedial training in the problem areas. Some of the problems that arise are: poor comprehension of
geography; poor radio skills; inability to apply the law; poor or no report
writing skills; poor officer safety skills; and poor judgment. Remediation
is a prescription to address the agency's concerns and can last from one to
four weeks.

THE SOCIALIZATION PROCESS

The process of becoming a police officer begins with the decision to enter
the profession. However, once the preemployment process begins, a candidate is drawn deeper into the process. The real shock and indoctrination
begins in the academy with the military style training, learning the law,
firearms, and beginning to understand that there is no other job on earth

like that of a police officer. Unlike other professions, this is truly a way of life; a police officer is a police officer 24 hours a day, 7 days a week (Ruiz & Hummer, 2007; Russell & Beigel, 1990).

Like many professions, policing is considered an institution, and the process of becoming an officer means that one is ultimately institutionalized (McNamara, 1999). McNamara offers a theory that police and military recruits are resocialized in that they are stripped of their identity when they enter training, and as they complete the training process they are molded to fit the shape of the institution in question (p. 3). This process includes the learning of new rules, expectations, professional standards, language, and a commitment to the profession and fellow officers.

Goffman (1961) argues that this resocialization occurs in what he describes as a **total institution.** Goffman describes the characteristics of a total institution as: all aspects of the profession are conducted under a single authority; all of the activities are carried out in the immediate company of others; all members are required to act alike and are treated the same; all activities are tightly scheduled and controlled by a command staff; and all the daily activities are designed to meet the goals of the organization (p. 6). An excellent example of the expectations that the total institution demands of its members can be found in General Order 26/17 from the Gainesville Police Department (1998), which provides the following:

> Members of this department will not associate with known offenders except in the lawful performance of their duty or with persons that they know are under criminal investigation or indictment, or persons who have a criminal reputation within the community. (p. 4)

It is because of resocialization and the expectations of the total institution that police officers develop a working personality that Skolnick (2004) describes as being comprised of two variables: danger and authority. However, psychologists have been unable to identify what is considered the perfect or ideal personality of a police officer (Barak, 2007; Bartol & Bartol, 2008; Kenney & Watson, 1999). There is a difference between the working personality and the ideal officer in that the working personality is developed over time and is a direct result of socialization.

total institution

an institution in which all aspects are under the control of a single authority, and all daily activities are designed to meet the needs and goals of the organization; policing is considered to be a total institution.

THE POLICE CAREER

Upon successful completion of the FTO program, probationary officers are assigned to shifts. New officers are assigned wherever the agency needs them, usually to fill holes in staffing. Most agencies bid shifts based on seniority; bid cycles can be every three, six, or twelve months, depending on the agency. A new officer will stay on his or her assigned shift until shift bids. The most popular shift for senior officers is the day shift because it provides some degree of normalcy when it comes to a personal life. The other two shifts are evenings and midnights where most of the officers with low seniority are assigned. Evening shift hours are 3:00 P.M. to 11:00 P.M. on an 8-hour shift or 4:00 P.M. to 2:00 A.M. on a 10-hour shift, and midnight shift hours are 11:00 P.M. to 7:00 A.M. for an 8-hour shift or 7:00 P.M. to 7:00 A.M. on a 12-hour shift.

Placing most of the junior officers on one of two shifts creates a problem because of their lack of experience. To address this issue, an agency will attempt to assign senior supervisors. However, supervisors bid for shift preference based on seniority, and as a result, the same problem exists—with one caveat: the junior supervisors are experienced officers and should have an excellent knowledge base to draw from.

CAREER DEVELOPMENT

All candidates have some idea about what they want to accomplish as they enter policing. Some find a niche in patrol and never leave it. Others have visions of assignments in homicide, narcotics, traffic, K–9, training, school resource officer, community-oriented policing, street crimes, SWAT/ERT, hostage negotiator, and/or to be promoted through the ranks and become a part of the administration. Policing is like any other profession in that there are many opportunities. See Chapter 11 for a detailed discussion of career development.

The purpose of career development is to enhance each employee's current job performance and enable individuals to take advantage of future job opportunities. Progressive agencies understand the importance of such a plan in the development and retention of their employees. Once off probation, an officer will identify his or her interests and career goals. While in patrol, the officer will be allowed to attend specialized training courses to prepare him or her for the future assignment.

A question that all candidates have is: how long do I need to be in patrol before I can transfer? The time frame is different for each agency; it could be as little as one year or as long as five years. Unless an officer has prior experience, leaving patrol after one or two years is a disservice to the agency and the officer, because new officers are just becoming comfortable with their newfound role. In fact, it takes about five years before new officers are considered seasoned/veterans because by this time they have experienced everything that patrol has to offer.

The aspect of career planning that is often overlooked is retirement. A law enforcement officer's career lasts on average twenty to twenty-five years. If an officer were to start his or her career at age 22 and retire after twenty years of service, the officer would retire at the age of 42. Retiring from law enforcement is similar to retiring from the military. Policing is an identity and a way of life. The problem is that no one needs a homicide investigator or a retired traffic cop except a police department or private attorney. Career planning is not complete unless it assists an officer in preparing for retirement/separation. This plan should begin approximately five years before the officer's planned retirement (Hutton & Mydlarz, 2001; Russell & Beigel, 1990). Five years is ideal because it provides enough time for an officer to complete a bachelor's or master's degree and/or become credentialed in another profession.

STAGES OF A POLICE CAREER

A police officer's career evolves through many stages. At the beginning, an officer is the idealist, with a personal constitution of saving the world. After years of service, officers lose their optimism and become cynics, lacking trust in both the organization and humanity. The change happens as a result of dealing with the public and all their idiosyncrasies as well as the departmental politics. Officers experience four identifiable stages throughout their career:

- *Stage one/rookie years:* During this stage, officers are very optimistic. They enter policing with the idea that they are going to save the world, do everything by the book, and protect life and the rights of individuals. Niederhoffer (1967) describes these years as an indoctrination where the rookie learns the language, rituals, patrolling zones, discretion and keeping the peace, issuance of citations, the temptations of receiving payoffs, and making arrests (pp. 54–76). This stage can last between one and five years.

- *Stage two/productive years:* During this stage, officers have developed the necessary skills and are very proficient at their job. In fact, they are comfortable with their assignment and find a tremendous amount of job satisfaction. This is often where an officer is deciding on a career path, be it patrol, traffic, detectives, or promotions and administration. Niederhoffer (1967) describes this stage as the five-year officer, in many cases, looking beyond patrol to do something different (pp. 77–78). Although the officers are satisfied, they have developed some degree of cynicism as a result of two factors:

crime and politics. This stage can begin as soon as the third year and last until the tenth year.

- *Stage three/cynical years:* These years can be created by several factors, such as being passed over for promotion or not getting an assignment the officer had planned for as part of his or her career development. In the cynical years, there is often resentment and bitterness that is born out of exchanges with the public and the administration. The cynicism impacts all officers, and what often brings about the change to a negative attitude is a new assignment, whether they want it or not. Every officer experiences cynicism, but it is unique to each individual based on the individual's personal feelings and satisfaction. This stage can begin as early as the fifth year and last until retirement.
- *Stage four/twilight years:* This is the end of an officer's career—the last four or five years. In most cases, officers have resolved any conflicts they had and their cynicism has leveled off. It would be safe to say that they have found their place within the organization and accept their role. Niederhoffer (1967) describes these officers as the old-timers who have put in fifteen or more years of service. Although these are called the twilight years, they can begin as soon as the tenth year and last until retirement.

In examining the stages, you will find that there are no absolutes and that they overlap. The design of these stages is akin to those in Maslow's theory on the hierarchy of needs or Freud's theory of psychosexual development.

A career is something that should flow smoothly with proper planning. Void of any mishaps, the transition from one stage to the next is simple. The one element in career planning that cannot be assessed, however, is human nature. In policing, the organization is fluid; there is constant change, and with change comes changes in the political climate—hence, the varying degrees of cynicism.

POLITICS IN POLICING

Politics and *policing* should create an oxymoron in that police are not to be influenced in their decision making. Nevertheless, three types of politics impact the profession:

1. *Interagency politics:* politics that occur between two agencies. The agencies will work together when it is to their benefit, but at times the relationship is tenuous. One of the most common relationships is between the prosecutor's office and the police department. It is not

uncommon for the prosecutor's office to dismiss a case without cause (Kleinig, 1996; Stanko, 1989).

2. *Intra-agency politics:* politics within the organization. Skolnick and Bayley (1988) argue that the institutional character plays a role in the relationship between the leadership and officers and the ability of a department to make strides or change (p. 7). The politics of an administration will determine how much support the organization receives from the rank and file. Some of the battles may include: bickering between commanders to gain favor of the sheriff/chief at the expense of fellow commanders; Internal Affairs being characterized as the administration's headhunters and showing preference to a select few; the promotional process allows the administration to promote their favorites despite scores. Unless the chief executive addresses such matters, intra-agency politics can divide an organization and ultimately destroy the agency's morale.

3. *Community-agency politics:* a form of politics that can have great influence on an agency and its ability to provide effective police services. This form of politics is excellent if the agency has taken the time to foster a working relationship with the community. However, it can and will backfire if the agency has done nothing to deal with community concerns. Community-oriented policing, problem-oriented policing, and zero tolerance are concepts of the police where the agency has enlisted the community. However, what is missing is civilian oversight of the operations, meaning that such programs are viewed by researchers as tools for police to gain information, but lacking in shared concern or investment by the police (Beckett & Sasson, 2004; Giles, 2002; Lyons, 2002).

POLICE PSYCHOLOGY

Policing and the field of psychology are at best an uncomfortable marriage. From a psychological standpoint, psychologists who practice **police psychology** view their role as very necessary in that it is an integral part of the preemployment process; is utilized in hostage negotiations; determines if an officer is fit for duty; and is part of critical incident debriefings, which are the debriefing and counseling of officers who have been involved in traumatic events and their aftermath (Bartol, 2005; McNally & Solomon, 1999; Scrivner & Kurke, 1995).

police psychology

specialized to meet the needs of police officers. It can be and is used in the preemployment process; is utilized in hostage negotiations; determines if an officer is fit for duty; and is used in critical incident debriefings to debrief and counsel officers who have been involved in traumatic events and their aftermath

On the other hand, police have little faith or trust in the field of psychology. In fact, a certain degree of paranoia exists in policing regarding the administration, which is based on the relationship the administration has with the officers. This fear translates into believing that management is attempting to find a way to force an officer off the department by declaring that he or she is a danger to society and/or to himself or herself (Ostrov, 1995; Rostow & Davis, 2004). The bottom line is that police officers see and do things of which the average human being cannot conceive, and this translates into stress in both their professional and personal lives. (See Scenario 4-1.)

SCENARIO 4-1: BURGLARY INVESTIGATION

You are on patrol and receive the following call Alpha 110, 10-65: Respond to 1221 W. Lafayette, apartment 201, reference a possible burglary. The complainant advises that she hears banging noises in apartment 201. The complainant states that the resident in 201 has left for work and that she has taken her 5-year-old son to the sitter and that no one is to be in the apartment. You arrive on scene, speak with the complainant, and she repeats exactly what she told dispatch. While you are talking to the neighbor, you hear knocking against the wall and hear something break. You advise dispatch regarding what you heard and check on your backup's arrival. You are advised that backup is at least six minutes away. You make the decision to check the apartment before backup arrives, fearful that the suspect will flee or that an innocent person is in the apartment and may be injured.

You check the door to 201 and it is unlocked. You enter the apartment; it is dark, and you hear someone in the back slamming what you believe are dresser drawers. You announce yourself and order the subject to come out with hands up. The suspect enters the dark living room and you observe a silhouette of the suspect holding a gun. You order the suspect to drop the gun, and he turns and points the gun at you. You fire two rounds, instantly killing the suspect.

When you secure the suspect, you determine that he is a child approximately 5 years of age and that the gun is a toy. The investigation reveals that the child is the 5-year-old who lives there and that his mother was unable to get a sitter for the day. The mother left the child at home by himself because she could not afford to miss work. She has done this in the past and there has never been a problem.

Analysis and Reflection

1. Did you have a legal right to investigate the suspicious circumstances? Yes. Based on the information that you received, you had every right to investigate the compliant, especially since the complainant had intimate knowledge of the occupants of 201.

2. Were you justified in entering the apartment and not waiting on backup? Your logic for entering the apartment was sound. It was based on exigent circumstances for fear that someone might be injured in the apartment. However, that decision may be questioned based on the information that you received in the call.

3. Once in the apartment, after challenging the suspect and he turned with what you believed to be a gun, did you have a right to use deadly force? Yes. You have a right to defend yourself and others in such situations. In fact, the law is on your side in the decision to use deadly force.

4. Does it matter that he was a child and pointing a gun at you? No. Once again the law does not discriminate when it comes to a potential threat. A 5-year-old can kill you the same as a 20-year-old. The difference in such a case is that 5-year-olds are limited in their capacity to understand right and wrong and the concept of death. What you perceive as a deadly encounter may in fact be a game to them.

5. Was the shooting justifiable? Yes. The shooting will be ruled justifiable, with one question: why didn't you wait for backup? The argument here may be that if you had waited, this might not have happened. This will be a question that you will have to reconcile. However, there is no guarantee that the outcome would have been any different.

6. The most difficult questions to follow are: How will this impact you in the future? Can you stay on the job and be effective? Or do you think it will be better to seek a medical retirement due to the prolonged stress that you will endure? Only you can answer these questions, and it will become very personal from here. The outcome depends on how the community deals with the issue; how the department handles the matter both internally and externally; how your peers receive you; how this impacts your family; and how you deal with the issue psychologically.

I would love to say that situations like that in Scenario 4-1 will never happen and that every aspect of policing will be clear, with no murky situations or tough decisions. However, no matter what the circumstances, police and first responders are always put in a unique situation in that they deal with human beings' inhumanity toward one another, and this creates stressors that impact their lives.

Herman (1992) paints a picture of psychological trauma as human nature meeting evil in the natural world and bearing witness to horrific events (p. 7). Police have a front-row seat to human misery and are left with the aftermath of humans' evil to humans: dead bodies, victims of rape, fatalities in car accidents, child abductions and murders, murder-suicides, and domestic violence (Regehr & Bober, 2005). The human psyche is not designed to handle a constant bombardment of such incidents without having some impact on an officer's personality (Dantzker, 2005). In addition to the horrors that officers witness, they have the burden of being hyper-vigilant because they are under the constant threat of becoming victims of violence themselves.

Policing as a profession is very stressful, and if officers are to be successful, they must develop a coping strategy. Falvo (2005) argues that

general adaptation
syndrome (GAS)

the body's physiological
response to stressors consisting of three stages: alarm,
resistance, and exhaustion.

coping is a series of acts that change over time and that they are individu-
alized (p. 4). Some officers work out while others pursue hobbies outside
of policing. The purpose of the coping strategies is to restore balance to
one's life when confronted with such encounters.

Coping begins with understanding and recognizing the physiological responses to stress, which are best described by Seyle (1976).
These responses are known as the **general adaptation syndrome
(GAS),** which is associated with the body's response of *fight or flight.*
During a fight-or-flight response, the body prepares itself for battle
or escape by moving blood from the small organs to the large muscle
groups, such as the arms and legs; increasing the heart rate and heavy
breathing; and increasing visual acuity to focus on the task at hand
(pp. 36–39).

Think of an officer's career as a cup; it is empty when the officer first
begins the job, and over time the cup gets full. Officers who have developed excellent coping strategies or mechanisms will be able to reconcile
the stressors and move on; otherwise, the impact will be long-lasting and
can manifest as posttraumatic stress disorder (Barry, 2002; Herman, 1992;
Regehr & Bober, 2005; Van Der Kolk & Saporta, 1991). Some of the coping strategies or mechanisms that officers use are humor, compartmental-
izing, and disassociation:

- *Humor:* Many officers have a morbid sense of humor, and most
  tell jokes at horrific crime scenes and car accidents to get themselves through the investigation and the shock of what they are
  witnessing.

- *Compartmentalize:* Many officers have the unique ability to compartmentalize their day. In fact, they separate policing from their personal lives. When they are off work, they do not bring the job home
  nor do they share it with their family members. This is an excellent
  tactic, but in doing this, officers often lose their ability to empathize with family members and are often described as distant and
  noncaring. The ability to adapt and compartmentalize is described
  as a bi-phasic personality (Keppel & Birnes, 1997; Seaward, 2005;
  Siebert, 1996).

- *Disconnect/disassociate:* Yochelson and Samenow (1976) describe
  this as a shutoff mechanism that allows one to push fears away and
  that acts as a critical psychological defense (p. 414). Yochelson and
  Samenow's description of the shutoff mechanism is associated with

violent criminals, but it is appropriate in this discussion because it explains how officers can cope with what they encounter. This mechanism has been discussed by Freud, Egger, and Lifton, all describing what appears to be some out-of-body experience or dissociative state. When officers utilize this as a coping mechanism, it allows them to function with no outward emotional attachment to the incident.

These coping mechanisms are considered adaptive behaviors, meaning that they allow officers to have longevity in their careers.

POLICE SUICIDE

With the discussion of stressors and coping strategies in mind, policing is a profession that is steeped in the tradition of not seeking help. In fact, in the policing profession, an officer is considered weak if he or she seeks counseling services (Carroll & Holloway, 1999; Greene, 2006). It is interesting that every agency recognizes that officers are subjected to trauma and may need help, and yet the officers themselves define individuals as weak if they seek help. Volanti (1995) argues that police agencies do not keep accurate statistics regarding police suicide and that some may be classified as something else, such as an accidental death caused while cleaning a firearm (p. 20).

There are several categories of stressors in policing: organizational, external, task-related, job, and personal (Bartol & Bartol, 2008; White & Honig, 1995). If an officer has poor or no coping mechanisms, these stressors often lead to destructive behavior. The inability to cope may manifest itself in divorce, domestic violence, substance abuse, health problems, acts of brutality, and finally suicide (Bonifacio, 1991; Ward, Fowler, & Curran, 1985; White & Honig, 1995). The cause of police suicide can be found in an officer's inability to effectively cope with the daily grind of police work, which goes beyond the calls for service and lends itself to cynicism and helplessness. It can best be described as a culmination of unresolved events, which causes a crisis in that officer's life. Pearlin and Schooler (as cited in Regehr & Bober, 1995) describe observable consequences of ineffective coping as emotional distress, impaired sense of self-worth, inability to enjoy interpersonal contacts, and impaired task performance (p. 29). (See Scenario 4-2.)

SCENARIO 4-2: POLICING OR FAMILY

You are a new officer. You have been with the agency approximately one year and just finished probation. You have been married for seven years and have one child. During the seven-year marriage, you and your spouse have experienced numerous problems. Your spouse is an alcoholic and, when drinking, becomes violent, depressed, self-destructive, and angry. On two occasions you have come home and found your spouse sitting in the dark with a loaded gun, saying, "I am going to kill myself." In each of these incidents, you were successful in convincing your spouse not to commit suicide. Your spouse has decided that he/she no longer likes the city, nor does he/she like you being a police officer and demands that you quit. When you refuse to move and to quit your job, he/she packs everything while you are at work, closes the bank accounts, takes your child, and moves.

As your separation extends, you discover that your spouse has maxed out all your credit cards. As you get the bills, you immediately contact the credit card companies and ask that your spouse be removed from the accounts or that the accounts be closed. The credit card companies advise you that they cannot do that unless your spouse agrees to close the accounts. The bottom line is that you have lost everything except your car, and you are $80,000 in debt.

Analysis and Reflection

1. Can you think of any reason why you did not get your spouse help as it relates to his/her alcoholism and threats of suicide? Yes. As crazy as it seems, to seek outside assistance in a law enforcement family is an indication that you are weak and cannot control all aspects of your life. In doing so, it may hurt your standing in the department, especially when it comes time for promotion.

2. Is this an agency problem or a personal problem? This problem is both. If it impacts you personally, it will have a direct impact on your professional life. The questions become: What are your coping mechanisms? Are they adaptive and positive or maladaptive and counterproductive?

3. Can you empathize with victims of crime or will you become the ultimate cynic? You may lose the ability to empathize and become totally cynical. In doing so, you will have lost your objectivity, and that will have an impact on your performance. On the other hand, you may become more enlightened and understanding, seeing that you have been in a similar situation.

4. Are you in a crisis situation? It depends on how you define crisis. This goes back to how you handle the situation. The key here is to recognize that you have a problem and seek help in sorting out the issues. This is the type of thing that supervisors need to be aware of so that they can help, even if that means reassigning you temporarily so that this situation does not manifest itself in some form of aberrant behavior.

5. Can you see how such an incident could cause suicide? Yes. You have lost everything—family, child, and financial security (the very things we work for all our lives)—not to mention how you have been embarrassed because of this incident.

COMBATING POLICE STRESS

A crisis can happen to anyone. For officers, it could be a call that they are not prepared to handle, or it could be a failing personal life that overwhelms them. One common characteristic of the profession that has been mentioned by many researchers as a stressor is danger (Bartol & Bartol, 2008; Dantzker, 2005; Herman, 1992; Skolnick, 2004; White & Honig, 1995). The element of danger requires that an officer be hyper-vigilant and ready to respond to a threat at a moment's notice. The public would like to think that an officer's response is a calculated measure of violence where he or she is in total control. However, White and Honig (1995) address one of the occupational stressors as a lack of training, which translates to lack of preparedness.

Meloy (2000) argues that violence can be categorized in one of two types: affective or predatory. *Affective violence* is a mode of violence that is intense and immediate, with the primary goal being threat reduction and displacement of the target. Here an officer lacks the proper preparation to respond appropriately to an act of aggression. Depending on the threat, the response could be inappropriate or excessive. *Predatory violence* can be described as being prepared for any potential threat, and in responding there is a lack of emotion, a lack of concern for the threat, because of preparation, with the ultimate goal of establishing control (p. 88). Although training budgets limit the frequency and type of training that an officer receives, much like fitness, this type of preparation on one's own time can relieve some of the stress associated with danger.

The key is not being afraid to seek assistance. In most cases, such assistance is confidential. The only time that the agency will have to be notified or even know is if the therapist feels that an officer is a threat to himself or herself or others. The avenues available to an officer include:

1. Department psychologist (usually found in large agencies).
2. Peer assistance, which are officers trained to provide counseling services after critical incidents; this is known as critical incident debriefing. They can also make referrals to department psychologists or employee assistance. The discussions that an officer has with peer counselors are completely confidential unless an officer reveals that he or she was involved in a criminal act.
3. Employee assistance programs, which are off-site counseling services that provide counseling services 24 hours a day. They are similar to the staff psychologist, but just provide services through a contract as opposed to being an employee of the department.

4. Adopting a healthy lifestyle and fitness, both of which keep an officer fit to deal with danger and provide healthy outlets for stressful situations. They are the safe alternative to alcohol.

CONCLUSION

The decision to become a police officer is one of the more difficult decisions that an individual will ever make because of the impact the profession has on one's personal life. This chapter has described the decision as one that loved ones often fear because of the perceived danger. Those in one's culture might fear the decision because of how the police are defined in one's particular community.

Once the decision to enter policing is made, the candidate must understand that it is a profession not suited to everyone. Beginning with candidate testing and through completion of the FTO program and the first year of probation, the process is one of elimination; agencies are looking for the most qualified candidates. The training is a process of socialization and, in many cases, enforced conformity.

After candidates have successfully navigated the initial pitfalls, they must concentrate on dealing with the stress of the profession. Policing is filled with periods of extreme boredom followed by periods of sheer terror. Officers have to deal with politics, and actively participate in and witness humans' inhumanity to one another. Police see the worst in our society. Ultimately, the mental health survival of police officers depends on their coping skills, along with the support group they have surrounded themselves with. Successful officers understand that there is a delicate balancing act between their professional and personal lives, and that to be successful at both, an officer must find that there is more to policing than the job.

 DISCUSSION QUESTIONS

1. The preemployment process is like climbing a mountain with a number of obstacles. Examine the process and determine where your obstacles are located, then develop a strategy that will allow you to overcome them.

2. As discussed in this chapter, developing standards for police fitness is a difficult task, as there is no "norm" regarding physical tasks performed by police officers. Consider this, and relate it to Downey and Roth's profile of a typical male police officer over a 25-year career. What factors can you attribute to this? What conclusions can you draw based on these statistics?

3. Reflect on the different phases of the FTO program, their purpose and their impact on the new officer. What do you think is the most important phase? Why?

4. Discussed in this chapter are four stages of a law enforcement officer's career. What personality characteristics do you think are most important for the officer to possess during each stage of his or her career? Explain.

5. Stress is a major issue in policing. How would you prevent yourself from falling into this trap? What coping mechanisms do you currently use when you find yourself in stressful situations, and do you believe they will be adequate in coping with the issues of policing? If not, what will you have to change?

 ## RESEARCH TOPICS

Following are two topics that are central to this chapter. Choose one, and research the topic based on the instructions of your professor.

- *Making the decision.* In the beginning of this chapter, there was a rather lengthy discussion on one's decision to become a police officer. Today you have decided that policing is your chosen profession. Research the agency that you believe to be the ideal agency and describe why you are the candidate for that agency. This will require you to research the history of that department, looking at its culture and traditions, and examine your personality traits to determine if you will be successful with that agency. Defend your answer.

- *Police officer stress.* It is said that one officer dies every 24 hours through suicide. Research the issue of police stress and what officers and agencies are doing to effectively combat this problem. In your research, determine if stress is simply an issue manufactured by the officer or if it is a real problem that agencies tend to ignore. Defend your answer.

BIBLIOGRAPHY

Avery, M., & Rudovsky, D. (1986). *Police misconduct: Law and litigation.* New York: Clark Boardman.

Aylward, J. (1985). Psychological testing and police selection. *Journal of Police Science and Administration, 13*(3), 201–210.

Bailey, W. G. (1996). *The encyclopedia of police.* New York: Garland.

Barak, G. (2007). *Battleground: Criminal justice.* Westport, CT: Greenwood.

Barker, J. C. (1999). *Danger, duty, and disillusion: The worldview of Los Angeles police officers.* Prospect Heights, IL: Waveland Press.

Barry, P. D. (2002). *Mental health and mental illness* (7th ed.). Philadelphia: Lippincott, Williams, & Wilkins.

Bartol, C. R. (2005). *Current perspectives in forensic psychology and criminal justice.* Thousand Oaks, CA: Sage.

Bartol, C. R., & Bartol, A. M. (2008). *Introduction to forensic psychology: Research and application* (2nd ed.). Los Angeles: Sage.

Beckett, K., & Sasson, T. (2004). *The politics of injustice: Crime and punishment in America.* Thousand Oaks, CA: Sage.

Bonifacio, P. (1991). *The psychological effects of police work: A psychodynamic approach.* New York: Plenum Press.

Brooks, M. E. (2001). Law enforcement physical fitness standards and Title VII. *FBI Law Enforcement Bulletin 70*(5), 26–31. Washington, DC: Department of Justice.

Browne-Marshall, G. J. (2007). *Race, law and American society.* Boca Raton, FL: CRC Press.

Burbeck, E., & Furnham, A. (1985). Personality and police selection: Trait differences in successful and non-successful applicants to the Metropolitan Police. *Journal of Personality and Individual Differences, 5*(3), 257–263.

Carroll, M., & Holloway, E. (1999). *Counselling supervision in context.* Thousand Oaks, CA: Sage.

Charles, M. T. (1982). Women in policing: The physical aspect. *Journal of Police Science and Administration 10*(2), 195–205.

Cooper, S. (2006). A closer look at racial profiling. In S. J. Muffler (Ed.), *Racial profiling: Issues, data and analyses* (pp. 25–30). Hauppauge, NY: Nova.

Cooper Institute for Aerobics Research. (2002a). *Common questions about physical fitness standards and programs in law enforcement.* Dallas, TX: Author.

Cooper Institute for Aerobics Research. (2002b). *Procedures and sequencing of physical fitness tests in law enforcement.* Dallas, TX: Author.

Confessore, N., & Cave, D. (2006, January 29). Even with rules friendly fire is a challenge. *New York Times.*

Dantzker, M. L. (2005). *Understanding today's police.* Monsey, NY: Criminal Justice Press.

Downey, R., & Roth, J. (1981). *Weapon retention techniques for officer survival.* Springfield, IL: Charles C. Thomas.

Dwyer, W. O., Prien, E. P., & Bernard, J. L. (1990). Psychological screening of law enforcement officers: A case of job relatedness. *Journal of Police Science and Administration, 17*(3), 176–182.

Fagen, P. W. (1992). Repression and state security. In J. E. Corradi, P. W. Fagen, & M. A. Garretón (Eds.), *Fear at the edge: State terror and resistance in Latin America* (pp. 39–71). Berkeley: University of California Press.

Fahy, R. F. (2005). *U.S. firefighter fatalities due to sudden cardiac death, 1995–2004.* Quincy, MA: National Fire Protection Association.

Falvo, D. R. (2005). *Medical and psychosocial aspects of chronic illness and disability.* Sudbury, MA: Jones & Bartlett.

Federal Bureau of Investigation (FBI). (2002). *Officers killed or assaulted.* Washington, DC: Author.

Florida Department of Law Enforcement (FDLE). (2000). *Basic recruit training program: Law enforcement academy course guide.* Tallahassee, FL: Author.

Florida Department of Law Enforcement (FDLE). (2003). *Field training officer program: Course 809: Instructor guide.* Tallahassee, FL: Author.

Gainesville Police Department. (1998). *Gainesville Police Department policy manual.* Gainesville, FL: Author.

Giles, H. (2002). *Law enforcement, communication, and community.* Amsterdam, Netherlands: John Benjamins.

Goffman, E. (1961). *Asylums.* Garden City, NY: Anchor Books.

Greene, J. R. (2006). *The encyclopedia of police science.* Boca Raton, FL: CRC Press.

Hadden, S. (2001). *Slave patrols: Law and violence in Virginia and the Carolinas.* Cambridge, MA: Harvard University Press.

Heinz, W. S., & Fruling, H. (1999). *Determinants of gross human rights violations by state and state-sponsored actors in Brazil, Uruguay, Chile, and Argentina, 1960–1990.* The Hague, Netherlands: Kluwer Law International.

Herman, J. L. (1992). *Trauma and recovery.* New York: Basic Books.

Holden, H. M. (2006). *To be a crime scene investigator.* St. Paul, MN: Zenith Press.

Hutton, D. B., & Mydlarz, A. (2001). *Guide to law enforcement careers.* Hauppauge, NY: Barron's Educational Series.

Kenney, D. J., & Watson, T. S. (1999). Intelligence and the selection of police recruits. In D. J. Kenney & R. P. McNamara (Eds.), *Police and policing: Contemporary issues* (pp. 15–36). Westport, CT: Praeger.

Keppel, R. D., & Birnes, W. J. (1997). *Signature killers: Interpreting the calling cards of the serial murderer.* New York: Pocket Books.

Kessler, R. (1993). *The FBI.* New York: Simon & Schuster.

Kleinig, J. (1996). *The ethics of policing.* New York: Cambridge Press.

Klinger, D. (2004). *Into the kill zone: A cop's eye view of deadly force.* San Francisco: Jossey-Bass.

Klockars, C. B., Ivković, S. K., & Haberfeld, M. R. (2006). *Enhancing police integrity.* New York: Springer.

Kops, D. (2007). *Open for debate: Racial profiling.* Tarrytown, NY: Marshall Cavendish Benchmark.

Krauss, C. (1994, August 26). In wake of shooting, Bratton appoints panel to study racial attitudes. *New York Times.*

Latting, C., & Deshazo, C. (2005). *Once a marine: Collected stories by enlisted Marine Corps Vietnam veterans: Their lives 35 years later.* Bloomington, IN: Author House.

Lee, J. C. (2007). Physical fitness in policing. In J. Ruiz & D. Hummer (Eds.), *Handbook of police administration* (pp. 289–304). Boca Raton, FL: CRC Press.

LeQuang, W. (2005). *How to become a peace officer.* Victoria, BC: Trafford.

Lyons, W. (2002). *The politics of community policing: Rearranging the power to punish.* Ann Arbor, MI: University of Michigan Press.

Massachusetts State Police Academy. (2006). *Report of the Massachusetts State Police Academy Commission.* Framingham, MA: Author.

McNally, V. J., & Solomon, R. M. (1999). The FBI's critical incident stress management program. *FBI Law Enforcement Journal, 68*(2), 20–26.

McNamara, R. P. (1999). The socialization of the police. In D. J. Kenney & R. P. McNamara (Eds.), *Police and policing: Contemporary issues* (pp. 1–14). Westport, CT: Praeger.

Meloy, J. R. (2000). *Violence risk and threat assessment: A practical guide for mental health and criminal justice professionals.* San Diego: Specialized Training Services.

Miller, S. L. (2007). *Criminal justice research and practice: Diverse voices from the field.* Lebanon, NH: University Press of New England.

Niederhoffer, A. (1967). *Behind the shield: The police in urban society.* Garden City, NY: Doubleday Books.

Ostrov, E. (1995). Legal, psychological, and ethical issues in police related forensic psychology evaluations. In M. I. Kurke & E. M. Scrivner (Eds.), *Police psychology into the 21st century* (pp. 133–145). Hillsdale, NJ: Lawrence Erlbaum.

Quire, D., & Blount, W. (1990). A coronary risk profile study of male police officers: Focus on cholesterol. *Journal of Police Science and Administration, 17,* 89–94.

Rafilson, F. M. (2003). *Police officer* (16th ed.). Laurenceville, NJ: Arco/Thomson.

Regehr, C., & Bober, T. (2005). *In the line of fire: Trauma in emergency services.* New York: Oxford University Press.

Reuss-Ianni, E. (1993). *Two cultures of policing: Street cops and management cops.* New Brunswick, NJ: Transaction.

Rostow, C. D., & Davis, R. D. (2004). *A handbook for psychological fitness-for-duty evaluations in law enforcement.* Binghamton, NY: Haworth.

Ruiz, J., & Hummer, D. C. (2007). *Handbook of police administration.* Boca Raton, FL: CRC Press.

Russell, H. E., & Beigel, A. (1990). *Understanding human behavior for effective police work* (3rd ed.). New York: Basic Books.

Schaefer, P., & Helm, M. (1996). *The incidence of heart disease in North Carolina officers.* Unpublished.

Schroeder, D. J., & Lombardo, F. A. (2001). *Police officer exam* (6th ed.). Hauppauge, NY: Barron's Educational Series.

Scrivner, E. M., & Kurke, M. I. (1995). Police psychology at the dawn of the 21st century. In M. I. Kurke & E. M. Scrivner (Eds.), *Police psychology into the 21st century* (pp. 3–30). Hillsdale, NJ: Lawrence Erlbaum.

Seaward, B. L. (2005). *Managing stress: Principles and strategies for health and well-being.* Sudbury, MA: Jones & Bartlett.

Seyle, H. (1976). *The stress of life.* New York: McGraw-Hill.

Siebert, A. (1996). *The survivor personality: Why some people are stronger, smarter, and more skillful at handling life's difficulties . . . and how you can be, too.* New York: Perigee.

Skolnick, J. (2004). A sketch of the police officer's "working personality." In B. W. Hancock & P. M. Sharp (Eds.), *Criminal justice in America: Theory, practice, and policy* (pp. 100–124). Upper Saddle River, NJ: Prentice Hall.

Skolnick, J. H., & Bayley, D. H. (1988). *The new blue line: Police innovation in six American cities.* New York: Simon & Schuster.

Skolnick, J. H., & Fyfe, J. J. (1993). *Above the law: Police and the excessive use of force.* New York: The Free Press.

Smith, D., & Natalier, K. (2005). *Understanding criminal justice: Sociological perspectives.* Thousand Oaks, CA: Sage.

Stanko, E. A. (1989). Missing the mark: Police battering. In J. Hanmer, J. Radford, & E. A. Stanko (Eds.), *Women, policing and male violence: An international perspective* (pp. 46–69). New York: Routledge.

Stevens, D. J. (2008). *An introduction to American policing.* Sudbury, MA: Jones & Bartlett.

Thomas, D. J. (2008). *College credit for completion of the police academy.* Fort Myers, FL: Unpublished.

Thomas, D. J., & Barringer, T. A. (2008). Developing fitness standards for police officers. *Public Safety Chronicles, 1*(1), pp. 23–27.

Truncale, J. J., & Smith, T. E. (1994). *MDTS: Monadnock defensive tactics system.* Fitzwilliam, NH: Monadnock PR-24 Training Council, Inc.

Van Der Kolk, B. A., & Saporta, J. (1991). The biological response to psychic trauma: Mechanisms and treatment of intrusion and numbing. *Anxiety Research, 4,* 199–212.

Volanti, J. M. (1995). The mystery within: Understanding police suicide. *FBI Law Enforcement Bulletin, 64*(2), 19–23. Washington, DC: Department of Justice.

Walker, S., & Katz, C. M. (2005). *The police in America: An introduction* (5th ed.). Boston: McGraw Hill.

Ward, R. H., Fowler, A., & Curran, J. T. (1985). *Police and law enforcement.* Brooklyn, NY: AMS Press.

White, E. K., & Honig, A. L. (1995). Law enforcement families. In M. I. Kurke & E. M. Scrivner (Eds.), *Police psychology into the 21st century* (pp. 189–206). Hillsdale, NJ: Lawrence Erlbaum.

Wilson, C. A. (1996). *Racism: From slavery to advanced capitalism.* Thousand Oaks, CA: Sage.

Yearwood, D. L. (2003). *Retention and recruitment study series: Sworn police personnel.* Raleigh, NC: North Carolina Criminal Justice Education & Training Standards Commission.

Yochleson, S., & Samenow, S. (1976). *The criminal personality: A profile of change.* Northvale, NJ: Jason Aronson.

CHAPTER **5**

THE POLICE ORGANIZATION

OBJECTIVES

After completing this chapter, the student will be able to:

- Define the term *jurisdiction* and describe the limitations of municipal, county, state, and federal law enforcement agencies.
- Discuss the importance of training as it relates to professionalism.
- Discuss the role of leadership within a police organization.
- Describe the role of the informal leader.
- Explain the three styles of policing and their relationship to agency culture.
- Describe the impact that a subculture has on an organization.
- Discuss the negative and positive aspects of affirmative action and its impact on policing.
- Define the terms *black tax* and *minority tax*.
- Discuss the impact of African Americans and women in policing and their hardships.

KEY TERMS

black tax/minority tax – minority groups have to perform at a higher level than their white peers.

brotherhood of the badge – describes policing as a male-dominated profession.

community-oriented policing (COP) – the development of external partnerships with community members and groups.

COMPSTAT (Computer Statistics or Comparative Statistics) – a management accountability tool. COMPSTAT offers a clear picture of crime and the crime-fighting efforts of the commanders. The focus is on results and sharing information.

core values – the beliefs that guide an organization and the behavior of its employees.

four-factor complexes – criteria developed by Shafter to determine how a police agency justifies its need for personnel.

home rule – limits the rights of the federal government and grants each state the ability to govern itself. That authority is further granted in state constitutions, extending the privilege to incorporated governments within the state.

ingredients of leadership – the five ingredients—guiding vision, passion, integrity, curiosity, and daring—that Bennis argues one should possess to be a successful leader.

intelligence-led policing – the application of criminal intelligence analysis as an objective decision-making tool in order to facilitate crime reduction and crime prevention through effective policing strategies and from external partnership projects drawn from an evidential base.

jurisdiction – police power in the United States is limited by geographical boundaries, which ensures that the local levels will control their respective police forces and which limits police authority.

legalistic-oriented agency – an agency that does not allow officers to use their discretion. The agency uses statistics to show how effective they are in their crime-fighting effort.

organizational culture – closely tied to the style of policing that the organization and the community embrace.

problem-oriented policing (POP) – a method of analysis and solving crime problems.

service-oriented agency – an agency that caters to the needs of the community.

watchman-oriented agency – the agency's role is maintenance of order. The officers use discretion in determining the seriousness of law violations.

DOC'S WORDS OF WISDOM

Like many things in America, its police organizations are unique in that they find their roots in the teachings of Sir Robert Peel. Yet the agencies are guided by the U.S. Constitution and the needs of the communities that they serve.

INTRODUCTION

Policing in the United States is unique in that it is fragmented; this is a design of the Constitution, and the framework can be found in the Tenth Amendment (Mawby, 1999; Ratcliffe, 2008; Stevens, 2008). The concept of the Tenth Amendment was to limit the rights of the federal government and grant each state the ability of **home rule.** This right is further extended to each governmental entity within a state, such as counties, townships, villages, and cities. The Tenth Amendment reads as follows:

> *The powers not delegated to the United States by the Constitution, nor prohibited by it to the states, are reserved to the states respectively, or to the people.*

As a result of the Tenth Amendment, each governmental entity is responsible for enacting laws and providing services for its constituents.

As discussed in Chapter 1, the need for policing in America was the direct result of urban growth and crime in the late 1700s. The city governments of New York and later Boston passed legislation that created municipal police departments (Monkkonen, 2004; Steverson, 2008). To understand law enforcement in the United States, we must begin by examining the responsibilities of each level of policing: the federal law enforcement, and the state, county, and municipal agencies. Law enforcement agencies in the United States share overlapping responsibilities and at times share jurisdiction over the same criminal act, such as bank robbery, Internet crimes, and drug trafficking (Dantkzer, 2005; Smith, 1999; Walker & Katz, 2005).

home rule

limits the rights of the federal government and grants each state the ability to govern itself. That authority is further granted in state constitutions, extending the privilege to incorporated governments within the state.

JURISDICTION

Police power in the United States is limited by geographical boundaries, which ensures that the local levels will control their respective police forces and which limits police authority (Dantkzer, 2005; Smith, 1990; Walker & Katz, 2005). For the novice, **jurisdiction** is one of the most confusing issues in American policing. Many believe that there is a hierarchy in policing that begins with federal law enforcement agencies, such as the Federal Bureau of Investigation (FBI), having the authority in any criminal case. Nothing could be further from the truth. American policing is a host of subsystems that consist of federal, state, county, and municipal/local agencies. Dantzker (2005) argues that because the systems are separate and yet intertwined, they should be studied in a systems approach (pp. 25–26). (See Figures 5-1, 5-2, and 5-3.)

jurisdiction

police power in the United States is limited by geographical boundaries, which ensures that the local levels will control their respective police forces and which limits police authority.

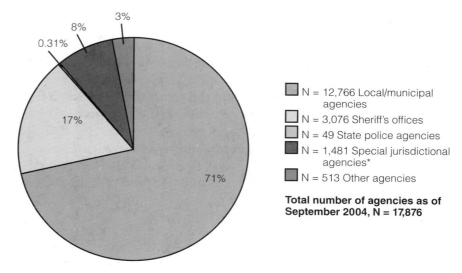

*Special jurisdictions are: transit police, port authority, airport police, university police, conservation officers/parks and recreation officers with arrest powers, criminal investigation, and special enforcement such as gaming, alcohol, and agriculture.

Figure 5-1   Number of State and Local Law Enforcement Agencies
(Data source: Bureau of Justice Statistics, Census of State and
Local Law Enforcement Agencies, 2004.)

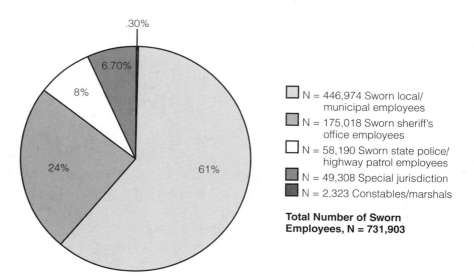

Figure 5-2   Number of Sworn Law Enforcement Officers in the United States
(Data source: Bureau of Justice Statistics, Census of State and
Local Law Enforcement Agencies, 2004.)

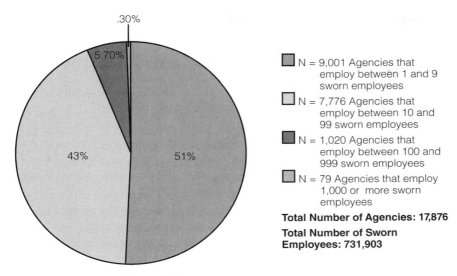

.30%

5.70%

43%

51%

N = 9,001 Agencies that employ between 1 and 9 sworn employees

N = 7,776 Agencies that employ between 10 and 99 sworn employees

N = 1,020 Agencies that employ between 100 and 999 sworn employees

N = 79 Agencies that employ 1,000 or more sworn employees

Total Number of Agencies: 17,876

Total Number of Sworn Employees: 731,903

Figure 5-3   Size of Local and State Agencies

(Data source: Bureau of Justice Statistics, Census of State and Local Law Enforcement Agencies, 2004.)

LOCAL/MUNICIPAL AGENCIES

The authority of local law enforcement agencies is granted by state statutes that grant local governments the right of home rule and allow for the creation of local law enforcement (e.g., North Carolina General Statute Chapter 13, 160a-281, 2008; Utah Code, Title 10-3-909 to 10-3-915). Since enforcement authority is granted by the state, most states require a minimum number of training hours for an officer to become certified at the basic level, which dates back to 1959.

The first state to mandate minimum training standards was New York, and later that year the state of California followed with voluntary standards (Greene, 2006; Russell, Conser, & Gingerich, 2005). The minimum standards are unique to each state and are developed to meet the needs of each state's citizenry. Police recruit training has many goals, the two most prominent being to prepare recruits for the job at hand and to raise the level of professionalism (Palombo, 1995). Vollmer (1936) argues that if any other profession recruited and hired candidates randomly and placed them on the job without training, it would be a catastrophe. Yet in 1936, that is what the profession of policing was allowed to do (pp. 230–231).

In evaluating the data in regard to local police agencies' size and the number of employees, the most striking detail is found in the number of small agencies: 13,214 of the 17,876 agencies have fewer than 25 employees. The Federal Bureau of Investigation (FBI) (2007) provides that the ratio of police to citizens is 2.4 officers per 1,000 residents in a community. The traditional standard has been one officer for every 1,000 residents; however, that number is not etched in stone by any group or statute, but is a baseline to assist cities in developing budgets and meeting the needs of their constituents (FBI, 1998).

A number of variables determine how many sworn personnel an agency will need, including number of residents, crime rate, type of crimes, and programs that an agency may be implementing. Slovak (1988) argues that it varies by region and provides an examination of three states: South Carolina, Ohio, and New Jersey. In reviewing Slovak's results, be mindful of the limitations of his study; it only addressed two regions of the country and three states. Slovak's study determined the following:

- City size and police department size are heavily correlated despite the crime control.
- In the south, South Carolina department size is determined by population.
- In the industrial northeast, Ohio and New Jersey, population and department size play a role and adjust accordingly based on the crime rate.

four-factor complexes

criteria developed by Shafter to determine how a police agency justifies its need for personnel.

On the other hand, Shafter (1961) noted in his study of two cities of similar size, with leaders who had similar ideals in regard to crime, that there were **four-factor complexes** that are dependent upon each other: ecological patterns, demographic conditions, traditions and attitudes, and fortuitous events. Shafter argues that if one of these factors changes, it will have an impact on the other three (pp. 344–346).

COUNTY POLICE/SHERIFF'S DEPARTMENTS

The next level in the tier of policing and police organizations is county law enforcement. County law enforcement is usually associated with the Office of the Sheriff. The sheriff is usually an office that is elected by the citizens of a county. However, in some states, sheriffs are appointed by the governor or the county government (Stevens, 2008).

There are two types of county agencies, and they have very different functions, depending on the region of the country. In some states, such as Georgia, Virginia, Maryland, and New York, you may find a Sheriff's Department and a County Police Department both residing within the same county. However, their duties and responsibilities are unique to that organization. An example of such a case is the Nassau County Police Department in Nassau County, New York. The police department is responsible for traditional policing and has the following divisions: Patrol, Detectives, Support Services, and Community Affairs. In comparison, the Nassau County Sheriff's Department is responsible for the following: County Corrections, Family Court Unit, and the serving of civil papers.

In contrast to the division of labor in Nassau County, the Chautauqua County Sheriff's Office just north of Buffalo provides traditional policing to the unincorporated areas of the county as well as contract services to incorporated municipalities, towns, and villages that do not have a police department—in addition to the traditional services they are mandated by statute to provide: the service of civil papers, courtroom security, county corrections, and boating and snowmobile patrols. The jurisdiction of a sheriff's department is the entire county, which includes all of the municipalities. However, if there is a local agency such as a police department, then the sheriff's department does not interfere with their operations.

STATE LAW ENFORCEMENT AGENCIES

The first state law enforcement agency was the Texas Rangers in 1835. Initially the Texas Rangers were a paramilitary organization formed to defend the borders of Texas and to deal with ongoing Indian problems due to the expansion west. The Texas Rangers were modified and disbanded on several occasions due to changing missions and the Civil War, and in 1901 they became a permanent police agency in the state of Texas (Fehrenbach, 2000; Gillett, 1943).

Today state law enforcement agencies are much like federal law enforcement in that they have many different enforcement arms that specialize. State law enforcement agencies are most recognized by their uniformed police known as state police, highway patrol, department of public safety, or state troopers. In the United States, there are forty-nine such agencies. The state of Hawaii does not have a state police organization. There is a distinct difference between a highway patrol and a state police organization. The primary duty of the highway patrol is limited to enforcing traffic laws. However, state police are responsible for delivering full police services in the unincorporated and rural areas of the state (Berg, 1999; Betchel, 1994).

An example of the differences can be found in the state of Florida. Florida has the Florida Highway Patrol (FHP), which is the enforcement arm of the Florida Division of Highway Traffic Safety and Motor Vehicles, with their primary responsibility of enforcing the traffic laws and investigating traffic crashes in the state of Florida. Florida does not have a state police but does have an investigative law enforcement body known as the Florida Department of Law Enforcement (FDLE), which is responsible for investigating all criminal activity at the state level; they also support local law enforcement with crime scene and crime lab functions, coordinating domestic security, conducting investigations of public officials, and so on. Other states have similar investigative agencies, many of which are known as a Bureau of Investigation. These agencies are much like the Federal Bureau of Investigation (FBI) and are responsible for investigating criminal violations of state law and assisting local law enforcement in their cases.

In contrast, the Indiana State Police is a full-service organization and provides the following services: patrol, commercial vehicle enforcement, criminal investigation, aviation, bomb disposal, emergency response, hostage negotiations, scuba, drug interdiction, and crime lab operation. Most if not all states have other categories of law enforcement officers that specialize in such areas as: Fish and Wildlife; Environmental Protection; Capitol Police; Transportation; and Alcohol and Tobacco (Hutton & Mydlarz, 2001; Stotler, 2002).

FEDERAL LAW ENFORCEMENT

The first federal law enforcement agency in the United States was the U.S. Marshals Service, which was established by the Federal Judiciary Act of 1789 (Bumgarner, 2006; Calhoun, 1991). The powers and duties of the Marshals Service are specified in Title 28, *United States Code*, Section 566: provide security and enforce all orders of the U.S. District Court, U.S. District Courts of Appeals, and the Court of International Trade; make arrests for felony violations of federal statutes; provide protection for federal jurists, court officers, and witnesses; and investigate fugitive matters (*United States Code*, 2008).

The most recognizable federal agency is the Federal Bureau of Investigation (FBI). Prior to 1908, the Department of Justice borrowed Secret Service Agents to complete their investigations. In 1908 the Sundry Civil Appropriation Bill was introduced and passed by Congress, and this forbade the Department of Justice from utilizing Secret Service Agents to assist in their investigations (Jeffreys-Jones, 2007; Miller, 1994). In March of 1909, the Bureau of Investigations was born, which later became known as the FBI (Gatewood, 1970; Koletar, 2006). The role and responsibilities of the FBI are found in many different sections of the *United States Code;*

however, the primary statute that grants it law enforcement authority is Title 18, *United States Code*, Section 3052, which provides that FBI agents can carry firearms and make arrests with warrants, as well as warrantless arrests with probable cause, for any offense committed against the United States (*United States Code*, 2008). The responsibilities of the FBI are constantly changing, much like those of local law enforcement agencies, based on the potential threats to the United States (Koletar, 2006).

The most recent set of data concerning federal law enforcement agencies was recorded by Reaves and Bauer (2002). As of 2002, there were sixty-seven federal law enforcement agencies and twenty-eight offices of the inspector general, totaling some 93,000 officers in fifty states (p. 1). This survey was concluded prior to the creation of the Department of Homeland Security (DHS), which transferred several agencies to the authority of DHS. Some of the federal agencies *not* impacted by the creation of DHS are: Federal Bureau of Investigation (FBI); Internal Revenue Service (IRS); Drug Enforcement Administration (DEA); National Park Service Police; Veterans Health Administration (VHA); Alcohol, Tobacco and Firearms (ATF); U.S. Postal Inspectors; U.S. Capitol Police; U.S. Fish and Wildlife, Law Enforcement Division; and the U.S. Marshals Service.

The Department of Homeland Security (DHS) was created with the enactment of the Homeland Security Act of 2002, combining several law enforcement agencies with a host of other federal agencies. The creation of DHS was the largest government reorganization since 1947 (Bullock, Haddow, & Coppola, 2006; LeMay, 2006). The statutory mandate of DHS is to: prevent terrorist attacks in the United States; reduce the vulnerability of the United States to terrorist attacks; minimize damage and assist in recovery that is a result of terrorism; be the focal point for manmade and natural crises; and monitor connections between drug traffickers and terrorists and sever those connections. The federal law enforcement agencies that were transferred to DHS include: U.S. Secret Service; Transportation and Security Administration, which includes Federal Air Marshals; U.S. Customs Service; Federal Protective Service; and Immigration and Naturalization (INS). The final two pieces of the DHS puzzle are the U.S. Coast Guard and the Federal Emergency Management Agency (FEMA), which provide services that are non–law enforcement in nature (Purpura, 2007; Thaler & Bea, 2005).

The federal law enforcement model provides for specialization, such as U.S. Fish and Wildlife; Drug Enforcement Administration; Treasury Department; and the U.S. Postal Inspectors Office. In examining the federal agencies, their titles provide you with some perspective of their specialty. Although they are all federal law enforcement officers, their responsibilities are very specialized. However, that does not preclude a federal law enforcement officer from making a felony arrest for a crime that is committed against the United States. A federal law enforcement officer's powers and authority are limited to federal crimes.

There is no doubt that there is a duplication of services or an overlap in jurisdiction. However, the issue of accountability resides on the community in which the agencies serve. The federal agencies have particular mandates under the *United States Code* (USC) which prohibits them from interfering in matters of the state, county, and municipal governments, except where there is a violation of civil rights or the officials are involved in illegal activity. If you go back and examine the discussions of the U.S. Marshals Service and the FBI, each of their duties has been specifically outlined in the USC, and each statute identifies their role in crimes against the United States (*United States Code,* 2008).

With that said, there are some crimes over which federal and local agencies have joint jurisdiction, such as bank robbery. Every state has a law that prohibits armed robbery, be it of a person or a business. However, banks are unique because they are insured by the Federal Deposit Insurance Corporation (FDIC), which insures all depositors' money up to $250,000 per account (Salinger, 2004). Theoretically, both agencies can investigate such crimes. However, it would be a waste of taxpayer dollars for both to investigate the crimes individually. In many cases, the agency heads make a decision as to which agency will have primary responsibility in the investigation, and that frees the other agency's investigators to pursue other cases.

One area of policing that has been the source of jurisdictional conflicts is illegal narcotics. To avoid such conflicts, some agencies have entered into agreements to create some type of task force. One interagency drug task force is the High Intensity Drug Trafficking Area Program (HIDTA). The HIDTA are regional task forces and are located in specific regions of the country based on the threat of narcotics within that region. Some of the major areas in which HIDTA concentrates their efforts are: Houston, Los Angeles, New York/New Jersey, South Florida, the Southwest Border, Washington/Baltimore, Puerto Rico/U.S. Virgin Islands, Atlanta, Chicago, and Philadelphia/Camden. The purpose of this effort is to correlate federal, state, and local law enforcement organizations so they will not be duplicating services and will accomplish what can and should be considered effective enforcement strategies regarding the drug problem (Hundall, 2004; Westphal, 2008).

Aslinger and Tomkins (1953) argue that in spite of task forces such as HIDTA, much of the responsibility for illegal narcotics rests on the shoulders of local law enforcement. Their role is to address the problem in the community, along with the host of crimes that are spawned from the illegal drug trade, such as burglary, robbery, theft, and forgery (pp.168–170).

POLICE ORGANIZATION

Historically organizational police models have followed the path of the traditional military model. However, many scholars and professionals are quick to point out that the model is paramilitary (Samaha, 2005; Skolnick & Fyfe, 1994) inasmuch as policing is based on a hierarchical structure: with a chief/sheriff at the top of the organization, then a host of commanders with numerous titles, and funneling down to first-line supervisors, officers, and civilian personnel who are responsible for the day-to-day operations of the organization, as well as the citizen contact (Regoli & Hewitt, 2007; Walma & West, 2002). The organization is designed to meet the needs of the administration and what they believe best accommodates the public. (See Figures 5-4 and 5-5.)

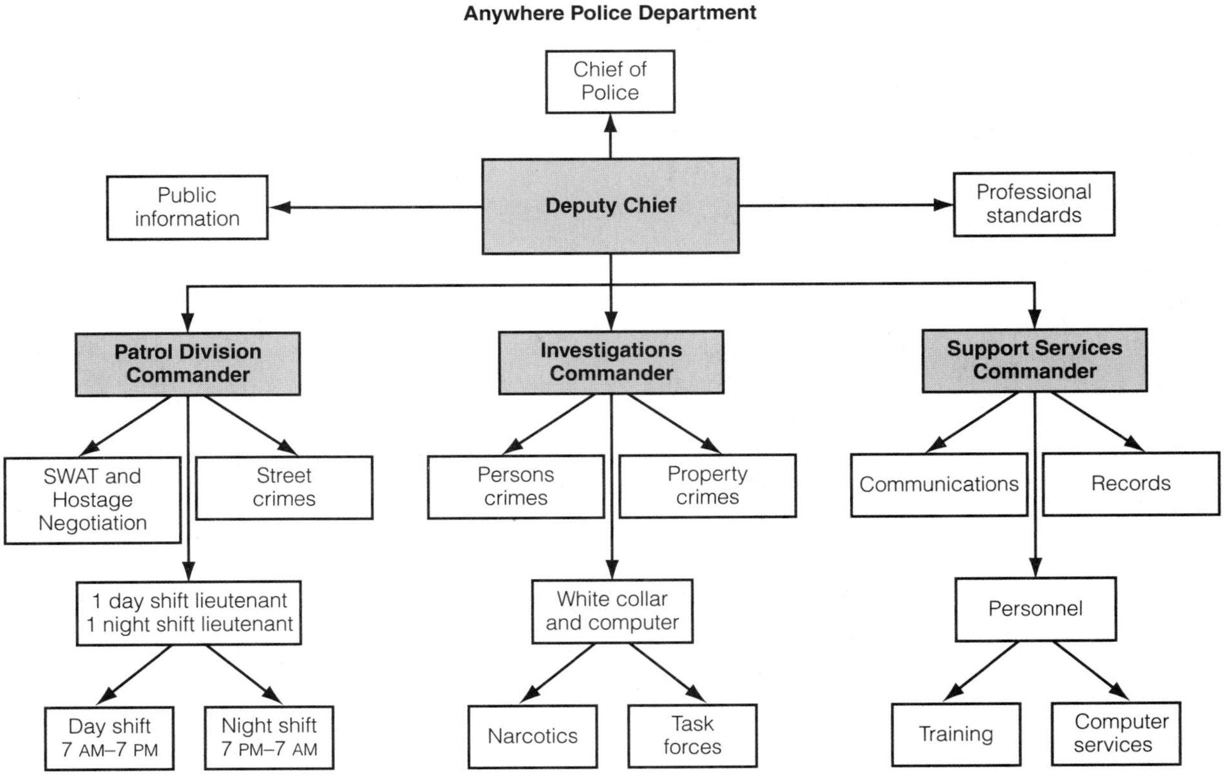

Anywhere Police Department

Figure 5-4 Local Agency Organizational Chart

Anywhere Sheriff's Office

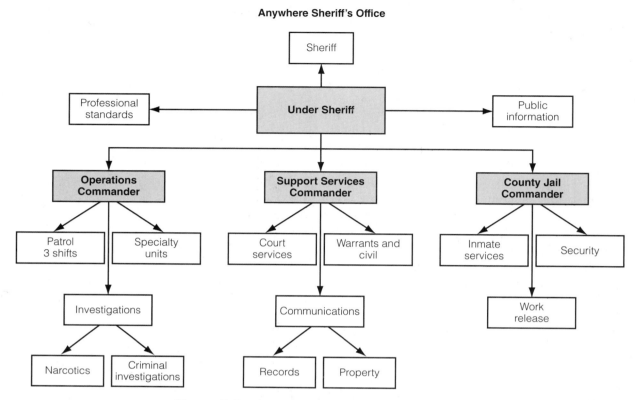

Figure 5-5   County Sheriff's Office Organizational Chart

The military organization featuring the chain of command is designed to address accountability. The police organization has several components: structure based on organizational size, accountability, and lines of communication. The other dynamics, which have a greater impact on the organization, are: leadership; core values; agency culture; training; and interaction with the community.

LEADERSHIP

A leader provides the roadmap for an organization. In almost every case, the culture of an agency is shaped by the message that the leader communicates to both the public and the subordinates. There is clearly a difference between police leaders and managers. Managers possess the skills that keep the organization operating daily, such as ability to budget, enforce policies and procedures, and delegate authority, as well as good communication skills. Adlam and Villiers (2003) agree that all leaders must have these skills as well, but note that they may be in conflict with them at times. These authors describe a leader as someone who generates and stimulates new ideas, seeks to replace given rules when necessary, supports subordinates even at a personal cost, and interprets the rules according to the ethical mandates set forth to guide the organization (p. 113).

Dantzker (2000) offers leadership characteristics similar to those presented by Adlam and Villiers, citing: intelligence, interest and aptitude, communication, mental and emotional stability, drive and motivation, cooperation, and administrative skills (pp. 21–23). Although not a police researcher, Bennis (1994) provides what he describes as the **ingredients of leadership** that can be applied universally to any leader in any profession: guiding vision, passion, integrity, curiosity, and daring (pp. 39–40).

ingredients of leadership
the five ingredients—guiding vision, passion, integrity, curiosity, and daring—that Bennis argues one should possess to be a successful leader.

Bennis, Adlam, and Villiers differentiate themselves from Dantzker in that they reference ethics or integrity in their descriptions. Without integrity, leaders fail before they even get started (Klockars, Ivkovic, & Haberfield, 2006; O'Hara, 2005). The job of executive leadership is both difficult and demanding, so much so that the average tenure of a metropolitan police chief is between 3.5 and 5 years (Maguire, 2003; Peak & Glensor, 1996). A formal part of the organizational leadership is the command staff, which is responsible for communicating the chief's message and expectations. A typical chain of command will have a deputy chief, possibly major(s) or captain(s), lieutenants, sergeants, and finally the line officers.

Informal Leader

No leadership model is effective without discussing the role of informal leaders and their impact on an agency. There are many different kinds of informal leaders; most are attached to one of the many subcultures within an organization, which will be discussed later in this chapter. Informal leaders are recognized by their peers, and they gain status because of their knowledge and skills, the successful outcome of an internal investigation, successfully challenging the administration or winning a grievance, and/or their knowledge of policy and law.

King (2005) supports the concept of informal leadership and posits that there are five hierarchies in police organizations, three of which are associated with peer recognition and two of which are associated with the administration; peer recognition hierarchies are skill sets, seniority, and status, whereas administrative hierarchies are rewards and authority (pp. 98–104). King points out that only one of these levels is classified as authority, and yet each one has an influence on the organization.

The informal leader's credibility is enhanced because he or she can be trusted and is uncompromising. The status of such leaders is validated even more if they refuse to become a part of the administration. Adlam and Villiers (2003) note that informal leaders are viewed as nonconformists, which is a part of their charisma (p. 130).

CORE VALUES

core values

the beliefs that guide an organization and the behavior of its employees.

Core values are closely associated with the terms *integrity* and *trust*. Palmiotto (2000) defines **core values** as the beliefs that guide an organization and the behavior of its employees (p. 245). The public expects the profession of policing to be an institution in which they can trust. Often what affects core values is the conflict between due process and crime control (Koenig & Dias, 2001; Tonry, 2000). However, as an institution, police actions have shaken the public's confidence due to corruption, poor investigations that have resulted in the loss of high-profile cases, and the inability to solve crimes (Banks, 2008; Smith & Henry, 2007). Before you move on, take a moment and make a short list of what you consider to be core values of a law enforcement organization, and then compare it to Vicchio's list in the discussion that follows.

Vicchio (1997) identifies seven core values that are essential to police organizations: prudence, trust, effacement of self-interests, courage, intellectual honesty, justice, and cognizance (pp. 10–12). If you compare these core values of an organization to Bennis's characteristics of leadership presented in our earlier discussion, you will find that the two correspond to one another.

AGENCY CULTURE

organizational culture

closely tied to the style of policing that the organization and the community embrace.

Organizational culture is closely tied to the style of policing that the organization and the community embrace (Slovak, 1988; Stevens, 2008). Professionalism in policing was defined in Chapter 1 as the ethical conduct of officers who meet the needs of the communities in which they serve. At issue with this definition is the police subculture and the organization and how they are influenced by their respective environments. A police officer's indoctrination into the subculture begins with the academy and is reinforced in the field training program (Engelson, 1999; McNamara, 1999). Schein (2004) asserts that behavior is a direct result of organizational culture, and it is accomplished through shared norms (p. 8).

Many police agencies fit into one of three categories; and these have a direct impact on the personality of the officer when the organization promotes its particular style of policing: service, watchman, and legalistic (Wilson, 1968).

- **Service-oriented agency:** one that caters to the needs of the community. This style works best in middle-class communities that are homogenous and where the residents are not divided by class or race. Police here are not seen as crime fighters and do not subscribe to the crime control model of policing (pp. 200–201). This agency's style of enforcement is by the *color of the law*, which means that an officer has discretion in the enforcement of the law.

- **Watchman-oriented agency:** one where the agency's role is the maintenance of order. The officers use discretion in determining the seriousness of the law violations, and their standards will differ based on the group being policed: one standard for the minority community, another standard for the rich and middle class; another for prostitutes; yet another for drug dealers; still another for drunk drivers; and so on (pp. 140–141). This is the type of discretion that has mandated law changes, such as mandatory arrests for acts of domestic violence. This agency's style of enforcement is by the color of the law, which means that an officer has discretion in the enforcement of the law; there is no universal standard, and enforcement action is taken based on the individual officer's belief system.

- **Legalistic-oriented agency:** an agency that does not allow officers to use their discretion. The agency uses statistics to show how effective they are in their crime-fighting effort. The most notable organizational problem is that with this style of policing, an officer's value within the agency is determined by the statistics generated each month. This agency's enforcement style is by the *letter of the law*, which means that there is no discretion and that an arrest is made for every violation of the law.

In Chapter 2, we discussed Scrivner (1994), who identified five profiles of officers who were involved in police brutality: chronic risk, job-related tendencies, early career stage problems, patrol style, and personal problems. Considering these personalities as they relate to brutality, ask yourself: Is there a typical police personality, and how is that impacted by the officer's environment, that is, the community and the agency?

Skolnick (2004) describes the working police officer's personality as being comprised of two variables: danger and authority. The element of danger makes an officer hyper-vigilant and suspicious, always looking for

service-oriented agency

an agency that caters to the needs of the community.

watchman-oriented agency

the agency's role is maintenance of order. The officers use discretion in determining the seriousness of law violations.

legalistic-oriented agency

an agency that does not allow officers to use their discretion. The agency uses statistics to show how effective they are in their crime-fighting effort.

law violations or acts of violence. The element of authority reinforces the element of danger in isolating a police officer. Because of their role in society, police officers are isolated, which leads to solidarity inasmuch as officers do not trust those outside the profession (pp. 101–111).

Racial composition of neighborhoods is predictive of police coercion (Hickman, 2008; Smith, 1986). In large police departments that are broken into districts and/or precincts, each varies in workload demands, community composition, leadership style, and workforce composition. In essence, this means that many different subcultures exist within the same agency, with each having a unique way of policing, and with the conduct and behavior of each being influenced by a host of variables (Hickman, 2008; Skogan, 2006; Smircich, 1983). Regardless of the message sent from the top, professionalism is controlled by crime rates, socioeconomic status, residential stability, and population heterogeneity (Hickman, 2008; Lanier & Henry, 2004; Meehan & Ponder, 2005).

It is because of officers' behavior, individual officer perceptions of their community/beats, and the lack of a universal standard of conduct that police officers and agencies lack professionalism and continue to have issues with certain communities that date back to the 1960s (Liska, 1992; Walker, 2005). Klein (2000) argues that all organizations are built to fail at some point for a variety of reasons, and notes that even great societies such as the Roman Empire have failed due to poor leadership, divided authority, corruption, poor management, internal conflict, and political behaviors (p. xv). Klein points out that public entities and institutions such as policing remain because of a lack of competition, but the aforementioned challenges are issues with which they must deal.

O'Hara (2005) argues that law enforcement organizations fail because some operation, employee, policy, or process produces results that deviate from expectations in substantial and disruptive ways (p. 15). O'Hara explains that failure of an organization falls into one of six categories: accidental, structural, oversight, organizational culture, institutionalization, or resource diversion.

OTHER STYLES OF POLICING

There is no question that the behavior of police officers and the organization is constantly in flux due to the environment, be it from forces inside the agency or outside the department. The minority and poor communities within a jurisdiction have grievances that have not changed much since the 1960s (Hickman, 2008; Skogan, 2006; Skolnick & Fyfe, 1993).

However, policing has tried to reinvent itself with a host of initiatives in an attempt to effectively deal with these grievances (Greene, 2000; Stevens, 2008).

Community Policing

The initial concept of community policing began in the late 1970s and early 1980s as an experiment to bring back old-fashioned foot patrols, or what is known as the "beat cop." The need for such a program was born out of two concerns from the community: a rise in the violent crime rate; and a series of volatile incidents that occurred nationally throughout African American communities. Most notable of the incidents was the shooting of unarmed black males who had committed nonviolent felonies and were fleeing the scene. It was not until 1985 and the celebrated case of *Tennessee v. Garner* that the fleeing felon rule was abolished. In essence, the return of foot patrols/beat cops had as much to do with public relations as it did with protection and security. Trojanowicz and Bucqueroux (1998) support the concept of public relations and partnerships as a win-win for all involved (p. 3).

Foot patrols/beat cops evolved into the philosophy that we now know as **community-oriented policing (COP).** Community policing includes the development of external partnerships with community members and groups. Additionally, community policing addresses organizational changes that should take place in a police agency (such as decentralized decision making, fixed geographic accountability, agency-wide training, and personnel evaluations) designed to support collaborative problem solving, community partnerships, and a general proactive orientation to crime and social disorder issues (Fielding, 1995; Stevens & Yach, 1995).

community-oriented policing (COP)

the development of external partnerships with community members and groups.

The concept is great in theory. However, it means different things to different agencies (Lord & Fiday, 2008; Maguire & Mastrofski, 2000). Skogan (2006) argues that community policing is not about fighting crime and reducing fear as much as it is about recapturing the legitimacy that police have lost in minority communities (p. 247). Using research that he conducted in Chicago, Skogan notes that the police agenda has not changed, and the department is in control of the decision making and agenda setting; as a result, the Chicago Police Department continues to employ traditional police tactics under the guise of community policing (p. 210).

Problem-Oriented Policing

Goldstein (1990) introduced the concept of **problem-oriented policing (POP),** a method of analysis and solving crime problems. POP begins

problem-oriented policing (POP)

a method of analysis and solving crime problems.

with defining the problem. It is important to differentiate between a cluster or series of problems as opposed to one or two incidents; a substantive community concern; and a unit of police business (p. 66). Simply stated, this would be the difference between a single residential burglary and a host of burglaries in a specific geographic area. Problems are identified in POP through an analysis of the problem and evaluation of the police response to achieve a clear understanding of the problem; agreement over the particular interests to be served and their order of importance; an agreed-upon method to be used to determine the extent to which each of these are met; a realistic assessment of police expectations; determination of short-term goals versus long-term goals; and a clear understanding of the legality and fairness of the responses (pp. 146–147).

Computer Statistics or Comparative Statistics (COMPSTAT)

The City of New York adopted this style of policing in response to a speech that Mayor Rudolph Giuliani delivered on February 24, 1998, entitled "The Next Phase of Quality of Life: Creating a More Civil City." The "quality of life" crusade was a hallmark of Giuliani's mayoralty and, coupled with the reported drops in serious crimes like murder and assault, gave him a national reputation as a hard-nosed urban reformer (Murphy, 2006).

COMPSTAT (Computer Statistics or Comparative Statistics)

a management accountability tool. COMPSTAT offers a clear picture of crime and the crime-fighting efforts of the commanders. The focus is on results and sharing information.

New York's focus was on petty crimes with the understanding that if you address those, that will stop a host of others. This was the beginning of **COMPSTAT (Computer Statistics or Comparative Statistics),** which is a management accountability tool. In New York, COMPSTAT involved weekly meetings of police commanders in New York City, with each presenting their accomplishments and activities. The commanders were closely questioned, and in some cases were interrogated by the police commissioner and several deputy commissioners. COMPSTAT offered a clear picture of crime and the crime-fighting efforts of the commanders. The focus was on results and sharing information. However, commanders who failed to achieve results or meet the grade sometimes found that they were no longer commanders (Henry, 2002).

COMPSTAT has been adopted throughout the United States as a crime-fighting tool, which has made managers and officers accountable; however, Harris (2007) argues that the implementation of COMPSTAT has had no real impact on the reduction of crime. Harris examines several studies and references of Eck and Maguire (2000), noting that the homicide rate began to drop three years prior to the NYPD's implementation of COMPSTAT (pp. 171–174). Willis, Mastrofski, and Weisburd (2003) conducted a study of COMPSTAT in Lowell,

Massachusetts, Minneapolis, Minnesota, and Newark, New Jersey, and found that the crime rate in all three cities began dropping before the implementation of COMPSTAT; in Lowell, the crime rate began to rise after the implementation of COMPSTAT, which supports the findings of Harris, and Eck and Maguire (p. 6). Knowing the results of the data, the question begs: Why do police continue to use COMPSTAT if the results are in question?

Intelligence-Led Policing

Intelligence-led policing is new to the field of policing, at least that is what Ratcliffe (2008) postulates. However, it relies on some of the same strategies that COMPSTAT and problem-oriented policing utilize. Ratcliffe (2008) defines **intelligence-led policing** "as the application of criminal intelligence analysis as an objective decision-making tool in order to facilitate crime reduction and crime prevention through effective policing strategies and from external partnership projects drawn from an evidential base" (pp. 84–85). There is one subtle difference from prior styles of policing: Intelligence-led policing allows organizations to target known felons in order to prevent crime. Newburn (2008) states that intelligence-led policing provides an up-to-date picture of crime and the offenders with the purpose of disrupting and removing the most prolific offenders (pp. 383–384). Intelligence-led policing is fed by four types of intelligence products: strategic assessment, tactical assessment, target profiles, and problem profiles (Alison, 2005; Newburn, 2008; Ratcliffe, 2008).

intelligence-led policing

the application of criminal intelligence analysis as an objective decision-making tool in order to facilitate crime reduction and crime prevention through effective policing strategies and from external partnership projects drawn from an evidential base.

RACE AND GENDER

Law enforcement as an institution is a subculture, and it is one that has a host of subcultures within the organization. They can be grouped by job tasks, such as detectives versus patrol officers, or sergeants versus administration; but the road less traveled in the discussion are the subcultures of race and gender, and the impact these have on the profession and particular agencies.

As you read the remainder of this chapter, keep in mind that this text is designed to make you aware of every aspect of the profession of policing. There is no doubt that every profession has a dark side, and such issues are not unique to policing. In fact, the issues of race and gender play out daily in corporate America. So do not be discouraged by what you read or by interactions you have in the classroom; instead, embrace these discussions and use them to evaluate your personal belief system and how it will impact your decisions as a law enforcement officer. In any profession you choose, it is important to understand your personal biases and how they will affect your personal and professional lives.

AFFIRMATIVE ACTION

The term *affirmative action* has a negative meaning in many circles. Today, it is being attacked in every state by Ward Connerly and the American Civil Rights Institute as it relates to education. When examining this initiative, ask yourself: Do I really understand affirmative action? In fact, take a moment before you move on and define *affirmative action*.

Conservatives argue that affirmative action is nothing more than reverse discrimination and that whites have been and will continue to be hurt by such pieces of legislation. Pincus (2003) argues that nothing could be further from the truth, pointing out that most arguments deal with race and race alone, and disregard the issue of women (pp. 79–81).

Affirmative action legislation was designed to give minorities and women an opportunity to enter the workforce in careers where access had been denied. The origins of affirmative action were in 1966 when President Lyndon B. Johnson issued Executive Order 11246. It was later passed into law in 1972 and is now known as the Equal Employment Opportunity Act, which extended coverage to state and local governments. The purpose of affirmative action was racial desegregation of the American workforce, access to skill and professional training, as well as granting a place in the hierarchy of the American workplace to those who had been previously denied a place in it (Dipboye & Colella, 2005; Eastland, 1997; Ezorsky, 1991).

There is no doubt that there have been governmental abuses when it comes to affirmative action and hiring and that affirmative action has been used as reverse discrimination, which has only fueled the debate. Agencies have been accused of hiring less qualified applicants to fill quotas. In fact, Edley (1996) states that polls of the American public support the misconception that the purpose of affirmative action is to fill quotas, and yet this is the single greatest misconception of affirmative action's purpose (p. 18). Edley (1996) also notes that there have been abuses, and these are some of the ways in which they have occurred: those responsible for implementing the policy have looked at it as a rigid policy with no flexibility, meaning they have devised quotas, when in essence the policy should be very flexible; race has become the lone determining factor, eliminating all of the other objectives; programs have been implemented that have had an adverse impact on the nonbeneficiaries of the program; and finally, such programs have invited fraud (pp. 18–20).

Understanding the complexities of affirmative action and an agency's need to be diverse begins by asking oneself: What makes one candidate more qualified than another? Examine the following questions and attempt to determine how would you make your selection, with all things being equal: What set of qualifications predicts success? Is it academics in the academy? Is it an unsullied lifestyle prior to entering the academy? Is it scoring in the upper 10% of new officer candidates on the entrance exam? Is it a college education? Is it common sense and good decision-making skills? Take a moment to play the role of administrator, and choose from this list of questions what you believe makes one candidate more qualified than another when it comes to success within your agency and the policing profession in general.

In regard to the literature, there is no one characteristic or set of characteristics that will determine a candidate's success. Sanders (2003) notes that agencies have used such traits as intelligence, dependability, common sense, interpersonal skills, good communication, sensitivity, empathy, and flexibility, to name a few; all have been discussed with some regularity in the literature, and yet there is no consistency (p. 314). In fact, numerous studies have found that there is a direct correlation between higher attrition rates and intelligence and/or education (Burbeck & Furnham, 1985; Trojanowicz & Nicholson, 1976).

Contrary to earlier studies that predicted attrition of educated officers, however, Aamodt (2004) completed a meta-analysis of data collected over the years and came to these conclusions regarding education and policing (Palombo, 1995; Russell, Cosner, & Gingerich 2005):

- Success in the academy is related to education. Also, there is a correlation between education and success in policing.
- Recruits with degrees have greater academic success in the academy than those without degrees.
- In the long term, officers with bachelor's degrees will outperform those with associate degrees and high school diplomas.
- There is no advantage to majoring in criminal justice. The key to success in policing is a bachelor's degree. (pp. 49–58)

(See Scenario 5-1.)

SCENARIO 5-1: IS THE POLICE DEPARTMENT RACIST?

You are a highly decorated black officer and have a reputation for being the best field training officer in the agency. The lieutenant in charge of the field training program trusts your judgment so much that he has asked you on several occasions to evaluate trainees to determine if they are worth salvaging or if they should be terminated. If they could be salvaged, the lieutenant has had you develop training plans to address their shortcomings. If they did not possess the necessary skills to become a successful officer, then the lieutenant has used your observations and reports as the means for termination.

You have been at the agency for 7 years and have 20 years of experience from working at other law enforcement agencies. You have been transferred to training to become the lead trainer, and you are responsible for the high-liability areas, including firearms, defensive tactics, and driving. During your tenure you are aware that the agency has hired less-than-qualified minorities. In fact, there have been accusations that these individuals were given the test questions after failing the entrance examination two or three times. There also have been allegations that the females who did not pass the test had sexual relationships with the personnel lieutenant and were hired.

While assigned to training, one of your fellow officers (Officer Smith) is in serious trouble. In fact, when he was hired, Officer Smith did not have to complete the field training program. He was moved directly to Neighborhood Services because they needed him for community outreach. In discussing the matter with personnel, it was determined that Officer Smith took the examination three times and failed miserably on the writing sample as well as the oral interview. However, on the third attempt, he passed each aspect of the exam with a score of 100%. The personnel lieutenant stated: "I helped him prepare but did not give him the answers."

You have been in training approximately six months, and there have been several budget cuts. The position in Neighborhood Services has been returned to patrol, and the captain can no longer protect Officer Smith. Officer Smith is ordered back to patrol with the caveat that he must first successfully complete the field training program. Now the accusations are flying around the department that the field training program is racist and, because of this, Officer Smith will never pass the process. You have been approached by the chief and the union to leave training and train Officer Smith for the first phase of his training, and to return for his final phase of training.

Analysis and Reflection

1. What is the police department attempting to do by removing you from training? They are attempting to head off a lawsuit before it begins. They realize that they made a tragic mistake by not making Officer Smith complete the field training program before being transferred. Also, by not requiring Officer Smith to do the training program, they created a dangerous precedent that could be seen and challenged as a form of reverse discrimination by white candidates who were terminated in field training.

2. How did the administration's actions impact the credibility of black officers within the department? Black officers have felt that they have had to be better than their white counterparts in order to be accepted. Because Officer Smith allowed this to happen, it made the group appear less than credible.

3. Can this scenario be categorized as one of the abuses discussed by Edley? Yes. After reviewing how Officer Smith obtained his position, it is clear that he was not qualified and that race became the determining factor in his selection. Also, in making such a selection, the agency acted in a manner that was fraudulent.

4. In asking you to leave training and train Officer Smith, is the agency making a statement about their practices? Yes. The first statement they are making is an admission that the system is racist and that the only way not to be seen as such is to use you to accomplish the goal. However, it is both your reputation as a trainer and the fact that you are black that the administration is attempting to use to its advantage. By using you, they are attempting to gain credibility with patrol officers and avert any potential lawsuits.

5. If you refuse to participate, do you believe that this will hurt your career? This is a personal decision, and it depends on where you want your career to go. Reflect on your answer.

AFRICAN AMERICANS AND WOMEN IN POLICING

As two of the many subcultures within policing, African Americans and females have felt as though they have had to prove themselves to be accepted by their white male counterparts. Two terms, **black tax** and **minority tax,** have been used to describe this phenomenon. Gates (2004) describes the black tax as a standard where blacks are running high hurdles or having to complete a series of much more difficult tasks than their white counterparts; a higher standard is used to make one prove that one belongs, and anything less means one has failed (p. 88). Caver (2002) argues that the issue of credibility is very difficult, with blacks having to constantly prove themselves, and that any decisions that they make are constantly being second-guessed (p. 103).

black tax/minority tax

minority groups have to perform at a higher level than their white peers.

It is this author's belief that all minorities experience this phenomenon to some degree—not just African Americans, but all minorities in a workplace. However, policing has its own set of circumstances because it has traditionally been viewed as a white male profession. Mankiller (1998) argues that as an occupation, policing has been characterized as an institution of white male privilege, which creates a series of special hurdles for women and people of color (p. 455).

The history of African Americans in law enforcement has not been well documented. The first African American police officers date back to the 1800s in New Orleans. Dulaney (2007) describes them as "free men of color," and their role was to regulate the behavior of "black slaves" and stop potential rebellions that might arise (pp. 9–10). Much like the state police organizations, African Americans in policing was a concept that vacillated from extinction to tolerating their presence until the 1960s.

Before the 1960s, African American police officers had limited power in that they could not arrest whites even if the crime was committed right in front of them (Dulaney, 2007; Hine & Jenkins, 2001; Karatnycky, 2001). After the riots of the 1960s, the Kerner Commission in 1968 (see Chapter 1) determined that police operations were one of the primary reasons for the riots. As a part of the solution, the commission recommended the hiring and promotion of Negro officers as well as establishing a "Community Service Officer Program" to attract Negros to the profession (p. 15). This truly marks the growth of African Americans in policing. However, with that said, there is no national database that can provide the exact number of minority males or minority females in policing. The *Uniform Crime Reports* (UCR) dating back to 1991 include only data on the number of female officers and male officers.

A subject that is rarely discussed outside the inner circle of black officers is that they often feel marginalized by two institutions. The first is the police department and the value system that it imposes regarding their worth to the organization. The second is the African American community, as some in the community view the officers as traitors to their race (Alex, 1969). Holmes (2000) argues that there is very little difference when it comes to acts of brutality within minority communities, noting that race is not a factor and that black officers are just as guilty as their white colleagues. Instead, acts of brutality are shaped by the organization, peer pressure, and/or challenges to an African American officer's authority (p. 350). This feeling of mistrust and contempt toward black police officers is detailed in a documentary filmed by Ormsby (2002) at Fredonia State University entitled *Behind the Badge:*

> Being a black police officer is difficult. My dad hated the fact that I became an officer. He stated: "You went to college to become a police officer; what a waste. In fact, all I can say is that you have become a useless piece of shit. You could do anything and you choose to be a cop; they have been beating our asses since the beginning of time. Why would you do something so stupid? Nothing good will ever come of this. I will pray that you come to your senses.

Bolton and Feagin (2004) note that several studies have been done regarding African American police officers and that they have been, at best, contradictory when it comes to how the African American community views black officers. Some studies suggest that black officers are viewed as having a positive impact on the black community, other studies report that black officers feel more respected by the white community, and other studies have found that community attitudes are shaped by the socioeconomic status of the community (pp. 22–23).

Women in Policing

The original role for all women in policing was they served as matrons; later they were moved to deal with juvenile assignments, and finally patrol

(Martin & Jurik, 1996; Schulz, 2004). Martin (1989) reports that the number of women entering policing has grown from 2% in 1972 to 8.8% in 1986. African American female officers experience some of the same issues as African American male officers, yet they are unique because of experiencing both color and gender discrimination. Pike (1992) states that there is a difference in being black as opposed being a black female (pp. 275–276). Martin and Jurik (1996) point out that cultural images and/or stereotypes differ between white and black women, and it is because of this that black women are treated differently based on those cultural norms and biases (p. 71). Black females are viewed as sexually aggressive or promiscuous, as seeking welfare or light-duty assignments, and as being less intelligent (Allard, 2005; Jarret-Macauley, 1996; Martin & Jurik, 1996).

In the hierarchy of subcultures within policing, the African American woman sees herself as being on the lowest rung on the ladder (Bolton & Feagin, 2004; Fletcher, 1995). Bolton and Feagin (2004) provide this statement summarizing the feelings of an African American female officer: she is the scum of the earth because she is female and black (p. 108).

All females are marginalized in policing because policing is seen as a masculine profession. Police officers are seen as crime fighters involved in two wars: a "War on Drugs" and a "War on Crime." This has led to the **brotherhood of the badge,** which enabled policing to exclude women throughout most of its history. It was not until the 1970s that we saw an increase in female police officers (Appier, 1998; Scarborough & Collins, 2002; Ziegler & Gunderson, 2005). The end result of this exclusion has been additional stress, and it has prevented women from receiving information and sponsorship vital to occupational success (Maguire & Radosh, 1996).

brotherhood of the badge

describes policing as a male-dominated profession.

What is most interesting regarding women in policing is that they are as competent as their male counterparts. As women entered policing, there was skepticism regarding their effectiveness as patrol officers. However, a 1974 study conducted by Bloch and Anderson found that women perform in patrol just as effectively as men and that citizens respect female officers as much as male officers. The researchers did note several differences, however: women were more effective at defusing violent situations and avoiding violence; women made fewer arrests and wrote fewer traffic citations; and women were less likely than men to engage in serious unbecoming conduct.

When it comes to promotions, women officers are usually viewed by the white males in the organization as a quota system showing preferential treatment to minority males and females, yet both groups consistently lag behind in management positions within police organizations (Schulz, 2004). There is a stigma attached to the accomplishments of a minority officer because of the exclusivity of the club (white males). If a black male or a female is promoted, the first thing that many of the club members will say is that he or she was promoted because of race or gender without looking at what that individual has accomplished as an officer (Fletcher, 1995). This goes back to the issue of the *minority tax:* How much does one have to pay in order to be accepted?

MEDIA AND POLICE

From an organizational standpoint, one of the more difficult tasks in policing is an agency's public persona and how it is viewed by the local and sometimes national media, depending on the media market. Often the media becomes law enforcement's greatest form of oversight, and the relationship between police and the media at best can be described as tenuous (Fisman & Hubbard, 2006; Martin 2007). Lovell (2003) argues that the mass media is responsible for the reform of police administration and practices because it has exposed such atrocities as the Rodney King incident (p. 4).

The media has changed over the last twenty years. In the 1960s, 1970s, and mid-1980s, our primary source of information was traditional media, either print or television, with a reporter interpreting the information for the consumer. Lawrence (2000) argues that traditional forms of media are influenced by the reporters and their use of words to influence a story or incite an audience (p. 21).

Today what we know as the media includes the World Wide Web, and what differentiates the Internet from traditional media sources is that everyone has instant access to the Internet through the use of a cell phone or a computer. The problem that this poses for government and police in particular is that raw video footage can be captured and uploaded to the Internet as an incident is in progress, leaving police and public officials having to explain police behavior after public opinion has been formed (Baron, 2003; Jiggins, 2007; Rabinowitz, 1994).

However, because there is instant access, there are no filters, and the footage is raw, the public needs to exercise caution in accepting Internet news as the gospel truth; anyone can post an opinion or a video. In some cases, it might be impossible to determine authenticity and whether it is fact or fiction. In fact, the release of the information may be to the benefit of the stakeholder. Owens (2004) recognizes the benefit of instant access but also notes that often such information is rife with content and factual inaccuracies, and unlike the traditional media, which we hold accountable, on the World Wide Web that just is not possible (p. 26).

Public Information Officer

Today many agencies employ a public information officer (PIO) to become the spokesperson for the police department. Munsell (2008) states that the PIO serves as a tool to disseminate information to the public and often becomes the face and the conscience of the organization, relating the agency's values and mission to the public (p. 39). Depending on the size of the agency, the PIO can be a sworn officer, an entire department, or a staff of professional civilians. In smaller agencies, the chief or sheriff may act as the PIO.

Staszak (2001) points out that the media is evolving; the print media is merging or going bankrupt, and news has become a for-profit business with an eye on ratings, subscriptions, and advertising dollars (p. 10). Because of this, the media and police may have two different agendas. Police will use the press to get information to the public, while the media needs a story for ratings and ultimately sales. Staszak notes that it is for this very reason that a police agency and, more importantly, the PIO needs to understand that they must become effective at packaging their message and making it media-worthy, but stop short of sensationalizing (p. 13).

Information Sources

In any story, the PIO is only going to release limited information focusing on the who, what, where, when, why, and how. However, depending on the nature of the crime, such as a sexual battery or where the victim is a juvenile, the law may forbid police from releasing such information. The state of Florida has an open public records law known as the Sunshine Law that makes all police reports open to the public with certain limitations (Florida State Statute 119.01), and other states release information based on the Freedom of Information Act. No matter the law, there will be limitations to the information released because certain facts need to remain confidential to maintain the integrity of an investigation or protect the identity of a witness or victim.

The skills of a good investigative reporter are not much different from those of a good police investigator. Both have confidential sources, know their beats and the residents, and may have to work undercover; and in some cases, an investigative reporter may have one up on the police investigator because the investigative reporter will have sources within the police department (Ettema & Glasser, 1998). The agenda of confidential sources within the department may be contrary to the official information and position of the department. Such was the case during the

Watergate scandal and investigation in 1972, which led to the resignation of President Richard Nixon in 1974. The source of the information to *Washington Post* reporters was known as Deep Throat. Deep Throat was identified in 2005 as former Deputy Director of the FBI William Mark Felt (Felt & O'Connor, 2006; Jenkins, 2003).

CONCLUSION

Police organizations have been striving for years to become more than a vocation and to become a profession. The challenge is multifaceted, beginning with the agencies' leaders and the values systems that they convey to their organizations. Perhaps the most significant observation in this chapter is that by Schein (2004) when he notes that behavior is a direct result of organizational culture and is accomplished through shared norms (p. 8). What Schein acknowledges is that there are a host of factors that leaders cannot control, many of which are embodied in the personalities of their employees and later assimilated into an organization's culture.

In the past, the belief systems have included racism, sexism, differences in leadership styles and policing styles, and different agency responses to officer misconduct, which have been reflected in, for example: racism—how minority communities are treated and how minority officers assimilate into organizations; sexism—how women are marginalized in the profession and not considered as equals; differences in leadership styles—from management to first-line supervisors, impacting the message to the officer on the street; differences in policing styles—sometimes conflicted, such as when the agency message is community policing but the agency is actually legalistic; and different agency responses to officer misconduct—sometimes permissive, with incidents being minimized, and sometimes the agency has taken action.

These challenges coexist in an environment that includes the scrutiny of the media, with their bottom line being profit. Failing to address any or all of these issues places the organization and the leader in a precarious situation. There is no doubt that an organization is heavily influenced by the leader's leadership style, and hence he or she must be beyond reproach. To be successful, a leader must possess excellent communication skills, have political savvy, and serve the organization and community with integrity. For an agency to be considered professional, the leadership must balance each of the aforementioned intangibles and work in concert with the community.

DISCUSSION QUESTIONS

1. Describe how and why policing in the United States is considered fragmented. Is this a positive thing or a negative thing? Give examples to illustrate your answer.

2. Discuss Schein's observations regarding the organizational culture. Do you believe that a leader can impact the subtleties that have caused conflict within organizations over the years? Defend your answer.

3. Do you believe there are similarities in the hardships faced by black police officers and female police officers? Discuss the impact of these hardships, and how they have changed the face of policing.

4. What is affirmative action? Do you think such a policy is antiquated, or does it still serve a purpose? Explain your answer.

5. What are the components of sound community relations? Explain how community relations affect police officers and patrol.

 # RESEARCH TOPICS

Following are two topics that are central to this chapter. Choose one, and research the topic based on the instructions of your professor.

- *Leadership.* In this chapter, much has been said about leadership and leadership qualities. Choose a historical figure, someone you admire, and discuss that person's leadership style, paying particular attention to issues such as integrity, courage, and vision. Explain why you chose this leader over all others. Defend your answer with research.

- *Other styles of policing.* Most police departments in the United States have adopted one or more of the styles of policing presented in this chapter, depending on the administrator, the demographics, and the agency's size. As an administrator of a 100-person police department, what style of policing would you adopt to meet the needs of your community? In your consideration, remember that the mission of policing has been expanded to incorporate homeland security and terrorism. Defend your answer.

BIBLIOGRAPHY

Aamodt, M. G. (2004). *Research in law enforcement selection.* Boca Raton, FL: Brown Walker Press.

Abel, R. L. (2006). *The black shields.* Bloomington, IN: Author House.

Adlam, R., & Villiers, P. (2003). *Police leadership in the twenty-first century: Philosophy, doctrine and developments.* United Kingdom: Waterside Press.

Allard, S. A. (2005). Media images and sociological perceptions of black women: The impact of race and gender in the law of self-defense and battered woman syndrome. In N. J. Sokoloff & C. Pratt (Eds.), *Domestic violence at the margins: Readings on race, class, gender, and culture* (pp. 194–205). New Brunswick, NJ: Rutgers University Press.

Alex, N. (1969). *Black in blue: A study of the negro policeman.* Englewood Cliffs, NJ: Prentice-Hall.

Alison, L. J. (2005). *The forensic psychologist casebook.* United Kingdom: Willan.

Appier, J. (1998). *Policing women: The sexual politics of law enforcement and the LAPD.* Philadelphia: Temple University Press.

Aslinger, H. J., & Tomkins, W. F. (1953). *The traffic in narcotics.* New York: Funk & Wagnalls.

Banks, C. (2008). *Criminal justice ethics* (2nd ed.). Los Angeles: Sage.

Baron, G. R. (2003). *Now is too late: Survival in an era of instant news.* Upper Saddle River, NJ: Financial Times–Prentice Hall.

Bennis, W. (1994). *On becoming a leader.* Reading, MA: Addison-Wesley.

Berg, B. L. (1999). *Policing in modern society.* Woburn, MA: Butterworth-Heinemann.

Betchel, H. K. (1994). *State police in the United States: A socio-historical analysis.* Westport, CT: Greenwood.

Bloch, P., & Anderson, D. (1974). *Policewomen on patrol: Final report.* Washington DC: Police Foundation.

Bolton, K., & Feagin, J. R. (2004). *Black in blue: African American police officers and racism.* New York: Routledge.

Bullock, J. A, Haddow, G. D., & Coppola, D. P. (2006). *Introduction to homeland security.* Burlington, MA: Elsevier Butterworth-Heinemann.

Bumgarner, J. B. (2006). *Federal agents: The growth of federal law enforcement in America.* Westport, CT: Greenwood.

Burbeck, E., & Furnham, A. (1985). Police officer selection: A critical review of the literature. *Professional Psychology, 5*(3), 257–263.

Calhoun, F. S. (1991). *The lawmen: United States Marshals and their deputies 1789–1989.* New York: Penguin Group.

Caver, K. A. (2002). *Leading in black and white: Working across the racial divide in corporate America.* San Francisco: Wiley.

Dantzker, M. L. (2000). The police executive. In W. G. Doerner & M. L. Dantzker (Eds.), *Contemporary police organization and management: Issues and trends* (pp. 15–28). Boston: Butterworth & Heinemann.

Dantzker, M. L. (2005). *Understanding today's police.* Monsey, NY: Criminal Justice Press.

Dipboye, R. L., & Colella, A. (2005). *Discrimination at work: The psychological and organizational bases.* Mahwah, NJ: Routledge.

Dulaney, W. M. (2007). The Texas Negro Peace Officers Association: The origins of black police unionism. In B. A. Glasrud & J. M. Smallwood (Eds.), *The African American experience in Texas: An anthology* (pp. 335–352). Lubbock TX: Texas Tech University Press.

Eastland, T. (1997). *Ending affirmative action: The case for colorblind justice.* New York: Basic Books.

Eck, J. E., & Maguire, E. R. (2000). Have changes in policing reduced violent crime? An assessment of the evidence. In A. Blumstein & J. Wallman (Eds), *The crime drop in America* (pp. 207–265). Cambridge: Cambridge University Press.

Edley, C. (1996). *Not all black and white: Affirmative action and American values.* New York: Hill & Wang.

Engelson, W. (1999). The organizational values of law enforcement agencies: The impact of field training officers in the socialization of police recruits to law enforcement organizations. *Journal of Police and Criminal Psychology, 14*(2), 11–19.

Ettema, J. S., & Glasser, T. L. (1998). *Custodians of conscience: Investigative journalism and public virtue.* New York: Columbia University Press.

Evan, W. (1973). Measuring the impact of culture on organizations. *International Studies of Management and Organizations, 5*(1), 91–113.

Ezorsky, G. (1991). *Racism and justice: The case for affirmative action.* Ithaca, NY: Cornell University Press.

Federal Bureau of Investigation (FBI). (1998). *Uniform Crime Reports: Crime in the United States—1998.* Washington, DC: Author.

Federal Bureau of Investigation (FBI). (2007). *Crime in United States 2007: Table 74.* Washington, DC: Author.

Fehrenbach, T. R. (2000). *Lone star: A history of Texas and Texans.* Cambridge, MA: DA Capo Press.

Felt, W. M., & O'Connor, J. (2006). *A g-man's life: The FBI, being "deep throat" and the struggle for honor in Washington.* New York: PublicAffairs.

Fielding, N. (1995). *Community policing.* New York: Oxford University Press.

Fisman, R., & Hubbard, R. G. (2006). The role of nonprofit endowments. In E. L. Glaeser (Ed.), *The governance of not-for-profit organizations* (pp. 217–234). Chicago: University of Chicago Press.

Fletcher, C. (1995). *Breaking and entering.* New York: Harper Collins.

Florida State Legislature. The Sunshine Law, Florida State Statute 119.01. Tallahassee, FL: Author.

Gates, H. L. (2004). *America behind the color line: Dialogues with African Americans.* New York: Warner Books.

Gatewood, W. B. (1970). *Theodore Roosevelt and the art of controversy; Episodes of the White House years.* Baton Rouge: Louisiana State University Press.

Gillett, J. B. (1943). *Six years with the Texas Rangers 1875–1881.* Chicago: The Lakeside Press.

Goldstein, H. (1990). *Problem oriented policing.* Hightstown, NJ: McGraw Hill.

Greene, J. R. (2000). *Community policing in America: Changing the nature, structure and function of police.* Rockville, MD: National Institute of Justice.

Greene, J. R. (2006). *The encyclopedia of police science.* Boca Raton, FL: CRC Press.

Greene, K. (2006, January 16). Retired black cops pressure Georgia for pension equity. *Wall Street Journal,* archives.

Harris, C. J. (2007). The police and soft technology: How information technology contributes to police decision making. In J. M. Byrne & D. J. Robevich (Eds.), *The new technology of crime, law and social control* (pp. 153–184). Monsey, NY: Criminal Justice Press.

Heidensohn, F. (1995). *Women in control?: Role of women in law enforcement.* New York: Oxford University Press.

Henry, V. E. (2002). *The COMPSTAT paradigm: Management accountability in policing, business and the public sector.* New York: Looseleaf Law Publications.

Hickman, M. J. (2008). On the context of police cynicism and problem behavior. *Applied Psychology in Criminal Justice, 4*(1), 1–45.

Hine, D. C., & Jenkins, E. (2001). *A question of manhood: A reader in U.S. black men's history and masculinity.* Bloomington: Indiana University Press.

Holmes, M. D. (2000). Minority threat and police brutality: Determinants of civil rights complaints in U.S. municipalities. *Criminology, 38*(2), 343–366.

Hundall, R. K. (2004). *No safe haven: Homeland insecurity.* El Paso, TX: Omega Press.

Hutton, D. B., & Mydlarz, A. (2001). *Guide to law enforcement careers* (2nd ed.). Hauppauge, NY: Barron's Educational Series.

Institute of Medicine. (1990). *Treating drug problems.* Washington, DC: National Academy Press.

Jarrett-Macauley, D. (1996). *Reconstructing womanhood, reconstructing feminism.* New York: Routledge.

Jeffreys-Jones, R. (2007). *The FBI: A history.* Lexington: University Press of Kentucky.

Jenkins, P. (2003). *Images of terror: What we can and can't know about terrorism.* New York: Aldine Transaction Press.

Jiggins, S. (2007). The news media. In M. Mitchell & J. Casey (Eds.), *Police leadership and management* (pp. 203–217). Leichhardt, Australia: Federation Press.

Karatnycky, A. (2001). *Freedom in the world: The annual survey of political rights and civil liberties.* Edison, NJ: Transaction Publishers.

Kerner Commission. (1968). *Report of the national advisory commission on civil disorders: Summary of report.* Washington, DC: Author.

King, W. R. (2005). Toward a better understanding of the hierarchical nature of police organizations: Conception and measurement. *Journal of Criminal Justice, 33*(1), 97–109.

Klein, J. I. (2000). *Corporate failure by design.* Westport, CT: Quorum Books.

Klockars, C. B., Ivković, S. K., & Haberfield, M. R. (2006). *Enhancing police integrity.* New York: Springer.

Koenig, D. J., & Dias, D. K. (2001). *International police cooperation.* Lanham, MD: Lexington Books.

Koletar, J. W. (2006). *The FBI career guide.* Saranac, NY: AMACOM.

Lanier, M., & Henry, S. (2004). *Essential criminology.* Boulder, CO: Westview Press.

Lawrence, R. G. (2000). *The politics of force: Media and the construction of police brutality.* Berkeley: University of California Press.

Leishman, F., & Mason, P. (2003). *Policing and the media: Facts, fictions and factions.* Portland, OR: Willan.

LeMay, M. C. (2006). *Guarding the gates: Immigration and national security.* Westport, CT: Greenwood.

LexisNexis. (2007). *Massachusetts criminal law and motor vehicle handbook.* Charlottesville, VA: Matthew Bender.

Liska, A. E. (1992). *Social threat and control.* Albany, NY: SUNY Press.

Lord, V. B., & Fiday, P. C. (2008). What really influences officer attitude toward COP? *Police Quarterly, 11*(2), 220–238.

Los Angeles Police Department. (1991). *Report of the independent commission on the Los Angeles police department.* Los Angeles: Author.

Lovell, J. S. (2003). *Good cop–bad cop: Mass media and the cycle of police reform.* Monsey, NY: Criminal Justice Press.

Maguire, B., & Radosh, P. F. (1996). *The past, present, and future of American criminal justice.* Walnut Creek, CA: AltiMira Press.

Maguire, E. R. (2003). *Organizational structure in American police agencies: Context, complexity, and control.* Albany, NY: SUNY Press.

Maguire, E. R., & Mastrofski, S. D. (2000). Patterns of community policing in the United States. *Police Quarterly, 3*(1), 4–45.

Mankiller, W. (1998). *The reader's companion to U.S. women's history.* New York: Houghton Mifflin.

Martin, D. (2007). Accountability mechanisms: Legal sites of executive-police relations—Core principals in a Canadian context. In M. E. Beare & T. Murray (Eds.), *Police and government relations: Who's calling the shots?* Toronto, ON: University of Toronto Press.

Martin, S. E. (1989). *Women on the move? A report on the status of women in policing.* Washington, DC: Police Foundation.

Martin, S. E., & Jurik, N. C. (1996). *Doing justice, doing gender: Women in law and criminal justice occupations.* Thousand Oaks, CA: Sage.

Massaquoi, H. J. (1991). How to stop police brutality. *Ebony Magazine, 46*(9), 58–60.

Mawby, R. I. (1999). *Policing across the world.* New York: Routledge.

McNamara, R. P. (1999). The socialization of police. In D. J. Kenney & R. P. McNamara (Eds.), *Police and policing: Contemporary issues* (2nd ed., pp. 1–14). Westport, CT: Praeger.

Meehan, A. J., & Ponder, M. C. (2005). Race and place: The ecology of racial profiling African American motorists. In S. L. Gabbidon & H. T. Greene (Eds.), *Race, crime and justice.* New York: Routledge.

Miller, N. (1994). *Theodore Roosevelt: A life.* New York: HarperCollins.

Monkkonen, E. H. (2004). *Police in urban America, 1860–1920.* New York: Cambridge University Press.

Munsell, J. (2008). PIO affiliate will help CEO mission and department bottom line. *Policy and Practice of Human Services, 66*(2), 39–43.

Murphy, J. (2006, April 18). Big crackdown on little crime. *Village Voice,* p. 1.

Newburn, T. (2008). *Handbook of policing.* United Kingdom: Willan.

North Carolina General Assembly. (2008). *General statute 160A-28: Cities and towns.* Raliegh: Author.

Office of National Drug Control Policy. (2001). *The high intensity drug trafficking area program: 2001 annual report.* Washington, DC: U.S. Government Printing Office.

O'Hara, P. (2005). *Why law enforcement agencies fail: Mapping the organizational fault lines in policing.* Durham, NC: Carolina Academic Press.

Ormsby, R. (Producer/Director). (2002). *Behind the badge.* (Documentary). Fredonia, NY: Fredonia State University.

Owens, R. (2004). *Voice of reason: Why the left and right are wrong.* Hoboken, NJ: Wiley.

Palmiotto, M. (2000). *Community policing: A policing strategy for the 21st century.* Gaithersburg, MD: Aspen.

Palombo, B. J. (1995). *Academic professionalism in law enforcement.* New York: Garland.

Peak, K. J., & Glensor, R. W. (1996). *Community policing and problem solving: Strategies and practices.* Upper Saddle River, NJ: Prentice Hall.

Pike, D. L. (1992). Women in police academy training: Some aspects of organizational response. In I. Moyer (Ed.), *Changing roles of women in the criminal justice system: Offenders, victims, and professionals* (2nd ed., pp. 261–280). Prospect Heights, IL: Waveland Press.

Pincus, F. L. (2003). *Reverse discrimination.* Boulder, CO: Lynne Rienner.

Purpura, P. P. (2007). *Terrorism and homeland security: An introduction with applications.* Burlington, MA: Butterworth-Heinemann.

Rabinowitz, P. (1994). *They must be represented: The politics of documentary.* Brooklyn, NY: Verso Books.

Ratcliffe, J. (2008). *Intelligence-led policing.* United Kingdom: Willan.

Reaves, B. A. (2004). *Census of state and local law enforcement agencies, 2004.* Washington, DC: Bureau of Justice Statistics.

Reaves, B. A., & Bauer, L. M. (2002). *Federal law enforcement officers, 2002.* Washington, DC: Bureau of Justice Statistics.

Regoli, R. M., & Hewitt, J. D. (2007). *Exploring criminal justice.* Sudbury, MA: Jones & Bartlett.

Russell, G. D., Conser, J. A., & Gingerich, T. (2005). *Law enforcement in the United States* (2nd ed.). Sudbury, MA: Jones & Bartlett.

Salinger, L. M. (2004). *Encyclopedia of white-collar and corporate crime.* Thousand Oaks, CA: Sage.

Samaha, J. (2005). *Criminal justice.* Belmont, CA: Thomson Wadsworth.

Sanders, B. A. (2003). Maybe there's no such thing as a "good cop": Organizational challenges in selecting quality officers. *Policing: An International Journal of Police Strategies and Management, 26*(2), 313–328.

Scarborough, K. E., & Collins, P. A. (2002). *Women in public and private law enforcement.* Boston: Butterworth & Heinemann.

Schein, E. (2004). *Organizational culture and leadership.* San Francisco: Jossey-Bass.

Schulz, D. M. (2004). Invisible no more: A social history of women in U.S. policing. In B. R. Price & N. J. Sokoloff (Eds.), *The criminal justice system and women: Offenders, prisoners, victims, and workers* (3rd ed., pp. 483–494). New York: McGraw-Hill.

Scrivner, E. (1994). *The role of police psychology in controlling excessive force.* Washington, DC: National Institute of Justice.

Shafter, A. J. (1961). Numerical strength of small police departments. *Journal of Criminal Law, Criminology, and Police Science, 52*(3), 344–346.

Skogan, W. G. (2006). *Police and community in Chicago.* New York: Oxford University Press.

Skolnick, J. H. (2004). A sketch of the police officer's "working personality." In B. W. Hancock & P. M. Sharp (Eds.), *Criminal justice in America: Theory, practice and policy* (3rd ed., pp. 100–124). Upper Saddle River, NJ: Prentice Hall.

Skolnick, J. H., & Fyfe, J. J. (1994). *Above the law: Police and the excessive use of force.* New York: The Free Press.

Slovak, J. S. (1988). *Styles of urban policing.* New York: NYU Press.

Smircich, L. (1983). Concept of culture and organizational analysis. *Administrative Science Quarterly, 28*(3), 339–359.

Smith, D. (1986). The neighborhood context of police behavior. In A. Reiss & M. Tonry (Eds.), *Communities and crime* (pp. 313–341). Chicago: University of Chicago Press.

Smith, D. J., & Henry, A. (2007). *Transformation of policing*. Burlington, VT: Ashgate.

Smith, G. D. (1999). *Combating terrorism*. New York: Routledge.

Staszak, D. (2001). Media trends and the public information officer. *FBI Law Enforcement Bulletin, 70*(3), 10–13.

Stevens, D. J. (2008). *An introduction to American policing*. Sudbury, MA: Jones & Bartlett.

Stevens, P., & Yach, D. M. (1995). *Community policing in action*. Cape Town, South Africa: Wyvern.

Steverson, L. A. (2008). *Policing in America: A reference handbook*. Santa Barbara, CA: ABC-CLIO.

Stotler, J. A. (2002). *California state law enforcement agencies*. Paducah, KY: Turner.

Thaler, W. M., & Bea, K. (2005). *Emerging issues in homeland security*. Hauppauge, NY: Nova Science.

Tonry, M. H. (2000). *The handbook of crime and punishment*. New York: Oxford University Press.

Trojanowicz, R., & Bucqueroux, B. (1998). *Community policing: How to get started*. Cincinnati, OH: Anderson.

Trojanowicz, R. C., & Nicholson, T. G. (1976). A comparison of behavioral styles of college graduate police officers. *Police Chief, 43*(8), 56–59.

U.S. Legislature. (2008). *United States code*. Washington, DC: Author.

Utah State Legislature. (2009). *Utah code, title 10-3-909 to 10-3-915*. Salt Lake City: Author.

Vicchio, S. J. (1997). Ethics and police integrity. *FBI Law Enforcement Bulletin, 66*(7), 8–12.

Vollmer, A. (1936). *The police and modern society*. Berkeley: Regents of the University of California.

Walker, S. (2005). *The new world of police accountability*. Thousand Oaks, CA: Sage.

Walker, S., & Katz, C. M. (2005). *Police in America: An introduction* (5th ed.). Boston: McGraw Hill.

Walma, M., & West, L. (2002). *Police powers and procedures*. Toronto, CA: Emond Montgomery.

Westphal, C. (2008). *Data mining for intelligence, fraud and criminal detection*. Boca Raton, FL: CRC Press.

Willis, J. J., Mastrofski, S. D., & Weisburd, D. (2003). *COMPSTAT in practice: An in-depth analysis of three cities*. Washington, DC: The Police Foundation.

Wilson, J. Q. (1968). *Varieties of police behavior*. Cambridge, MA: Harvard University Press.

Ziegler, S. L., & Gunderson, G. G. (2005). *Moving beyond G.I. Jane: Women and the U.S. military*. Lanham, MD: University Press of America.

CHAPTER 6

PATROL OPERATIONS

OBJECTIVES

After completing this chapter, the student will be able to:

* Discuss the role of patrol in society.
* Describe the role of police in American society.
* Describe the three types of patrol styles.
* Explain the patrol experiments.
* Describe the advantages and disadvantages of shift assignments.
* Discuss the advantages and disadvantages of one-person versus two-person patrol units.
* Explain the characteristics associated with officer safety and an officer's area of responsibility.
* Discuss the primary calls associated with service in patrol.
* Discuss the pros and cons of police pursuits.
* Describe the role of patrol officers in narcotics enforcement.

KEY TERMS

call boxes – originally these were a direct line to the police station, and officers had a special key to access the boxes for calls for service; later they were open to the public so anyone could access them and call police anytime they were needed.

children in need of services – children who are found living in deplorable conditions or who are truant from school, constantly run away from home, or have behavior problems in school.

crime-fighting model – not proactive in nature; associated with traditional reactive policing, that is, responding to calls for service after the crime has been committed.

hot spot policing – focusing patrol attention on locations (hot spots) where clusters of crime and disorder occur in an environment that fosters the readiness associated with the decision to commit a crime.

Kansas City patrol experiment – found that the three experimental patrol conditions did not appear to affect crime, service delivery, or citizen feelings of security in ways the public and the police often assume that they do.

officer-to-citizen ratio – the number of officers who work for a particular agency, which is determined by the level and nature of crime, as compared to the number of citizens. On a national average, there are 2.4 officers for every 1,000 citizens.

post-9/11 project – convened in 2004 and attended by the International Association of Chiefs of Police (IACP), the National Sheriff's Association (NSA), the National Organization of Black Law Enforcement Executives (NOBLE), and the Police Foundation with a goal of assisting state and local law enforcement in the management of an ever-changing police environment.

proactive policing – an attempt to prevent crime before it happens through the use of methods such as crime analysis, COMPSTAT, problem-oriented policing, community policing, and intelligence-led policing.

routine activity theory – holds that for a personal or property crime to occur, there must be at the same time a perpetrator, a victim, and the absence of a guardian to prevent the attack.

shifting eras and mission reconfiguration – recognizes that the police mission has changed since 9/11, and yet the traditional policing models of crime control and community policing cannot be ignored.

team policing – a team of officers is assigned to a geographical area of the city and held accountable for crimes in that area. It is the forerunner to community policing and requires officers to work in conjunction with the community.

triad of tactical thinking – the business of assessing every situation and analyzing it as if it were a threat by being cognizant of three concepts: problem areas, areas of responsibility, and any potential threat.

Doc's Words of Wisdom

Patrol is the backbone of every law enforcement organization. In fact, if you take a moment and think about it, uniform patrol is the only visible form of government that is responsible for the public at large.

INTRODUCTION

Patrol has many purposes, including acting as a deterrent, the detection and apprehension of criminals, advising the public, traffic enforcement, and maintaining public order (American Bar Association, 1972; Horton, 1989). Many who enter the profession believe that it involves going from one emergency call to another, always on the hot seat, experiencing an adrenaline rush, and the ultimate prize or trophy is the bad guy. There is no doubt that television has glamorized policing, but those who work in the profession find that they are challenged more with boredom than excitement, often entangled in tons of paperwork and administrative duties (Ericson, 1982; Vila & Taiji, 1999; Waddington, 1994).

Other newcomers to the profession who have watched shows like *Law and Order* believe they have the "right stuff" and can skip patrol and move immediately into the specialized units such as narcotics or detectives. The truth is that in order to be a good police officer, you must pay your dues in patrol. Patrol provides every officer with the foundation for many of the skills needed in police specialties such as investigations and traffic (Dantzker, 2005; McConnell, 2009). Patrol is considered the backbone of the department because they are first responders, take most of the initial crime reports, make on-view arrests, are the gateway to the criminal justice system, and are the most visible form of local government (Dantzker, 2005; Schroeder & Lombardo, 2004; Stering, 2004; Steverson, 2008).

DEVIANCE

Take a moment and reflect on how and why police have evolved to what we know today. Tromanhauser (2003) argues that deviance is a characteristic of civilization and that if we were isolated on an island with no social interaction, there would be no need for police or the law (p. 82). In examining Tromanhauser's statement, we must be cognizant of the following:

1. The growth of society and the human need to interact are the foundations for deviant behavior.

2. As a result of this deviant behavior, which is considered a violation of social norms and/or law, there is an inherent need for society to respond to these violations.

3. Hence, throughout history protective forces have been formed, be it the sentries who guarded the walls of ancient Rome, night watchmen, sheriffs, town marshals, or finally law enforcement as we know it today.

However, understand that if suspects are determined to commit crimes, they will do so no matter what. Criminologists offer a number of theories as to why some of us commit crimes and others choose not to. For those who refuse to commit crimes, the best argument is the theory of deterrence: those who refuse to pursue a life of crime have something to lose and fear jail (Bachman & Schutt, 2007). On the other hand, many believe that those who commit crimes do so because they have made a rational choice to do so (Tunnell, 2004). So many variables influence one's decision to enter a life of crime that it is virtually impossible to identify one cause of crime or why one makes the choice unless a suspect is perfectly honest upon reflection.

We may not know the specific causes of crime, but we do know that the benefits of committing crime outweigh the probability of getting caught. A meta-analysis of the Federal Bureau of Investigation's (FBI's) *Uniform Crime Reports* (UCR) between the years 1995 and 2006 provides the following data in regard to police clearance rates on a national level, which vary from agency to agency. Note that these data are limited by the quality of information that agencies provide to the FBI and captures only crimes reported to the police; also note that these data are associated with the specific crimes of murder, forcible rape, robbery, aggravated assault, burglary, larceny, and motor vehicle theft. On average, during this twelve-year period, police cleared 33% of the crimes reported annually, with murder being the most often cleared and motor vehicle theft being the least.

THE PURPOSE OF PATROL

Today patrol is designed to be the first responder to those who have a need of police services; there is the perception that police officers are crime fighters, and society's first line of defense against the criminal element

(Banks, 2009; Fyfe, 1993; Richardson, 1974). Patrol has evolved from the 1700s when citizens patrolled the streets as night watchmen, to beat officers walking foot patrol in the 1800s, to the various forms of patrol we have today (Steverson, 2008). The first foot patrol officers were on their own because there was no form of communication. They often relied on the *hue and cry*, which dates back to 1066 in Britain, or on being contacted by citizens in need as they passed on their beat (Chu, 2001; Dias, 2002). It was not until the 1800s that police began to use call boxes, which were strategically placed on the officers' beats.

The first call boxes were telegraph boxes, which later became phones. The original **call boxes** were a direct line to the police station, and officers had a special key to access the boxes for calls for service. Later the call boxes were open to the public so that anyone could access them and call police anytime they were needed (Oslin, 1999; Safir & Whitman, 2003; Steverson, 2008). Eventually technology provided two-way communications in patrol cars, and then portable radios. Today communication is faster, digitized, and includes computers.

With the advent of technology, growth of urban and rural communities, and the need for fast mobile response times, patrol moved from the beat officer to what became known as the rapid-response or **crime-fighting model.** Many scholars argue that it is at this point that patrol became reactive rather than proactive. However, if you examine the inefficient ways police were contacted in the 1800s, the model then was nothing more than reactive. The only advantage of beat officers on foot is that they knew the members of their respective beats and had an opportunity to solve some of the problems. There are three basic types of patrol:

- *Preventative patrol* utilizes the marked patrol unit and uniformed officers assigned to a designated zone or district. The unit is responsible for all calls for service within that zone and patrols the area randomly to act as a deterrent to future criminal acts (Grieve, Harfield, & MacVean, 2007; Sherman & Wisebud, 1995; Zimring, 2007). Preventative patrol primarily uses automobiles; other transportation forms are foot, bicycle, horse, and scooter. Depending on the jurisdiction, specialty forms may be demanded, such as marine patrol, beach patrol, air patrol, snowmobile patrol, and agricultural patrols.
- *Reactive patrol* is the traditional patrol response. Police respond to calls after they have occurred and investigate the incidents. This is the least effective way of policing because there is no attempt to prevent or anticipate activity before it occurs. This type of patrol is synonymous with preventative patrol (Reiss, 1971; Sung, 2002; Websdale, 2001).

call boxes

originally these were a direct line to the police station, and officers had a special key to access the boxes for calls for service; later they were open to the public so anyone could access them and call police anytime they were needed.

crime-fighting model

not proactive in nature; associated with traditional reactive policing, that is, responding to calls for service after the crime has been committed.

- *Proactive patrol* is an attempt to prevent crime before it happens through the use of crime analysis, COMPSTAT, problem-oriented policing, community policing, and intelligence-led policing. These are all methods of **proactive policing** (Braga, 2008; Skogan & Frydl, 2004; Vogel, 1997). Each requires that police analyze information, develop a plan of action, implement the plan, complete the plan, and then analyze what happened to determine the success or failure of the plan. The idea is that if executed properly, the plan will eliminate problems in the long term. Analysis is very important here because it should show if criminal activity has been *displaced*—that is, moved to another location because of the police activity (Cornish & Clark, 2006; Hope, 1994; Newburn, 2007; Smith, 2003).

proactive policing

an attempt to prevent crime before it happens through the use of methods such as crime analysis, COMPSTAT, problem-oriented policing, community policing, and intelligence-led policing.

PATROL EXPERIMENTS

It has long been held that the purpose of patrol is to act as a deterrent against crime. This assumption dates back to Sir Robert Peel and the Peelian Reform. As mentioned earlier, patrol is the backbone of policing, and based on the meta-analysis of the UCR we know that national clearance rates are dismal. In order to become more effective and efficient, policing has studied the impact of patrol through experiments and different methods of deployment.

Operation 25, New York City Police Department, 1954

Operation 25 was one of the first studies regarding the impact of increased patrol on crime. It was conducted for four months in a single Harlem precinct. The number of officers in the precinct doubled from 188 to 440. Foot patrol officers were assigned to a single street, patrolling four blocks. There was a 55% decrease in reported felonies as compared to the same time period a year prior. This study had many flaws in that it did not address displacement or cost-effectiveness, and it relied only on official crime reports (Ross & LaFree, 1985; Zimring & Hawkins, 1973). The reality of such an experiment, however, is that no agency can afford to deploy the number of resources used in this experiment for any length of time.

20th Precinct Project, New York City Police Department, 1963–1967

The 20th Precinct Project was designed to determine if an increase of sworn personnel by 40% (100 officers) would have an impact on crime in the 20th precinct and if the addition of the personnel and increased police activity would displace crime to adjacent precincts. It is important to note that this was not an actual experiment; there were no controls and no replication. In all ten crimes were analyzed, including burglary, robbery, grand larceny, felonious assaults, auto theft, and misdemeanors, as well as the number of arrests for felonies and misdemeanors. Adjustments were made for seasonal changes in crime, and the data collected were compared to data gathered before the study began. The data analysis confirmed that there was a decrease in crime in all categories except the total number of misdemeanor violations and the only significant increase in crime displacement was in Central Park, which is adjacent to the 20th precinct (Press, 1971, pp. iii, v–vi).

Kansas City Preventative Patrol Experiment, 1972–1973

One of the first scientific studies of uniform patrol effectiveness was conducted by Keeling, Pate, Dieckman, and Brown (1974) in conjunction with the Police Foundation and the Kansas City, Missouri, Police Department. The research, conducted between October 1, 1972, and September 30, 1973, was designed to test the impact that patrol has on two very common hypotheses: visible police presence prevents crime by deterring potential offenders and uniform patrol reduces the public's fear of crime (p. vii).

The study lasted for one year and was structured with three types of beats for comparison: reactive, proactive, and control. The reactive beats had officers only respond to calls for service in their beats but not patrol the beat once the call was handled. The proactive beats had two to three times the number of patrol units actively patrolling those beats. The control beats consisted of the usual number of cars (one per beat) randomly patrolling and taking calls for service. The **Kansas City patrol experiment** found that the three experimental patrol conditions did not appear to affect crime, service delivery, or citizen feelings of security in ways the public and the police often assume that they do (p. 2).

Kansas City patrol experiment

found that the three experimental patrol conditions did not appear to affect crime, service delivery, or citizen feelings of security in ways the public and the police often assume that they do.

San Diego Field Interrogation Study, 1975

The San Diego experiment was designed to see if stopping field interviews and frisking would have a noticeable impact on street crime. In one area of the city, field interrogations were stopped for a seven-month period. During that time, the number of crimes committed in that area rose by one-third. The crimes in question were robbery, burglary, theft, auto theft, malicious mischief, disturbances, and sex crimes. When field interrogations were reintroduced for a nine-month period, the number of crimes dropped back to the original number. Boydstun (1975) argues that because there was a noticeable drop after the reintroduction of police activity, noticeable police activity does have a deterrent impact on criminal activity.

Team Policing, 1970s

Team policing is truly decentralizing decision making and leaving it in the hands of the team leader, usually a sergeant or above; it should be done cooperatively with the community. A team of officers is assigned to a geographical area of the city; it could be a particular zone, but it works better if the area is scaled down so that the team has greater impact. The officers are held accountable for crime control and disorder within the area. In cities where team policing was implemented, there was a reduction in crime (Brown, 1988; Maguire & Wells, 2002; McDavid & Hawthorn, 2005; Skolnick & Bayley, 1988). The officers were also responsible for meeting with neighborhood leaders and addressing their needs. Brown (1988) argues that officers who were involved in team policing were much more aggressive than officers who did not participate in these experiments, with an increased number of arrests (pp. 300–301). Team policing was the forerunner to community policing.

Hot Spot Patrolling

Hot spots are locations where clusters of crimes occur. The decision to commit a crime is associated with readiness. Criminal readiness is not constant and varies over time and place, dependent upon the suspect's background and site-specific situations (Brantingham & Brantingham, 1993). Simply put, certain locations within a jurisdiction allow for order or disorder to take place on a regular basis; in a disordered environment (hot spot), crimes flourish. One method of patrol is to focus attention on these areas, which is known as **hot spot policing.** Associated with hot spots is the **routine activity theory** (Felson, 1998), which holds that for a personal or property crime to occur, there must be at the same time a perpetrator, a victim, and the absence of a guardian to prevent the attack (p. 123). Locations of possible hot spots are open-air drug markets, abandoned buildings, city parks, and locations where alcohol is sold and/or consumed. Hot spots can be identified through crime mapping, COMPSTAT, intelligence-led policing, or crime analysis.

PATROL ZONES/BEATS

To understand the significance of the patrol function, Reaves and Goldberg (1996) report that nationally about 70%, or 286,000, of full-time

---

team policing

a team of officers is assigned to a geographical area of the city and held accountable for crimes in that area. It is the forerunner to community policing and requires officers to work in conjunction with the community.

hot spot policing

focusing patrol attention on locations (hot spots) where clusters of crime and disorder occur in an environment that fosters the readiness associated with the decision to commit a crime.

routine activity theory

holds that for a personal or property crime to occur, there must be at the same time a perpetrator, a victim, and the absence of a guardian to prevent the attack.

sworn local police personnel were uniformed officers on patrol or otherwise regularly assigned to respond to calls for service.

A patrol zone/beat is an area of responsibility for an individual patrol unit where a patrol car is assigned to a specific geographic area and is responsible for calls that occur in that area. Depending on the agency, officers may or may not be allowed to roam into other zones. Another important note regarding the zones is that they vary in size based on demographics, the nature of the crimes that occur within the area, the availability of personnel, and the type of agency (Rubin, 1982; Vinzant & Crothers, 1998).

The size of an organization defines the structure and size of uniform patrol. In addition to the agency size, population is a key factor in determining the size of a law enforcement agency. However, this does not translate into the number of officers assigned to the patrol function (Dantzker, 2005). In fact, if an agency has three hundred officers, only one hundred may be assigned to patrol. Other assignments include detectives, personnel, training, forensics, narcotics, school resources, and administration. The FBI's *Uniform Crime Report, 2006* provides the following data: For every 1,000 residents in the United States, there are 2.4 sworn officers; this is known as the **officer-to-citizen ratio.** The numbers provided by the *Uniform Crime Report* have limitations because the officer-to-citizen ratio is based on a national average.

A municipal agency's patrol division that is responsible for 100,000 residents may be structured in an entirely different way from that of a county with the same number of residents. In such cases, geography may define the size of the patrol zones. The Gainesville Police Department Gainesville, Florida, has 100,000 residents located in a geographic area of 48 square miles, and the agency employs 314 sworn officers with approximately 100 officers assigned to the patrol division. In contrast, the Alachua County Sheriff's Office in Alachua County, Florida, is responsible for a geographic area of 965 square miles, including the city of Gainesville. If you exclude the city of Gainesville's population and landmass, the Alachua County Sheriff's Office is responsible for approximately 108,000 residents and 917 square patrol miles. The Alachua County Sheriff's Office has approximately 270 sworn deputies with 160 assigned to patrol.

officer-to-citizen ratio

the number of officers who work for a particular agency, which is determined by the level and nature of crime, as compared to the number of citizens. On a national average, there are 2.4 officers for every 1,000 citizens.

PATROL SHIFTS

Patrol provides services 24 hours per day, 7 days a week. In most agencies, shifts are determined by seniority where officers bid for a particular shift every three months, four months, six months, or annually. This bid cycle depends on the agency and the collective bargaining agreement. The three most common schedules in law enforcement today are the traditional eight-hour, ten-hour, and twelve-hour schedules. The goals of scheduling are a delicate balance between meeting the needs of the community and taking care of employee needs and include: providing optimal coverage within the specified jurisdiction during peak demands for service; providing officers with backup during the peak service times; and attempting to provide a schedule that takes into account the use vacation and sick leave (Stering, 2007; Thierry & Jansen, 1998; Wedderburn, 1995).

Eight-Hour Schedule

The eight-hour schedule is the most common in the American workforce, with each employee working 40 hours per week with the traditional two days off per week. In policing, especially patrol, weekends off are rare because Friday and Saturday are two of the busiest days, since those are the days when the rest of society enjoys free time. Traditionally an eight-hour schedule would be comprised of three shifts: day shift from 7:00 A.M. to 3:00 P.M.; evening shift from 3:00 P.M. to 11:00 P.M.; and the midnight shift from 11:00 P.M. to 7:00 A.M. However, in policing it is wise to add a fourth overlapping shift to address increased demand for services. In most jurisdictions, those hours are between 10:00 P.M. and 3:00 A.M. To meet these needs, it would be important to have an overlapping shift that works between the hours 8:00 P.M. and 4:00 A.M.

Ten-Hour Schedule

In policing, the ten-hour schedule has been the most revered in that it allows officers to work four 10-hour days, with three days off each week. As in the eight-hour schedule, the most difficult days off are Friday, Saturday, and Sunday because the first priority is the community and meeting their demands for service. A traditional ten-hour schedule is comprised of three shifts: day shift from 7:00 A.M. to 5:00 P.M.; evening shift from 4:00 P.M. to 2:00 A.M.; and midnight shift from 10:00 P.M. to 8:00 A.M. Unlike the traditional eight-hour shift where you have to build in the overlap shift, this naturally occurs with the ten-hour schedule. The overlap of the ten-hour shift provides optimal staffing during the busiest times on the evening and midnight shifts, which are between 11:00 P.M. and 3:00 A.M. (Bureau of Alcohol, Tobacco, and Firearms, 2004; Zawitz et al., 1993). This allows an agency to double its coverage during peak service hours.

Twelve-Hour Schedule

The twelve-hour shift has become another staple in law enforcement with its most redeeming quality being that it provides a three-day weekend every other weekend. To many officers, this is the closest they will ever get to a normal life while assigned to patrol. The days off on this schedule rotate weekly and are as follows:

1. *Week One*
   a. *Work* Monday–Tuesday
   b. *Off* Wednesday–Thursday
   c. *Work* Friday, Saturday, and Sunday
2. *Week Two*
   a. *Off* Monday–Tuesday
   b. *Work* Wednesday–Thursday
   c. *Off* Friday, Saturday, and Sunday

Although the twelve-hour shift provides great time off, it poses some unique problems. The first is that it is very similar to the eight-hour shift in that it provides no overlap and requires that an overlap shift be created to address peak hours of service. Officers assigned to the day shift work 7:00 A.M. to 7:00 P.M.; the night shift works from 7:00 P.M. to 7:00 A.M.

Although the twelve-hour schedule provides for more time off, it can create havoc for those who work nights when it comes to attending court during the day. It is not unusual for officers to work all night and then spend the first four hours of the morning in court. When this happens, it can turn the traditional twelve-hour day into fifteen or sixteen hours, with little time for rest before they have to return to duty. This can easily lead to increased use of sick time and/or burnout.

ONE-OFFICER VERSUS TWO-OFFICER PATROL UNITS

One of the great debates regarding the deployment of patrol units is whether two-officer units provide a greater degree of safety than one-person patrol units. From a managerial standpoint, one-officer units allow an agency to deploy more units at any given time, increasing the presence of officers on patrol. Boydstun, Sherry, and Moelter (1977) determined that one-officer patrol units are more efficient, provide a better quality of service, and are safer because officers take fewer chances (pp. 4–5). Upon completion of the Boydstun et al. study of the San Diego Police Department, it was determined that one-officer units were just as effective as two-officer units. The analysis of the data revealed that the use of two-officer units as regular patrol units did not appear to be justified in San Diego (p. 5).

In contrast to Boydstun et al., Kaplan (1979) argues that the decision to move to one-officer patrol units has been based on speculation and that the true implications of such a decision are unknown (p. 325). Kaplan evaluated a number of performance measures in the argument of one-officer versus two-officer units (expected area covered by patrol, response time from the nearest vehicle to a randomly occurring incident, expected frequency of patrol, visibility of patrol, probability of intercepting a crime in progress, probability of officer injury, and comparative costs) and determined that the benefits of a two-officer unit far outweigh those of a one-officer unit (pp. 349–350).

OFFICER SAFETY

The number one priority of every officer is: "Come home alive at the end of every shift." With that credo comes survival and winning every encounter. All officers understand that they are not immune to an attack. In fact, officers do best when they are hyper-vigilant in both their preparation and observations. A note regarding hyper-vigilance, however: There needs to be a balance, which provides an officer with self-control. Lack of control due to fear or anger is void of thinking and can result in either a mental stall that stops the officer from recognizing a threat, causing an officer's injury or death, or the use of excessive force. The keys in developing the necessary skills to have balance are training and mental rehearsal (Desmendt, 1982; Green, 2000; Hickey, 2003).

It is important to understand that suspects have the advantage tactically in almost any situation because they know if they are armed, if they are wanted, and if they have committed a crime; and they assume that officers know those things as well, or why would they be contacting them? Remsberg (1986) asserts that officers should go about the business of assessing every situation and analyzing it as if it were a threat by utilizing what he terms the *triad of tactical thinking*. The **triad of tactical thinking** requires an officer to be cognizant of three concepts on every call: problem areas, areas of responsibility, and any potential threat (pp. 55–58).

Let's revisit the number one priority of every sworn police officer: "Come home alive at the end of every shift." The FBI's *Officers Killed and*

triad of tactical thinking

the business of assessing every situation and analyzing it as if it were a threat by being cognizant of three concepts: problem areas, areas of responsibility, and any potential threat.

Assaulted (2006) provides some definitive data regarding officers feloniously killed and assaulted between the years 1995 and 2006 (See Figure 6-1):

- A total of 562 officers were feloniously killed during this ten-year period.
- Of the 562 killed, 68 were killed while working a two-officer patrol unit, and 165 were killed while working a one-officer patrol unit.
- Of the 562 killed, 134 were killed while being assisted by backup patrol units.
- Victim officer profile: White male, 37 years of age, 5'11, 199 lbs, with ten years of service.
- Suspect profile: White male, 18–24 years of age, 5'10, 176 lbs, either under the supervision of the court or a convicted felon.
- Most dangerous calls for service in order: disturbance; effecting an arrest; ambush; traffic; and the investigation of suspicious persons or incidents.

There is no doubt that death is the ultimate sacrifice in policing. However, officers are assaulted daily by suspects, and the most common weapons

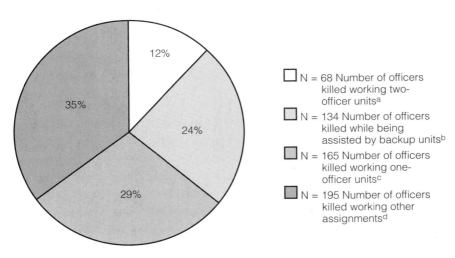

12%

35%

24%

29%

☐ N = 68 Number of officers killed working two-officer units[a]

☐ N = 134 Number of officers killed while being assisted by backup units[b]

☐ N = 165 Number of officers killed working one-officer units[c]

☐ N = 195 Number of officers killed working other assignments[d]

a. Total number of officers feloniously killed during the ten-year period 1995–2006 was N = 562.
b. N = 367 of the deaths were officers assigned to patrol.
c. N = 299 of the deaths were associated with one-person patrol units.
d. N = 195 of the deaths occurred while officers were assigned to some other unit (e.g., SWAT, warrants, or detectives).

Figure 6-1   Officers Feloniously Killed, 1995–2006

(Data source: Federal Bureau of Investigation, *Officers Killed and Assaulted*, 2006.)

are hands, fists, and feet. The numbers of such assaults have remained consistent over the last ten years; annually there have been (See Figure 6-2.):

- 59,000 assaults upon officers
- 10,500 assaults upon officers assigned to two-officer patrol units
- 15,000 assaults upon officers assigned to one-officer patrol units
- 21,500 assaults upon officers assigned to one-officer patrol units who responded as backup

These data offer some interesting insights into the nature of assaults on police, especially when discussing one-officer versus two-officer patrol units. In regard to actual deaths, the numbers over the ten-year period provide insight into suspects' aggressive behavior. When two officers arrive on a scene together in one unit, the officers appear to have the tactical advantage, and the suspect believes that he or she is less likely to get away after the encounter. In fact, an analysis of the data shows that a two-officer unit is a deterrent against assaults and deaths.

The most interesting analysis of the data arises when you compare one-officer units to one-officer units with assistance/backup. The one-

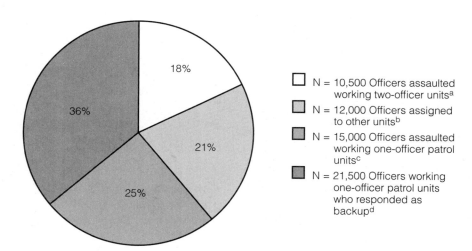

a. N = 59,000: total number of officers assaulted annually from 1995 to 2006.
b. E.g., SWAT, warrants, or detectives.
c. N = 36,500: total number of officers assaulted annually working one-person patrol unit.
d. Data supports concept that two-officer patrol units are safer than one-officer patrol units.

Figure 6-2   Officers Assaulted by Suspects with Hands, Fists, and Feet, 1995–2006 (Data source: Federal Bureau of Investigation (FBI), *Officers Killed and Assaulted,* 2006).

officer unit pits an individual officer's skills against a suspect's skills. In this situation, a suspect has to believe that the playing field is at least level and that he or she has an excellent chance of not being apprehended after an attack. However, of even greater interest are the number of deaths and assaults that occur when an officer has backup. These data indicate that the first officer on a scene engages a suspect before the second unit arrives, which may occur for any number of reasons: for example, on a traffic stop, the officer makes the stop and then requests backup, or the first officer to arrive on the scene of a shooting or a disturbance decides to engage the suspect, knowing that backup is on the way. By acting as an individual rather than waiting for a backup unit, the first officer on the scene has made a decision that may result in catastrophic consequences for both officers. The backup has no choice but to assist the first unit on the scene in resolving the encounter. In this situation, the tactical advantage goes to the suspect because he or she has an opportunity to deal with the two officers at different times, as opposed to the one unified body presented by the two-officer patrol unit.

One final observation regarding this topic: If we do an analysis of the victim officer, what do age and years of experience say about the officer's decision making? One can only deduce that because an officer has ten years of experience, the officer understands the importance of waiting for backup. However, what the research shows is that officers are overconfident in handling these situations, primarily because they have been involved in them hundreds of times during their tenure. (See Scenario 6-1.)

SCENARIO 6-1: DOMESTIC DISTURBANCE

You are on patrol, working a one-person patrol unit, and receive the following call: Charlie 5, 10-65: The complainant located at 805 Franklin Ave. S.E. advises that she can hear a disturbance coming from the next-door neighbor's house, 807 Franklin Ave. S.E. The complainant advises that she can hear yelling and screaming and heard a female scream "stop hitting me." The complainant also advises that she has personally witnessed the neighbor's boyfriend strike the neighbor in the past and that the victim dismisses the abuse by stating: "That's how he shows he loves me." Charlie 3 has been sent as your backup and advises that he is three minutes away. You arrive at the scene before Charlie 3. Upon your arrival, you park two houses away and can hear the fighting.

Because the arguing is so loud, you make the decision to approach the house and look through the window to see what you can observe. When you get to the window, you can see through the living room and into the kitchen. You observe a W/F standing with a large butcher knife in her hand, drawn back over

(continued)

(continued)

her head, and a W/M cowering on the floor in the corner of the kitchen. The front door is standing open. You make the decision to enter the house and challenge the W/F with your weapon drawn. You order the female to put the knife on the table. She complies with your request. Just as she places the knife on the table, your backup arrives.

Analysis and Reflection

1. Do you believe that you did the right thing by not waiting for backup? This is a personal decision that many officers make. If you examine the data regarding the potential for assault, as an individual officer, statistically you would have been better off waiting for backup.

2. As you observe the woman with the knife, do you believe that if you fail to intervene, it will cost the W/M his life? In cases like this, you don't

know the answer to such questions, and your information is limited to what you have received from dispatch. However, you do know that there is a potential that the male will be stabbed if you don't do something. Most officers feel compelled to intervene; however, it needs to be understood that this is very dangerous, especially in a domestic situation like this, where both individuals could turn and attack the officer.

3. Could it be that responding to this situation without waiting for backup is a violation of departmental policy? Yes. Your agency may have a policy that requires you to wait for backup before intervening. Such a policy is designed for one thing: officer safety. In this case, the decision to intervene may have had a successful outcome; however, you still may be disciplined for violating department policy.

NATURE OF PATROL

This section begins with a question. As you read this question, take a moment and reflect on your answer: *What is the role of police in our society?* The most common answer is: "To protect and serve the citizens." For the purpose of this exercise, this answer is unacceptable. Take a moment and jot down some ideas. You will probably find this task to be more difficult than you originally expected.

In 1972, the American Bar Association attempted to describe the police role in America. Following are some of the police responsibilities they outlined: identify and apprehend criminal offenders; preventive patrol; aid individuals who are in danger; protect constitutional guarantees; traffic direction enforcement; conflict resolution; identify problems that impact police and government; create a feeling of security in the community; order of maintenance; and provide services on an emergency basis (p. 9).

The role of police in American society is difficult to identify. The reality is that police have no definitive role in American society. In fact, the role is one that is defined by law, politics, economics, and the needs of the community in which officers serve. In essence, the role is ever changing because of the demands of American society and individual communities (Waddington, 1994; White, 2004). One of the best examples, and the one that has had the greatest impact on policing, is the events of September 11, 2001 (9/11). The role of the police in that situation was as first responders to a crisis, with the objective of assisting the fire department in saving lives. That responsibility was nothing new, but there are other considerations.

Prior to the events of 9/11, policing had embraced the concept of community policing. Cronkhite (2007) notes that pre-9/11, law enforcement had strong community ties and was successful in crime reduction, and public trust was strong (p. 327). After 9/11, the police mission changed. This change was identified in the *post-9/11 project*. The **post-9/11 project** was convened in 2004 and attended by the International Association of Chiefs of Police (IACP), the National Sheriff's Association (NSA), the National Organization of Black Law Enforcement Executives (NOBLE), and the Police Foundation with a goal of assisting state and local law enforcement in the management of an ever-changing police environment (pp. i–ii).

The conference members identified and developed a host of objectives and goals for post-9/11. One idea that stands out in regard to combining traditional police operations with post-9/11 responsibilities is **shifting eras and mission reconfiguration,** which recognizes that the police mission has changed since 9/11, and yet the traditional policing models of crime control and community policing cannot be ignored. It is believed that American policing should transition from the community policing model to a domestic security model (p. ii).

Terrorism is the latest national crisis, and it has had an impact on the police role in American society. Other crises that preceded it include: landmark court decisions that outline or place limits on police behavior, such as *Miranda* and *Tennessee v. Garner;* the civil rights movement; the inner city riots of the 1960s; the National Organization of Women and their push for protection in cases of domestic violence; the closing of mental hospitals in the 1960s and the release of mental patients to community mental health; Mothers Against Drunk Driving and their campaign for greater enforcement; the proliferation of gang violence; the introduction of cocaine, then crack cocaine, and now methamphetamines; HIV/AIDS; technology; and police misconduct and brutality cases. Each of these issues has had an impact on the identity of American policing, and because the police role is determined by the community at large, it will continue to be molded and fluid.

The debate regarding the role of police centers on whether they are crime fighters, peacekeepers, or responsible for maintenance of order. The list of issues affecting the role of police in American society demonstrates that the question is complex. The reality is that it encompasses all of the monikers, and if you take a moment to reflect on the role of police, you can probably add to this list.

post-9/11 project

convened in 2004 and attended by the International Association of Chiefs of Police (IACP), the National Sheriff's Association (NSA), the National Organization of Black Law Enforcement Executives (NOBLE), and the Police Foundation with a goal of assisting state and local law enforcement in the management of an ever-changing police environment.

shifting eras and mission reconfiguration

recognizes that the police mission has changed since 9/11, and yet the traditional policing models of crime control and community policing cannot be ignored.

CALLS FOR SERVICE

An assignment in patrol offers more diversity than any other aspect of policing, because a patrol officer is exposed to every type of call as a first responder and not a specialist. For trainees, it becomes the foundation of their entire career. It is important to understand that officers spend a great deal of their time on calls that have nothing to do with enforcing the law; these are considered service calls. The primary role of patrol officers is to investigate the array of calls to which they have been dispatched. To help you understand the diversity of patrol, read the following list of calls, organized by category and types of crime:

1. *Disturbance:* armed disturbance, civil dispute, domestic violence, physical fight, verbal dispute, neighbor problems, and landlord-tenant disputes.

2. *Traffic:* DUI/DWI, crash/accident investigation, directing traffic, issuing parking/traffic citations, disabled vehicles, and vehicle pursuits.

3. *Persons crimes:* assault/battery, aggravated assault/battery, robbery (armed, bank, unarmed, and carjacking), sex crimes, rape/sexual battery, child/elderly abuse, stalking, attempted murder/murder, attempted suicide/suicide, and other death investigations.

4. *Property crimes:* burglary/residence/business/vehicle, trespass, criminal mischief, theft (motor vehicle, gas drive-offs, and shoplifters), forgery/counterfeiting, and lost/found property.

5. *Suspicious activity:* suspicious person, vehicle, activity, mail, substance, prowler, or unsecured conditions at a business or residence.

6. *Alarms:* burglar, vehicle, panic, robbery, lifeline, and fire alarms.

7. *Juvenile problems:* truancy, tobacco violations, runaway, and alcohol violations.

8. *Miscellaneous:* bomb threats and explosive devices, marine incidents, aircraft incidents, trash dumping, harassing phone calls, special details, information complaints, mentally ill, panhandling, the homeless, and medical emergencies. (Alachua County Sheriff's Office Combined Communication Center, 2009)

This list is comprehensive, but by no means complete. If you examine it closely, it is clear that a number of investigations have nothing to do with criminal activity. (See Scenario 6-2.)

SCENARIO 6-2: ATTEMPTED SUICIDE

You are on patrol, working a one-officer unit, and receive the following call: Alpha 1, the complainant located at 335 S. Main advises that her son has been recently diagnosed with HIV and is threatening suicide. The complainant states that her son has cut both wrists and made the statement: "I want to die. The Lord is punishing me for my sins and I refuse to suffer. You might as well let me die, and if you call the goddamn police, then I will infect them and take them with me." The complainant advises that her son does not have a history of mental problems and this is the first time that he has ever threatened suicide. Be advised that Alpha 2 has been sent as backup.

Analysis and Reflection

1. What is your responsibility once you arrive at the scene? The first responsibility is to yourself and the safety of others. It is not advisable to enter the house unless you are attempting to get an innocent party out whom the subject may be attempting to infect.

2. Do you have the necessary equipment to avoid being contaminated by the subject's blood? In most cases, police do not. Recently agencies have been providing officers with suits for terrorist attacks, and this equipment may be suitable. The fire department and paramedics are equipped to handle this type of situation. The fear is that no matter who enters the house, the subject will become combative and attempt to tear off the protective gear, especially since he has made the statement that he intends to infect anyone who intervenes.

3. Could the intent of the subject be *suicide by cop?* This is very possible. The subject cut himself, knowing that emergency personnel have a responsibility to save his life. Keep in mind that this was done so that his mother would be able to contact authorities. It could be that he has made up his mind that once police arrive at the scene and he attacks them, they will have no choice but to use deadly force. This happens when subjects do not have the courage to kill themselves and use police to do so. There have been a number of cases where subjects have pointed toy or unloaded guns at police, knowing the response would be deadly force.

4. What is the best course of action on this call? The best course of action is to let the subject bleed out if there are no other threats. Once there is sufficient blood loss, the subject will become unconscious, and then emergency personnel can enter, secure, treat, and transport the subject to the hospital.

TRAFFIC ENFORCEMENT

One of the duties of a patrol officer is traffic enforcement. The tasks are many and include issuing moving and nonmoving traffic citations, directing traffic, investigating and arresting for violations of driving under the influence, and investigating traffic accidents. The primary reason for traffic enforcement is public safety (Hurst, 2001;

Transportation Research Board, 1998). Traffic safety is so important that agencies have specialized traffic units with their primary purpose as traffic enforcement.

One of the most dangerous acts that arises from traffic enforcement is the *police pursuit* or *high-speed chase.* Many pursuits are initiated when subjects refuse to stop because they have a suspended driver's license. The question needs to be asked: Is an officer's or innocent motorist's life worth the apprehension of a driver who flees because of a suspended driver's license? Hill (2002) argues that traffic accidents constitute the most common terminating event in a police pursuit (p. 14).

The National Highway and Traffic and Safety Administration (NHSTA) supplied the Georgia Association of Chiefs of Police (GACP, 2006) with the following data regarding police pursuits during the ten-year period from 1994 to 2004:

- Average number of deaths due to pursuits: 352.2 per year, totaling 3,877 fatalities
- Total number of suspects killed: 2,510
- Total number of occupants of other vehicles killed: 1,182
- Total number of nonoccupants killed: 129
- Total number of officers killed: 56

The GACP noted clearly that very little is known about police pursuits because there is no mandatory reporting system, and there are limitations to the data that are supplied, since of those that do report, the NHSTA may alter the numbers. However, if you review the numbers, it is clear that approximately 50% of the fatalities that occur are a direct result of pursuits that unintentionally involve innocent motorists.

Because of the dangers, many agencies have adopted restrictive pursuit policies that mirror the use-of-deadly-force policies. A number of the model policies offer for consideration that before an officer begins a pursuit, the pursuing officer must come to the conclusion that the suspect is of greater danger to the officer and public than the pursuit itself (GACP, 2006; IACP, 1996).

JUVENILES AND PATROL

Juvenile violence in the United States has reached epidemic proportions (Kennedy, 2002; Martin, 2005; Quinn, 2004). The problem that we have as a society is we are not sure what we want to do with delinquent youths. The dilemma lies in the debate of punishment versus treatment (Conrad, Allen, Cox, & Hanser, 2007; Sacks & Reader, 1992). It is believed that if we punish them for violent acts, we lose them for life. On the other hand, there is no proof that treatment and rehabilitation are the answer, especially since the juveniles are returned to the same environment upon completion of treatment.

Many believe that when the crime is violent, the juvenile should be adjudicated as an adult and sent to adult prison. Fondacaro and Fasig (2005) argue that in the new age of the twenty-first century, we are of the belief that everyone should be responsible for their crimes, even children as young as 12 years of age; however, in taking this approach, we fail to recognize that juveniles are developmentally immature and therefore should not be treated as adults (p. 368).

The juvenile problem is more than an issue of police encounters or a child who simply chooses to commit crimes. It is difficult to determine the cause of any crime, let alone juvenile crime. If researchers had a crystal ball, the prescription would be easy; instead, we have a host of theories as to the causes of juvenile crime.

Kelley, Loeber, Keenan, and DeLamatre (1997) have identified three basic overlapping pathways in the development of disruptive child behavior. The study was conducted by the Office of Juvenile Justice and Delinquency Prevention. The cities that participated in the study were: Rochester, New York; Denver, Colorado; and Pittsburgh, Pennsylvania. The study had 4,000 participants (boys) over a ten-year period. The results of the study note that preventing delinquency requires accurately identifying risk factors that increase the likelihood of delinquent behavior, and developing a plan of action to intervene and change the behavior patterns (p. 1). The limitation of this study is that it focused only on boys. The three pathways that were identified should be viewed as developmental steps:

- *Authority conflict* is the first pathway, which applies to boys before the age of 12 (if they begin after the age of 12, they will start at the third stage of authority avoidance). Authority conflict is comprised of three stages:
  1. Stubborn behavior
  2. Defiance—refusal and disobedience
  3. Authority avoidance (e.g., truancy and running away from home)

- *Covert* is the second pathway and is comprised of three stages:
  1. Lying and shoplifting
  2. Property damage, which can include vandalism and fire setting
  3. More serious property crimes such as burglary

- *Overt* is the third pathway, with increasing aggressive acts of violence. It is comprised of three stages:
    1. Minor aggression such as annoying others and/or bullying
    2. Physical fighting including gang violence
    3. Violent crimes such as robbery, rape, or aggravated battery

(Howell, 1997; Kelley et al., 1997).

Snyder and Sickmund (2006) provide insight into the enormity of the problem with the following data for the year 2003 for juveniles between the ages of 10 and 17: over 2 million arrests, with 92,300 of the arrests for violent crimes; African American youth accounted for a disproportionate number of the arrests; and there are an estimated 24,000 youth gangs with approximately 760,000 members (p. 125).

Unlike adults, juveniles pose a unique set of problems for law enforcement. The rules for handling them are much different from those for adults. From a practical perspective, there are usually three dispositions when police make contact with juveniles (See Scenario 6-3.):

1. *Counsel and release:* Here no formal charges are filed. These are usually status offenses, meaning that they are crimes for juveniles but not crimes for adults: possession of tobacco products, curfew violations, truancy, runaways, and minor in possession of alcohol.

2. *Detain and release to parent/responsible adult:* There are no formal charges. However, an officer will bring the juvenile to the police station or transport the juvenile home. The officer makes the parent/responsible adult aware of the incident. These are usually minor offenses as well and can include status offenses; this category also includes criminal violations such as fighting, runaways, and trespass.

3. *Arrest:* In this case, the juvenile is arrested and formally charged with a crime. However, unlike adults who are transported to the local jail, juveniles may be processed and released. The determining factor in detaining or releasing a juvenile is the sole discretion of juvenile officials or the seriousness of the crime. If the crime is a felony with violence, then the juvenile will probably be detained. One note regarding the release of juveniles: in most states, there are no bond proceedings; the juvenile is released to the custody of a parent or responsible adult (Musick, 1995; Piliavin & Briar, 1974; Quinney & Tervino, 2001).

children in need of services

children who are found living in deplorable conditions or who are truant from school, constantly run away from home, or have behavior problems in school.

SCENARIO 6-3: CHECK ON THE WELFARE

You are assigned to the day shift and receive the following call: Delta 8, 10-65: Meet the complainant at Thomas Elementary School regarding check on the welfare of two students who did not come to school today and have missed the last week. Upon your arrival, you meet with the complainant, who is the principal, in addition to the school counselor. The complainant advises that Rick and Tina Ford, ages 8 and 10, have missed school the entire week and the parents have not called to say that they would be out. The complainant and the counselor have called the house multiple times and have not gotten an answer. Both advise that they have been concerned regarding the welfare of the children because they have been wearing dirty clothes to school, have poor hygiene, and have no winter clothes, yet it is snowing. In fact, the complainant advises that he contacted Ms. Ford regarding winter clothes and offered to get the children the necessary clothing, but Ms. Ford told the complainant to stay out her family's business. The complainant is fearful that something has happened to the children and requests that you check on their welfare.

You arrive at the Ford residence at 1200 hrs. It is 25 degrees with three inches of snow on the ground, and it is dark and overcast. You knock on the door and there is no answer. However, the door is unlocked. You open the door and announce yourself and there is no response. The house is dark, and when you attempt to turn the hall light on, the bulb is out. The temperature in the house is the same as the temperature outside. The hall is full of dirty clothes. You enter the kitchen and begin to walk toward a closed door where you hear children's voices. As you walk through the kitchen, it is dark and you hear something crunching under your feet. You turn on your flashlight and see that the floor is moving around you. You examine it closer and realize that what you are stepping on is a floor full of roaches. As you examine the kitchen further, it is full of dirty dishes and open garbage bags full of rotting food, and there are roaches everywhere. You continue to where you hear the voices, and you find Rick and Tina playing in their bedroom.

Analysis and Reflection

1. Do you have legal right to enter the house? Yes. You have a legal right to enter the house. The reason you are there is to *check on the welfare* of two children, and since there is no response to your repeated knocks, coupled with the fact that the door is unlocked, the circumstances should be considered *suspicious* and you have a right to investigate further. Once you enter the house and hear the voices, it is incumbent upon you to dispel any fears that you may have. Remember, you are there regarding the children's welfare, and not because of a criminal act.

2. Once you locate the children, do you have the right to take custody of them because they have been neglected? Yes. Once you find the children, you must address their living conditions, which include: no heat, open garbage, roaches and vermin throughout the house, dirty clothes strewn about the floor, and feces and urine on the floor. In addition, the principal and counselor have shared their concerns and observations. Your obligation is to contact Protective Services and turn the children over to them. In this case, they are considered **children in need of services** (CINS).

3. Can you charge the parents with a crime once they have been located? Yes. Depending on the state, at the very least the parents can be charged with *child abuse and neglect.*

PATROL AND NARCOTICS

One effort that patrol has been saddled with since the introduction of drugs in the 1960s and the open-air drug markets that were created with the explosion of crack cocaine in the 1980s is drug enforcement. Invariably patrol officers will come in contact with illegal drugs as a matter of routine enforcement activities like traffic stops, during field interviews or *Terry* stops, or in response to a call for service in a residence (Boland & Healey, 1993; Chaiken, Chaiken, & Karchmer, 1990). The impact that patrol officers have on street-level narcotics in many cases is limited because they are responsible for calls for service and do not have the time to develop the necessary resources to be effective in this battle. To be effective at narcotics enforcement, an officer needs to be able to develop informants and work undercover, and needs the resources and support to complete the mission (Hagan, 1996; Woodiwiss, 2001).

One area where patrol has proven its value is the interdiction of narcotics. In some cases, agencies have developed specialized interdiction units to work the highways using a profile and building the narcotics case from the initial stop or using police canine units to search the exterior of the vehicle during the stop (Steffen & Candelaria, 2003). This has been most effective, but two problems have come to the forefront since the inception of interdiction: racial profiling and policing for profit.

Barak (2007) states that racial profiling is the association of criminality and minorities, most often associated with drugs during traffic stops by law enforcement (p. 605). The Leadership Conference on Civil Rights (2000, p. 2) noted that the practice of racial profiling was widespread in the 1990s, and some of the more notable cases are:

- *Maryland State Police and the I-95 corridor:* Under a federal court decree during a two-year period, it was determined that 70% of the drivers stopped and searched by the Maryland State Police were black, while only 17.5% of the drivers, including speeders, were black.

- *Volusia County, Florida, 1992:* 70% of the drivers stopped on a central Florida highway were black or Hispanic, and yet only 5% of the drivers were black or Hispanic.

- *New Jersey Turnpike:* 46% of those stopped were black, and yet only 13.5% of the cars on the road had a black driver or passenger, and there was no significant difference in the driving patterns of whites and blacks.

Woodiwiss (2001) argues that police have begun to use interdiction and forfeiture as a means of profit, using the monies to fund additional resources and equipment. He notes that the cases are about maximizing profits rather than eradicating narcotics (pp. 356–357). Duke (2000) supports this argument and states that giving police and prosecutors control over forfeited assets insults good government (p. 59).

This country has an interesting history with substance abuse that dates back to the late 1800s. America's attitudes and moral values have evolved regarding the use of drugs from the nineteenth century to the twenty-first century. Caulkins, Rueter, Iguchi, and Chiesa (2005) argue that the evidence regarding the war on drugs is lost and based on changing moral values (p. 2). Beckett (2003) argues that America sees drugs as a form of crime and that is why they have become a primary concern. She states that the American perception of drugs as a pressing problem is confirmed in several surveys, noting that in April of 1986 only 3% of those polled believed that it was a problem and in 1989 the figure had jumped to 64%; and she argues that the moral conscience of this country changed because the White House politicized the problem (pp. 71–74).

The Institute of Medicine (1990) noted that a 1986 national survey indicated that state and local law enforcement had spent 18.2% of their budget on narcotics enforcement, which amounted to $3.8 billion out of every $21 billion in state and local law enforcement efforts (p. 103). It is believed that these types of expenditures will have to change so that law enforcement can deal with the rise in violent crime (Russell, Gingerich, & Cosner, 2005). Caulkins et al. (2005) note that enforcement efforts have limited possibilities because sellers are replaced as quickly as they are arrested; that the mass market makes it impossible to police effectively; and that a million dollars spent on enforcement buys less of a drop in drug consumption than the previous million spent (pp. 36–37).

Narcotics enforcement is but one of the many skills that a patrol officer must master. Those effective at making drug arrests have excellent knowledge of the law and avoid unprofessional behavior such as racial profiling and violations of civil rights. Keys to successful enforcement are a working knowledge of the drugs, their delivery systems, and the physical and psychological effects, as well as the ability to identify the common drugs abused within one's jurisdiction.

CONCLUSION

Patrol is the most visible form of government that we have today. Patrol officers are usually the first on the scene of major crimes, and because they have some degree of autonomy, they are considered the gateway to the criminal justice system.

Patrol is also the place where officers begin skill development and determine their specialized interests for future career aspirations. Patrol can be either boring or a smorgasbord of activity. The activity is what everyone craves, and it is also where officers learn about human behavior and develop survival and threat assessment skills.

As first responders, patrol is the backbone and the life blood of every law enforcement agency in the United States. With that said, patrol sets the tone for community-police relations, depending upon the style of policing, demographics, size, and the demands of the leadership.

 # DISCUSSION QUESTIONS

1. Describe how television has glamorized policing. Discuss the differences between real policing and that seen on television. In your discussion, make a determination if television has had a positive or negative impact on the profession.
2. Describe the many patrol experiments. In your discussion, choose which one you believe is most effective, and describe why.
3. Explain how 9/11 has impacted policing in the United States.
4. "Police officers should be allowed to engage in vehicle pursuits regardless of the crime." Do you agree or disagree with this statement? Defend your position.
5. Drug enforcement has its limitations for patrol officers. Describe these limitations.

 # RESEARCH TOPICS

Following are two topics that are central to this chapter. Choose one, and research the topic based on the instructions of your professor.

- *Effective patrol style.* There has been extensive discussion regarding the personality of a police department, meaning that a department adopts an organizational method of operation. There are times when this method or style is not in concert with the community, and many conflicts have resulted throughout our history. Research one of these conflicts, noting how the organization failed the community and the eventual outcomes. Defend your answer.

- *Officer safety.* There has been lengthy discussion regarding the issue of one-officer versus two-officer units. You are an administrator, and currently your agency uses one-officer patrol units. However, the union has filed a grievance demanding that you authorize two-person patrol units because in the last year, several officers have been seriously injured and two have been killed in the line of duty. Research the subject and take a position, understanding that you have limited capital resources. How will you address the demands of the union? Defend your answer.

 BIBLIOGRAPHY

Alachua County Sheriff's Office. (2009). *List of dispatch signals and 10 codes.* Gainesville, FL: Author.

American Bar Association. (1972). *Standards relating to the urban police function.* New York: Institute of Judicial Administration.

Bachman, R., & Schutt, R. K. (2007). *The practice of research in criminology and criminal justice.* Thousand Oaks, CA: Sage.

Banks, C. (2009). *Criminal justice ethics: Theory and practice* (2nd ed.). Thousand Oaks, CA: Sage.

Barak, G. (2007). *Battleground criminal justice.* Westport, CT: Greenwood.

Beckett, K. (2003). Setting the public agenda: "Street crime" and drug use in American politics. In J. D. Orcutt & D. R. Ruby (Eds.), *Drugs, alcohol, and social problems* (pp. 71–92). Lanham, MD: Rowman & Littlefield.

Boland, B., & Healey, K. M. (1993). *Prosecutorial response to heavy drug case loads: Comprehensive problem-reduction strategies.* Darby, PA: Diane Publishing.

Boydstun, J. E. (1975). *San Diego field interrogation: Final report.* Washington, DC: Police Foundation.

Boydstun, J. E., Sherry, M. E., & Moelter, N. P. (1977). *Patrol staffing in San Diego: One- or two-officer units.* Washington, DC: Police Foundation.

Braga, A. A. (2008). *Problem-oriented policing and crime prevention.* Monsey, NY: Criminal Justice Press.

Brantingham, P. L., & Brantingham, P. J. (1993). Environment, routine, and situation: Toward a pattern theory of crime. In R. V. G. Clarke & M. Felson (Eds.), *Routine activity and rational choice* (pp. 259–294). New Brunswick, NJ: Transaction Publishers.

Brown, M. K. (1988). *Working the street: Police discretion and the dilemmas of reform.* New York: Russell Sage Foundation.

Bureau of Alcohol, Tobacco, and Firearms. (2004). *Violent crime impact: Best practices.* Darby, PA: Diane Publishing.

Caulkins, J. P., Rueter, P., Iguchi, M. Y., & Chiesa, J. (2005). *How goes the "war on drugs"? An assessment of U.S. drug problems and policy.* Santa Barbara, CA: Rand Corporation.

Chaiken, J., Chaiken, M., & Karchmer, C. (1990). *Multijurisdictional drug law enforcement strategies: Reducing supply and demand.* Darby, PA: Diane Publishing.

Chu, J. (2001). *Law enforcement information technology: A managerial, operational, and practical guide.* Boca Raton, FL: CRC Press.

Conrad, J. G., Allen, J. M., Cox, S. M., & Hanser, R. D. (2007). *Juvenile justice: A guide to theory, policy, and practice.* Thousand Oaks, CA: Sage.

Cornish, D. B., & Clark, R. V. (2006). The rational choice perspective. In S. Henry & M. Lanier (Eds.), *The essential criminology reader.* Cambridge, MA: Westview Press.

Cronkhite, C. L. (2007). *Criminal justice administration: Strategies for the 21st century.* Sudbury, MA: Jones & Bartlett.

Dantzker, M. L. (2005). *Understanding today's police* (4th ed.). Monsey, NY: Criminal Justice Press.

Desmendt, J. (1982). *The physical intervention paradigm for enforcement and corrections.* Nokesville, VA: Protective Safety Systems.

Dias, G. A. (2002). *Honolulu cop: Reflections on a career with HPD.* Honolulu, HA: Bess Press.

Duke, S. (2000). The drug war and the Constitution. In T. Lynch (Ed.), *After prohibition: An adult approach to drug policies in the 21st century* (pp. 41–60). Washington, DC: Cato Institute.

Ericson, R. V. (1982). *Reproducing order: A study of police patrol work.* Toronto, Canada: University of Toronto Press.

Federal Bureau of Investigation (FBI). (2006). *Crime in the United States, 2006.* Washington, DC: Department of Justice.

Federal Bureau of Investigation (FBI). (2006). *Officers killed and assaulted, 2006.* Washington, DC: Department of Justice.

Felson, M. (1998). *Crime and everyday life* (3rd ed.). Thousand Oaks, CA: Sage.

Fondacaro, M. R., & Fasig, L. G. (2005). Judging juvenile responsibility: A social ecological perspective. In N. E. Dowd, D. G. Singer, & R. F. Wilson (Eds.), *Handbook of children, culture and violence* (pp. 355–374). Thousand Oaks, CA: Sage.

Fyfe, J. J. (1993). "Good" policing. In B. Frost (Ed.), *The socio-economics of crime and justice* (pp. 269–290). Armonk, NY: M.E. Sharpe.

Georgia Association of Chiefs of Police (GACP). (2006). *Law enforcement pursuits in Georgia: Review and recommendations.* Duluth, GA: Author.

Germann, A. C., Day, F. D., & Gallati, R. R. J. (1978). *Introduction to law enforcement and criminal justice.* Springfield, IL: Charles C. Thomas.

Gould Publications. (2005). *Texas criminal and traffic law manual* (2005–2006 edition). Charlottesville, VA: Matthew Bender.

Green, M. (2000). How long does it take to stop? Methodological analysis of driver perception–brake times. *Transportation Human Factors, 2*(3), 195–216.

Grieve, J., Harfield, C., & MacVean, A. (2007). *Policing.* Thousand Oaks, CA: Sage.

Hagan, J. (1996). Why is there so little criminal justice theory? Neglected macro- and micro-level links. In G. S. Bridges, J. G. Weis, & R. D. Crutchfield (Eds.), *Criminal justice: Readings.* Thousand Oaks, CA: Pine Forge Press.

Hamilton-Smith, N. (2002). Anticipated consequences: Developing a strategy for the targeted measurement of displacement and diffusion of benefits. In N. Tilley (Ed.), *Evaluation for crime prevention.* Monsey, NY: Criminal Justice Press.

Hickey, E. W. (2003). *Encyclopedia of murder and violent crime.* Thousand Oaks, CA: Sage.

Hill, J. (2002). High-speed police pursuits: Dangers, dynamics, and risk reductions. *FBI Law Enforcement Bulletin, 71*(7), 14–17.

Hope, T. J. (1994). Problem-oriented policing and drug market locations: Three case studies. In R. V. Clark (Ed.), *Crime prevention studies.* Monsey, NY: Criminal Justice Press.

Horton, C. (1989). Good practice and evaluating policing. In R. Morgan & D. J. Smith (Eds.), *Coming to terms with policing* (pp. 31–48). New York: Routledge.

Howell, J. C. (1997). *Juvenile justice and youth violence.* Thousand Oaks, CA: Sage.

Hurst, J. W. (2001). *The growth of American law: The law makers.* Boston: Little, Brown.

Institute of Medicine. (1990). *Treating drug problems: A study of the evolution, effectiveness, and financing of public and private drug treatment services.* Washington, DC: National Academy Press.

International Association of Chiefs of Police (IACP). (1996). *Sample policy of vehicular pursuits.* Washington, DC: Author.

International Association of Chiefs of Police (IACP). (2005). *Post 9-11 policing: The crime control–homeland security paradigm. Taking command of new realities.* Washington, DC: Author.

Kaplan, E. H. (1979). Evaluating the effectiveness of one-officer versus two-officer patrol units. *Journal of Criminal Justice Press, 7,* 325–355.

Keeling, G. L., Pate, T., Dieckman, D., & Brown, C. E. (1974). *The Kansas City preventive patrol experiment: A summary report.* Washington, DC: Police Foundation.

Kelley, B. T., Loeber, R., Keenan, K., & DeLamatre, M. (1997). *Developmental pathways in boy's disruptive and delinquent behavior.* Washington, DC: Office of Juvenile Justice and Delinquency Prevention.

Kennedy, D. M. (2002). A tale of one city: The Boston gun project. In G. S. Katzman (Ed.), *Securing our children's future: New approaches to juvenile justice and youth violence* (pp. 229–261). Washington, DC: Brookings Institute.

Ksir, C. J. J., Ray, O. S., & Hart, C. L. (2006). *Drugs, society, human behavior.* New York: McGraw Hill.

Leadership Conference on Civil Rights/Education Fund. (2000). *Justice on trial: Racial disparities in the American criminal justice system.* Washington, DC Author.

Maguire, E. R., & Wells, W. (2002). Community policing as communication reform. In H. Giles (Ed.), *Law enforcement, communication, and community* (pp. 33–66). Philadelphia: John Benjamins.

Martin, G. (2005). *Juvenile justice: Process and systems.* Thousand Oaks, CA: Sage.

McConnell, E. H. (2009). Interview with Harold L. Hurtt, chief of police, city of Houston police department, Houston, Texas, USA. In D. K. Das & O. Marenin (Eds.), *Trends in policing: Interviews with police leaders across the globe* (pp. 231–250). Boca Raton, FL: CRC Press.

McDavid, J. C., & Hawthorn, L. R. L. (2005). *Program evaluation and performance measures: An introduction to practice.* Thousand Oaks, CA: Sage.

Musick, D. (1995). *An introduction to the sociology of juvenile delinquency.* Albany, NY: SUNY Press.

Newburn, T. (2007). *Criminology.* Portland, OR: Willan.

Oslin, G. P. (1999). *The story of telecommunications.* Macon, GA: Mercer University Press.

Piliavin, I., & Briar, S. (1974). Police encounters with juveniles. In L. Rainwater (Ed.), *Social problems and public policy: Deviance and liberty.* Edison, NJ: Aldine Transaction.

Press, S. J. (1971). *Some effects of an increase in police manpower in the 20th precinct of New York City.* New York: Rand Institute.

Purnick, J. (1996, June 20). Metro matters: Quality of life works 2 ways in arrests. *New York Times,* archives.

Quinn, W. H. (2004). *Family solutions for youth at risk: Applications to juvenile delinquency, truancy, and behavior problems.* New York: Psychology Press.

Quinney, R., & Tervino, A. J. (2001). *The social reality of crime.* Edison, NJ: Transaction.

Reaves, B. A., & Goldberg, A. L. (1996). *Census of state and local law enforcement agencies, 1996.* Washington, DC: Department of Justice.

Reiss, Jr., A. J. (1971). *The police and the public.* New Haven, CT: Yale University Press.

Remsberg, C. (1986). *The tactical edge: Surviving high-risk patrol.* Northbrook, IL: Calibre Press.

Richardson, J. F. (1974). *Urban police in the United States: A brief history.* Port Washington, NY: Kennikat Press.

Ross, H. L., & LaFree, G. D. (1985). Deterrence in criminology and social policy. In N. J. Smelser & D. R. Gerstein (Eds.), *Behavioral and social science: Fifty years of discovery: In commemoration of the fiftieth anniversary of the "Ogburn Report," recent social trends in the United States.* Washington, DC: National Academies Press.

Rubin, I. (1982). *Running in the red: The political dynamics of urban fiscal stress.* Albany, NY: SUNY Press.

Russell, G., Cosner, T., & Gingerich, R. P. J. (2005). *Law enforcement in the United States* (2nd ed.). Sudbury, MA: Jones & Bartlett.

Sacks, H., & Reader, W. D. (1992). History of the juvenile court. In M. G. Kalogerakis & American Psychiatric Association Workgroup on Psychiatric Practice in the Juvenile Court (Eds.), *Handbook of psychiatric practice in the juvenile court* (pp. 13–20). Washington, DC: American Psychiatric Publications.

Safir, H., & Whitman, E. (2003). *Security: Policing your homeland, your city, yourself.* New York: MacMillan.

Schroeder, D. J., & Lombardo, F. A. (2004). *Police sergeant exam* (4th ed.). Hauppauge, NY: Barron's Educational Series.

Sherman, L. W., & Wisebud, D. (1995). Does patrol prevent crime? The Minneapolis hot spot experiment. In K. Miyazawa & S. Miyazawa (Eds.), *Crime prevention in the urban community* (pp. 87–98). New York: Springer.

Skogan, W. G., & Frydl, K. (2004). *Fairness and effectiveness in policing: The evidence.* Washington, DC: National Academies Press.

Skolnick, J. H., & Bayley, D. H. (1988). *The new blue line: Police innovation in six American cities.* New York: Simon & Schuster.

Skolnick, J. H., & Fyfe, J. J. (1993). *Above the law: Police and the excessive use of force.* New York: The Free Press.

Smith, M. J. (2003). Exploring target attractiveness in vandalism: An experimental approach. In M. J. Smith & D. B. Cornish (Eds.), *Theory for practice in situational crime prevention* (pp. 197–236). Monsey, NY: Criminal Justice Press.

Snyder, H. N., & Sickmund, M. (2006). *Juvenile offenders and victims: 2006 national report.* Washington, DC: Department of Justice.

Steffen, G. S., & Candelaria, S. M. (2003). *Drug interdiction: Partnerships, legal principles, and investigative methodologies for law enforcement.* Boca Raton, FL: CRC Press.

Stering, R. (2004). *Police officer's handbook: An introductory guide.* Sudbury, MA: Jones & Bartlett.

Stering, R. S. (2007). *Police officer's handbook: An analytical and administrative guide.* Sudbury, MA: Jones & Bartlett.

Steverson, L. A. (2008). *Policing in America: A reference handbook.* Santa Barbara, CA: ABC-CLIO.

Sung, H. E. (2002). *The fragmentation of policing in American cities: Toward an ecological theory of police-citizen relations.* Westport, CT: Praeger.

Thierry, H., & Jansen, B. (1998). Work time and behavior at work. In P. J. D. Drenth, H. Thierry, & C. J. Wolff (Eds.), *Handbook of work and organizational psychology: Work psychology* (pp. 89–120). United Kingdom: Psychology Press.

Transportation Research Board. (1998). *Managing speed: Review of current practice for setting and enforcing speed limits.* Washington, DC: Author.

Tromanhauser, E. (2003). Comments and reflections on forty years in the American criminal justice system. In I. A. Ross & S. C. Richards (Eds.), *Convict criminology* (pp. 81–94). Belmont, CA: Thomson/Wadsworth.

Tunnell, K. D. (2004). Choosing crime: Close your eyes and take your chances. In B. W. Hancock & P. M. Sharp (Eds.), *Criminal justice in America: Theory, practice, and policy* (pp. 39–51). Upper Saddle River, NJ: Prentice Hall.

Vila, V., & Taiji, E. Y. (1999). Police work hours, fatigue, and officer performance. In D. J. Kenney & R. P. McNamara (Eds.), *Police and policing: Contemporary issues.* Westport, CT: Praeger.

Vinzant, J. C., & Crothers, L. (1998). *Street-level leadership: Discretion and legitimacy in front-line public service.* Washington, DC: Georgetown University Press.

Vogel, R. K. (1997). *Handbook of research on urban politics and policy in the United States.* Westport, CT: Greenwood.

Waddington, P. A. J. (1994). *Liberty and order: Public order policing in a capital city.* London, England: UCL Press.

Websdale, N. (2001). *Policing the poor: From slave plantation to public housing.* Lebanon, NH: University Press of New England.

Wedderburn, A. (1995). Shiftwork. In N. Brewer & C. Wilson (Eds.), *Psychology and policing* (pp. 341–366). Hillsdale, NJ: Lawrence Erlbaum.

White, J. R. (2004). *Defending the homeland: Domestic intelligence, law enforcement and security.* Belmont, CA: Wadsworth.

Wilson, C. (1990). *Research on one and two person patrols: Distinguishing fact from fiction.* Sydney: Australian Centre for Policing Research.

Woodiwiss, M. (2001). *Organized crime and American power: A history.* Toronto, ON: University of Toronto Press.

Zawitz, M. W., Klaus, P. A., Bachman, R., Bastian, L. D., DeBerry, Jr., M. M., Rand, M. R., & Taylor, B. M. (1993). *Highlights from 20 years of surveying crime victims: The national crime victimization survey, 1973–92.* Darby, PA: Diane Publishing.

Zimring, F. E. (2007). *The great American crime decline.* New York: Oxford University Press.

Zimring, F., & Hawkins, G. (1973). *Deterrence.* Chicago: University of Chicago Press.

CHAPTER 7

INVESTIGATIONS

OBJECTIVES

After completing this chapter, the student will be able to:

- Describe the differences in preliminary, primary, and follow-up investigations.
- Describe the process of crime scene investigation and its relationship to corroborating a case.
- Discuss the importance of a detailed investigation and why answering these six basic questions is essential: who, what, where, when, how, and why.
- Describe the resources of information utilized in a follow-up investigation.
- Discuss problems associated with eyewitness testimony and its limitations.
- Describe the differences between an interview and an interrogation.
- Discuss the laws associated with interrogation and the limitations that they place on police.
- Describe empathy statements and how they may be used in an interrogation.

KEY TERMS

confession – the acknowledgment or admission of the commission of all elements of a crime and the defendant's involvement in the act.

crime analysis – the examination of data associated with criminal acts to determine their nature, to provide information to uniformed officers and investigators in an attempt to prevent and/or suppress criminal activity, and to assist in the apprehension of criminal suspects, and the allocation of personnel and resources.

crime scene processing – the collection of evidence that should corroborate the chain of events as outlined by witnesses and complainants.

custody – defined in terms of police interrogation, the subject is *not* free to leave at any time during the interrogation.

false confession – a confession to a crime obtained from an innocent party through coercion, spoon-feeding a subject the facts, internal self-doubt, or memory errors.

getting into the well – a process of meeting and understanding the defendant at his or her level of anger, frustration, or criminal intent.

informants – people who choose to work with police and provide them with information in regard to criminal activity. They must be reliable in regard to the information they provide, and it is important to understand their motivation.

interrogation – the questioning of a person suspected of having committed an offense or who is reluctant to make full disclosure of information that is pertinent to an investigation.

interview – a conversation held to generate information from a person who has knowledge of a situation or crime so that an investigation can be continued or concluded; a form of fact finding.

moving forward – the point in an interrogation where rapport has been established between the interrogator and the suspect, and where cooperative behavior and confessions begins.

neighborhood canvassing – going door-to-door in the area of a crime to determine if those in the area heard or saw anything in reference to the crime.

on-view police activity – police see a crime or suspicious activity and stop to investigate, as opposed to police activity generated by witnesses stopping police when they have observed suspicious activity or a call to dispatch.

preliminary investigation – used to determine if a crime has been committed, and if there is a suspect, to determine if he or she committed the crime in question.

primary investigation – occurs once an officer determines that a crime has been committed; officer is responsible for initial investigation, identifying possible suspects, and making an arrest where possible.

stop-snitching campaign – a campaign employed by drug dealers to allow their atrocities to go unpunished.

> ### Doc's Words of Wisdom
>
> *The most successful investigators are those who pay particular attention to detail, use every resource at their disposal, and follow the law. In any investigation, it is not the end result but the process that will be scrutinized.*

INTRODUCTION

The basics of every investigation begin with the first officer on the scene, which is usually a uniformed patrol officer. He or she must have the ability to determine if a crime has occurred, classify that crime, collect the evidence that corroborates the commission of the crime, and make the arrest if it is possible (Fisher, 2003; Geberth, 2006; Hawthorne, 1999). The involvement of the first officer will vary depending on the nature of the case and if a suspect is still present. Since most police agencies have fewer than ten officers, the first officer on a scene may become the primary investigator of the crimes to which he or she is assigned, which means officers may have investigative duties in addition to patrol duties in smaller agencies that have no investigators.

TYPES OF INVESTIGATION

Many investigations begin with a complainant who calls dispatch requesting police to investigate what he or she believes to be a crime, something suspicious, a motor vehicle accident, or something as simple as a loud/unusual noise (e.g., glass breaking or a gunshot). In Chapter 6, we identify eight categories of calls to which an officer may respond. The call-taker in the communications center asks a series of questions in an attempt to clarify the nature of the call so that officers do not enter the call blindly (Peterson, 1993; Roberts, Madsen, & Desai, 2007). The role of the call-taker in dispatch is critical in deciphering the information, and often it becomes a source or frustration for the complainant because of the numerous questions the call-taker asks (Herbert, 2006; Shepherd & Rothenbuhler, 2001).

Although many preliminary investigations begin with dispatch, there are limitations to their abilities. Dispatchers and call-takers are highly trained, but they are not police officers and are not always correct in the determination of every call. Another issue that may impair a call-taker's ability is whether the complainant is cooperative; in some cases, call-takers have to call back many times to obtain information for the responding officers. To offset these limitations, the call-taker and dispatcher must continually gather, assess, and update information for responding units (Gonzalez, 2002; Sanders, 2003; Tracy & Agne, 2002). Examine the dialogue in Scenario 7-1 to understand the importance of information gathering and how it impacts the police response in terms of personnel needed.

SCENARIO 7-1: ROBBERY OR IS IT?

Caller: I have just been robbed. I need the police here now.

Call-taker: Ma'am! What is your address?

Caller: Don't you have caller ID?

Call-taker: Ma'am, I need to know the address where you are right now so I can send police.

Caller: 1225 S. Division Ave.

Call-taker: Ma'am, police are on the way! Ma'am, is the suspect still there?

Caller: No.

Call-taker: Was he armed or did he have a weapon?

Caller: What are you talking about? Someone broke into my house and stole everything. I was robbed!!!

Caller: Let me get this straight. Someone broke into your house and they were gone when you arrived?

Caller: Yes. They took everything!!!!

Call-taker: Police are on the way, ma'am. What time did you leave the house today?

Caller: I have been at work since 8:00 this morning and just got home at 5:00.

Analysis and Reflection

1. At the beginning of the dialogue, you believe that a robbery has just occurred. Why? The victim does not know the difference between a robbery and a burglary. In fact, what has happened is a burglary.

2. Why is it important to know the difference and get the correct information to responding units? It will make a difference in the response. If it is a robbery that just occurred or a burglary in progress, the officers will get there as quickly as possible, and may even go with lights or lights and siren, depending on department protocol. If the crime has just occurred, there is an increased possibility that the suspects might still be in the area.

3. As the call-taker obtains more information, what does he or she learn about the burglary? The victim was at work between 8:00 A.M. and 5:00 P.M. This provides a time frame for the crime. The investigating officer might be able to narrow the time down by canvassing the neighborhood to determine whether the neighbors heard or saw anything suspicious.

4. Is it important to send two patrol cars? Yes, it is important, especially if the caller has not checked the house to see if anyone is still there. If two units are sent, they will search and secure the house before taking a report. In some cases, a victim comes home and the suspect hides and waits for an opportunity to flee; in other cases, the suspect will hide and wait to harm the victim. So a thorough search is necessary.

Preliminary Investigation

Preliminary investigation is the first category of a criminal investigation. Bautista (2003) notes that the purpose of a **preliminary investigation** is to determine if a crime has been committed, and if there is a suspect, to determine if he or she committed the crime in question (pp. 38–39). For patrol officers, preliminary investigations begin with information from one of several sources. **On-view police activity** means the police see a crime or suspicious act and stop to investigate. Other times, witnesses stop police on the street to report what they believe to be suspicious activity or a crime. Sometimes the police activity begins with a call to dispatch. Each of these sources requires police action.

The second phase of the preliminary investigation begins when the first officer arrives at the scene. This officer is responsible for ensuring his or her safety and the safety of others before doing anything else. The first officers at a scene survey the scene by scanning the surrounding houses, making a mental note of bystanders on the street, injured persons, or suspicious vehicles (Carney, 2004; Gardner, 2004). The idea here is to address these issues before entering the scene because they could be related to the crime. Caution should always be exercised here. Often police become complacent, rely on the information provided by dispatch, and stroll right up to a door without making this survey; as a result, some have fallen victim to an ambush (Murray, 2004; Stering, 2004).

During phase two of the preliminary investigation, the officer has the following tasks: determining the true nature of the call; securing the crime scene if necessary; determining if other resources are needed (e.g., medical, crime scene, or investigators); interviewing witnesses, canvassing the neighborhood; and making an arrest if possible, or providing the complainant with a series of solutions and/or outcomes (Euale, Martin, Rock, & Sadek, 1998; Fisher, 2003; Sonne, 2006). (See Scenario 7-2.)

Crime Scene Investigation

The final stage of any investigation is processing the crime scene. **Crime scene processing** should corroborate the chain of events as outlined by witnesses and complainants (Bevel & Gardner, 2001; Lee, Palmbach, & Miller, 2001; Prior, 2004). In some cases, the evidence will detail or outline an entirely different set of facts, which may bear witness to false statements, facts, and/or testimony (Graham, 2003; Walton, 2008). To better understand how crime scene investigation corroborates a case, we will examine intricate facts from Scenario 7-2, Shots Fired, and correlate them to the evidence.

preliminary investigation

used to determine if a crime has been committed, and if there is a suspect, to determine if he or she committed the crime in question.

on-view police activity

police see a crime or suspicious activity and stop to investigate, as opposed to police activity generated by witnesses stopping police when they have observed suspicious activity or a call to dispatch.

crime scene processing

the collection of evidence that should corroborate the chain of events as outlined by witnesses and complainants.

SCENARIO 7-2: SHOTS FIRED

You are on patrol working David 2, a two-person unit, and you receive the following call: David 2, 10-65: The complainant at 1011 Franklin Street advises that she heard at least six gunshots coming from her next-door neighbor's house. The address is 1013 Franklin S.E.; it is a single-family dwelling. The complainant also advises prior to the shooting she observed a car pull in front of her house and saw a B/M drag a B/F from the passenger side of the vehicle, pulling the B/F out of the driver's side of the car. The driver's door of the vehicle is still open on the street side. The B/M dragged the B/F into 1013 Franklin.

Upon your arrival, you discover the vehicle unoccupied and the driver's door open into the street as the complainant described. You park your patrol car out of sight and run the license plate to the vehicle. The vehicle is owned by a couple whose house you have been called to numerous times regarding domestic violence; in fact, you have arrested the husband on several occasions. Just as the registration comes back, the suspect drags the victim out of the house. The suspect is holding a semi-auto pistol in his right hand and holding the victim's arm with his left. As they get to the driver's side of the vehicle, the suspect strikes the victim in the head several times with the pistol; she collapses and is forced into the car. Your partner cuts the suspect vehicle off with your patrol car, leaving the only path of escape by backing down the street.

You and your partner exit the patrol vehicle, draw your weapons, and order the suspect to drop his gun and release the victim. Immediately the suspect places his gun to the victim's head and states: "If you don't move the car, I'll kill her." The victim snatches her arm from the suspect's grip and falls out the passenger side door. The victim runs across the street and collapses in front of 1013 Franklin. As the suspect is reaching for the victim, his foot slips off the brake and the suspect vehicle strikes your patrol car; neither you nor your partner are in danger of being hit. The suspect then

exits the vehicle and stands behind the passenger side rear. His hands are hidden from plain view. You repeatedly order the suspect to drop his weapon. After a short period of time, he complies. You secure the suspect and his weapon, and call for backup. This situation unfolded so fast that you were unable to call for backup until the suspect was in custody.

Once backup and EMS arrive, you must check 1013 Franklin where the shots were fired to determine if there are any victims. When you knock on the door, the victim's sister answers and advises the following: The suspect and victim are husband and wife. Tonight the suspect brought the victim to 1013 in an attempt to determine if the victim was cheating on the suspect. Witnesses to the incident were the victim's sister, brother, and mother. The family members told the suspect that he was crazy and that the victim had not been cheating. The victim's brother attempted to get the suspect to calm down and the two began to struggle. In the struggle, the suspect's gun fell from his waistband onto the floor.

The suspect then grabbed the gun, fired several shots into the ceiling, and ordered the family members to stand back, stating: "If you attempt to stop me, I'll kill all of you right here." The suspect grabbed the victim and, using her as a shield, panned his gun back and forth at the family members while dragging the victim from the house. They watched the incident as you pulled up in the patrol car and will give witness statements to what they observed both in the house and outside.

Analysis and Reflection

1. Did dispatch give you good information and as much as they possibly could based on the nature of the call? Yes. They did everything humanly possible. Often when they have an incident address, they will look it up and advise you of who lives there. In addition, they will advise if police have

been to that address and the nature of the previous calls. In this case, they were unable to do this because of your arrival time and the fact that the incident began to unfold before they could get back to you.

2. Why didn't you call for backup when you saw the suspect exit the house and attack the victim? In this case, the incident unfolded so fast that you did not have time to call for backup. You had a responsibility to intervene, which began when you blocked the exit path of the vehicle. However, you did leave the suspect an escape route, and that was to back his vehicle down the street. In many departments, leaving an escape route is necessary so as not to corner suspects, leaving them with no option except a deadly encounter.

3. What are your responsibilities once the scene is under control?
   • After the suspect is in custody, call for EMS, backup units, and crime scene.
   • Next check on the victim and render first aid until EMS arrives.
   • Once backup arrives, have them stand by with your prisoner while you check on the occupants in 1013 Franklin where the complainant heard the shots.
   • If no one is injured, then the primary investigation begins. In a case such as this, you will not call detectives; you are the investigating officer from start to finish.

4. In regard to reports, who is responsible for what?
   • You will be responsible for the primary report, and your partner has to complete a supplemental report. In addition, each officer who arrived on the scene and assisted you must complete a supplemental report detailing their role.
   • Crime scene is called to the scene, and they will complete a crime scene report based on the pictures and evidence that they collect.
   • A unit will be required to take an accident report, since the suspect vehicle struck your vehicle.
   • You will need witness statements from the complainant who called in the initial report, and from each of the victims/witnesses who were in 1013 Franklin. You will also need to follow-up with the victim at the hospital and take her statement.

5. What criminal charges will arise from this case? The charges in this case could be: *aggravated battery/domestic violence* (depending on the state); *kidnapping/false imprisonment* (depending on the state); three counts of *aggravated assault* (depending on the state); *possession of a firearm by a convicted felon*; and *discharging a firearm within city limits* (depending on jurisdiction).

• *Fact 1:* The complainant at 1011 Franklin Street advises that she heard at least six gunshots coming from her next-door neighbor's house. The address is 1013 Franklin S.E.; it is a single-family dwelling. Also, the victims in 1013 stated the following: "In the struggle, the suspect's gun fell from his waistband onto the floor. The suspect then grabbed the gun and fired several shots into the ceiling."

   a. *Corroborating evidence:* Upon entry into 1013 Franklin, you observe several bullet holes in the ceiling and fresh plaster on the floor from the bullet holes; and the three witnesses confirm the suspect fired the gun in the house.

   b. *Crime scene technician's responsibility:* Take photographs of the ceiling and recover the projectiles from the ceiling and photograph them.

- *Fact 2:* The victim's brother attempted to get the suspect to calm down, and the two began to struggle. In the struggle, the suspect's gun fell from his waistband onto the floor.

  a. *Corroborating evidence:* The brother's clothes are torn as a result of the struggle, and he has a bloody lip with several scratches on his face and neck that are fresh wounds.

  b. *Crime scene technician's responsibility:* Take photographs of the brother's scratches, bloody lip, and torn clothing.

- *Fact 3:* The suspect then grabbed the gun, fired several shots into the ceiling, and ordered the family members to stand back, stating: "If you attempt to stop me, I'll kill all of you right here." The suspect grabbed the victim, using her as a shield, and panned his gun back and forth at the family members.

  a. *Corroborating evidence:* You have verified that the suspect fired the shots into the ceiling. There is no way to positively confirm that the suspect pointed the weapon at all three victims in 1013 Franklin; however, each of the victims, who were interviewed separately, described the incident the same. Based on how quickly the incident unfolded, it is unlikely that the victims had an opportunity to discuss what they would say to the police before the interview. This supports the criminal charge of *aggravated assault.*

  b. *Crime scene technician's responsibility:* The crime scene technician has no responsibility here. However, you as an officer have the responsibility to take written statements of each of the victims in the residence.

- *Fact 4:* Just as the registration comes back, the suspect is dragging the victim out of the house. The suspect is holding a semi-auto pistol in his right hand and holding the victim's arm with his left hand. As they get to the driver's side of the vehicle, the suspect strikes the victim in the head several times with the pistol; she collapses and is forced into the car.

  a. *Corroborating evidence:* You observe the suspect exiting the house holding a semi-auto pistol and dragging the victim. Also, you observe the suspect commit the aggravated battery with the firearm when he strikes the victim in the head several times before she collapses. This supports the criminal charge of *aggravated battery (domestic violence).*

  b. *Crime scene technician's responsibility:* Take photographs of the victim's head injuries. Although you witnessed the attack, the victim's statement is needed to detail the entire incident including being struck in the head.

- *Fact 5:* You and your partner exit the patrol vehicle, draw your weapons, and order the suspect to drop his gun and release the victim. Immediately the suspect places his gun to the victim's head and states: "If you don't move the car, I'll kill her."

  a. *Corroborating evidence:* You are the witness to the suspect taking the victim hostage and keeping her against her will. The suspect pointed the gun at her head and advised that he would kill her. This supports the criminal charges of *false imprisonment* and *kidnapping.*

  b. *Crime scene technician's responsibility:* The suspect's vehicle should be processed for fresh blood from the victim's head wounds. You have a responsibility in detailing this in your report, as well as getting a complete statement from the victim. Keep in mind that there may be things that she does not remember, so it is important not to coax or coach her in taking her statement.

- *Fact 6:* As the suspect is reaching for the victim, his foot slips off the brake and the suspect vehicle strikes your patrol vehicle; neither you nor your partner is in danger of being hit. The suspect then exits the vehicle and stands behind the passenger side rear; his hands are hidden from plain view.

  a. *Corroborating evidence:* The incident occurred in a car, which is substantiated when the suspect's vehicle struck your car. The suspect was armed with a firearm, which was recovered after the suspect was taken into custody.

  b. *Crime scene technician's responsibility:* Take photographs of the firearm on the ground, and then secure and recover the firearm. Take any blood samples that may be on the firearm from striking the victim.

An important note regarding securing firearms at the scene: In a house where only police officers remain after a scene has been secured, it will be safe to leave a firearm in its place so that the technicians can photograph, secure/unload, and collect it as evidence. However, on the street where a scene is fluid and at times almost impossible to completely secure, it is best that the first officer on the scene secure the weapon and, in the process, attempt to avoid contaminating the evidence. This is a matter of officer safety.

Primary Investigation

The incident in Scenario 7-2 changed from a preliminary investigation to a primary investigation. The difference between a preliminary investigation and a **primary investigation** is that in a primary investigation, an officer has determined that a crime has occurred and that he or she is now responsible for articulating the following details in an investigative report:

primary investigation

occurs once an officer determines that a crime has been committed; officer is responsible for initial investigation, identifying possible suspects, and making an arrest where possible.

1. Who are the parties involved in this incident?
   - Who is the suspect(s)?
   - Who is the victim(s)?
   - Who is the complainant if there is one, and does this person wish to remain anonymous?
   - Who is the witness(es), if any?

2. What happened during this incident?
   - What did the suspect(s) do or say?
   - What did the victim(s) do or say?
   - What did the witness(es) do or say?

3. Where did this incident occur?

4. When did the incident occur?
   - Is it several hours old?
   - Is it in progress?
   - Did it just occur?

5. How did the suspect commit the crime?
   - In a burglary, did he or she break a door to enter, or was entry through an unlocked door?
   - In a kidnapping, did he or she use a gun or just verbal threats?
   - In an assault, was it with a fist or with an object such as a bat?

6. Why did the suspect commit this crime? In some cases, *why* is an attempt to address motive. In burglaries where property was stolen, this question is very easy. In Scenario 7-2, where the suspect accused his wife of cheating, is the *why* understandable? What about a sense-less murder where the victimology shows no ties to any gang, no bad relationship, no criminal history, and no illegal activity? In any case, understanding victimology will assist an investigator in understanding motive—the *why* in a crime.

See Figure 7-1 which outlines the four phases of an investigation.

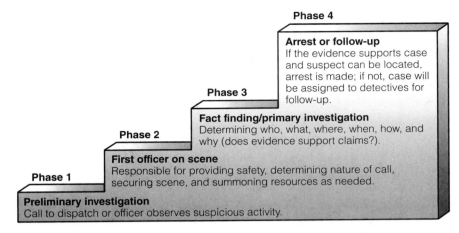

Figure 7-1   Criminal Investigative Process for Patrol Officers

Follow-Up Investigations

Most follow-up investigations are conducted by detectives, because responding officers are unable to complete an investigation that would in turn lead to an arrest. Gottschalk (2006) notes that investigations are divided into two areas of responsibility: the preliminary investigation, which is usually carried out by patrol, and the follow-up investigation, which is usually carried out by detectives. The detectives are responsible for recovering stolen property, gathering criminal intelligence, and preparing criminal cases for trial (p. 135).

The need for follow-up investigations can be found in a meta-analysis that was discussed in Chapter 6. An analysis of the data from the Federal Bureau of Investigation's (FBI's) *Uniform Crime Reports* between the years 1995 and 2006 provides a picture of police clearance rates on a national level. The data are associated with the following crimes: murder, forcible rape, robbery, aggravated assault, burglary, larceny, and motor vehicle theft. On average during this twelve-year period, police cleared 33% of the crimes reported annually, with murder being the most often cleared and motor vehicle theft being the least.

Nationally, the crimes most often needing follow-up investigation because of their low clearance rate are classified as property crimes. Spelman (1994) argues that some of the reasons for poor performance in police clearance rates are: the victims wait too long to contact police; criminal intelligence is vague or poor; and too few police are protecting all the potential targets (p. 174). Officers use a number of investigative tools to assist them in solving the crimes, including crime analysis, neighborhood canvassing, and informants.

Crime analysis is the examination of data associated with criminal acts to determine their nature, to provide information to uniformed officers and investigators in an attempt to prevent and/or suppress criminal activity, and to assist in the apprehension of criminal suspects, and the allocation of personnel and resources. There are three main types of crime analysis: *tactical,* which identifies immediate crime trends, patterns, and hot spots; *strategic,* which identifies long-range problems and projections of long-term increases and decreases in patterns of crime trends; and *administrative,* which involves the presentation of data from crime research for use as an information tool by police administration, city officials, and citizens in planning police budgets and justifying and allocating resources (Boba, 2005; Osborne & Wernicke, 2003; Vellani & Nahoun, 2001). (See Scenario 7-3.)

Neighborhood canvassing is going door-to-door in the area of a crime to determine if those in the area heard or saw anything in reference to the crime. Often neighbors will hear or see something that they will not associate with a criminal act. Such information may provide a time, a physical description of a suspect, direction of flight, or a vehicle description (Eck & Wisebud, 1995; Palmiotto, 2004; Walton, 2006).

A relatively new phenomenon that hinders police efforts in the African American community is the **stop-snitching campaign** employed by drug dealers to allow their atrocities to go unpunished (Asante, 2008). Kitwana (2003) argues that the use of informants in the black neighborhood is akin to a conspiracy and perpetuates a race war. The targets of the race war are African American drug dealers and their families, friends, and gang members, who are snitching on them in exchange for a reduced sentence (pp. 70–71). This argument minimizes responsibility and fails to recognize the damage that drugs have done to the African American community. This stop-snitching campaign has become an even greater concern today because the hip-hop generation has taken a vow not to snitch.

Informants are a great source of information. However, they must be reliable in regard to the information they provide, and it is important to understand their motivation, which may be revenge, money, or to have existing criminal charges dropped (Becker, 2008; Brown, 2001; Lyman, 2006). The standard of informant reliability was outlined in three court cases:

- *Agulair v. Texas,* 378 U.S. 108 (1964), established a two-pronged test: the credibility of the informant must be established, and the reliability of the informant's information must be established.

---

crime analysis

the examination of data associated with criminal acts to determine their nature, to provide information to uniformed officers and investigators in an attempt to prevent and/or suppress criminal activity, and to assist in the apprehension of criminal suspects, and the allocation of personnel and resources.

neighborhood canvassing

going door-to-door in the area of a crime to determine if those in the area heard or saw anything in reference to the crime.

stop-snitching campaign

a campaign employed by drug dealers to allow their atrocities to go unpunished.

informants

people who choose to work with police and provide them with information in regard to criminal activity. They must be reliable in regard to the information they provide, and it is important to understand their motivation.

SCENARIO 7-3: CRIME ANALYSIS: SEXUAL BATTERY

You are a detective assigned to the *persons squad*, which means you investigate all crimes against persons, including: murder, rape, robbery, aggravated battery/assaults, and assaults/battery. Your zone of responsibility is *Charlie*. In the last month, your zone has been hit with ten rapes. However, you check with the other detectives on the squad and only one other zone has seen a similar impact. That zone is *David*, which has recorded six rapes during this same thirty-day period. *David* is the adjoining zone to the south. Patrol has utilized every investigative tool, but there is no information on the street regarding the suspect.

Analysis and Reflection

Crime analysis provides the following information:

1. The victims are all girls between the ages of 8 and 10.

2. All of the rapes occurred between the hours 4:00 P.M. and 6:00 P.M.

3. Each rape was outside; two occurred during a storm in 20-degree temperatures.

4. There have been a total of sixteen rapes in four weeks. The suspect is averaging four rapes per week.

5. Unique to each rape is that the suspect takes the victim's panties with him.

6. There is no DNA because the subject uses a condom in each attack and takes it with him.

7. Although each scene was processed, no evidence has been located.

8. Each of the rape kits were negative except to show that the suspect used a condom with lubricant, which is common in many condoms.

9. The suspect is described as a B/M, approximately 5'11, 200 lbs, with a beard and a strong odor of an alcoholic beverage on his breath.

10. In each case, the victim was walking alone when the suspect appeared from bushes or an alley, grabbed the victim, and stated: "If you scream, I'll kill you."

11. The geographical area in which he perpetrates his crimes is roughly ten square miles and is predominately African American or Latino. The subject blends well into the community.

12. A computer check of similar incidents within the city shows five suspects who have a paraphernalia specific to preteen-aged girls. Three of the suspects are currently in prison, the fourth is dead, and the fifth was released from prison three months ago.

13. In reviewing past police reports, the change to his MO is that in these cases he took the females' panties. In previous cases, he did not and was convicted because of a pubic hair recovered in the panties of one of the victims.

14. The suspect's parole officer advises that the suspect is wanted because he has not reported. You have a name and warrant for David Jerome Clark, B/M, 40 years old.

- *Spinelli v. United States*, 393 U.S. 410 (1969), established that corroboration can be used to support informant information. Corroboration can be obtained through surveillance, neighborhood canvassing, record checks, and body mikes.

- *Illinois v. Gates*, 462 U.S. 213 (1983), abolished the two-pronged test established by *Agulair* and *Spinelli* and established that a search warrant can be issued on the totality of the circumstances, which is the same criteria for establishing probable cause.

WITNESSES

Witnesses play an important role in assisting officers in chronologically detailing an incident. However, witnesses pose several challenges, the first of which is perspective. In any investigation, an officer needs to understand the role that attention, perception, and memory play on recall of an incident (Brewer, Weber, & Semmler, 2007; Hardy & Heyes, 1999; Kapardis, 2003). Warden, Armbrust, and Linzer (2001) argue that "erroneous eyewitness testimony—whether offered in good faith or perjured—no doubt is the single greatest cause of wrongful convictions in the U.S. criminal justice system" (p. 1). Wells, Wright, and Bradfield (1999) note that three variables control the accuracy of eyewitness testimony: the age of the witness, the intensity of the incident, and the aftermath (pp. 58–59).

Another issue regarding the effectiveness of eyewitness identification is the use of police lineups and photo show-ups. The questions begin with: how similar are the physical characteristics of the suspect and the innocents? Another question is: if officers are using a photo show-up, are all the pictures similar (i.e., are they all driver's license photos, Polaroids, or jail pictures)? Finally, what instructions are given to the eyewitness who is viewing the lineup or show-up? If the police tell the eyewitness that the suspect is in the lineup or show-up, he or she will be pressured to select a person (Acker & Brody, 2004; McCann, Shindler, & Hammond, 2004; Schacter, 2002; Sporer, 1994).

Wells and Seelau (1995) outline the following strategies to assist in the reduction of false identification: inform the witness that the guilty party may not be in the lineup or show-up; the suspect should not stand out from the other individuals, and in a show-up, there should be some degree of similarity as described in the photo selection; have the lineup or show-up administered by someone who has no knowledge of the suspect; and assess the level of confidence the eyewitness has in the identification of a suspect before administering the lineup or show-up (p. 765).

INTERVIEW AND INTERROGATION

The strength of any case depends on probable cause and evidence. There are two forms of fact finding utilized by the police: the police interview, which is designed to obtain information about a case and possibly identify a suspect, and police interrogation, which involves questioning a suspect in an attempt to obtain a confession. The most damning piece of evidence that an investigator can obtain is a confession from the defendant. Brainerd and Reyna (2005) argue that confession evidence is so central to the prosecution that it strengthens criminal cases where there may be little or no evidence. This assertion is supported in post-trial interviews where jurors state that they assign a great deal of weight to a confession (p. 260).

Interview

An **interview** is defined as a conversation held to generate information from persons who have knowledge of a situation or crime so that an investigation can be continued or concluded. In essence, an interview is a form of fact finding. There are several stages to a police interview: preparation; establishing rapport, or a good relationship, between interviewer and interviewee; a description of the rules regarding the interview process; identifying defense mechanisms and disarming them; use of open-ended questions; enlisting the full cooperation of the witness; understanding the witness version and being cognizant of his or her vantage point; and summarizing and verifying the statement (Henry, 2004; Powell, Fisher, & Wright, 2007; Vadackumchery, 1999).

interview

a conversation held to generate information from a person who has knowledge of a situation or crime so that an investigation can be continued or concluded; a form of fact finding.

Interrogation

An **interrogation** is the questioning of a person suspected of having committed an offense or who is reluctant to make full disclosure of information that is pertinent to an investigation (Abernathy & Perry, 1993; Brooks, 2001; Leo, 1998). The investigator must be cognizant that both the interview and the interrogation are forms of fact finding. However, the most significant difference between the two is that an interview is not governed by such court decisions as *Miranda*. The conduct of a sworn officer during an interrogation is outlined in several landmark cases that were detailed in Chapter 3. The most significant case regarding the suspect's rights when in custody is *Miranda v. Arizona* (1966).

interrogation

the questioning of a person suspected of having committed an offense or who is reluctant to make full disclosure of information that is pertinent to an investigation.

When Are Police Required to Read Miranda?

In reviewing the *Miranda* decision, the court repeated one phrase consistently: *custodial interrogation*. Take a moment and contemplate that phrase. Does it mean that a suspect has been placed under arrest? Does it mean that every person must be read Miranda prior to any questioning? What does *custody* mean?

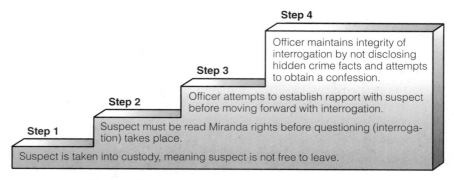

Step 4

Officer maintains integrity of interrogation by not disclosing hidden crime facts and attempts to obtain a confession.

Step 3

Officer attempts to establish rapport with suspect before moving forward with interrogation.

Step 2

Suspect must be read Miranda rights before questioning (interrogation) takes place.

Step 1

Suspect is taken into custody, meaning suspect is not free to leave.

Figure 7-2   The Interrogation and Confession Process

custody

defined in terms of police interrogation, the subject is *not* free to leave at any time during the interrogation.

Custody defined in terms of police interrogation means the subject is *not* free to leave at any time during the interrogation. The issue can best be explained by the case of *Oregon v. Mathiason,* 429 U.S. 492 (1977), which can be summed up in this statement: "Miranda warnings are required only where there has been such a restriction on a person's freedom as to render him 'in custody.'" It is that sort of coercive environment to which *Miranda* by its terms has been made applicable, and to which it is limited. A simple formula to remember regarding the reading of Miranda warnings is: *Custody + Interrogation = Miranda Warnings.* (See Figure 7-2.)

CONFESSIONS

confession

the acknowledgment or admission of the commission of all elements of a crime and the defendant's involvement in the act.

Integral to interview and interrogation is the term *confession.* A **confession** is the acknowledgment or admission of the commission of all elements of a crime and the defendant's involvement in the act (Brown, 2001; Inbau, Reid, Buckley, & Jayne, 2001; Palmiotto, 2004).

false confession

a confession to a crime obtained from an innocent party through coercion, spoon-feeding a subject the facts, internal self-doubt, or memory errors.

During the course of the interrogation, an investigator should not offer any of the facts to the suspect. This is important because if an innocent party is feeling pressured, he or she may provide a **false confession** with facts that match the crime because they were provided by the investigator (Cohen, 2003; Euale & Turtle, 1999; Zulawski & Wicklander, 2001). The facts of a case that only you and the suspect know are referred to as *hidden crime facts.* The suspect should have the ability to articulate each of the facts. In high-profile cases, the media may leak some of the common facts of a case to the public. The suspect's confession should include facts that the police have not released to the public and that were not discussed during the interview.

Obtaining the Confession

To obtain a confession, an investigator needs to develop good communication skills, develop active listening, and, most important, understand human behavior (Brooks, 2001; Leo, 2006). When investigators begin an interrogation, they have no control over the hand that they have been dealt. It is important to reconcile personal feelings regarding the case or the crime before the interrogation begins. It is not uncommon for an officer to personalize acts of violence when the victim is a child, female, or another officer. Failure to reconcile any personal issues that an officer has before beginning the interrogation may impede the process even if a suspect is willing to discuss the case openly.

Knudson (1999) describes the process of meeting and understanding the defendant at his or her level of anger, frustration, or criminal intent as **getting into the well.** Another term associated with getting into the well is *empathy*. Martinovski, Traum, and Marsella (2007) note that most of the research on empathy is focused on the ability or skill of giving empathy, but the acceptance or rejection of empathy should be seen as coping strategies, and when one introduces the skill set, it is dependent on the offender's state of mind at the time (p. 61).

When discussing individuals under duress, Jones (2000) explains that the art of interrogation/negotiation must follow a four-step process before an investigator can claim success. The process is called **moving forward** and articulates that cooperative behavior must be established between the investigator and the defendant. Once cooperative behavior is established, a sense of *us* emerges over *me*, the individual. The defendant becomes cooperative because of the bond that has been established, and power and control are no longer issues.

getting into the well

a process of meeting and understanding the defendant at his or her level of anger, frustration, or criminal intent.

moving forward

the point in an interrogation where rapport has been established between the interrogator and the suspect, and where cooperative behavior and confessions begins.

CONCLUSION

Many sources can initiate police investigations. The first officer on the scene has the responsibility of arriving safely, surveying the crime scene before entering it, and investigating what has occurred. The first officer on the scene also has the responsibility of determining if a crime has been committed and what resources are needed to complete an investigation.

After arriving safely on the scene and taking care of those who are injured, the most important thing that the first officer on the scene has to do is complete a police report answering six questions: who, what, where, when, how, and why. The importance of detailing an incident completely cannot be stressed enough, as an officer's reports will be scrutinized by supervisors, detectives in follow-up investigations, prosecutors in developing charging documents, judges, and juries.

Obtaining the confession is an art that is usually predicated by one's experience. Police officers go through several phases of development during the course of their career. When they begin their career, they are placed in an environment where survival and coming home at the end of the night are the dominant themes. Those themes are difficult to balance with concepts like empathy and understanding. The key is to never lose sight of the primary objectives: safety, thoroughness, quality service, and exemplifying professionalism in every facet of the job.

 ## DISCUSSION QUESTIONS

1. A call-taker in many instances is the beginning of a police investigation. Describe the importance of the call-taker's role in the investigation process. Also discuss how a call-taker's information gathering is often considered a police officer's lifeline, and why.

2. Describe the differences between a preliminary investigation and a primary investigation.

3. Describe the importance of physical evidence and witness statements in corroborating the facts in a criminal investigation.

4. Describe the differences between an interview and an interrogation. In your discussion, explain the rules associated with each and whether it is ethical for an investigator to misrepresent or omit facts during an interrogation.

5. This chapter states that according to national averages, police are poor at solving crimes. Discuss the many tools police officers have at their disposal to assist them in solving crimes.

 ## RESEARCH TOPICS

Following are two topics that are central to this chapter. Choose one, and research the topic based on the instructions of your professor.

- *Clearance rates.* This chapter discusses the dismal clearance rates for all crimes throughout the United States. A number of case management tools are available to assist officers in solving crimes. Research the concept of case management and describe the process you would implement to enhance your clearance rate. Defend your answer.

- *Obtaining confessions.* Two of the chapters have discussed confessions. Research a criminal from history whom you find intriguing, and use that information in researching the art of confessions. Detail the skill set and possible pitfalls that would be involved in obtaining a confession from your suspect. Defend your answer.

 ## BIBLIOGRAPHY

Abernathy, M. G., & Perry, B. A. (1993). *Civil liberties under the Constitution* (6th ed.). Columbia: University of South Carolina Press.

Acker, J. R., & Brody, D. C. (2004). *Criminal procedure: A contemporary perspective.* Sudbury, MA: Jones & Bartlett.

Agulair v. Texas, 378 U.S. 108 (1964).

Asante, M. K. (2008). *It's bigger than hip-hop: The rise and fall of the hip-hop generation.* New York: St. Martin's Press.

Bautista, A. R. (2003). *Basic criminal procedure.* Manila, Philippines: Rex Bookstores.

Becker, R. F. (2008). *Criminal investigation* (3rd ed.). Sudbury, MA: Jones & Bartlett.

Betts v. Brady, 316 U.S. 455 (1942).

Bevel, T., & Gardner, R. M. (2001). *Bloodstain pattern analysis: With an introduction to crime scene reconstruction* (2nd ed.). Boca Raton, FL: CRC Press.

Boba, R. (2005). *Crime analysis and crime mapping.* Thousand Oaks, CA: Sage.

Brainerd, C. J., & Reyna, V. F. (2005). *The science of false memory: An integrative approach.* New York: Oxford University Press.

Brewer, N., Weber, N., & Semmler, C. (2007). Eyewitness identification. In N. Brewer & K.D. Williams (Eds.), *Psychology and law: An empirical perspective* (pp. 177–221). New York: Guilford.

Brooks, P. (2001). *Troubling confessions: Speaking guilt in law and literature.* Chicago: University of Chicago Press.

Brown, M. F. (2001). *Criminal investigation: Law and practice* (2nd ed.). Boston: Butterworth-Heinemann.

Brown v. Mississippi, 297 U.S. 278 (1936).

Carney, T. P. (2004). *Practical investigation of sex crimes: A strategic and operational approach.* Boca Raton, FL: CRC Press.

Cohen, S. (2003). *The wrong men: America's epidemic of wrongful death row convictions.* New York: Carroll & Graff.

Eck, J. E., & Wisebud, D. (1995). *Crime and place: Crime prevention studies.* Monsey, NY: Criminal Justice Press.

Escobedo v. Illinois, 378 U.S. 478 (1964).

Euale, J., Martin, D., Rock, N., & Sadek, J. (1998). *Principles of evidence for policing.* Toronto, Canada: Edmond Montgomery Publications.

Euale, J., & Turtle, J. W. (1999). *Interviewing and investigation.* Toronto, Canada: Edmond Montgomery.

Fisher, B. A. J. (2003). *Techniques of crime scene investigation.* Boca Raton, FL: CRC Press.

Gardner, R. M. (2004). *Practical crime scene processing and investigation.* Boca Raton, FL: CRC Press.

Geberth, V. J. (2006). *Practical homicide investigation; Tactics, procedures, and forensic techniques* (4th ed.). Boca Raton, FL: CRC Press.

Gideon v. Wainwright, 372 U.S. 335 (1963).

Gonzalez, L. P. (2002). New media, new behaviours: Emerging conversational patterns in computer mediated communication. In A. S. Macarro (Ed.), *Windows on the world: Media discourse in English.* Valencia, Spain: University of Valencia.

Gottschalk, P. (2006). *Knowledge management systems in law enforcement: Technologies and techniques.* Hershey, PA: Idea Group.

Graham, M. H. (2003). *Cleary and Graham's handbook of Illinois evidence* (8th ed.). Riverwoods, IL: Aspen.

Hardy, M., & Heyes, S. (1999). *Beginning psychology* (5th ed.). New York: Oxford University Press.

Hawthorne, M. R. (1999). *First unit responder: A guide for physical evidence collection for patrol officers.* Boca Raton, FL: CRC Press.

Henry, V. E. (2004). *Death work: Police, trauma, and the psychology of survival.* New York: Oxford University Press.

Herbert, S. K. (2006). *Citizens, cops, and power: Recognizing the limits of community.* Chicago, IL: University of Chicago Press.

Illinois v. Gates, 462 U.S. 213 (1983).

Inbau, F. E., Reid, J. E., Buckley, J. P., & Jayne, B. C. (2001). *Criminal interrogations and confessions* (4th ed.). Sudbury, MA: Jones & Bartlett.

Jones, J. (2000). *F.I.R.E. model of crisis negotiation.* Gainesville, FL: Author.

Kapardis, A. (2003). *Psychology and law: A critical introduction.* New York: Cambridge University Press.

Kitwana, B. (2003). *The hip hop generation: Young blacks and the crisis in African American culture.* New York: Basic Civitas Books.

Knudson, M. L. (1999). *Alachua County Crisis Center training manual.* Gainesville, FL: Alachua County Crisis Center.

Lee, H., Palmbach, T., & Miller, M. T. (2001). *Henry Lee's crime scene handbook.* San Diego: Elsevier.

Leo, R. A. (1998). From coercion to deception: The changing nature of police interrogation in America. In R. A. Leo & G. C. Thomas (Eds.), *The Miranda debate: Law, justice and policing*. Lebanon, NH: University Press of New England.

Leo, R. A. (2006). The third degree and the origins of psychological interrogation in the United States. In D. Lassiter (Ed.), *Interrogations, confessions, and entrapment* (pp. 37–84). New York: Springer.

Lyman, M. D. (2006). *Practical drug enforcement* (3rd ed.). Boca Raton, FL: CRC Press.

Martinovski, B., Traum, D., & Marsella, S. (2007). Rejection of empathy in negotiation. *Group Decision and Negotiation, 16*, 61–76.

McCann, J. T., Shindler, K. L., & Hammond, T. R. (2004). The science and pseudoscience of expert testimony. In S. O. Lilienfeld, S. J. Lynn, J. M. Lohr, & C. Tavris (Eds.), *Science and pseudoscience in clinical psychology* (pp. 77–108). New York: Guilford.

Miranda v. Arizona, 384 U.S. 436 (1966).

Murray, K. R. (2004). *Training at the speed of life, volume one: The definitive textbook for military and law enforcement reality based training*. Gotha, FL: Armiger.

Oregon v. Mathiason, 429 U.S. 492 (1977).

Osborne, D., & Wernicke, S. (2003). *Introduction to crime analysis. Basic resources for criminal justice practice*. Philadelphia: Haworth.

Palmiotto, M. (2004). *Criminal investigation* (3rd ed.). Lanham, MD: University Press of America.

Peterson, L. (1993). *Emergencies: Emergencies*. Lawrenceville, NJ: Thomson-Peterson.

Powell, M. B., Fisher, R. P., & Wright, R. (2007). Investigative interviewing. In N. Brewer & K. D. Williams (Eds.), *Psychology and law: An empirical perspective* (pp. 11–42). New York: Guilford.

Prior, I. (2004). The ballistics expert at the scene. In J. Horswell (Ed.), *The practice of crime scene investigation*. Boca Raton, FL: CRC Press.

Roberts, K. H., Madsen, P., & Desai, V. (2007). Organizational sensemaking during a crisis. In C. M. Pearson, C. Roux-Dufort, & J. Clair (Eds.), *International handbook of organizational crisis management*. Thousand Oaks, CA: Sage Publications.

Sanders, R. E. (2003). Applying the skills concept to discourse and conversation: The remediation of performance defects in talk-in-interaction. In J. O. Greene & B. R. Burleson (Eds.), *Handbook of communication and social interaction skills* (pp. 221–256). Mahwah, NJ: Lawrence Erlbaum.

Schacter, D. L. (2002). *The seven sins of memory: How the mind forgets and remembers*. New York: Houghton Mifflin Harcourt.

Shepherd, G. J., & Rothenbuhler, E. W. (2001). *Communication and community*. Mahwah, NJ: Lawrence Erlbaum.

Sonne, W. J. (2006). *Criminal investigation for the professional investigator.* Boca Raton, FL: CRC Press.

Spelman, W. (1994). *Criminal incapacitation.* New York: Springer.

Spinelli v. United States, 393 U.S. 410 (1969).

Sporer, S. L. (1994). Decision times and eyewitness identification accuracy in simultaneous and sequential lineups. In D. F. Ross, J. D. Read, & M. P. Toglia (Eds.), *Adult eyewitness testimony: Current trends and developments* (pp. 300–327). New York: Cambridge University Press.

Stering, R. (2004). *Police officers handbook: An introductory guide.* Sudbury, MA: Jones & Bartlett.

Tracy, K., & Agne, R. R. (2002). "I just need to ask somebody some questions": Sensitivities in domestic dispute calls. In J. Cotterill (Ed.), *Language in the legal process* (pp. 75–90). New York: MacMillan.

Vadackumchery, J. (1999). *Professional police-witness interviewing.* New Delhi, India: APH Publishing.

Vellani, K. H., & Nahoun, J. D. (2001). *Applied crime analysis.* Boston: Butterworth-Heinemann.

Walton, D. N. (2008). *Witness testimony evidence: Argumentation and the law.* New York: Cambridge University Press.

Walton, R. H. (2006). *Cold case homicide: Practical investigative techniques.* Boca Raton, FL: CRC Press.

Warden, R., Armbrust, S. M., & Linzer, J. (2001, May). *How mistaken and perjured eyewitness identification testimony put 46 innocent Americans on death row.* Paper presented at Andrews University, Berrien Springs, MI.

Wells, G. L., & Seelau, E. P. (1995). Eyewitness identification: Psychological research and legal policy on lineups. *Psychology, Public Policy, and Law, 1,* 765–791.

Wells, G. L., Wright, E. F., & Bradfield, A. L. (1999). Witnesses to crime: Social and cognitive factors governing the validity of people's reports. In R. Roesch, S. D. Hart, & J. R. P. Ogloff (Eds.), *Psychology and law: The state of discipline.* New York: Springer Science & Business.

Zulawski, D. E., & Wicklander, D. E. (2001). *Practical aspects interview and interrogation.* Boca Raton, FL: CRC Press.

CHAPTER 8

USE OF FORCE

OBJECTIVES

After completing this chapter, the student will be able to:

- Describe where an officer obtains the statutory authority to use physical force in making arrests.
- Explain the purpose of a force continuum and discuss the levels of resistance versus the level of force.
- Discuss why an officer uses force.
- Discuss the importance of *Graham v. Connor* and the reasonable officer doctrine.
- Discuss the impact of *Tennessee v. Garner* on a police officer's use of deadly force.
- Explain the impact that reaction time has on an officer's ability to respond to a threat.
- Discuss Grossman's model of *fight or flight, posture or submit* and how it is applied to policing.
- Discuss *sudden custody death syndrome* and the problems that it presents to police in making arrests.

KEY TERMS

escalation and **de-escalation** – terms that identify an officer's need to use force to establish control. Officers can escalate their use of force to establish control of a subject; however, they must de-escalate once control is established.

excited delirium – associated with drug abuse and/or mental illness; the symptoms are extreme agitation and restlessness, incoherent and rambling speech, hallucinations, delusions with paranoid features, disorganized thought content, bizarre behavior, and combativeness.

fleeing felon rule – a common law rule that provides officers with the ability to use deadly force to stop a person who flees after the commission of a felony whether that person is a threat or not.

officer-subject factors – an officer's evaluation of a subject prior to a confrontation, which may involve a number of variables based on the officer's observations, assessment of the subject, and beliefs at the time of the incident.

positional asphyxia – the occurrence of asphyxia when the position of the body interferes with respiration.

positional restraint asphyxia – the occurrence of asphyxia when a subject is placed in the hogtie position (i.e., subject's feet are restrained by handcuffs, flexcuffs, or a hobble restraint; subject's hands are handcuffed behind his or her back; and subject's feet are pulled to the center of subject's back and connected to his or her hands—subject is then placed on his or her stomach on the ground and later in the patrol car for transport).

reaction time – an officer's ability to assess a threat and respond with the appropriate level of force.

reasonable officer doctrine – requires an examination of the facts as the officer perceived them at the time, not after the fact. The *Graham* decision prescribed the following criteria for determining reasonableness: the severity of the crime; whether the suspect poses an immediate threat to officers or others; and whether the suspect is resisting arrest or attempting to evade arrest by flight.

sudden custody death – a death that occurs immediately after an arrest in which there is a violent struggle.

targeted violence – any incident of violence where a known or knowable attacker selects a particular target prior to a violent attack.

Tennessee v. Garner – a case in which the Supreme Court ruled that officers *cannot* use deadly force to apprehend a nonviolent felon and also stipulated that officers can use force only in defense of themselves or others.

use of force – dictated by circumstances; usually involves police reacting to a situation or attempting to prevent further damage or harm.

use-of-force matrix or force continuum – a visual tool used to explain the concept of force; these are usually created by an agency and are unique to the agency's needs.

DOC'S WORDS OF WISDOM

One of the most difficult choices an officer has to make during a use-of-force encounter is the selection of the appropriate weapon or skill in a split-second decision for the sole purpose of establishing control of a subject.

INTRODUCTION

Every time an officer uses force, the public wonders: why? Since the advent of video, we are accustomed to seeing the atrocities committed by officers. These scenes have been viewed on television dating back to the 1960s, detailing officers' actions in the civil rights movement, antiwar demonstrations, and more recently incidents such as Rodney King. What most people do not understand is that the use of force is dictated by a subject's actions and that the force used must be fair and reasonable for that confrontation (Alpert & Dunham, 2004; Rahtz, 2003; Schneider, Gruman, & Coutts, 2005).

AUTHORITY TO USE FORCE

An officer's ability to use force is defined in state statutes. It is most often associated with making an arrest for a criminal violation. Most state statutes read in a way that is similar to Florida State Statute 776.05, *Use of Force in Making an Arrest*, which specifies three circumstances in which an officer is justified in using force:

1. In defense of self or another while making an arrest
2. When retaking felons who have escaped
3. In arresting felons fleeing from justice

As you analyze the circumstances in which an officer can use force, can you conceive of a situation where force is not associated with an arrest? Concepts associated with the uniformed police officer are identification, deterrence, and the first level of force when an officer arrives on a scene (Box, 1983; Olsen, 2001; Shpayer-Makov, 2002).

WHAT IS FORCE?

The **use of force** is dictated by a series of circumstances. In most cases police are reacting to a situation or attempting to prevent further damage or harm. The most important component associated with the use of force is the concept of *reasonableness*, which can have infinite interpretations. In essence, the term *reasonable* is void of meaning, but it was addressed by the U.S. Supreme Court in *Graham v. Connor*, 490 U.S. 386 (1989). The *Graham* decision established a doctrine that could be called the **reasonable officer doctrine** (Lippmann, 2006; Urbonya, 1998; Williams, 2005). The doctrine requires an examination of the facts as the officer perceived them at the time, not after the fact. The *Graham* decision prescribed the following criteria for determining reasonableness: the severity of the crime; whether the suspect poses an immediate threat to officers or others; and whether the suspect is resisting arrest or attempting to evade arrest by flight.

One of the more common categories of force is known as *police defensive tactics*. Police defensive tactics encompass a number of empty-hand skills, the use of intermediate weapons, and ultimately the use of deadly force (Alpert & Dunham, 2004; Rahtz, 2003; Thomas, 1989; Walker, 2005). Although many of the empty-hand techniques taught to police are taken from martial arts, police still have to abide by the rule of reasonableness in establishing control. In almost any instance, a kick to the groin or a strike to the throat would stop an aggressor, but this may not be an acceptable defensive tactic technique; such techniques can be deployed only under certain sets of circumstances (Dantzker, 2005; Kennedy, 1995; Lawrence, 2000; Waddington, 1991).

As you examine the officer response levels, understand that *no tactic is 100% effective,* and this includes a firearm. Often an escalation of force is required by an officer to establish control of a subject. The type and level of force an officer uses is dictated by the subject's actions. Today, force is best defined by using a **use-of-force matrix or a force continuum.** Most if not all continuums have been developed by trainers, agencies, or state training commissions as visual tools to explain the concept of force and are unique to their respective needs (Dantzker, 2005; Neyroud, 2008; Walker, 2005). However, all define force and resistance using similar terms and definitions. Thomas (1989) identifies and defines a subject's level of resistance and an officer's response to the subject's resistance.

---

use of force

dictated by circumstances; usually involves police reacting to a situation or attempting to prevent further damage or harm.

reasonable officer doctrine

requires an examination of the facts as the officer perceived them at the time, not after the fact. The *Graham* decision prescribed the following criteria for determining reasonableness: the severity of the crime; whether the suspect poses an immediate threat to officers or others; and whether the suspect is resisting arrest or attempting to evade arrest by flight.

use-of-force matrix or force continuum

a visual tool used to explain the concept of force; these are usually created by an agency and are unique to the agency's needs.

Subject's Levels of Resistance

1. *Verbal resistance:* occurs once police arrive at a scene when the subject becomes verbally abusive or begins to challenge the officer's authority.

2. *Passive physical resistance:* subject fails to respond to police requests but offers no overt physical acts of aggression toward the officer, nor does the subject attempt to flee. *Example:* A crowd is involved in an unlawful assembly. The officers order the crowd to disperse, and the crowd responds by sitting in the middle of the street blocking traffic. They offer no physical resistance other than sitting.

3. *Pulling away resistance:* occurs when an officer has made physical contact with a subject with the intent to arrest the subject, and the subject responds by pulling away. The subject offers no overt physical aggression toward the officer. The subject is attempting to defeat an officer's attempt at making an arrest by pulling away from the officer's grasp or control.

4. *Combative physical resistance:* the subject's level of violence has escalated and the subject is now attacking the officer with hands, fists, or feet. The objective is to injure the officer and get away.

5. *Armed physical resistance:* the subject's level of violence is such that the subject intends to cause great bodily harm or death to the officer. The subject may use a variety of weapons: knife, firearm, bludgeon, automobile, and so on.

Officer's Levels of Response

1. *Officer presence:* the officer's arrival at a scene or call for service. This could also be interpreted as deterrence while on patrol. The key here is that the officer has not attempted dialogue, and this level of force is associated with the officer's uniformed presence.

2. *Verbal direction:* the officer directs a subject to do something. Examples: "Move over here so we can talk." "Leave or go to jail." "Place your hands behind your back; you're under arrest." "Get on the ground." "Stop resisting."

3. *Control techniques:* these techniques require physical contact with a subject and are often utilized to establish control when the subject is offering some form of physical resistance. The techniques can be categorized in the following manner:

a. *Pain compliance:* techniques that are used to get a subject to stop resisting. They are often used when a subject engages in forms of pulling away resistance. These techniques are not designed to cause injury, just compliance. Examples are nerve pressure points and joint locks.

b. *Takedowns:* techniques that require an officer to physically take a subject to the ground. The probability of injury increases based on the technique employed, how aggressively the technique is applied, how actively the subject resists, and the surface that the suspect and officer are going to land upon.

c. *Striking:* techniques that are the most violent of the empty-hand techniques employed. Strikes include kicks, punches, and the use of elbows and knees. The areas that an officer can strike are nonlethal. However, if officers need to stop an attack that could cause great bodily harm or death, they can escalate and attack targets that are considered lethal/deadly in nature. Examples of lethal/deadly targets are groin, eyes, temple, spine, throat, and so on.

4. *Intermediate weapons:* weapons an officer deploys to stop an aggressive threat. Since the turn of the century, there has been a trend to move intermediate weapons above empty-hand control techniques based on the belief that once verbal resistance begins, it will soon be followed by some form of physical resistance. By deploying intermediate weapons early in the confrontation, control is established sooner, reducing the potential for injury to the officer and the subject. The categories of intermediate weapons are:

a. *Impact weapons:* weapons that an officer uses to strike a subject. Until the 1960s, these were known as *night sticks.* Today the correct term is *baton,* and the officer has many choices. However, the type of baton and system used with it are often dictated by an agency's policy. Potential for injury is minimal if the officer strikes muscle mass. However, if the targets become bones and joints, the potential for serious injury is greatly enhanced. Baton strikes do not work each time a baton is deployed; sometimes multiple strikes are required. Examples of impact weapons are the side-handle baton, straight baton, and collapsible baton.

b. *Oleoresin capsicum (OC)/pepper spray:* an aerosol spray that is sprayed into the subject's face. The focal points of the spray are the nose, the eyes, and the top of the head. The objective of the spray is to temporarily incapacitate a subject by affecting his or her ability to breathe and see. Depending on the manufacturer, incapacitation is temporary and lasts at best one-half hour. Like batons, OC spray is not effective in every case. In fact, once OC spray is deployed, an officer should wait until the subject is affected before attempting to establish control. Potential for injury or long-term aftereffects is minimal. However, there has been some controversy surrounding the use of OC spray, associating its deployment with a resisting subject's death. Chan, Vilke, Clausen, Clark, Schmidt, Snowden, and Neuman (2001) reported in a National Institute of Justice study that "OC exposure and inhalation do not result in significant risk for respiratory compromise or asphyxiation, even when combined with positional restraint" (p. 3). It should be noted that this study was completed in controlled laboratory conditions with the participants wearing goggles and void of the stressful conditions a subject experiences during an arrest. The question remains, why has death been associated with the use OC spray?

5. *Electronic devices:* designed to disrupt a subject's neuromuscular systems and render the subject helpless by sending an electrical current through the subject's body. Electromuscular disruption devices are designed to limit the potential for serious injury to the officer and the subject. However, as with OC spray, there is controversy surrounding the use of electronic devices. Most if not all of the controversy is associated with subjects who have died during the deployment of an electrical device. A 2008 National Institute of Justice study indicates that such weapons are not risk-free, but there is no conclusive medical evidence that indicates a high risk of serious injury or death due to the deployment of an electronic device (p. 3). Studies conducted by Taser International have all been done in a lab and during police training conditions that are sterile. Again, the sterile laboratory environment does not take into account the fear and anxiety subjects experience when resisting arrest.

6. *Deadly force:* employing a weapon with the intent to cause great bodily harm or death. Deadly force is the last resort and is only deployed if the officer has no other options. In most cases, deadly force is associated with the use of a firearm. However, other options can include the use of empty-hand techniques, baton strikes, and in rare cases the use of a motor vehicle.

See the use-of-force continuum in Figure 8-1.

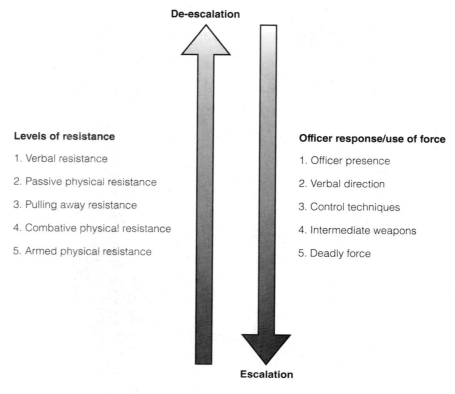

Figure 8-1   Use-of-Force Continuum

WHY IS FORCE USED?

The primary purpose of the use of force is to *establish control*. From a legal standpoint, there really is no other purpose for an officer's actions (Alpert & Dunham, 2004; Ivkovich, 2000; Tyler & Huo, 2002). Florida State Statute 776.05 identifies three conditions in which an officer can use force: to stop a threat, to stop a felon who has escaped, or while arresting a felon who is fleeing. The statute is specific to felons, but all arrests, be they felonies or misdemeanors, may require that some force be used. It may be as simple as verbal direction or the application of handcuffs where there is no resistance, or as severe as the use of deadly force.

The concept of control carries with it two important components: **escalation** and **de-escalation.** Officers can escalate their use of force to establish control of a subject; however, they *must* de-escalate once control is established (Dobkin, 1996; Geller & Toch, 2005; Goodwin, 2002; Walker 2005). (See Scenario 8-1.)

escalation and **de-escalation**

terms that identify an officer's need to use force to establish control. Officers can escalate their use of force to establish control of a subject; however, they must de-escalate once control is established.

SCENARIO 8-1: USE OF A CONTROL TECHNIQUE

An officer attempts to make an arrest for shoplifting. As the officer attempts to apply the handcuffs, the suspect snatches away from the officer's grasp and attempts to run. The officer catches the suspect and takes the suspect to the ground using a takedown technique. Once on the ground, the suspect offers no more resistance. If the suspect offers no more physical resistance, the encounter is over.

HOW IS DEADLY FORCE UTILIZED?

Prior to 1985, most states allowed officers to use deadly force based on English common law, which was interpreted as the *fleeing felon rule*. The **fleeing felon rule** defined in its simplest terms means that whenever subjects have committed any felony, they can be shot to stop their escape (Fyfe, 1996; Kleinig, 2008; Lippman, 2007; Walker, Spohn, & DeLone, 2007). (See Scenario 8-2.) The state of Michigan has a statute entitled "Larceny (Theft) in a Building, MCL750.360 (Felony)"; there is no dollar value associated with the act of larceny. The statute reads:

> Any person who shall commit the crime of larceny by stealing in any dwelling house, house trailer, office, store, gasoline service station, shop, warehouse, mill, factory, hotel, school, barn, granary, ship, boat, vessel, church, house of worship, locker room or any building used by the public shall be guilty of a felony.

The change came about in a 1985 landmark Supreme Court decision known as ***Tennessee v. Garner***, 471 U.S. 1 (1985). The circumstances of the *Garner* case were similar to those in Scenario 8-2. In that decision, the Supreme Court ruled that officers *cannot* use deadly force to apprehend a nonviolent felon and also stipulated that officers can use force only in defense of themselves or others (pp. 7–22).

Why the change in policy and law? At the time our forefathers adopted *English common law*, there were very few felonies. Today our society has evolved, and so have our sense of morals and our value of life. Put simply, a candy bar and chips are much less valuable than the life of a nonviolent offender. In essence, the fleeing felon rule shocked the conscience of our society and was archaic in principle, and thus the courts mandated a change.

fleeing felon rule

a common law rule that provides officers with the ability to use deadly force to stop a person who flees after the commission of a felony whether that person is a threat or not.

Tennessee v. Garner

a case in which the Supreme Court ruled that officers *cannot* use deadly force to apprehend a nonviolent felon and also stipulated that officers can use force only in defense of themselves or others.

SCENARIO 8-2: LARCENY IN A BUILDING

You are on patrol prior to 1985 and the fleeing felon rule is in effect. You are dispatched to the local 7-11 with reference to a kid stealing candy from the store. You are just around the corner, and dispatch gives you a physical description of B/M, approximately 10 years old, 5'0, 100 lbs, wearing a red plaid shirt and blue jean shorts. Dispatch also advises that the subject has no weapons and has not threatened the clerk. As you arrive, you observe the subject running from the store with what appears to be a candy bar in one hand and a bag of potato chips in the other. The store clerk steps outside and states: "That's him, officer, stop him!" You order the subject to stop, and he continues to run. You shoot the subject in the back, killing him.

Analysis and Reflection

1. Was this shooting a justifiable shooting prior to 1985? Yes, unless your agency had a policy that forbade the use of deadly force in such incidents. These types of shootings were common in minority communities in the 1960s and 1970s and created a lot of tension between the community and police.

2. If you actually were the officer who killed this kid, who was unarmed, over a bag of chips and a candy bar, how would you feel? The greater question here is: what is the value of a human life if a subject is not a threat to anyone else? These are personal questions that you have to answer. It is important to understand under what circumstances you can use deadly force and when you will personally feel comfortable in using it. The standard is different for every officer, and it is highly personal regardless of the law and/or department policy.

When discussing deadly force, however, it is not enough to address *Garner*. The next logical step is to examine circumstances in which deadly force is used and attempt to answer the age-old question: Are police trained to shoot to kill? As you ponder this question, think about some of the circumstances in which officers would deploy their firearms.

Now examine some of the situations that officers find themselves in: man with a gun; woman attacking an officer with a knife; officer being beaten with a pipe; suspect is biting an officer's thumb off and the officer is going unconscious; suspect stabbing a woman upon the officer's arrival; and suspect has taken a hostage and threatened to shoot the hostage. The list of possible situations is infinite. Place yourself in the officer's shoes in any one of the aforementioned situations, and ask yourself the question: Are police trained to shoot to kill? The correct answer is "No." Police are trained to stop the threat (Hatch, 2002; Holbrook, 2004).

Police deadly force training, however, encompasses shooting at the largest part of the human anatomy, the torso. The reasoning for such training is that under stressful situations, it would be difficult to focus on an arm or a leg in an attempt to shoot it (Fyfe, 1996; Klinger, 2004; Waddington, 1991). In addition, there is a physiological response to these incidents that affects an officer's visual acuity and causes a loss of fine motor skills and a greater reliance on gross motor skills (Dutton, 1985; Murray, 2004). Further, in most deadly force encounters, the subject is moving, which makes smaller targets even more difficult to acquire. Finally, most deadly force encounters occur at a distance of less than ten feet (FBI, 2007; Sweeney & Ferguson, 2004). In this situation, it would be impossible to focus on a small part of a subject's anatomy because of the immediacy of the threat and potential for harm to the officer.

FACTORS INFLUENCING USE OF FORCE

In addition to those already discussed, a number of factors influence an officer's decision about whether to use force, including: officer-subject factors, threat assessment, circumstances, the human element, and fight-or-flight syndrome. These are discussed in the sections that follow.

Officer-Subject Factors

Desmendt (1982) describes what has come to be known as **officer-subject factors,** arguing that the use of less-than-lethal force may involve a number of variables, which are evaluated based on the confrontation, the officer's observations, assessment of the subject, and beliefs at the time of the incident. Desmendt's argument is supported by the U.S. Supreme Court decision of *Graham v. Connor,* which is discussed earlier in this chapter. The *Graham* decision went one step further and applied reasonableness to all use-of-force encounters, with the most important being the officer and his or her interpretation of the encounter (Arrigo & Shipley, 2004; Blum, 2000; Florida Department of Law Enforcement, 2008; Michigan State Police Training Academy, 2004; Rahtz, 2003). Walker (2005) notes that there is more to an officer's use of force than officer-subject factors and argues that the use of force is closely correlated to the nature and calls for service, race of the suspect, and the suspect's actions (p. 189).

officer-subject factors

an officer's evaluation of a subject prior to a confrontation, which may involve a number of variables based on the officer's observations, assessment of the subject, and beliefs at the time of the incident.

Threat Assessment

Threat assessment is a term associated with terrorism, executive protection details, stalking, domestic violence, and serial killers. However, it goes far beyond the scope of those entities. In every officer-subject encounter, there is some degree of assessing the potential threat to an officer.

As discussed earlier, officers are at a disadvantage because subjects have intimate knowledge of their past deeds. The subject will know if an arrest warrant exists, if he or she has just committed a crime, or if he or she is currently involved in a crime that officers have stumbled upon. Holbrook (2004) argues that threat assessment is fluid, ever-changing, and unique to a particular situation or set of circumstances (p. 555). Examine Scenarios 8-3 and 8-4 and determine the initial threat in each incident. If you were an officer at these scenes at those given times, is there anything that you would have done differently?

Threat assessment begins with the suspect's intentions and the term *targeted violence.* This term evolved from the U.S. Secret Service's reference of the behavior of individuals who have attempted or carried out

SCENARIO 8-3: THE TRAFFIC STOP

You are working the midnight shift and on patrol. It is 2:00 A.M. and you observe a black van run a red light at the intersection of Hall and Division. The vehicle is westbound and there is no other traffic. It has been your experience based on the time of day and the nature of the violation that the driver is probably a drunk driver. You stop the vehicle two blocks from the intersection. As you approach the vehicle, the driver is excited and sweating profusely. Before you can ask the driver any questions regarding the violation, the driver states: "Ok, officer, you got me. I did it. I killed her. The girl is in the back. You caught me. I was on my way to get rid of the body. Damn, you're good. You caught me. How did you know? How did you know?"

SCENARIO 8-4: THE AMBUSH

You are on patrol and it is 3:00 A.M. in the morning. You receive a call at a local sporting goods store. You have responded to this alarm many times in the past, and it has always been false. However, you always proceed with caution because this store sells guns, which have great value on the street. Upon checking the exterior of the building you discover that the front door is smashed in and you can hear someone inside. As you prepare to enter the building with your partner, you hear a shot that comes from behind you. Your partner standing next to you drops dead, with a bullet wound to the head. Before you can react, you are shot in the back. You survive the shooting, but the suspects get away. The investigation reveals that a subject with a rifle was waiting in the trees one hundred yards behind you. You never had a chance. The subjects had planned to kill anyone who responded to the alarm.

lethal attacks on public officials or prominent individuals. The term was later refined in 1992 in a published report entitled the *Exceptional Case Study Project*. Vossekuil, Reddy, and Fein (2000) define **targeted violence** as any incident of violence where a known or knowable attacker selects a particular target prior to a violent attack (p. 13).

During any encounter, an officer must read the subject's behavioral cues. The process begins with a visual scan of the subject's outer clothing, looking for any unusual bulges that might identify a weapon, for example, an outline of a gun under a shirt. The next most important component is the subject's hands: are they visible? Finally, attention is given to the subject's verbal and nonverbal cues, which are possible indicators of violence. The verbal cues are a loud angry tone of voice, profanity, and/or threatening words. The nonverbal cues include a red flushed face, hyperventilation, rigid body, clenched fists, and/or shaking. Note that these are *possible* indicators; nothing is absolute (Florida Department of Law Enforcement, 2008; Garwood, 2005; Murray, 2004). (See Figure 8-2.)

Threat assessment is essential in an officer's ability to react to a situation. If officers are unable to assess a situation properly or are not mentally prepared, it inhibits their ability to react to the threat. Therefore, reaction time is an integral component of the use-of-force equation and is associated with one's ability to process information cognitively (Lachman & Butterfield, 1979). **Reaction time** is an officer's ability to assess a threat and respond with the appropriate level of force. Many studies of reaction

targeted violence

any incident of violence where a known or knowable attacker selects a particular target prior to a violent attack.

reaction time

an officer's ability to assess a threat and respond with the appropriate level of force.

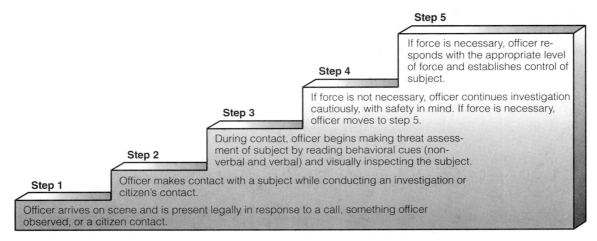

Step 5
If force is necessary, officer responds with the appropriate level of force and establishes control of subject.

Step 4
If force is not necessary, officer continues investigation cautiously, with safety in mind. If force is necessary, officer moves to step 5.

Step 3
During contact, officer begins making threat assessment of subject by reading behavioral cues (nonverbal and verbal) and visually inspecting the subject.

Step 2
Officer makes contact with a subject while conducting an investigation or citizen's contact.

Step 1
Officer arrives on scene and is present legally in response to a call, something officer observed, or a citizen contact.

Figure 8-2   Threat Assessment Process During Officer-Subject Contacts

This graphic was developed as a visual interpretation of the threat assessment process. It is not intended to be used as an absolute in the officer's use-of-force decision making. Use-of-force decision making is dynamic and changes constantly until control has been established.

time have been conducted by traffic engineers regarding accident avoidance and with pilots in simulators responding to a crisis with an aircraft; however, many of these concepts apply to policing and threat assessment. Green (2000, p. 200) defines reaction time as a series of stages, which he has applied to accident avoidance and brake application, but which can be applied to police reaction time as follows:

- *Mental processing time:* the time it takes the responder to perceive that a signal has occurred and to decide on a response. Mental processing is comprised of three components:
  a. *Sensation:* the time it takes to detect assaultive action.
  b. *Perception:* the time needed to recognize the meaning of the sensation.
  c. *Response selection and programming:* the time necessary to decide which, if any, response to make and to mentally program the movement. Response time slows when an officer is faced with multiple choices. Conversely, practice decreases the required response time.
- *Movement time:* the time it takes the officer's muscles to perform the programmed movement.
- *Device response time:* the time it takes for the physical device to perform its response.

Under What Circumstances Does an Officer Use Force?

We have defined *force* and addressed the guidelines on the use of force. It would be great if our discussion could be limited to those factors, but it cannot be so limited. The most important ingredients are the officer and the subject at the time they cross each other's paths. In our society, there is an expectation that officers will act professionally in the execution of their duties. This expectation involves a false perception that officers do not possess biases, do not take issues personally, and are always objective. If this were the case, then why are officers charged with brutality?

The Human Element

Take a moment and think about this question: under what circumstances might an officer be justified in using force? Possible answers might be: in making an arrest; to stop an attack; to stop a crime in progress, such as a burglary; to stop a riot; to remove a subject from a business establishment or domicile; and so on.

The officer-subject encounter becomes much more complex than a set of circumstances, however, because the human element offers an infinite number of possibilities. Thomas (1989) argues that when an officer encounters a suspect, the officer may face one of three possible personality types: cooperative, potentially uncooperative, or combative. Remsberg (1986) describes these personality types as yes, no, and maybe. Thompson (1993) classifies these personalities as the nice, the difficult, and the wimp. In knowing that you will encounter one of the three personalities, would you treat each person the same or would you adjust your behavior to that of the subject? As you ponder this question, remember that the subject has the advantage at the beginning of most encounters.

Fight or Flight

When faced with an encounter with each other, officers and subjects alike have to deal with the human physiological and psychological response known as *fight or flight* (Cotton, 1990; Pfaff, 2006). Since the police are on the front line and called upon to protect the public in need, they have no duty to retreat and in many cases must perform their duty (Waddington, 1991). The subject has options, and the most daunting of tasks is to challenge the officer both verbally and physically. If the subject is a true predator, then he or she may be better prepared than the officer in any encounter.

Grossman (1996) adds two additional not previously discussed components to the fight-or-flight syndrome. Grossman's model describes the human encounter as *fight or flight, posture or submit* (pp. 5–7). As the encounter begins, rather than flee, the subject postures and argues with the officer. During this phase, the subject shows that there is no respect for the officer and his or her authority. This is a decision point for many officers: if there is no arrestable offense, what are the officer's options? In many cases, an officer will respond by giving the suspect two options: leave or go to jail. The officer knows that there is no violation of the law, but the subject's actions are leading the officer down a path rarely discussed outside police culture; it is known as "pissing off the police (POP)" or "contempt of cop (COP)" (Rudovsky, 1997; Zeisel & Kaye, 1997).

If the subject continues to argue and challenge the officer's authority, the subject is often arrested and charged with a minor misdemeanor similar to *breach of the peace* or *disorderly conduct*. Two things have occurred during the posturing phase: the subject's challenge to the officer's authority, and the officer's challenge to the subject's credibility on the street. The bottom line is a loss of respect or an attempt to "save face." Thompson

(1993) addresses the issue of face-saving by attempting to get officers to understand that they will always have the last action, the ability to make an arrest. By allowing the subject to blow off steam and leave, an officer allows the subject to save face (pp. 76–77).

If during the posturing phase an arrest is imminent, then the options are flight, fight, or submit. If the suspect leaves before the officer announces that the suspect is under arrest, then the situation is resolved. During the arrest, the subject has two options, fight or submit. Submission is the preferred method; however, when examining the statistics from the FBI's *Uniform Crime Report: Officers Killed and Assaulted* between the years 1991 and 2001, it is clear that resistance is a road often taken. The number of assaults that occurred during this ten-year period totaled 658,306. This number includes every category of assault.

SUDDEN CUSTODY DEATH SYNDROME

In this chapter, we have discussed all the variables associated with the use of force, the decision-making process, the socialization of an officer, and the issues associated with police brutality. Is it possible for an officer to do everything right and once control has been established, the suspect dies? (See Scenario 8-5.)

Situations like that in Scenario 8-5 happen in the real world, but not only with police; these kinds of deaths occur in psychiatric units, hospital emergency rooms, and jails/prisons as well. Often they are wrongly associated with police brutality. This nature of death is known as *police custody death syndrome* or *in-custody death syndrome*. Several underlying factors are associated with this type of death, including excited delirium, positional asphyxia, positional restraint asphyxia, and sudden custody death.

Excited delirium is associated with drug abuse and/or mental illness. Tennant and Groesbeck (1972) have termed this phenomenon a post–drug impairment syndrome and cite many of the same characteristics that have been identified by Wetli and Fishbain in their 1985 research. Di Maio and Di Maio (2005) describe the symptoms of excited delirium as extreme agitation and restlessness, incoherent and rambling speech, hallucinations, delusions with paranoid features, disorganized thought content, bizarre behavior, and combativeness (p. 103).

Positional asphyxia and *positional restraint asphyxia* are closely related terms. Reay, Fligner, Stilwell, and Arnold (1992) define **positional asphyxia** as asphyxia when the position of the body interferes with respiration. They assert that in all cases of positional asphyxia, one or more

excited delirium

associated with drug abuse and/or mental illness; the symptoms are extreme agitation and restlessness, incoherent and rambling speech, hallucinations, delusions with paranoid features, disorganized thought content, bizarre behavior, and combativeness.

positional asphyxia

the occurrence of asphyxia when the position of the body interferes with respiration.

SCENARIO 8-5: THE MENTAL PATIENT

You and your partner are dispatched to 1215 Los Alamos Drive regarding a mental patient who has not been taking his medication. The patient's name is Dave Hall, and you have been to his house on several occasions. In the past you have had to commit Dave to the local crisis stabilization unit for psychological evaluation so he can be placed back on his medication.

He has a history of violence and extreme paranoia when off his medication. Upon your arrival, you meet with Mrs. Hall, Dave's mother, and she advises that Dave has not taken his medication for the past week and has become increasingly violent, exhibiting fits of rage that are evidenced by damaged chairs, a broken coffee table, and a smashed china cabinet and china.

You locate Dave in the basement. He is cowering in a corner, exhibiting signs of extreme anxiety and wildly swinging into the air as if to stop something from attacking him. As you look around the basement and visually inspect Dave's outer clothing, you see no weapons.

Since you have a history with Dave, you approach him and begin a dialogue. Dave is very irrational and delusional, stating that snakes and alligators are attacking him. After a ten-minute dialogue, you get Dave to stand up and come out of the corner. You tell Dave

that you and your partner are going to transport him to the crisis unit for evaluation. Dave is fine and offers no resistance. However, as you begin to ascend the stairs, Dave becomes agitated but continues to comply.

Once you get to the patrol car, you advise Dave that he must be handcuffed before you can place him in your car. Without warning, Dave explodes violently, attacking your partner. Your partner is kicked in the head and knocked unconscious. You fight with Dave using only empty-hand skills, which include wrestling and control holds of the arms. You are unable to get to your baton, OC spray, or electromuscular disruption weapon. Mrs. Hall observes the struggle, calls 911, and backup is enroute. Before the other units arrive, you are able to establish control and handcuff Dave. You set him upright against the car, and then check on your partner's well-being.

The struggle with Dave has lasted for approximately four minutes, and you are exhausted. As the other units arrive, you ask them to place Dave in your car so you can transport him to the crisis unit. The backup officers approach Dave, attempt to get him on his feet, and determine that he is not breathing. They begin CPR as you call for an ambulance. Dave is pronounced dead fifteen minutes later at the local hospital.

contributory factors provide an explanation of the victim's inability to breathe; these include: alcohol/drug intoxication, concussive head injury, entrapment, restraint, and some form of physical disability (p. 94). Positional asphyxia is often associated with the situation where officers who are wrestling with a combative subject use their body weight to control the subject by pressing a knee into the subject's back, restricting the subject's ability to breathe. Another situation in which it occurs is when several officers apply their body weight on the back of a subject to establish control and restrict the subject's airway.

Violently combative subjects have often been placed in a position known as the *hogtie position*. Hogtying occurs when a subject's feet are restrained by handcuffs, flexcuffs, or a hobble restraint; the subject's hands are handcuffed behind his or her back; and the subject's feet are pulled to the center of his or her back and connected to the hands. The subject is then placed on his or her stomach on the ground and later in the patrol car for transport (Di Maio & Di Maio, 2005; Dolinak, Matshes, & Lew, 2005; Hatch, 2002; Reay et al., 1992; Shepherd, 2005).

The hogtie position is used to keep subjects from kicking officers, kicking out patrol car windows, or hurting themselves by slamming their head into the windows, doors, or cage that separates the subject from the officer. As a result of the hogtying and placing the subject on his or her stomach, the subject can experience **positional restraint asphyxia.** The primary difference between positional asphyxia and positional restraint asphyxia is the application of restraints in the hogtie position.

Di Maio and Dana (1998) define **sudden custody death** as a death that occurs immediately after an arrest in which there is a violent struggle. Di Maio et al. note that as long as there is a struggle and there is contact between the officer and the deceased, no matter what the cause of death, even a heart attack, it will most likely be ruled a homicide. They have concluded that most deaths occurring during the arrest occur after the struggle and are a combination of the physiological effects of the stress of the struggle and the action of drugs (pp. 499–506).

CONCLUSION

The use of force is a complex dynamic. An officer's judgment is influenced by the law, skill development, officer survival, the field training program, and the agency. All of these guiding forces in the decision-making process must be meshed with an officer's personal value system in deciding when and how much force an officer is willing to use in an encounter. The unknown variable in any encounter is the suspect, his or her abilities, and whether the suspect suffers from a disorder or medical condition that could lend itself to death in a less-than-lethal situation.

The use of force is a difficult balancing act and at times can become a tightrope, even when an officer has done everything correctly. To obtain success in any officer-subject encounter, officers must understand the rules, properly assess the threat, and use force that is reasonable for the confrontation.

---

positional restraint asphyxia

the occurrence of asphyxia when a subject is placed in the hogtie position (i.e., subject's feet are restrained by handcuffs, flexcuffs, or a hobble restraint; subject's hands are handcuffed behind his or her back; and subject's feet are pulled to the center of subject's back and connected to his or her hands—subject is then placed on his or her stomach on the ground and later in the patrol car for transport).

sudden custody death

a death that occurs immediately after an arrest in which there is a violent struggle.

DISCUSSION QUESTIONS

1. Discuss the impact of *Graham v. Connor,* and describe the elements of the reasonable officer doctrine.

2. Describe the fleeing felon rule and the importance of *Tennessee v. Garner* in the use of deadly force.

3. What is a force continuum, and how is it used to define force?

4. Discuss the importance of threat assessment when officers arrive on a scene.

5. What is sudden custody death syndrome, and what are the contributing factors?

RESEARCH TOPICS

Following are two topics that are central to this chapter. Choose one, and research the topic based on the instructions of your professor.

- *Excessive force.* This chapter details the proper use of force and how decisions should be made in all encounters. Research a famous excessive force case. Examine the officer's actions and determine what should have been the correct course of action. Defend your answer.

- *Less than lethal.* There are a number of weapons and empty-hand control techniques that are considered less than lethal; some examples are: neck restraint (empty-hand technique), neuromuscular disruption devices, and pepper spray. However, each has been associated with claims of death when they have been deployed in confrontations with suspects. Research one of these less-than-lethal options, and take a position on why it should or should not be utilized by police. Defend your answer with research.

BIBLIOGRAPHY

Alpert, G. P., & Dunham, R. G. (2004). *Understanding police use of force: Officers, suspects and reciprocity.* New York: Cambridge University Press.

Arrigo, B. A., & Shipley, S. L. (2004). *Introduction to forensic psychology: Issues and controversies in crime and justice* (2nd ed.). Burlington, MA: Elsevier Academic Press.

Blum, L. N. (2000). *Force under pressure: How cops live and why they die.* New York: Lantern Books.

Box, S. (1983). *Power, crime, and mystification.* New York: Tavistock.

Chan, T., Vilke, G. M., Clausen, J., Clark, R., Schmidt, P., Snowden, T., & Neuman, T. (2001). *Pepper spray's effects on a suspect's ability to breathe.* Washington, DC: National Institute of Justice.

Cotton, D. H. G. (1990). *Stress management: An integrated approach to theory.* New York: Brunner/Mazel.

Dantzker, M. L. (2005). *Understanding today's police.* Monsey, NY: Criminal Justice Press.

Desmendt, J. (1982). *The physical intervention paradigm for enforcement and corrections.* Nokesville, VA: Protective Safety Systems.

Di Maio, T., & Di Maio, V. J. M. (2005). *Excited delirium syndrome: Cause of death and prevention.* Boca Raton, FL: CRC Press.

Di Maio, V. J. M., & Dana, S. E. (1998). *Handbook of forensic pathology.* Georgetown, TX: Landes Bioscience.

Dobkin, B. A. (1996). Video verité: Language and image in the interpretation of power. In M. E. Stuckey (Ed.), *The theory and practice of political communication research* (pp. 84–94). Albany, NY: SUNY Press.

Dolinak, D., Matshes, E. W., & Lew, E. O. (2005). *Forensic pathology: Principles and practice.* Burlington, MA: Elsevier Academic Press.

Dutton, D. G. (1985). The public and the police: Training implications of the demand for a new model police officer. In J. C. Yuille (Ed.), *Police selection and training: The role of police psychology* (pp. 141–158). New York: Springer.

Federal Bureau of Investigation (FBI). (2001). *The FBI uniform crime report: Officers killed and assaulted.* Washington, DC: Department of Justice.

Federal Bureau of Investigation (FBI). (2007). *2007 Law enforcement officers killed and assaulted.* Washington, DC: Department of Justice.

Florida crimes, motor vehicles, and related laws with jury instructions. (2004). Longwood, FL: Gould Publications.

Florida Department of Law Enforcement. (2008). *Florida basic recruit training program. Vol. 2: High liability* (2008:4). Tallahassee, FL: Author.

Fyfe, J. J. (1996). Police use of deadly force. In G. S. Bridges, J. G. Weis, & R. D. Crutchfield (Eds.), *Criminal justice: Readings* (pp. 187–194). Thousand Oaks, CA: Pine Forge Press.

Garwood, R. J. (2005). *Thanks for listening.* Bloomington, IN: AuthorHouse.

Geller, W. A., & Toch, H. (2005). *Police violence: Understanding and controlling police abuse of force.* New Haven, CT: Yale University Press.

Goodwin, C. (2002). Professional vision. In D. Weinberg (Ed.), *Qualitative research methods* (pp. 281–312). Hoboken, NJ: Wiley-Blackwell.

Graham v. Connor, 490 U.S. 386 (1989).

Green, M. (2000). How long does it take to stop? Methodological analysis of driver perception–brake times. *Transportation Human Factors, 2*(3), 195–216.

Grossman, D. (1996). *On killing: The psychological cost of learning to kill in war and society.* Boston: Little, Brown.

Hatch, D. E. (2002). *Officer involved shooting and use of force: Practical investigative techniques.* Boca Raton, FL: CRC Press.

Holbrook, R. M. (2004). *Political sabotage: The LAPD experience, attitudes towards understanding police use of force.* Victoria, BC, Canada: Trafford.

Holtz, L. E. (2001). *Contemporary criminal procedure: Court decisions for law enforcement* (7th ed.). Longwood, FL: Gould Publications.

Ivkovich, S. K. (2000). Challenges of policing democracies: The Croatian experience. In O. Marenin & D. K. Das (Eds.), *Challenges of policing democracies: A world perspective* (pp. 45–86). The Netherlands: Gordon & Breach.

Kennedy, E. A. (1995). Teaching martial arts to law enforcement personnel. In C. A. Wiley (Ed.), *Martial arts teachers on teaching* (pp. 131–141). Berkeley: Frog Books.

Kleinig, J. (2008). *Ethics and criminal justice: An introduction.* New York: Cambridge University Press.

Klinger, D. (2004). *Into the kill zone: A cop's eye view of deadly force.* San Francisco: Jossey-Bass.

Klockars, C. B. (1995). A theory of excessive force and its control. In W. A. Geller & H. Toch (Eds.), *And justice for all: Understanding and controlling police abuse of force* (pp. 11–29). Washington, DC: Police Executive Research Forum.

Krosch, C., Binkerd, V., & Blackborne, B. (1992). *Final report of the custody death task force.* San Diego: San Diego Police Department.

Lachman, J. L., & Butterfield, E. C. (1979). *Cognitive psychology and information processing: An introduction.* Hillsdale, NJ: Lawrence Erlbaum.

Lawrence, R. G. (2000). *The politics of force: Media and the construction of police brutality.* Berkeley: University of California Press.

Lippmann, M. R. (2007). *Contemporary criminal law: Concepts, cases, and controversies.* Thousand Oaks, CA: Sage.

Michigan State Police Training Academy. (2004). *Criminal law and procedure: A manual for Michigan police officers.* Lansing, MI: Author.

Murray, K. R. (2004). *Training at the speed of life. Vol. 1: The definitive textbook for military and law enforcement reality based training.* Gotha, FL: Armiger.

National Institute of Justice. (2008). *Study of deaths following electro muscular disruption: Interim report.* Washington, DC: U.S. Department of Justice.

Neyroud, P. (2008). Policing and ethics. In T. Newburn (Ed.), *Handbook of policing* (2nd ed., pp. 666–692). Portland, OR: Willan.

Olsen, M. (2001). *State trooper: America's state troopers and highway patrolmen.* Paducah, KY: Turner.

Pfaff, D. W. (2006). *Brain arousal and information theory: Neural and genetic mechanisms.* Cambridge, MA: Harvard University Press.

Rahtz, H. (2003). *Understanding police use of force.* Monsey, NY: Criminal Justice Press.

Reay, D. T., Fligner, C. L., Stilwell, A. D., & Arnold, J. (1992). Positional asphyxia during law enforcement transport. *American Journal of Forensic Medicine and Pathology, 13*(2), 90–97.

Reiss, A. J. (1968). Police brutality: Answers to key questions. *Transaction, 5*(8), 10–19.

Remsberg, C. (1986). *The tactical edge: Surviving high-risk patrol.* Northbrook, IL: Calibre Press.

Ross, M. M. (1998). *Sword and shield revisited: A practical approach to section 1983.* Chicago: American Bar Association.

Rudovsky, D. (1997). Police abuse: Can the violence be contained? In M. D. McShane & F. P. Williams (Eds.), *Law enforcement operations and management* (pp. 249–286). New York: Garland.

Schneider, F. W., Gruman, J. A., & Coutts, L. M. (2005). Defining the field of applied social psychology. In F. W. Schneider, J. A. Gruman, & L. M. Coutts (Eds.), *Applied social psychology: Understanding and addressing social and practical problems* (pp. 1–18). Thousand Oaks, CA: Sage.

Shepherd, R. (2005). Deaths in custody. In M. Stark (Ed.), *Clinical forensic medicine: A physician's guide* (2nd ed., pp. 327–350). Totowa, NJ: Humana Press.

Shpayer-Makov, H. (2002). *The making of a policeman: A social history of a labour force in Metropolitan London, 1829–1914.* United Kingdom: Ashgate.

Stratton, S. J., Rogers, C., & Green, K. (1995). Sudden death in individuals in hobble restraints during paramedic transport. *Annals of Emergency Medicine, 25*(5), 710–712.

Sweeney, P., & Ferguson, T. (2004). *Modern law enforcement: Weapons and tactics* (3rd ed.). Iola, WI: Krause.

Tennant, F. S., & Groesbeck, C. J. (1972). Psychiatric effects of hashish. *Archives of General Psychiatry, 33,* 383–386.

Tennessee v. Garner, 471 U.S. 1 (1985).

Thomas, D. (1989). *Defensive tactics manual* (2nd ed.). Grandville, MI: Author.

Thompson, G. J. (1993). *Verbal judo: The art of gentle persuasion.* New York: Quill.

Tyler, T. R., & Huo, Y. J. (2002). *Trust in the law: Encouraging public cooperation with the police and courts.* New York: Russell Sage Foundation.

Urbonya, K. R. (1998). Dangerous misperceptions: Protecting police officers, society, and the Fourth Amendment right to personal safety. In M. M. Ross & American Bar Association (Eds.), *Sword & shield revisited: A practical approach to 1983* (pp. 259–349). Chicago: American Bar Association.

Vossekuil, B., Reddy, M., & Fein, R. (2000). *Safe school initiative: An interim report on the prevention of targeted violence in schools.* Washington, DC: U.S. Secret Service.

Waddington, P. A. J. (1991). *The strong arm of the law: Armed and public order policing.* New York: Oxford University Press.

Walker, S. (2005). *The new world of police accountability.* Thousand Oaks, CA: Sage.

Walker, S., Spohn, C., & DeLone, M. (2007). *The color of justice: Race, ethnicity, and crime in America* (4th ed.). Belmont, CA: Thomson/Wadsworth.

Wetli, C. V. (1999, May). The pathology of drug abuse: Discussions of case histories. In C. Wetli (Chair), *Current topics in forensic pathology.* Symposium conducted at the meeting of the American Society of Clinical Pathologists, New Orleans, LA.

Wetli, C. V., & Fishbain, D. A. (1985). Cocaine induced psychosis and sudden death in recreational cocaine users. *Journal of Forensic Science, 30,* 873–880.

Williams, G. T. (2005). *Force reporting for every cop.* Sudbury, MA: Jones & Bartlett.

Yuille, J. C. (1985). *Police selection and training: The role of police psychology.* New York: Springer.

Zeisel, H. Z., & Kaye, D. H. (1997). *Prove it with figures: Empirical methods in law and litigation.* New York: Springer.

CHAPTER 9

TERRORISM

OBJECTIVES

After completing this chapter, the student will be able to:

- Discuss the origins of terrorism and the Sicarii.
- Describe the typologies of terrorism.
- Discuss terrorist motivations.
- Discuss the psychology of terrorism.
- Describe the role of group dynamics in killing.
- Discuss weapons of mass destruction.
- Describe the differences in CBRN weapons (chemical, biological, radiological, and nuclear weapons).
- Discuss domestic terrorism and terrorists groups of the 1960s and 1970s.
- Describe the FBI Counterintelligence Program and its abuses between the years 1956 and 1971.
- Discuss the significance of *The Turner Diaries* in regard to domestic terrorism in the United States.
- Discuss right-wing extremism as it relates to the United States.
- Discuss the key components of the Patriot Act.
- Describe the role of the Department of Homeland Security.
- Discuss the role of the FBI and CIA in counterterrorism.
- Describe the changes that the New York City Police Department has made since 9/11 regarding counterterrorism.

KEY TERMS

April 19 – the anniversary of significant events in U.S. history, recognized by militia groups within the United States as a special day. The events in question are: the Oklahoma City bombing; the FBI assault on the Branch Davidians in Waco, Texas; and the federal government's initial surveillance of Randy Weaver at Ruby Ridge. It is also the date of the attack outlined in *The Turner Diaries*.

biological weapons –disease-causing microorganisms such as bacteria, viruses, and fungi that can be produced by humans or derived from plants, animals, or microorganisms.

chemical weapons – human-made substances designed to harm or kill an enemy; such products would likely be used against civilian populations because most military organizations have the equipment to combat such attacks.

Counterintelligence Program (COINTELPRO) – program operated by the FBI between 1956 and 1971, and charged with targeting foreign intelligence agencies operating in the United States during the Cold War.

dirty bomb – a device that combines a conventional explosive, such as dynamite, with radioactive material; used to disrupt life rather than destroy it. A dirty bomb is classified as a *radiological dispersal device (RDD)*.

group think – a theory that groups affected by group think ignore alternatives and make irrational decisions, which includes dehumanizing other groups. What happens during the group dynamics is a process known in psychological circles as projection.

jihad – the European translation is "holy war," but in traditional Arabic, the term comes from the term *jahada,* which is defined as a struggle or effort against some type of power, usually depicted as a visible enemy, the devil, or one's inner desires.

lone wolf – a person who espouses the beliefs of right-wing extremism, yet does not openly discuss his or her beliefs. Lone wolves become members of the U.S. establishment, local and state governments, and law enforcement organizations; they influence politics and decision making as well as wait for the call to rise to power.

post-9/11 project – convened in 2004 and attended by the International Association of Chiefs of Police (IACP), the National Sheriff's Association (NSA), the National Organization of Black Law

Enforcement Executives (NOBLE), and the Police Foundation, with a goal of assisting state and local law enforcement in the management of an ever-changing police environment.

radiological weapons – weapons that rely on radiation rather than a blast to cause death and casualties; with the right delivery system, such a weapon could make large amounts of real estate uninhabitable.

shifting eras and mission reconfiguration – recognizes that the police mission has changed since 9/11, and yet the traditional policing models of crime control and community policing cannot be ignored. It is believed that American policing should transition from the community policing model to a domestic security model.

terrorism – the calculated use of unexpected, shocking, and unlawful violence against noncombatants (including, in addition to civilians, off-duty military and security personnel in peaceful situations) and other symbolic targets perpetrated by a clandestine agent(s) for the psychological purpose of publicizing a political or religious cause and/or intimidating or coercing a government(s) or civilian population into accepting demands on behalf of the cause.

The Turner Diaries – a fictional book that details overthrowing the U.S. government and the rise of "White America."

weapons of mass destruction – weapons that are capable of creating mass casualties through one or a series of actions.

DOC'S WORDS OF WISDOM

The key to successfully combating terrorism is in understanding your enemy's motivations. The life blood of such a war is the ability to collect, analyze, and share intelligence information. This task is compounded because the rights of U.S. citizens weigh in the balance.

INTRODUCTION

Police have many roles in American society, and these roles are constantly changing based on the needs of the community that an organization serves. The most recent change in identity is associated with the aftermath of September 11, 2001 (9/11). Some of the questions that local law enforcement has been looking to answer are (Davis et al., 2004; Forest, 2006a; Schertzing, 2007):

1. Where do local and state police fit into the equation of domestic and international terrorism?

2. Do they have a role in the investigation and apprehension of terror suspects?

3. What will/should be the mission of local law enforcement in the detection and prevention of terrorist acts in local communities?

4. Is the role of local and state law enforcement intelligence gathering and information sharing or crime suppression?

5. What will happen to the crime rate if the mission of local law enforcement changes?

6. Where will an organization get the funding and personnel to sustain both fronts—their responsibility in terrorism intelligence gathering and providing optimal police service to the local community?

post-9/11 project

convened in 2004 and attended by the International Association of Chiefs of Police (IACP), the National Sheriff's Association (NSA), the National Organization of Black Law Enforcement Executives (NOBLE), and the Police Foundation, with a goal of assisting state and local law enforcement in the management of an ever-changing police environment.

shifting eras and mission reconfiguration

recognizes that the police mission has changed since 9/11, and yet the traditional policing models of crime control and community policing cannot be ignored. It is believed that American policing should transition from the community policing model to a domestic security model.

The role of police in American society is difficult to identify because in reality they have no definitive role. Their role is defined by law, politics, economics, and the needs of the community in which they serve. In essence, the role is ever-changing because of the demands of American society and individual communities (Waddington, 1994; White, 2004).

One of the best examples, and one that has had the greatest impact, is the events of 9/11. The role of police in that situation was correct: they were first responders to a crisis with the objective, in conjunction with the fire department, to save lives. That responsibility was nothing new for police. Prior to 9/11, policing had embraced the concepts of community policing. Cronkhite (2007) notes that pre-9/11 law enforcement had strong community ties and was successful in crime reduction, and public trust was strong (p. 327). After 9/11, however, the police mission changed and was identified in the *post-9/11 project*.

The **post-9/11 project** was convened in 2004 and attended by the International Association of Chiefs of Police (IACP), the National Sheriff's Association (NSA), the National Organization of Black Law Enforcement Executives (NOBLE), and the Police Foundation, with a goal of assisting state and local law enforcement in the management of an ever-changing police environment (pp. i–ii). The conference members identified and developed a host of objectives and goals for post-9/11. One idea that stands out in regard to combining traditional police operations with post-9/11 responsibilities is **shifting eras and mission reconfiguration.** Mission reconfiguration recognizes that the police mission has changed since 9/11, and yet the traditional policing models of crime control and community policing cannot be ignored. It is believed that

American policing should transition from the community policing model to a domestic security model (p. ii).

In the late 1980s and through the 1990s, local law enforcement was experiencing satisfaction because the violent crime rate dropped and agencies had finally begun connecting with their local communities through the efforts of such programs as community policing. It was not until September 11, 2001, that a new role was thrust upon local agencies. However, that role is confounded by the fact that local law enforcement is fragmented due to the jurisdictional limitations, as discussed in Chapter 5. The Tenth Amendment of the U.S. Constitution limits the authority of the federal government and authorizes and provides for home rule by the states.

BRIEF HISTORY OF TERRORISM

Historically terrorism dates back to the beginning of humans and the formation of societies. The first known terrorists were the Sicarii and Zealots, Jewish groups active during the Roman occupation of the Middle East, which dates back to before the year 66 (King, 2007; Laqueur, 1999). Victoroff (2006) states that there were organized groups committed to systematic terrorism early in recorded time, including the Jewish faction known as the *Sicarii* (pp. 10, 11).

Thomas Hobbes, a seventeenth-century philosopher, argued that when humans enter a social contract, they must give up some of their personal freedoms and give the government the authority to enforce laws and agreements. In addition, Hobbes argued that the state of nature is equivalent to anarchy because there are no rules (Ibbetson, 2001; McClelland, 1996; Williams & Arrigo, 2008). Understanding the concepts of Hobbes is important because they underscore the motivation for many terrorist acts in that there is a clash of ideological principles/agendas, which may be political, religious, cultural, or any combination thereof.

TYPOLOGIES OF TERRORISM

There are many forms of terrorism, and each has its unique definition. However, simply defining the term *terrorism* is very difficult. In an analysis of the literature, it appears that the definition varies based on the needs of the organization or researcher. Lutz and Lutz (2004) assert that a universal definition is lost because governmental entities in some cases are reluctant to use a definition and others will only classify certain acts as terrorism (p. 237). Before you move on in this chapter, take a moment and attempt to define *terrorism* in your own words, without using examples such as 9/11.

Hudson (1999) asserts that an act of violence that is regarded in the United States as terrorism may not be viewed as such in other countries, and describes **terrorism** as a calculated act of violence perpetrated against noncombatants where the targets are symbolic and the goal is either political or religious (p. 18). The Federal Bureau of Investigation (2001) classifies terrorism by using the following typologies: domestic, international, narco, cyber, environmental, or eco (pp. ii–iii). Mani (2004) classifies the typologies by agent or actor: non-state, state-supported, and the collusion of state and non-state actors (p. 220).

Regardless of the typologies, Laqueur (1999) argues that a change has taken place at the close of the twentieth century. He states that terrorism from the left is declining and that terrorism from the right is on the increase, and that its purpose is the destruction of society and elimination of large portions of a population; he describes the actions of the new terrorists as madness (p. 81).

PSYCHOLOGY OF TERRORISM

Have you ever wondered what a terrorist looks like? Take a moment and try to picture the physical features of a terrorist. Many in the United States believe that terrorists are of Middle Eastern descent, because of the perpetrators of 9/11. However, nothing could be further from the truth. Using such logic is dangerous and very similar to the logic that Cesare Lombroso used in creating his theories of the born criminal. Lombroso (2006/1876) theorized that born criminals had different characteristics such as: large jaws, canine teeth, and an arm span greater than height, like apes. It is clear that people come in all colors, different shapes, with large jaws and small teeth, small jaws and large teeth, and different arm lengths (pp. 51–53). The reality is that none of these principles apply. We look to find simple answers to complex questions.

Since we cannot identify a terrorist by physical characteristics, then there is little left to examine except psychology in understanding what defines a terrorist. The psychology of terrorism does not reveal major psychopathologies, and in fact the most outstanding characteristic of terrorists is their normality (Goodin, 2006; Laqueur, 1999; McCauley, 2007; Post, 1998). Hudson (1999) supports these findings and asserts that there seems to be general agreement among psychologists that no particular psychological attribute can be used to describe the terrorist, nor is there any "personality" that is distinctive to terrorists (p. 67).

The power and psychology of terrorism begin with transforming one's belief system to match that of a group that has similar interests; in

terrorism

the calculated use of unexpected, shocking, and unlawful violence against noncombatants (including, in addition to civilians, off-duty military and security personnel in peaceful situations) and other symbolic targets perpetrated by a clandestine agent(s) for the psychological purpose of publicizing a political or religious cause and/or intimidating or coercing a government(s) or civilian population into accepting demands on behalf of the cause.

essence, it is the group dynamics (see Figure 9-1). Bion (as cited in Post, 1998) states that groups rarely work in a conflict-free environment and that, in their functioning, they often sabotage their stated goals. Bion has identified three psychological symptoms of groups: the fight-flight group, which justifies its existence based on perceived threats; the dependency group, which is dependent upon the direction of an influential leader; and the paring group, which believes its acts will bring a new messiah (p. 32).

The power of group in time of war is described by Grossman (1995) where he states that when in battle, the most powerful commitment is not self-preservation but the sense of accountability to a soldier's fellow comrades. Grossman further states that group actions allow for anonymity, as opposed to an individual committing a similar act (p. 149).

Grossman's observation is supported by Janis and his theory of **group think.** Janis (1972) offers that groups affected by group think ignore alternatives and make irrational decisions, which includes dehumanizing other groups. What happens during the group dynamics is a process known in psychological circles as projection. In this case, their belief system/ideology allows the group to project every negative trait known to humankind upon their enemy.

Group think furthers a group's cause and strengthens cohesion amongst the members. Although this creates the perception of injustice, which is the cry of almost every group, such thinking occurs in a vacuum and provides a skewed perception of reality. The symptoms of group think are: the illusion of invulnerability; collective efforts to rationalize; belief in inherent morality; stereotyped views of enemy leaders; direct pressure; self-censorship of deviation; illusion of unanimity; and self-appointed mindguards (pp. 197–198). A final note regarding the importance of a group and acts of terrorism: often it is not about the cause, but rather

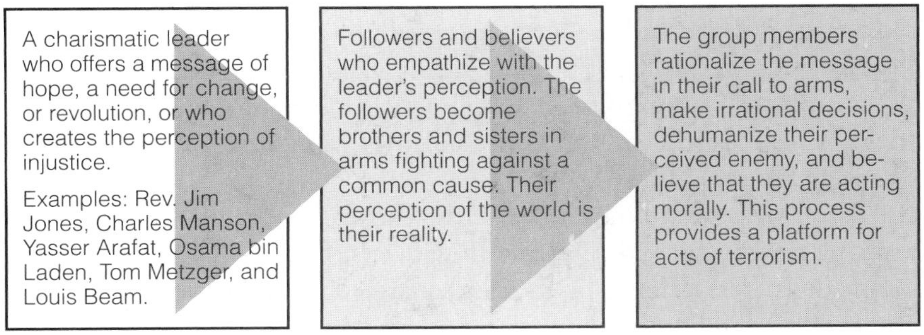

group think

a theory that groups affected by group think ignore alternatives and make irrational decisions, which includes dehumanizing other groups. What happens during the group dynamics is a process known in psychological circles as projection.

A charismatic leader who offers a message of hope, a need for change, or revolution, or who creates the perception of injustice.

Examples: Rev. Jim Jones, Charles Manson, Yasser Arafat, Osama bin Laden, Tom Metzger, and Louis Beam.

Followers and believers who empathize with the leader's perception. The followers become brothers and sisters in arms fighting against a common cause. Their perception of the world is their reality.

The group members rationalize the message in their call to arms, make irrational decisions, dehumanize their perceived enemy, and believe that they are acting morally. This process provides a platform for acts of terrorism.

Figure 9-1   Group Dynamics of Terrorism

about the group; and their ideology rationalizes their acts of terrorism (Bergman, 2003; Martin, 2007; Post, 1998).

ISLAM AND *JIHAD*

In the United States, *jihad* is a term that means "holy war," at least that is the way it has been described to citizens of the United States, both before September 11 and continuing today. It is important to understand the origin of the word and its many meanings, as well as how the United States became the center of a *jihad*.

White (2006) explains that the interpretation of ***jihad*** as a holy war is a European translation, not Arabic. In traditional Arabic, *jihad* comes from the term *jahada*, which is defined as a struggle or effort against some type of power, usually depicted as a visible enemy, the devil, or one's inner desires (p. 104). Kamrava (2005) describes that the Islamic fundamentalist world is divided into good versus evil, the oppressed versus the oppressor, and the abode of Islam versus the abode of war; the best way to achieve their goals is the *jihad* or holy war (p. 326).

The United States became the focus after the Afghan/Soviet War. Islam's international holy war was first conceived by Abdullah Azzam, a legendary mullah (Emerson, 2003; Jewett & Lawrence, 2004; Shay, 2008). Originally Azzam's vision of the *jihad* was to rid Muslim nations of their oppressors and return them to traditional Islamic beliefs. The belief was and is that if the *jihadists* could defeat the Soviets, then they would be able to defeat the United States (Allen, 2006; Dreyfuss, 2005; Laqueur, 2004). Azzam was killed by a car bomb in 1989 while driving in Islamabad. However, his message lives on.

Emerson (2003) conducted several interviews that detail the belief system of *jihadists*. In one such interview, Salih, the interviewee, argues that the United States has supported tyrannical regimes in the Arab world, most notably, Israel and the Jews. As a result of that support, *jihadists* view Jews as being in control of the U.S. media. Salih also argues that Jews are responsible for shaping U.S. national policies. In essence, the two countries are seen as one and the same, and they cannot oppose one without opposing the other (p. 70).

A final note regarding the *jihad*: the United States was responsible for assisting the Afghans in defeating the Soviets. The United States assisted indirectly in the training of the Afghan freedom fighters; in the development of a funding mechanism for an underground arms network; and in allowing Islamic charities the freedom to support the war effort. At

jihad

the European translation is "holy war," but in traditional Arabic, the term comes from the term *jahada,* which is defined as a struggle or effort against some type of power, usually depicted as a visible enemy, the devil, or one's inner desires.

the conclusion of the Afghan/Soviet War, the United States abandoned Afghanistan (Dreyfuss, 2005; White, 2006). In an effort to defeat Communism, the United States created a network that terrorists use today to fund the *jihad*.

WEAPONS OF MASS DESTRUCTION

Weapons of mass destruction are weapons that are capable of creating mass casualties through one or a series of actions. Langford (2004) describes weapons of mass destruction as weapons that kill people in more horrible ways than bullets and that have effects other than the destruction of buildings, with the purpose of spreading panic and fear, understanding that the effect and casualties are limited because of the delivery system (p. 1). These objectives could be achieved through the deployment of a dirty bomb, contaminating water and/or food sources, or through the development of a delivery system that will allow the dispersal of an airborne pathogen(s).

Many governmental entities have this ability with nuclear weapons, long-range missiles, and biological weapons. What Western and European governments fear is that terrorists and/or the states that are sympathetic to terrorist agendas will someday be armed with weapons of mass destruction and attack targets that they oppose, very similar to the September 11 attacks (Barnaby, 2004; Davis, 2006; Enders & Sandler, 2006). Note that any time a regime is overthrown, a political agenda changes from communism to democracy (e.g., Russia), or a radical faction of Islam comes into power, the United States and its allies are posturing to protect their interests at home and abroad. Litwak (2007) argues that such regime changes threaten international order, and the fear is that because of the change, weapons of mass destruction will fall into the wrong hands (pp. 15–18).

Hoffman (1993) notes that the most common forms of terrorist tactics are: bombs; attacks on installations, which include drive-by shootings, attacks with hand grenades, arson, and sabotage; assassinations; kidnappings; hijackings; and hostage situations, with the most common of the six being bombs (p. 13). Although the goal of the modern terrorist is to acquire weapons of mass destruction, terrorists have not found them to be readily accessible due to their limited/lack of technological ability, restricted access to weapons-grade nuclear materials, or their inability to develop a delivery system that allows the materials to remain stable during deployment (Pahwa, 2004; Steven & Gunarata, 2004). As a result, the failure of the tactics of terrorism remains in those areas described by Hoffman.

weapons of mass destruction

weapons that are capable of creating mass casualties through one or a series of actions.

With that said, it is important to understand that the future threat to the United States and governments with similar ideologies is weapons of mass destruction. Public safety and civil defense personnel must receive proper training and information. There are four categories of weapons of mass destruction: chemical, biological, radiological, and nuclear; the acronym CBRN is used to represent these four types. As stated, weapons of mass destruction are not readily accessible to terrorists.

Chemical Agents

chemical weapons

human-made substances designed to harm or kill an enemy; such products would likely be used against civilian populations because most military organizations have the equipment to combat such attacks.

Langford (2004) defines **chemical weapons** as human-made substances designed to harm or kill an enemy; such products would likely be used against civilian populations because most military organizations have the equipment to combat such attacks (p. 4). The Organisation for the Prohibition of Chemical Weapons (2005) has a similar definition but adds the elements of a device and munitions that can disperse the chemical (p. 3). The chemical weapons outlined in this definition should not be confused with the chemical weapons that law enforcement utilizes such as pepper spray and tear gas.

Chemical weapons were used in World War I with the deployment of mustard gas; in World War II in the gas chambers of German concentration camps; and in the Vietnam War by deploying Agent Orange as a defoliant to destroy the jungles of Vietnam. The by-products to those exposed to Agent Orange were cancer and birth defects. Saddam Hussein deployed chemical weapons against the Kurds in the late 1980s. Common types of chemical weapons are: mustard gas, phosgene gas, arsenic gas, sarin gas, GB gas, and VX gas (Brezina, 2005).

biological weapons

disease-causing microorganisms such as bacteria, viruses, and fungi that can be produced by humans or derived from plants, animals, or microorganisms.

Biological Weapons

Forsberg, Driscoll, Webb, and Dean (1995) define **biological weapons** as disease-causing microorganisms such as bacteria, viruses, and fungi that can be produced by humans or derived from plants, animals, or microorganisms (p. 13). Common types of biological weapons are smallpox, anthrax, and the plague (Langford, 2004).

radiological weapons

weapons that rely on radiation rather than a blast to cause death and casualties; with the right delivery system, such a weapon could make large amounts of real estate uninhabitable.

Radiological Weapons

Sauter and Carafano (2005) describe **radiological weapons** as weapons that rely on radiation rather than a blast to cause death and casualties; with the right delivery system, such a weapon could make large amounts of real estate uninhabitable (p. 168). Radiological weapons are often associated with a dirty bomb. Murray (2008) describes a **dirty bomb** as a device that combines a conventional explosive, such as dynamite, with radioactive

dirty bomb

a device that combines a conventional explosive, such as dynamite, with radioactive material; used to disrupt life rather than destroy it. A dirty bomb is classified as a *radiological dispersal device (RDD)*.

material; such a device is used to disrupt life rather than destroy it. A dirty bomb is classified as a *radiological dispersal device (RDD)* (p. 239).

The blast radius from a dirty bomb is limited to the ability of the delivery system. Since a dirty bomb requires the use of conventional explosives such as dynamite, the damage and death toll from the explosion may be greater than death and contamination from the radiation. In effect it would be limited to a few blocks or a few miles on the outside (Cockerham, Walden, Dallas, Mickley, & Landauer, 2007; Murray, 2008; Saha, 2006).

In contrast, the fallout from a nuclear bomb would be hundreds miles because of the mushroom cloud. It is because of these limitations that dirty bombs or radiological weapons are not considered weapons of mass destruction. Although they are not weapons of mass destruction, if detonated, dirty bombs achieve two objectives of terrorism: fear and disruption.

Low-level forms of radioactive material can be found in hospitals, research facilities, and construction sites. They are used for such purposes as diagnosing/treating illnesses, sterilizing equipment, and inspecting welding seams (Bullock, Haddow, Coppola, Ergin, Westerman, & Yeletaysi, 2006; Saha, 2006).

Nuclear Weapons

If the goal of Islamic fundamentalists is to defeat and destroy their oppressors, then the ultimate weapon would be a nuclear bomb. Pilisuk and Rountree (2008) describe the destructive force of a 120-megaton nuclear bomb as creating a crater large enough to engulf twenty city blocks, and deep enough to hide a twenty-story building. All brick and wood frame houses would be destroyed within a 7.7-mile radius; there would be 200,000 separate fires; a wind velocity of 150 miles per hour would be created; the infrastructure of food, water, power, and medical would be destroyed; and radiation damage would have a negative impact on all living things for 240,000 years (p. 8).

Nuclear weapons were successfully deployed in World War II when the United States dropped atomic bombs on the Japanese cities of Hiroshima and Nagasaki. The worst nuclear accident to date was in Chernobyl, Ukraine, at a nuclear power plant.

DOMESTIC TERRORISM

The FBI provides a definition of *domestic terrorism*. The term refers to activities involving acts dangerous to human life that are a violation of the criminal laws of the United States or of any state; that appear to be intended to intimidate or coerce a civilian population; that are intended to influence the policy of a government by mass destruction, assassination, or kidnapping; and that occur primarily within the territorial jurisdiction of the United States based on federal statute (18 U.S.C. § 2331(5)).

In the United States, acts of terrorism date back to the Revolutionary War. The definition of an act as terrorism depends on how one views the cause. There is an often-used saying: "One man's terrorist is another man's freedom fighter." Before you move on, take a moment and reflect on that statement and describe what it means to you.

Although each of us firmly believes that we understand terrorism, we seem to lose sight of why such acts occur. Here are a few examples that are of importance in U.S. history. How would you classify these actors—as freedom fighters or terrorists?

- When George Washington led the thirteen colonies in the Revolutionary War, was he a terrorist, as described by the British military, or a freedom fighter?
- In 1859 when abolitionist John Brown raided a federal arsenal at Harpers Ferry, Virginia, with the intent of arming slaves to fight for their freedom, Brown was arrested and convicted of treason. Would you consider him a terrorist or freedom fighter?
- Dr. Martin Luther King, Jr., led a nonviolent movement. Was he a freedom fighter or terrorist?
- The Ku Klux Klan was introduced in 1866 and rose to power thereafter. Are the members freedom fighters or terrorists?

There have been many such acts and organizations in the United States over the years. Following is a list of some of the organizations and causes and what they have stood for in the United States:

- *Ku Klux Klan:* Historically, there are three eras to the Klan.

  1. The first era was post–Civil War when the Klan was founded as a social fraternity in Pulaski, Tennessee, in 1866. In 1867, General Nathan Bedford Forrest, the Grand Wizard of the Empire, converted the Klan into a paramilitary force developed to directly oppose reconstruction of the South. The Klan terrorized recently freed slaves through coercion, intimidation, cross burnings, beatings, murder, and lynching (Chalmers, 1987).
  2. The second era of the Klan began in 1915 and is considered the World War I Era. The group rose to prominence advocating

patriotism and white Protestant supremacy, which produced an anti-Catholic sentiment. There were a host of new ideas, the publication of Thomas Dixon's novel *The Clansman* (1905), and in 1915 the release of the movie *Birth of a Nation* by D.W. Griffith; out of these events, a new Klan emerged (Quarles, 1999).

3. The third era of the Klan is associated with the rise of the civil rights movement in the 1960s and is still occurring today. The Klan was responsible for a number of atrocities, including the bombing of the Sixteenth Street Baptist Church in Birmingham, Alabama, that killed three little girls (Fleming, 2004); the 1964 kidnapping and murder of three members of the Congress of Racial Equality (CORE) in Neshoba County, Mississippi (Gray, 2007); the 1981 beating, murder, and hanging of Michael Donald in Birmingham, Alabama (Waldrep, 2006); and the 1998 dragging death of James Byrd, Jr., in Jasper, Texas, by members of the Confederate Knights of America (Shenk, 2003). Although the last act listed dates back to 1998, there is another issue rising to the forefront in U.S. politics and Americanism: immigration law and immigration reform. The Klan will use topics such as these as a platform for patriotism with an underlying message of white supremacy to solidify their political agenda.

• *Armed Forces of Puerto Rican National Liberation,* or in Spanish, *Fuerzas Armadas Liberacion Nacional Puertoriquena (FALN):* This group is a Puerto Rican clandestine terrorist group that has advocated independence for Puerto Rico and claimed responsibility for numerous bombings and robberies, causing a reign of terror in both the United States and Puerto Rico. Smith (1994) notes that the FALN claimed responsibility or was blamed for one hundred bombings, mostly in New York and Chicago, in the 1970s and early 1980s (p. 114).

• *Black Panther Party:* Originally known as the Black Panther Party for Self-Defense, this group was founded in October 1966 in Oakland, California, on a ten-point platform demanding employment, housing, education, freedom, justice, and an end to police brutality. The party ran a number of community-based programs that included, along with a host of others: child development center, consumer education classes, free medical programs, free breakfast for children, and legal aid (Smith, 1999). Baldwin (2006) posits that Panther Party members were considered angry black revolutionaries beginning with their dress, which consisted of black berets, black leather jackets, black pants, and black shoes. In addition, they legally armed themselves to defend the black community (pp. 67–68).

- *Weather Underground:* This was a splinter group of the Students for a Democratic Society. The Weather Underground used violence as a means for social and political change because of a 1969 Chicago police raid where they killed Black Panther leader Fred Hampton and Mark Clark. As a result of this incident, the Weathermen were formed. In 1970, the Weather Underground publicly announced a declaration of war against the United States. In that same month, a bomb that they were manufacturing accidentally detonated in a New York townhouse. The bomb was to be detonated at a military dance hall. In June 1970, they detonated a bomb at the New York City Police Department headquarters (Berger, 2006; Jacobs, 1997; Varon, 2004).

- *Symbionese Liberation Army (SLA):* This group began in the fall of 1973 when no more than a dozen white, college-educated children of middle-class families adopted a seven-headed snake as their symbol, a black ex-convict as their leader, and the phrase "Death to the fascist insect that preys upon the life of the people" as their slogan. They came to prominence by assassinating the Oakland, California, school superintendent with cyanide-tipped bullets. In February 1974, the SLA kidnapped newspaper heiress Patricia Hearst, who claimed that she was brainwashed; in March 1974, she was involved in a bank robbery with SLA members. Hurst was arrested in 1975 and later convicted of the bank robbery. Other members remained free until 2002 when they were convicted of a murder that occurred in 1975 (Martin, 2007; Perl, 2003).

FBI Counterintelligence Program (COINTELPRO)

Some may wonder why many Americans are leery of the Patriot Act and giving law enforcement unfettered access to personal records, the ability to use wire tapping without warrants, and the ability to declare someone an enemy combatant of the state and place him or her in jail void of due process. Some of the apprehension arises out of the activities of the FBI's **Counterintelligence Program (COINTELPRO),** which operated between 1956 and 1971, and was charged with targeting foreign intelligence agencies operating in the United States during the Cold War (Davis, 1992; Stone, 2008).

Members of COINTELPRO not only spied on Dr. Martin Luther King, Jr., but also used counterintelligence propaganda to discredit his

Counterintelligence Program (COINTELPRO)
program operated by the FBI between 1956 and 1971, and charged with targeting foreign intelligence agencies operating in the United States during the Cold War.

activities and the civil rights movement. An FBI memorandum dated December 1964 revealed subversive efforts by the FBI to get Dr. King to remove himself from the civil rights movement by meeting with Negro leaders and supplying them with information showing that Dr. King was a threat to the success of the movement. In turn, the leaders would seek to get Dr. King to step down. The FBI even prepared and sent an anonymous message suggesting that Dr. King commit suicide (Churchill & Vander Wall, 2002).

On another occasion, a special unit of the Cook County Police raided the headquarters of the Illinois chapter of the Black Panther Party. When the raid was over, the police fired between 82 and 99 shots, and the occupants only fired one. An FBI internal memorandum takes credit for being the sole source of information that led to the raid, and it knew that the weapons inside were purchased and possessed legally (Carroll, 1990; Churchill & Vander Wall, 2002).

Such activities were not limited to the FBI. In 1980 it was discovered that the Michigan State Police had the largest cache of files in the United States on its citizens; they were called the *Red Squad Files*. The Michigan State Police and the Detroit Police Department collected information and kept files on factory workers and their union activity, as well as students and their campus affiliations. The records contained information obtained from utilities, employers, landlords, and third-party informants (Donner, 1992; Heineman, 1994). In 1980, then Governor Milliken signed into law a bill entitled "Michigan's Interstate Law Enforcement Intelligence Organizations Act," stating: "I signed this act into law in order to protect the privacy of individual citizens and, at the same time, provide law enforcement agencies with the tools they need" (*Detroit Free Press*, p. 10A).

The Turner Diaries and Its Role in U.S. Domestic Terrorism

The Turner Diaries is a fictional book that details overthrowing the U.S. government and the rise of "White America." The text presents a series of cataclysmic events that are put into motion by a group known as The Organization; these events occur between the years 1991 and 1993. The book was written in 1978 by William Luther Pearce III, who published it using the pseudonym Andrew Macdonald. The book does not recognize the past, only its great victory and the future; the chronology of time is sorted into two categories:

1. BNE – Before the New Era, which denotes before the revolution
2. NE – The New Era, which denotes after the revolution

The Turner Diaries

a fictional book that details overthrowing the U.S. government and the rise of "White America."

The revolution described in *The Turner Diaries* begins in the United States and later spreads throughout the world.

The Turner Diaries details a series of fictitious assaults that are closely related to the loss of rights and the egregious attacks on privacy by the government. One incident that stands out is the bombing of the J. Edgar Hoover Building in Washington, DC. The details of the bombing are similar to those of the Oklahoma City bombing. For many, *The Turner Diaries* was a blueprint for the Oklahoma City bombing (Jenkins, 2003; Lief & Caldwell, 2006; Wright, 2007). The book describes a fictitious gun control law entitled the Cohen Act, which called for seizing weapons of all Americans. The passage of the Brady Bill in 1993 stipulating a five-day waiting period, banning assault-type weapons, and limiting magazine capacity was seen by many as a step in the direction of the fictitious Cohen Act.

ANNIVERSARY DATES AND HOMEGROWN TERRORISM

Anniversary dates are important to terrorist organizations. These dates may identify a celebration of victory, or may identify when a government has perpetrated some form of aggression against the organization, its members, or their belief system. Ganor (2005) states that various organizations celebrate anniversary dates to mark a historic event, religious or national holiday, key dates in the organization's past, significant offensive action where the organization or members were lost, or large attacks perpetrated by the organization or a sympathizing organization (p. 36). Ganor notes that it may not be the anniversary date that is the motive, but the date is used as a symbol to remind the public and to send a message of fear and show who is in control.

Schrich (2005) notes that **April 19** is the anniversary of significant events in U.S. history, and is recognized by militia groups within the United States as a special day. The events in question are: the Oklahoma City bombing; the FBI assault on the Branch Davidians in Waco, Texas; and the federal government's initial surveillance of Randy Weaver at Ruby Ridge. It is also the date of the attack outlined in *The Turner Diaries* (p. 70). A description of the Ruby Ridge and Waco, Texas, events follows.

- *Ruby Ridge, 1991:* Randy Weaver, a devout white supremacist, was wanted on warrants for gun running. FBI agents and the U.S Marshals Service were surveilling Weaver's residence with no identifying

April 19

the anniversary of significant events in U.S. history, recognized by militia groups within the United States as a special day. The events in question are: the Oklahoma City bombing; the FBI assault on the Branch Davidians in Waco, Texas; and the federal government's initial surveillance of Randy Weaver at Ruby Ridge. It is also the date of the attack outlined in *The Turner Diaries*.

markers that they were police or the FBI. The agents killed Weaver's dog, and there was an exchange of gunfire in which Weaver's 14-year-old son Samuel and Deputy U.S. Marshall Degan were killed. Subsequently, an FBI sniper killed Weaver's wife while she was holding their 10-month-old infant (Burns, Peterson, & Kallstorm, 2005; Hamm, 1997; Spitzer, 2001). Dees (1996) quotes Weaver as saying: "We have nothing to lose; if we die we win, because we become martyrs and that furthers the cause" (p. 10).

- *Waco, Texas, April 19, 1993:* This event began in a similar way to the Ruby Ridge incident. It stemmed from a botched attempt to arrest Branch Davidian Leader David Koresh and several of his followers on weapons charges and the execution of a search warrant for the Branch Davidian complex. Alcohol, Tobacco, and Firearms (ATF) agents attempted their initial assault on February 28, 1993. During the February 28 assault, four ATF agents were killed and sixteen others were wounded. The number of Branch Davidians that were wounded and/or killed was unknown. The FBI took command of the scene upon the death of the ATF agents; the incident lasted for 51 days and culminated in a final assault on April 19. On that day, the FBI announced to all in the compound that they were under arrest and that the FBI intended to deploy tear gas. The FBI used a combat engineering vehicle to breach the compound and deploy large quantities of tear gas. The FBI reported that fires were set on the inside of the compound by the Branch Davidians, and they also reported hearing gunfire from inside, which they believed came from the members either committing suicide or killing each other. Nine Davidians fled the scene as the fires started and were arrested (Beckwith, 1994; Biet-Hallahmi, 2002; Wagner-Pacifici, 2000).

RIGHT-WING EXTREMISM

This chapter has discussed extremist groups of the 1960s and 1970s. Today, the list of such groups is ever-changing, and they may well number into the hundreds.

Right-wing groups in the United States are in a constant state of flux (Martin, 2007; Michael, 2003). Smith (1994) offers some very important characteristics concerning right-wing extremists: they are anticommunist, very religious, and separatists who live in compounds. In fact, many use Christianity in their title, such as the Christian Patriots Defense League and the Church of the Creator (pp. 39–40). Quinley and Glock (1983) note that right-wing groups' ideology includes prejudice and hatred toward minorities, the cultivation of extremist politics, economic disconnects or inequalities, preservation of the good old days before America became diverse, hatred for the liberal press, and xenophobia and homophobia (pp. 174–175).

Although Smith provides that right-wing groups live in compounds and in rural areas, many right-wing extremists follow a much different credo, known as the *lone wolf*. A **lone wolf** is a person who espouses the beliefs of right-wing extremism, yet does not openly discuss his or her beliefs. Lone wolves become members of the U.S. establishment, local and state governments, and law enforcement organizations; they influence politics and decision making as well as wait for the call to rise to power. The idea is that they will be so deeply entrenched with power and influence, they can force change through either violence or political influence. This concept is advocated by Louis Beam, Grand Dragon of the Texas Knights of the Ku Klux Klan, and Tom Metzger, leader of the White Aryan Resistance (W.A.R.), and is known as leaderless resistance (Gerstenfeld, 2004; Michael, 2003; Reynolds, 2004). With no leader, the members of such groups cannot be identified.

You may wonder how many actual terrorist incidents occur in the United States annually. Between the years 1980 and 2005, there was a total of 318 terrorist incidents committed in the United States, according to the FBI (2006, p. 11), which translates to an average of 12.72 incidents per year during these years. Some question, however, whether the number may be higher.

Although the list of right-wing groups is vast, the problem in identifying the number of incidents in which they are involved may lie in how their acts are classified. Some of the crimes in question may be classified and prosecuted as hate crimes or other crimes such as robberies, murder, criminal mischief, arson, or bombings, which precludes them from being classified as terrorist incidents (Christian, 2004). The reason why many of these acts are prosecuted and classified as crimes may lie in the terrorism legislation and the specific definitions. For example, New York State Statute 490, the Anti-Terrorism Act of 2001, defines *terrorism crimes* as:

> Commit terrorist acts, Make terrorist threats, Solicit or provide support for terrorist acts, or Hinder the prosecution of terrorists. In New York, a person is now guilty of the crime of "Terrorism" when he or she commits a "specified offense" with the intent to accomplish one of three goals: Intimidate or coerce a civilian population; Influence the policy of a unit of government; or Affect the conduct of a unit of government.

lone wolf

a person who espouses the beliefs of right-wing extremism, yet does not openly discuss his or her beliefs. Lone wolves become members of the U.S. establishment, local and state governments, and law enforcement organizations; they influence politics and decision making as well as wait for the call to rise to power.

The problem with such legislation is that it requires *specific intent* and requires the prosecution to prove each of the elements associated with terrorism beyond a reasonable doubt. Therefore, it is easier to prosecute an individual under commonly used criminal offenses.

HOMELAND SECURITY AND INTELLIGENCE GATHERING

Before the attacks on September 11, 2001, the United States was protected by a number of individual government entities that acted as if they were solely responsible for protecting the borders of the United States from foreign aggression and terrorist acts. In an industry where intelligence information is a country's life blood, intelligence sharing was nonexistent. In essence, each agency worked in an intelligence vacuum, which resulted in the 9/11 catastrophe (Best, 2008; Gill & Phythian, 2006; Ratcliffe, 2008; Zegart, 2007). In response to the agencies' failure, the federal government moved swiftly by passing two pieces of legislation: the Uniting and Strengthening America by Providing Appropriate Tools Required to Intercept and Obstruct Terrorism Act of 2001 (USA Patriot Act) on October 26, 2001; and the Homeland Security Act of 2002, which established the Department of Homeland Security. In December 2004, the Intelligence Reform and Terrorism Prevention Act (IRTPA) was passed, which established the National Counterterrorism Center (NCTC).

The moves made by the federal government were supported by Priest and Eilperin (2002), who reported that during closed-door hearings of the House-Senate Intelligence Committee investigating the September 11th attacks, there was no smoking gun or single piece of evidence that would have prevented the attacks (p. A01). The 9/11 Commission noted that to prevent further attacks, the U.S. intelligence infrastructure needed to be strengthened, making five recommendations for organizing the government's response. At the top of the list was the coordination and sharing of information and knowledge as key to success in preventing future attacks (p. 571).

Patriot Act of 2001

Prior to the Patriot Act, the FBI's actions during the Counterintelligence Program (COINTELPRO) severely hampered their ability to investigate American citizens and terrorist activity after 1971 (Goldstein, 2001; Powers, 2004). After the September 11, 2001, attacks, it was clear that change was necessary in order to protect U.S. interests, and thus the Patriot Act was passed forty-five days after the attacks. The Patriot Act provided the following provisions for federal law enforcement: Enhancing Domestic Security Against Terrorism, Enhanced Surveillance Procedures, International Money Laundering Abatement and Anti-Terrorist Financing Act, Protecting the Border, Removing Obstacles to Investigating Terrorism, Providing for Victims of Terrorism, Increased Information Sharing for Critical Infrastructure Protection, Strengthening Criminal Laws Against Terrorism, and Improved Intelligence. In 2006 the Patriot Act was reauthorized and provided the following additions: an Assistant Attorney General for National Security, Terrorism Financing, Protects Mass Transportation, and the Combat Methamphetamine Epidemic Act of 2005.

It is agreed that these tools are necessary to protect the United States from extremists, be they right-wing/homegrown, left-wing/single-issue, or Muslim extremists who look to destroy the United States and/or convert its citizens to Islam. However, many Americans fear that these tools will be abused as they were by COINTELPRO. A system of checks and balances was created with the 2006 reauthorization providing for an Assistant Attorney General for National Security (Raskin, Spero, & Ehrenreich, 2007; Wechsler, 2003). Remember, all major court cases that direct and/or control police behavior are a direct result of a lack of rules or guidance by the courts that allowed police abuses; this is why a system of checks and balances must be in place.

Department of Homeland Security

The next step in protecting the United States came with the passage of the Homeland Security Act of 2002, which established the Department of Homeland Security (DHS). The mission of DHS, as prescribed by the act, is to: prevent terrorist attacks within the United States; reduce the vulnerability of the United States to terrorism; minimize the damage, and assist in the recovery, from terrorist attacks that do occur within the United States; carry out all functions of entities transferred to the department, including by acting as a focal point regarding natural and human-made crises and emergency planning; ensure that the functions of the agencies and subdivisions within the department that are not related directly to securing the homeland are not diminished or neglected except by a specific explicit act of Congress; ensure that the overall economic security of the United States is not diminished by efforts, activities, and programs aimed at securing the homeland; and monitor connections between illegal drug trafficking and terrorism, coordinate efforts to sever such connections, and otherwise contribute to efforts to interdict illegal drug trafficking.

In defining DHS's mission, the act is very specific regarding the investigation and prosecution of terrorists. The law prohibits DHS as a whole from participation in such activities except for those law enforcement agencies that had the authority before they were transferred to DHS. The statute provides that primary responsibility for investigating and prosecuting acts of terrorism shall be vested not in the department, but rather in federal, state, and local law enforcement agencies with jurisdiction over the acts in question.

The creation of DHS combined a host of organizations, with each bringing to the table a particular specialty. The agencies that make up DHS were established long before 9/11 and are known to all Americans: U.S. Customs and Border Protection, Transportation Security Administration, U.S. Citizenship and Immigration Service, U.S. Immigration and Customs Enforcement, U.S. Secret Service, U.S. Coast Guard, and Federal Emergency Management Agency.

The one agency in DHS that has become suspect is the Federal Emergency Management Agency (FEMA) because of its actions regarding the city of New Orleans during and after Hurricane Katrina. In response to FEMA's failure and much public criticism in 2007, the Post-Katrina Emergency Management Reform Act was passed, which added: the U.S. Fire Administration (USFA), the Office of Grants and Training (G&T), the Chemical Stockpile Emergency Preparedness Division (CSEP), the Radiological Emergency Preparedness Program (REPP), and the Office of National Capital Region Coordination (NCRC). The addition of these agencies is designed to help FEMA provide a more efficient and coordinated attack during times of disaster.

Federal Bureau of Investigation (FBI)

The FBI has always been a lead investigative agency regarding domestic and international terrorism. Since the September 11th attacks, their priority has been the prevention of terrorism. In order to accomplish this goal, they have shifted their resources from traditional criminal investigations to terrorism; increased the number of intelligence analysts and linguists; and increased the number of Joint Terrorism Task Forces and information-sharing capabilities with state and local agencies, including law enforcement agencies (Alexander & Kraft, 2007; Byman, 2007).

As mentioned earlier, a major failure of U.S. intelligence organizations was that they operated in an intelligence vacuum, void of sharing information. As a result of the pre–September 11th snafu, the FBI participates in the National Counterterrorism Center (NCTC), which is responsible for integrating intelligence related to terrorism; conducts strategic operational planning; serves as central repository for terrorism intelligence; provides intelligence support government-wide; and allows connectivity and access to information technology systems/databases of participating agencies. The agencies who participate in the NCTC with the FBI are the Central Intelligence Agency (CIA), Department of Defense (DOD), Department of Homeland Security (DHS), Department of Energy (DOE), Health and Human Services (HHS), Nuclear Regulatory Commission (NRC), and the Capitol Police (Bolton, 2007; Posner, 2005).

In addition to the NCTC, the FBI also participates in the Foreign Terrorist Tracking Task Force with the CIA, DOD, Immigration and Customs Enforcement (ICE), and the Office of Personnel Management (OPM). This task force provides information that helps keep foreign terrorists and their supporters out of the United States or leads to their removal, location, detention, surveillance, or prosecution (Alexander & Kraft, 2007; Forest, 2006b; Steven & Gunaratna, 2004).

The final piece of intelligence information sharing is the Terrorist Screening Center (TSC). The TSC provides a single comprehensive database of known or suspected terrorists (both domestic and international) and manages one, consolidated watch list available in real-time to federal, state, and local officers 24/7, accessible through the National Crime Information Center (NCIC) (Ball, 2004; Sims & Gerber, 2009).

Central Intelligence Agency (CIA)

The National Security Act of 1947 charged the CIA with coordinating the nation's intelligence activities and correlating, evaluating, and disseminating intelligence affecting national security. In December 2004, the Intelligence Reform and Terrorism Prevention Act created the position of Director of National Intelligence (DNI), which oversees the intelligence community and the National Counterterrorism Center (NCTC), discussed previously in the section on the FBI.

NEW YORK POLICE DEPARTMENT'S RESPONSE TO TERRORISM

Since the attacks of September 11th, the New York City Police Department (NYPD) has developed a Counterterrorism Unit equivalent to that of federal law enforcement with the understanding that a city cannot rely solely on the efforts of the federal government (Safir & Whitman, 2003). This was clearly the case during Hurricane Katrina and its aftermath. The message to all local officials is that they need to be as prepared as possible with the necessary resources.

The Office of Deputy Commissioner of Counterterrorism is complete with a host of specialists to direct the mission. It is divided into seven subunits, each with its own specialty: Terrorism Threat Analysis Group, Training Section, Critical Infrastructure Protection Section and the Transportation Security Section, CBRNE Policy and Planning Section, Special Projects Unit, NYPD SHIELD Unit, and Emergency Response and Planning Section (Horowitz, 2003).

In addition to the command structure, the NYPD has members of its agency assigned to the Joint Terrorism Task Force. The unit also strategizes and deploys teams of officers to disrupt terrorist plots with massive shows of force in such locations as bridges and tunnels, subways, and the financial district. They also have officers assigned in other countries, which is a testament to their resolve in preventing future attacks in New York. Currently officers are stationed in Sydney, Australia; Amman, Jordan; Santo Domingo, Dominican Republic; Toronto; Montreal; Singapore; London; Interpol headquarters in Lyons, France; and Tel Aviv, Israel (Dickey, 2009).

CONCLUSION

Now that you have completed this chapter, take a moment and reflect on this question: What should the role of law enforcement be in regard to terrorism? Should they be proactive like the city of New York? The role of police in American society is so vast that it is difficult to tie it to one task or a series of tasks. In fact, their role in terrorism prevention, intelligence gathering, and as first responders should just be considered in the realm of their assigned duties, with one caveat: information sharing.

The key to successfully combating terrorism is in understanding the enemy's motivations. The life blood of such a war is the ability to collect, analyze, and share intelligence information. This task is compounded because the rights of U.S. citizens weigh in the balance.

 DISCUSSION QUESTIONS

1. Explain the change in the role of local law enforcement agencies subsequent to September 11, 2001. What is the reason for this change?

2. Can you describe a correlation between the Patriot Act and the social contract described by Thomas Hobbes? Relate the concepts of Hobbes's social contract to the components of the Patriot Act.

3. Which of the five forms of terrorism do you believe presents the greatest danger to modern American society? Explain.

4. In Grossman's description of the power of the group in time of war, he states: "when in battle the most powerful commitment is not self-preservation but the sense of accountability to fellow comrades." Explain how this may apply to both terrorist cells and the military units that combat them.

5. What is the significance of anniversary dates to terrorism? Describe the significance of April 19 to right-wing extremists in the United States.

 ## RESEARCH TOPICS

Following are two topics that are central to this chapter. Choose one, and research the topic based on the instructions of your professor.

- *Motivations for homegrown terror.* This chapter has a rather lengthy discussion regarding homegrown terror in the United States. In many of these instances, the groups state that they love this country. Select one organization that you have an interest in, and research its history and message. Determine the motivations for the group members' acts. Are they truly terrorists or heroes? Defend your answer.

- *Group think.* This chapter discusses the concept group think. Pick an act of violence in which police have been involved or acts committed against this country by a terrorist organization, and research the concept of group think as it applies to their decision making. In your research, describe how the group arrived at a consensus to perpetrate the act(s) of violence in which they were involved. Defend your answer.

 ## BIBLIOGRAPHY

Alexander, Y., & Kraft, M. (2007). *Evolution of U.S. counterterrorism policy.* Westport, CT: Greenwood.

Allen, C. (2006). *God's terrorists: The Wahhabi cult and the hidden roots of modern Jihad.* Cambridge, MA: Da Capo Press.

American Legislative Exchange Council. (2003). *Animal and ecological terrorism in America.* Washington, DC: Author.

Anti-Defamation League. (1996). *Danger: Extremism: The major vehicles and voices on America's far-right fringe.* New York: Author.

Baldwin, B. (2006). In the shadow of the gun: The Black Panther Party, the Ninth Amendment, and discourses of self-defense. In J. Lazerow & Y. R. Williams (Eds.), *In search of the Black Panther Party: New perspectives on a revolutionary movement* (pp. 67–95). Durham, NC: Duke University Press.

Ball, H. (2004). *The USA Patriot Act of 2001: Balancing civil liberties and national security: A reference handbook.* Santa Barbara, CA: ABC-CLIO.

Barnaby, F. (2004). *How to build a nuclear bomb: And other weapons of mass destruction.* New York: Nation Books.

Beckwith, C. (1994). What went wrong in Waco? Poor planning, bad tactics result in botched raid. In J. R. Lewis (Ed.), *From the ashes: Making sense of Waco.* Lanham, MD: Rowman & Littlefield.

Berger, D. (2006). *Outlaws of America: The Weather Underground and the politics of solidarity.* Oakland, CA: AK Press.

Bergman, W. (2003). Pogroms. In W. Heitmeyer & J. Hagan (Eds.), *International handbook of violence research* (pp. 351–368). Dordrecht, The Netherlands: Kluwer Academic Press.

Best, Jr., R. A. (2008). Sharing law enforcement and intelligence information: The congressional role. In G. M. Kessler (Ed.), *Law and law enforcement issues* (pp. 197–212). New York: Nova Science.

Biet-Hallahmi, B. (2002). Rebirth and death: The violent potential of apocalyptic dreams. In C. E. Stout & K. Schwab (Eds.), *The psychology of terrorism: Theoretical understandings and perspectives* (pp. 163–190). Westport, CT: Greenwood.

Bolton, M. K. (2007). *U.S. national security and foreign policymaking after 9/11: Present at the re-creation.* Lanham, MD: Rowman & Littlefield.

Boyle, L. C. (2007). The U.S. terrorist screening center: Connecting the dots for law enforcement agencies at all levels. *Police Chief, 74*(10).

Brezina, C. (2005). *Weapons of mass destruction: Proliferation and control.* New York: Rosen.

Bullock, J. A., Haddow, G. D., Coppola, D., Ergin, E., Westerman, L., & Yeletaysi, S. (2006). *Introduction to homeland security* (2nd ed.). New York: Butterworth-Heinemann.

Burns, V., Peterson, K. D., & Kallstorm, J. K. (2005). *Terrorism: A documentary and reference guide.* Westport, CT: Greenwood.

Byman, D. (2007). *The five front war: The better way to fight global jihad.* Danvers, MA: John Wiley & Sons.

Caldwell, E. (1976, February 23). Symbionese liberation army: Terrorism from left. *New York Times,* p. 63.

Carroll, P. N. (1990). *It seemed like nothing happened: America in the 1970s.* New Brunswick, NJ: Rutgers University Press.

Chalmers, D. M. (1987). *Hooded Americanism: The history of the Ku Klux Klan.* Durham, NC: Duke University Press.

Christian, W. (2004). Defining terrorism in national and international law. In C. Walter, S. Voneky, V. Roben, & F. Schorkopf (Eds.), *Terrorism as a challenge for national and international law; Security versus liberty* (pp. 23–44). New York: Springer.

Churchill, W., & Vander Wall, J. (2002). *The COINTELPRO papers.* Cambridge, MA: South End Press.

Cockerham, L. G., Walden, Jr., T. L., Dallas, C. E., Mickley, Jr., G. A., & Landauer, M. A. (2007). Ionizing radiation. In A. W. Hayes (Ed.), *Principles and methods of toxicology.* Boca Raton, FL: CRC Press.

Committee on Assessment of Security Technologies for Transportation. (2006). *Defending the U.S. air transportation system against chemical and biological attacks.* Washington, DC: National Academies Press.

Committee on the Judiciary, United States Senate, 108th Congress. (2003). *Narco-terrorism: International drug trafficking and terrorism: A dangerous mix.* Washington, DC: U.S. Government Printing Office.

Craddock, B. J. (2005). *Posture statement of General Brantz J. Craddock, U.S. Army.* Washington, DC: Government Printing Office.

Cronkhite, C. L. (2007). *Criminal justice administration: Strategies for the 21st century.* Sudbury, MA: Jones & Bartlett.

Davis, J. A. (2006). Over a decade of counterproliferation. In B. R Schneider & J. A. Davis (Eds.), *Avoiding the abyss: Progress, shortfalls, and the way ahead in combating the MD threat* (pp. 1–18). Westport, CT: Greenwood.

Davis, J. K. (1992). *Spying on America: The FBI's domestic counterintelligence program.* Westport, CT: Praeger.

Davis, L. M., Riley, J. K., Ridgeway, G., Pace, J., Cotton, S. K., Steinberg, P. S., Damphousse, K., & Smith, B. L. (2004). *When terrorism hits home: How prepared are state and local law enforcement agencies?* Santa Monica, CA: Rand Corporation.

Dees, M. (1996). *The gathering storm.* New York: Harper Collins.

Dickey, C. (2009). *Securing the city: Inside America's best counterterror force: The NYPD.* New York: Simon & Schuster.

Donner, F. (1992). *Protectors of privilege: Red squads and police repression in urban America.* Berkeley: University of California Press.

Dreyfuss, R. (2005). *Devil's game: How the United States helped unleash fundamentalist Islam.* New York: Macmillan.

Elkies, L. (2005, November 3). NYPD is Australia-bound, Kelly says. *New York Sun Times.*

Emerson, S. (2003). *American jihad: The terrorists living among us.* New York: The Free Press.

Enders, W., & Sandler, T. (2006). *The political economy of terrorism.* New York: Cambridge University Press.

Federal Bureau of Investigation (FBI). (2001). *Terrorism 2000/2001*. Washington, DC: U.S. Department of Justice.

Federal Bureau of Investigation (FBI). (2006). *Terrorism 2002–2005*. Washington, DC: U.S. Department of Justice.

Ferguson, C. D., Kazi, T., & Perera, J. (2003). *Commercial radioactive sources: Surveying the security risks.* Monterey, CA: Monterey Institute of International Studies.

Fleming, C. G. (2004). *In the shadow of Selma: The continuing struggle for civil rights in the rural South.* Lanham, MD: Rowman & Littlefield.

Forest, J. J. F. (2006a). *Homeland security: Borders and points of entry.* Westport, CT: Praeger Security International.

Forest, J. J. F. (2006b). *Homeland security: Public spaces and social institutions.* Westport, CT: Praeger Security International.

Forsberg, R., Driscoll, W., Webb, D., & Dean, J. (1995). *Nonproliferation primer: Preventing the spread of nuclear, chemical, and biological weapons.* Cambridge, MA: MIT Press.

Ganor, B. (2005). *The counter-terrorism puzzle: A guide for decision makers.* New Brunswick, NJ: Transaction.

Gerstenfeld, P. B. (2004). *Hate crimes: Causes, controls, and controversies.* Thousand Oaks, CA: Sage.

Gill, P., & Phythian, M. (2006). *Intelligence in an insecure world.* Malden, MA: Polity Press.

Goldstein, R. J. (2001). *Political repression in modern America from 1870 to 1976.* Champaign, IL: University of Illinois Press.

Goodin, R. E. (2006). *What's wrong with terrorism?* Cambridge, UK: Polity.

Gray, S. P. (2007). Mississippi burning. In S. M. Chermak & F. Y. Bailey (Eds.), *Crimes and trials of the century* (pp. 247–268). Westport, CT: Greenwood.

Grossman, D. (1995). *On killing: The psychological cost of learning killing in war and society.* New York: Back Bay Books.

Hamm, M. S. (1997). *Apocalypse in Oklahoma: Waco and Ruby Ridge avenged.* Lebanon, NH: Northeastern University Press.

Heineman, K. J. (1994). *Campus wars: The peace movement at American state universities during the Vietnam era.* New York: NYU Press.

Hoffman, B. (1993). Terrorists targeting: Tactics, trends, and potentialities. In C. C. Harmon & P. Wilkinson (Eds.), *Technology and terrorism* (pp. 12–29). New York: Routledge.

Horowitz, C. (2003, January 27). The NYPD's war on terror. *New York Magazine*, archives.

Hudson, R. A. (1999). *Who becomes a terrorist and why: The 1999 government report on profiling terrorists.* Guilford, CT: The Lyons Press.

Ibbetson, D. J. (2001). *A historical introduction to the law of obligations.* Cary, NC: Oxford University Press.

International Association of Chiefs of Police (IACP). (2005). *Post 9-11 policing: The crime control–homeland security paradigm. Taking command of new realities.* Washington, DC: Author.

Jacobs, R. (1997). *The way the wind blew: A history of the Weather Underground.* Brooklyn, NY: Verso.

Janis, I. L. (1972). *Victims of groupthink.* New York: Houghton Mifflin.

Jenkins, P. (2003). *Images of terror: What we can and can't know about terrorism.* Edison, NJ: Aldine Transaction.

Jewett, R., & Lawrence, J. S. (2004). *Captain America and the crusade against evil: The dilemma of zealous nationalism.* Grand Rapids, MI: Wm. B. Eerdmans.

Kamrava, M. (2005). *The modern Middle East: A political history since the First World War.* Berkeley: University of California Press.

Kean, T. L., National Commission on Terrorist Attacks upon the United States, Hamilton, L. H., & New York Times Company. (2004). *The 9/11 report: The National Commission on Terrorist Attacks upon the United States.* New York: MacMillan.

King, S. C. (2007). *Seeds of war.* Bloomington, IN: AuthorHouse.

Kirk, M., McLeod, M., & Levis, K. (Producers). Kirk, M. (Director). (1995). *Waco: The inside story.* United States: Public Broadcasting Service.

Langford, B. E. (2004). *Introduction to weapons of mass destruction: Radiological, chemical, and biological.* Hoboken, NJ: John Wiley & Sons.

Laqueur, W. (1999). *The new terrorism: Fanaticism and the arms of mass destruction.* New York: Oxford University Press.

Laqueur, W. (2004). *Voices of terror: Manifestos, writings, and manuals of Al Qaeda, Hamas, and other terrorists from around the world and throughout the ages.* New York: Reed Press.

Lengel, A. (2005, September 16). Little progress in FBI probe of anthrax attacks: Internal report compiled as agents hope for a break. *Washington Post.*

Lief, M. S., & Caldwell, H. M. (2006). *The devil's advocate: Greatest closing arguments in criminal law.* New York: Simon & Schuster.

Litwak, R. (2007). *Regime change: U.S. strategy through the prism of 9/11.* Baltimore: Johns Hopkins University Press.

Lombroso, C. (2006). *Criminal man.* (M. Gibson & N. H. Rafter, Trans.). Durham, NC: Duke University Press. (Original work published 1876).

Lutz, J. M., & Lutz, B. L. (2004). *Global terrorism.* New York: Routledge.

Macdonald, A. (1978). *The Turner diaries.* New York: Barricade Books.

Mani, R. (2004). The root causes of terrorism and conflict prevention. In J. Bolden & T. G. Weiss (Eds.), *Terrorism and the UN before and after September 11* (pp. 219–242). Bloomington, IN: Indiana University Press.

Martin, G. (2007). *Essentials of terrorism: Concepts and controversies.* Thousand Oaks, CA: Sage.

McCauley, C. (2007). Psychological issues in understanding terrorism and the response to terrorism. In B. M. Bongar, L. M. Brown, L. E. Beutler, & P. G. Zimbardo (Eds.), *Psychology of terrorism* (pp. 13–31). New York: Oxford University Press.

McClelland, J. S. (1996). *A history of Western political thought.* New York: Routledge.

Michael, G. (2003). *Confronting right-wing extremism and terrorism in the USA.* New York: Routledge.

Michigan should disconnect from matrix system. (2004, August 5). *Detroit Free Press,* p. A10.

Murray, R. L. (2008). *Nuclear energy: An introduction to the concepts, systems, and applications of nuclear processes.* Burlington, MA: Butterworth-Heinemann.

New York State Statute 490, Anti-Terrorism Act of 2001.

Organisation for the Prohibition of Chemical Weapons. (2005). *Convention on the prohibition of the development, production, stockpiling, and use of chemical weapons and their destruction.* The Netherlands: Technical Secretariat of the Organisation for the Prohibition of Chemical Weapons.

Pahwa, P. K. (2004). The nuclear dimension. In R. Menon (Ed.), *Weapons of mass destruction: Options for India* (pp. 21–29). Thousand Oaks, CA: Sage.

Perl, L. (2003). *Terrorism.* Tarrytown, NY: Marshall Cavendish.

Pilisuk, M., & Rountree, J. A. (2008). *Who benefits from global violence and war: Uncovering a destructive system.* Westport, CT: Praeger Security International.

Posner, R. A. (2005). *Remaking domestic intelligence.* Stanford, CA: Hoover Institution Press.

Post, J. M. (1998). Terrorist psycho-logic: Terrorist behavior as a product of psychological forces. In W. Reich (Ed.), *Origins of terrorism: Psychologies, ideologies, theologies, and states of mind* (pp. 25–40). Washington, DC: Woodrow Wilson Center Press.

Post, J. M. (2004). *Leaders and their followers in a dangerous world: The psychology of political behavior.* Ithaca, NY: Cornell University Press.

Powers, R. G. (2004). *Broken: The troubled past and the uncertain future of the FBI.* New York: Simon & Schuster.

Priest, D., & Eilperin, J. (2002, July 11). Panel finds no smoking gun of 9/11 intelligence failures. *Washington Post,* p. A01.

Quarles, C. L. (1999). *The Ku Klux Klan and related American racialist and anti-Semitic organizations: A history and analysis.* Jefferson, NC: McFarland.

Quinley, H. E., & Glock, C. Y. (1983). *Anti-Semitism in America.* New Brunswick, NJ: Transaction Books.

Raskin, M., Spero, R., & Ehrenreich, B. (2007). *The four freedoms under siege: The clear and present danger from our national security state.* Westport, CT: Greenwood.

Ratcliffe, J. (2008). *Intelligence-led policing.* Portland, OR: Willan.

Reynolds, M. (2004). Virtual Reich. In R. Griffin & M. Feldman (Eds.), *Fascism: Post-war fascisms* (pp. 339–351). New York: Routledge.

Safir, H., & Whitman, E. (2003). *Security: Policing your homeland, your city, yourself.* New York: Macmillan.

Saha, G. B. (2006). *Physics and radiobiology of nuclear medicine.* New York: Springer.

Sauter, M., & Carafano, J. J. (2005). *Homeland security: A complete guide to understanding, preventing, and surviving terrorism.* New York: McGraw-Hill Professional.

Schertzing, P. D. (2007). Historical perspectives on the role of federal, state, and local law enforcement agencies in the United States in domestic intelligence operations. In S. Ozeren, I. D. Gunes, & D. M. Al-Badayneh (Eds.), *Understanding terrorism: Analysis of sociological and psychological aspects* (pp. 190–206). Amsterdam, The Netherlands: IOS Press.

Schrich, L. (2005). *Ritual and symbol in peacebuilding.* Bloomfield, CT: Kumarian Press.

Shay, S. (2008). *Islamic terror and the Balkans.* Piscataway, NJ: Transaction.

Shenk, A. H. (2003). Victim-offender mediation: The road to repairing hate crime injustice. In P. B. Gerstenfeld & D. R. Grant (Eds.), *Crimes of hate: Selected readings* (pp. 299–309). Thousand Oaks, CA: Sage.

Sims, J. E., & Gerber, B. (2009). *Vaults, mirrors, and masks: Rediscovering U.S. counterintelligence.* Washington, DC: Georgetown University Press.

Smith, B. (1994). *Terrorism in America: Pipe bombs, and pipe dream.* Albany, NY: State University of New York Press.

Smith, J. B. (1999). *An international history of the Black Panther Party.* New York: Garland.

Spitzer, R. J. (2001). *The right to bear arms and rights and liberties under the law.* Santa Barbara, CA: ABC-CLIO.

Steven, G. C. S., & Gunaratna, R. (2004). *Counterterrorism: A reference handbook.* Santa Barbara, CA: ABC-CLIO.

Stone, G. R. (2008). The Vietnam War: Spying on Americans. In D. Farber (Ed.), *Security v. liberty: Conflicts between civil liberties and national security in American history* (pp. 95–116). New York: Russell Sage Foundation.

U.S. Code, Title 18, Section 2331(5).

U.S. Congress. (2001). *Uniting and strengthening America by providing appropriate tools required to intercept and obstruct terrorism act (USA Patriot Act) of 2001* (Pub. Law 107-56). Washington, DC: Author.

U.S. Congress. (2002). *Homeland security act of 2002* (Pub. Law 107-296). Washington, DC: Author.

U.S. Congress. (2007). *The post-Katrina emergency management reform act* (Pub. Law 109-295). Washington, DC: Author.

U.S. Department of Justice. (2004). *Census of state and local law enforcement agencies, 2004.* Washington, DC: U.S. Government Printing Office.

Varon, J. (2004). *Bringing the war home: The Weather Underground, the Red Army Faction, and revolutionary violence in the sixties and seventies.* Berkeley: University of California Press.

Victoroff, J. I. (2006). *Tangled roots: Social and psychological factors in the genesis of terrorism.* Amsterdam, The Netherlands: IOS Press.

Waddington, P. A. J. (1994). *Liberty and order: Public order policing in a capital city.* London, England: UCL Press.

Wagner-Pacifici, R. E. (2000). *Theorizing the standoff: Contingency in action.* New York: Cambridge University Press.

Waldrep, C. (2006). *Lynching in America: A history in documents.* New York: NYU Press.

Wechsler, W. (2003). Law in order: Reconstructing U.S. national security. In E. R. Wittkopf & J. M. McCormick (Eds.), *The domestic sources of American foreign policy: Insights and evidence* (pp. 271–282). Lanham, MD: Rowman & Littlefield.

White, J. R. (2004). *Defending the homeland: Domestic intelligence, law enforcement and security.* Belmont, CA: Thomson/Wadsworth.

White, J. (2006). *Terrorism and homeland security.* Belmont, CA: Thomson/Wadsworth.

Williams, C. R., & Arrigo, B. A. (2008). *Ethics, crime, and criminal justice.* Upper Saddle River, NJ: Pearson/Prentice Hall.

Wilson, C. (2003). *Computer attack and cyber terrorism: Vulnerabilities and policy issues for Congress.* Washington, DC: Congressional Research Service, Library of Congress.

Wright, S. A. (2007). *Patriots, politics, and the Oklahoma City bombing.* New York: Cambridge University Press.

Zegart, A. B. (2007). *Spying blind: The CIA, the FBI, and the origins of 9/11.* Princeton, NJ: Princeton University Press.

CHAPTER 10

EDUCATION

OBJECTIVES

After completing this chapter, the student will be able to:

- Discuss the major historical events detailing the rise of education in law enforcement.
- Discuss the value of higher education.
- Discuss the career ending what ifs.
- Explain opportunities that education provides in the field of criminal justice.
- Describe the concept of law enforcement as a business.
- Discuss the necessity of higher education and its impact on a law enforcement career.
- Explain the significance of attending an accredited college/university.
- Describe the advantages/disadvantages of a two-year degree versus a four-year degree.
- Discuss the many fields of study associated with law enforcement and criminal justice.
- Discuss the pros and cons of online learning versus a traditional setting.

KEY TERMS

academic rigor – a strong level of academics in higher education provided by accredited institutions.

certifiable – means that a candidate has completed the academy and is eligible to take the state examination to become certified, and then will be able to be hired by an agency.

certified – means that once the candidate completes the academy, he or she can get a job immediately and not take a state examination.

diploma mill – sells college degrees and requires nothing more than a student's money.

DOC'S WORDS OF WISDOM

> *For those who enter law enforcement the value of education is often misunderstood. The old-timers complain that those who graduate from college are book smart and street dumb. Law enforcement managers argue that they need the college-educated officer to move the organization forward.*

INTRODUCTION

The concept of educating police dates back to the early 1900s and the efforts of Chief August Vollmer, who was the first chief to require that his police officers obtain college degrees. He was also responsible for the University of California at Berkeley establishing a criminal justice program in 1916 (Carte & Carte, 1975). However, it was not until the passage of the Law Enforcement Assistance Act in 1965 and the establishment of the Law Enforcement Education Program (LEEP) that education began to have real meaning in policing (Morn, 1995; Newman, 1993; Russell, Cosner, Gingrich, & Paynich, 2005). Education, however, is still a bone of contention; the debate within the profession in regard to the value of education remains, since most state training commissions still require only a high school diploma or GED to become a police officer (Blau, 1994; Dantzker, 2005).

Old-timers and street cops often ask: How will a degree save your ass when someone is shooting at you? This common sentiment is reflected in the introductory quotation: "The old-timers complain that those who graduate from college are book smart and street dumb." Yet, they forget that practical application begins when one graduates from the academy. In fact, very few officers are street smart at the beginning; this knowledge is acquired with experience. At best, with or without a degree, an agency can only hope that the people they select have common sense, the ability to reason, and at times can think abstractly (Vito, Maahs, & Holmes, 2006).

VALUE OF EDUCATION

Rowley and Hurtado (2002) state that the nonmonetary individual benefits of higher education include the tendency for postsecondary students to become more open-minded, more cultured, more rational, more consistent, and less authoritarian; these benefits are also passed along to succeeding generations. Palombo (1995) asserts that the higher the level of secondary education that officers have before entering policing, the more there exists a positive impact on their probationary period, academic status once employed, and a positive impact on the professional attitude of an officer (see Figure 10-1). Palombo also notes that education has a greater positive impact on officer attitudes before entering policing as compared to those who have no degree or obtain their degree after employment (pp. 144–145).

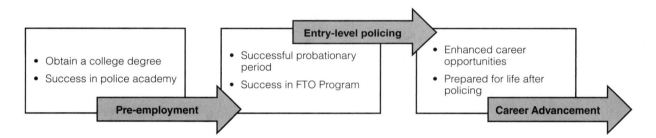

Figure 10-1   Value of a College Education
A college education has a positive impact on the future of an officer. It should not be looked upon as just getting a degree; rather, a college education should be valued as an investment toward a future in or out of policing.

For many who become law enforcement officers, that is the only job they have ever wanted. Some are drawn to the field because they think it is exciting. Others look to law enforcement for a career change. The reality is that people from all walks of life enter the profession, and for each there is a different motivation (Blank, 1990; Dellattre, 2002). Everyone who enters the profession has the idea that it is something they want to do, and they look forward to being successful. However, what many fail to consider before entering the academy are the potential pitfalls. Sure, everyone wonders about academics and the physical demands, but often that is where their self-doubt begins and ends. There are other obstacles that many do not consider.

Figure 10-2 provides a list of questions that come from the author's observations after twenty years of service as an officer, trainer, and mentor. These observations are based on encounters with those who entered the profession and ran into a series of obstacles for which they were not prepared.

1. What happens if you are eliminated in the preemployment process?

2. What happens if you fail the academy academically?

3. What happens if you are passed over during the hiring process because another applicant has a degree and you do not?

4. What happens if you get injured in the academy and can never work as a police officer?

5. What happens if you end up hating law enforcement?

6. What happens if you fail the FTO program?

7. What happens if your personal life demands that you quit?

8. What happens if you get laid off due to budget cuts?

9. What happens if you are terminated because of some action on the job?

10. What happens when you want to get promoted to sergeant or lieutenant and the requirements are that you must have a four-year degree?

Figure 10-2   Career-Ending What Ifs

The "what ifs" presented in Figure 10-2 represent some of the more common reasons that people are eliminated or decide that policing is no longer what they want to do. These individuals are left with a void and must decide on a new career path. Often those entering the profession never look at the possibility that their career could end at the drop of a hat or that they could be injured and never work as an officer again.

Law enforcement is very specialized and in actuality prepares one for very little in the civilian world. Those who come from another profession will always have that profession to return to as long as they maintain their credentials. For others who obtain a college degree before entering the profession, their degree can open a host of other career opportunities. A degree in criminal justice, for example, will offer opportunities in corrections, juvenile justice, forensics, compliance, parole and probation, homeland security, the courts, human services, child protection investigations, and so on (Belknap & Potter, 2007; Lambert & Regan, 2007).

LAW ENFORCEMENT AS A BUSINESS

To be a law enforcement officer, one does not have to major in criminal justice. It is important to think of law enforcement and the organization as a business. In order for the organization to function, there must be a host of support services, which support the agency's primary mission. Some of the support services are budget, training, forensics, communications, crime analysis, personnel, victim advocate, research and development, records, property and evidence, public information, accreditation, and crime prevention. Many of these positions are staffed by civilian personnel or by a combination of civilian personnel and sworn officers (Morgan, 2000; Seberhagen, 1995; Stinchcomb, 2002).

Policing has as its mission to become a profession, and one aspect of professionalism is education (Kleinig, 1996; Plebanski & Garner, 2006). A college degree will be used in the preemployment process, allowing an agency to take what it believes to be the greater-qualified individual. In other cases, the lack of a degree will keep officers from being promoted. In fact, a degree in many instances will be a requirement before a candidate qualifies for promotion to sergeant or lieutenant. If the degree requirement is not met, then an officer's career becomes stagnant (Champion, 1998; Palmiotto, 2000; Samaha, 2005). The officer is either forced to go to school, accept the fact that he or she will never be promoted, or go to another agency that does not have the same requirement. Carter and Wilson (2006) argue that the value of higher education in the police profession is difficult to measure, but education does provide the skills that are the hallmark of professionalism (pp. 42–43). (See Scenario 10-1.)

SCENARIO 10-1: KNEE PROBLEMS

You have been employed by your agency for ten years and have had a very successful career. In your tenure, you have been a Field Training Officer, Hostage Negotiator, SWAT Team Member, assigned to the most successful Community Policing Team in the city, DUI Specialist, and finally assigned to Training.

During the course of your career, you have had knee problems. In fact, you have had five knee surgeries to date. The first occurred two years after you were employed. You were injured while chasing an armed suspect on foot when you jumped a ten-foot fence and landed, tweaking your left knee. After surgery, the surgeon stated: "Your career is over. You don't belong on the street because of the damage. I cannot in good conscience recommend that you go back to full duty." You pled with the surgeon, stating:

(continued)

(continued)

"I would be lost if I didn't have policing in my life. This is all that I am prepared to do. We don't have light-duty assignments, so they will make me retire and I am only 25." After several meetings and while you were still off work, the surgeon agreed to sign the papers releasing you back to full duty, but said: "You will be back here in two years and it will be worse."

Two years later you arrested a drunk driver. During the arrest, you got into a fight and had to transport the suspect to the hospital for treatment. While at the registration desk, the suspect began to resist by jumping up and attempting to run. You grabbed the suspect and forced him back into the swivel chair. He began to twist in the chair, and as you held onto him, the lower part of your left leg got stuck, and the top of the leg rotated, tearing the anterior cruciate ligament (ACL). As a result of this injury, you were off work for one year. You had two more surgeries on that knee, and you had no more problems for several years.

Then you were assigned to the academy and ran with your class daily. Your right knee began to hurt, so you saw the same surgeon. He advised that you had a torn cartilage and that he would have you back to full duty in four weeks. After surgery, however, he met with you and stated: "Your right knee was shredded like it had been run through a paper shredder. You have been lucky so far. In fact, I am not sure how you have worked and taught at the academy with your left knee being so bad. With this injury, you will never be able to run again. You have torn all the cartilage off the

femur and the kneecap. They will have to find a place for you inside. You can plead all you want; however, your body will not let you do this, and there is nothing that I can do." During that consultation, you realized that your career is over, because your agency has no light-duty assignments. You must retire after ten years.

Analysis and Reflection

1. You have been with the department for ten years. How do you feel about retiring? This situation is one of those what ifs, and unless you are prepared for a life outside of policing, the transition will be difficult.

2. What would have been the best way for you to prepare for life outside policing—because someday your career was going to end, whether you did twenty years, or in this case, ten years? Because you are injured, you will get a police pension. However, the amount that you receive each month is determined by the pension board and the retirement system. Often it is a only a portion of the full pension; it can range from as little as 40% of your three highest paid years to a full pension. The most difficult aspect about retiring for police is that with the career goes an identity.

3. Will you be prepared? Only you can know the answer to that question. Everyone entering policing should have something other than policing to fall back on.

COLLEGE ACCREDITATION

The concept of college accreditation is often misunderstood. When many read that an institution is accredited, they assume that the institution has been validated by an outside organization that has developed a set of universally accepted standards and criteria. Lenn (1992) notes that part of the problem in the United States is that there is no ministry of education as in other countries that sets educational standards and establishes regulations for enforcing standards, which means that the higher education system in the United States is as fragmented as policing (p. 161).

The U.S. higher education standard for accreditation is based on peer review, voluntary compliance, and self-regulation. For the consumer, this poses a problem because there are a number of diploma mills that allow an individual to buy a degree. This observation is supported by Thomas (2005), who notes that a **diploma mill** sells college degrees and requires nothing more than a student's money (p. 238). The explosion of diploma mills has been especially troublesome since the advent of the Internet and has challenged the credibility of online education (Daniel, Mackintosh, & Diehl, 2007).

diploma mill

sells college degrees and requires nothing more than a student's money.

There is one accrediting body that all state universities, colleges, and community colleges use as the standard for accreditation. All these institutions are members of the Council for Higher Education Association (CHEA), which has as its primary membership a staple of eight regional accrediting bodies:

- Middle States Association of Colleges and Schools Middle States Commission on Higher Education
- New England Association of Schools and Colleges Commission on Institutions of Higher Education
- New England Association of Schools and Colleges Commission on Technical and Career Institutions
- North Central Association of Colleges and Schools The Higher Learning Commission
- Northwest Commission on Colleges and Universities
- Southern Association of Colleges and Schools Commission on Colleges
- Western Association of Schools and Colleges Accrediting Commission for Community and Junior Colleges
- Western Association of Schools and Colleges Accrediting Commission for Senior Colleges and Universities

There are other accrediting bodies that are members of CHEA, but for practical purposes, an institution of higher education should be accredited by one of these eight because it guarantees that the institution will provide a certain level of **academic rigor.** The same accrediting bodies accredit online programs as well as traditional colleges and universities. Note, however, that because a college or university is regionally accredited, this does not mean your credits will automatically transfer from one regionally accredited institution to another.

academic rigor

a strong level of academics in higher education provided by accredited institutions.

COLLEGE CREDITS AND THE POLICE ACADEMY

Besides receiving college credit through traditional degree-granting institutions, there is an assessment process that local police academies can request that allows the academy curriculum to be assessed for academic rigor and assigns college credit for the courses taught. This process may be completed by a state's department of education or by an individual college or university.

TWO-YEAR VERSUS FOUR-YEAR DEGREES

Criminal justice education can involve either a two-year or four-year degree. The benefit of obtaining either a two- or four-year degree is that it will help in meeting the entry requirements of many agencies, although most states require only a high school diploma.

Obtaining a four-year degree offers additional benefits. It opens doors outside law enforcement if there is an abrupt alteration in one's life plan. Remember also that education has now become the cornerstone of the promotional process in most agencies.

Two-Year Criminal Justice Degree

In pursuit of a two-year degree, a student is looking to graduate with an Associate of Arts or an Associate of Science degree. A community college usually provides two different tracks of study that reflect the following degree outcomes:

1. Track one is Liberal Arts and Sciences, which is designed for those who plan to move on to a four-year institution. Those who graduate will receive an Associate of Arts degree. Completion of this degree format ensures that all of the core basic education courses have been completed. Most, if not all, of the credits taken in this format will be transferable to a state college or university. To receive this degree, a student usually must complete 60–62 credit hours based on the school and the state education requirements.

2. Track two is Career and Professional Development, which is designed for those who are looking to enter the workforce upon completion of their program. These programs are usually integrated with a specialization or certification, and upon graduation the student is eligible to take a certification examination. The degree that one receives at the completion of this program is an Associate of Science degree. Because this degree is considered terminal, all of

the credits are not transferable to a four-year institution. In fact, if a student graduates with an Associate of Science Degree and later decides to get a bachelor's degree, he or she must complete a series of general education courses that were not required for the Associate of Science degree. To receive this degree, a student usually must complete 60–62 credit hours based on the school and the state education requirements. In this situation, the academy may account for as many as 30 credit hours toward the Associate of Science degree.

It is possible to be a criminal justice major and receive an Associate of Arts degree with the intent to attend a four-year institution and eventually obtain a bachelor's degree. Students who go this route may, upon receiving a bachelor's degree, attend an academy at the local community college by one of two ways:

1. Sponsoring themselves, which means that they are responsible for their tuition and receive no pay and benefits while attending the academy.
2. Applying to an agency, getting hired, and allowing the agency to sponsor them. The benefit of being hired and having agency sponsorship is that the candidate is a paid employee of that agency.

As outlined in Chapter 4, Police Socialization, one of the most popular formats in academy training is integrating the police academy into an academic program. The college-affiliated academies often are run by local community colleges and in some cases universities. Most candidates who attend these academies pay for their training and are not sponsored by an agency. Law enforcement agencies like this approach because it saves them tremendous amounts of money. Since these academies are not affiliated with an agency, some run their own assessment centers, which means that the college provides the preemployment screening services before candidates enter the academy. The models vary from state to state. Some have developed a curriculum that meets two educational goals: first, upon completion of the two-year program, students will graduate with an Associate of Science degree; and second, the graduates will have completed the police academy and be *certifiable* or *certified*, depending on the state.

- **Certifiable** means that a candidate has completed the academy and is eligible to take the state examination to become certified, and then will be able to be hired by an agency.
- **Certified** means that once the candidate completes the academy, he or she can get a job immediately and not take a state examination.

certifiable

means that a candidate has completed the academy and is eligible to take the state examination to become certified, and then will be able to be hired by an agency.

certified

means that once the candidate completes the academy, he or she can get a job immediately and not take a state examination.

Four-Year Criminal Justice Degree

The four-year degree is very similar to the two-year degree in that there are two categories: the Bachelor of Arts and the Bachelor of Science degrees.

1. In obtaining a Bachelor of Arts degree, students are required to complete a number of core courses in declaring their major, and they may have a choice in declaring a minor. The key lies in the fact that with this degree, a student has the opportunity to experience other disciplines because there are not as many required courses for the major. The benefit to the student is that he or she has an opportunity to examine other disciplines and see how they relate to the chosen field of study.

2. In obtaining a Bachelor of Science degree, the field of study is more concentrated/intense in that the student will be required to take more classes in his or her major. This is especially true in the natural sciences (e.g., forensics). However, for students majoring in criminal justice, the question here is: what would be the benefit unless the field is a hard science such as forensics? An argument can be made against such a concentration for those who want to become police officers because they will learn the science of policing in the academy. Law enforcement is not a field of study where upon graduation a student will be able to walk out the door and immediately begin the job.

Every four-year institution has a different take on the police academy. Some colleges/universities run their own police academy, which could be the last semester of the senior year of college, or even during the summer months limiting enrollment to juniors and seniors. The foundation for limiting such a program to upper-class persons is based on the state certification requirements and length of eligibility once they graduate from the academy. Other colleges/universities may grant college credit for completion of the academy; this system varies based on the institution, with some offering as few as 6 credit hours and others offering as many as 15 credit hours.

As a student who wants to enter the profession, be wary of meeting with law enforcement recruiters until you are in your last year or last semester of college, depending on the length of the preemployment process. Leaving college with a year to go can become an impossible hurdle to overcome. Understand that law enforcement is very demanding, and to be successful requires that you eat, sleep, and drink policing. The academy is usually between three and eight months in duration. Academically, it is just like college, with the added stress of learning to conform to the pressures of a new profession. The FTO program averages fourteen weeks of intense scrutiny with daily performance evaluations. Your first shift assignment will probably be evenings or nights, which leaves little time for school, not to mention other variables such as a family and/or personal life. At this point, education can easily take a back seat and the degree can become something you wish you had completed when life was less complicated.

OBTAINING ADVANCED DEGREES

A four-year degree is quickly becoming the standard for anyone entering the profession. The debate that students often have is: Should I get an advanced degree, and if I do, what field should it be in? Most advanced degrees are very specialized. In fact, as one moves from a bachelor's degree to a master's degree, the course of study becomes very specific to that discipline. Most programs will offer a series of core academic courses and some electives within the field. If an officer were to obtain a master's degree in Criminal Justice, the core courses might include ethics, leadership, public policy, and law. On the other hand, depending on the institution, the specialties are endless, with options such as homeland security, forensics, behavioral analysis, management, juvenile justice, forensic psychology, forensic computing, and public administration.

The best advice when it comes to the pursuit of such a degree is to pursue an advanced degree in a subject for which you have a passion and interest. Master's and PhD degrees will open doors beyond law enforcement and provide a number of options, especially for officers whose careers come to an abrupt end and for officers when they retire.

MANAGEMENT SCHOOLS

Another trend in law enforcement is to send current and future managers to management schools that provide them with the necessary skills to lead an organization. There are a host of such schools throughout the United States, each with a similar mission to educate managers in the profession. The FBI National Academy states the following regarding its mission "to support, promote, and enhance the personal and professional development of law enforcement leaders by preparing them for complex, dynamic, and contemporary challenges through innovative techniques, facilitating excellence in education and research, and forging partnerships throughout the world" (FBI, 2007).

These schools usually offer multiple tracks of study and may include course offerings in crime lab management, administration, law, behavioral sciences, special topics, and ethics. Depending on the program, those who attend can receive undergraduate or graduate credit. Unlike attending the local college or university, to enter these programs you must be sent by your agency. The FBI National Academy and the Southern Police Institute are two of the oldest and most respected law enforcement management programs in the country. Each requires residency at their respective schools for the ten- or twelve-week session. A relative newcomer in this field is St. Leo University, and what makes it unique is that it brings the program to the agency.

The FBI National Academy, Southern Police Institute, Northwestern University School of Police and Command Staff, and St. Leo University's Command School offer college credit for completing their programs of study. This list of programs is but a sampling of what is available for command-level officers, and is by no means a complete or exhaustive list.

POTENTIAL FIELDS OF STUDY

Completion of the academy provides a new officer with the journeyman's license that he or she needs to enter the profession. In essence, it provides the tools necessary to do the job. However, what it does not provide is the background on why things are done a particular way or even the history behind the many systems in policing. Education, on the other hand, provides information on topics such as: the history of the FTO program and its necessity; shift and zone assignments; two-person versus one-person units; police fitness; the socialization process; career development; politics in policing; police psychology; fragmentation of American policing; police organization; leadership; agency culture; and so on. Each of these topics is relevant in understanding the nuts and bolts of the profession—the *why*, if you will. Education also provides managers with the tools to challenge traditional theories if they choose to be innovative.

The fields of study and majors are many, and as mentioned earlier, education is something for which a student should have passion. A student needs to understand that the educational process is priceless and offers a perspective that exceeds the here and now. Some of the common majors include: Criminal Justice, Forensic Science, Crime Scene Investigation, Behavioral Crime Analysis, Police Administration, Juvenile Justice, Public Administration, Criminology, Sociology, Psychology, Forensic Psychology,

Corrections, Court Administration, Political Science/Terrorism, and Homeland Security. This list is just a sampling of many concentrations.

ONLINE VERSUS TRADITIONAL DEGREES

There was a time that online degrees were not valued by the profession or traditional educational institutions. The debate continues even today, with the diehard traditionalist believing that one must sit in a classroom in order to learn. The traditionalist will argue that online education has no academic rigor and that something is lost without personal contact with professors.

On the other hand, online education proponents argue that online professors are required to respond to students' questions daily; that class size is limited to thirty students, as opposed to state universities that have class sizes in the hundreds; and that there is more academic rigor than in a traditional classroom because students are researching and writing weekly. In addition, online programs offer a format where professors can provide weekly lectures and students can log in at any time to review them. Hislop (1999) found, in his study of the online learning environment, that 87% of the students who participated in the study found online education more convenient; 95% felt that they had better access to their professors; and 43% felt that they had communicated more than in a traditional class (p. 388).

No matter which side students take, they must be cognizant of their own learning style (Verdu, Regueras, Verdu, de Castro, & Perez, 2008). In a traditional setting, a student is required to participate in class and complete a number of assignments during the course of the semester. Many are satisfied in this setting and do well. However, when they venture into the world of online learning, they are often lost because in most situations, classes do not meet on a weekly basis, and the student is responsible for making sure that the assignments are completed and turned in on time. The benefit is access to the classroom anytime; the downfall is that greater responsibility falls on the learner, which requires discipline. Hislop (1999) noted that students agreed there was more work in an online class (p. 388).

The benefits of online learning are flexible scheduling, which accommodates full-time work, and availability of courses and programs of study that may not be offered locally. In contrast, the negatives of online learning are a lack of in-person interaction with fellow students; a lack of in-person interaction with professors; the degree may not be perceived as the equivalent of a traditional degree by some individuals/employers; cheating may be easier, leading to doubts about the degree; and it is difficult to sort out quality programs from less rigorous ones.

Many traditional colleges/universities have entered the online arena, and for the traditionalist, this may be the way to go. All degrees can be obtained though several formats:

1. Traditional in-the-classroom format, with weekly class meetings, usually sixteen weeks in length.

2. Online, with the entire class facilitated through online instruction and the instructional format delivered through one of many programs, depending on the format chosen by the institution. The most common are Angel and Web-CT.

3. Hybrid, which is a combination of traditional course instruction and online instruction. This format reduces the number of times that a class has to meet.

Before committing to any online program, be cautious and make sure the program is accredited, meets your educational needs, and provides academic rigor equivalent to that of a traditional university. Education is big business, with many predators looking to take your dollar. The benefits of education are clear, yet "The buyer must beware."

CONCLUSION

A college degree is the first step in professionalizing law enforcement. It also provides options both in and out of law enforcement. As much as one might like to say that a college education does not matter, it would be foolish to think that you will have the ability to advance within an agency without a degree. Failure to obtain a degree can limit your promotional potential and options within the organization. Also, a law enforcement career can end at any time for any reason. Obtaining a degree is a way to provide options if your career should end abruptly, and for the future when you retire.

 DISCUSSION QUESTIONS

1. Discuss the historical events that led to education being considered an important factor in law enforcement.

2. List some differences between traditional college degrees and online programs. Which type of program do you believe is more suitable to your personal goals? Explain your answer.

3. Why should law enforcement be considered a "business"? Give examples of law enforcement as a business.

4. Does education provide a police officer with greater opportunities within an organization? Why or why not? Defend your answer.

5. Choose one field of study associated with law enforcement and criminal justice mentioned in this chapter. Explain the career opportunities available to individuals who pursue this field of study.

RESEARCH TOPICS

Following are two topics that are central to this chapter. Choose one, and research the topic based on the instructions of your professor.

- *Education and professionalism.* This chapter explains the benefits of education in policing. This book is dedicated to a discussion of professionalism and policing. Research professionalism and determine whether postsecondary education is the foundation of police professionalism. Defend your answer.

- *A future beyond policing.* Many people enter policing in their early 20s and are eligible to retire in their 40s or 50s. We know that the health of a police officer deteriorates exponentially upon retirement. Research the causes of this decline, and offer solutions. What would enhance a retired officer's quality of life upon retirement? Defend your answer.

BIBLIOGRAPHY

Belknap, J., & Potter, H. (2007). Introduction: From passion to practice. In S. L. Miller (Ed.), *Criminal justice research and practice: Diverse voices from the field* (pp. 3–20). Hanover, MA: University Press of New England.

Blank, B. (1990). Bureaucracy: Power in details. In J. Bellush & D. Netzer (Eds.), *Urban politics, New York style* (pp. 107–142). Armonk, NY: M. E. Sharpe.

Blau, T. H. (1994). *Psychological services for law enforcement.* New York: John Wiley & Sons.

Carte, G. E., & Carte, E. H. (1975). *Police reform in the United States: The era of August Vollmer, 1905–1932.* Berkeley: University of California Press.

Carter, L., & Wilson, M. (2006). Measuring professionalism of police officers. *Police Chief, 73*(8), 42–44.

Champion, D. J. (1998). *Criminal justice in the United States* (2nd ed.). Chicago: Nelson Hall.

Daniel, J., Mackintosh, W., & Diehl, W. C. (2007). The mega-university response to the moral challenge of our age. In M. G. Moore (Ed.), *Handbook of distance education* (2nd ed., pp. 609–620). New York: Routledge.

Dantzker, M. L. (2005). *Understanding today's police* (4th ed.). Monsey, NY: Criminal Justice Press.

Dellattre, E. J. (2002). *Character and cops: Ethics in policing* (4th ed.). Washington, DC: AEI Press.

Federal Bureau of Investigation (FBI). (2007). *The FBI national academy.* (Retrieved December 18, 2007, from http://www.fbi.gov/).

Hislop, G. W. (1999). Anytime, anyplace learning in an online graduate professional degree program. *Group Decision and Negotiation, 8,* 385–390.

Institute for Higher Education Policy. (1998). *Reaping the benefits: Defining the public and private value of going to college. The new millennium project on higher education costs, pricing, and productivity.* Washington, DC: Author.

Kleinig, J. (1996). *The ethics of policing* (2nd ed.). New York: Cambridge University Press.

Lambert, S., & Regan, D. (2007). *Great jobs for criminal justice majors* (2nd ed.). New York: McGraw-Hill Professional.

Lenn, M. P. (1992). The U.S. accreditation system. In A. Craft (Ed.), *Quality assurance in higher education: Proceedings of an international conference* (pp. 161–168). New York: Routledge.

Morgan, M. (2000). *Careers in criminology.* New York: McGraw-Hill Professional.

Morn, F. (1995). *Academic politics and the history of criminal justice education.* Westport, CT: Greenwood.

Newman, D. J. (1993). The American Bar Foundation and the development of criminal justice higher education. In L. E. Ohlin & F. J. Remington (Eds.), *Discretion in criminal justice: The tension between individualization and uniformity* (pp. 279–341). Albany, NY: State University of New York Press.

Palmiotto, M. (2000). *Community policing: A policing strategy for the 21st century.* Gaithersburg, MD: Aspen.

Palombo, B. J. (1995). *Academic professionalism in law enforcement.* New York: Garland.

Plebanski, D., & Garner, R. (2006). Police and the globalizing city: Innovation and contested reinvention. In J. P. Koval, L. Bennett, M. I. J. Bennett, F. Demissie, R. Garner, & K. Kim (Eds.), *The new Chicago: A social and cultural analysis* (pp. 259–268). Philadelphia: Temple University Press.

Porter, K. (2002). *The value of a college degree.* Washington, DC: Eric Clearinghouse on Higher Education. (ERIC ED470038).

Rowley, L. L., & Hurtado, S. (2002). *The non-monetary benefits of an undergraduate education.* University of Michigan: Center for the Study of Higher and Postsecondary Education.

Russell, G. D., Cosner, J. A., Gingrich, T., & Paynich, R. (2005). *Law enforcement in the United States.* Boston: Jones & Bartlett.

Samaha, J. (2005). *Criminal justice* (7th ed.). Belmont, CA: Thomson-Wadsworth.

Seberhagen, L. W. (1995). Human resources management. In M. I. Kurke & E. M. Scrivner (Eds.), *Police psychology into the 21st century* (pp. 435–466). Hillsdale, NJ: Lawrence Erlbaum.

Senna, J. J. (1974). Criminal justice higher education: Its growth and directions. *Crime and Delinquency, 20,* 389–397.

Stinchcomb, J. D. (2002). *Opportunities in law enforcement and criminal justice careers* (2nd ed.). New York: McGraw-Hill Professional.

Thomas, R. M. (2005). *High-stakes testing: Coping with collateral damage.* New York: Routledge.

Verdu, E., Regueras, L. M., Verdu, M. A., de Castro, J. P., & Perez, M. A. (2008). Telematic environments and competition based methodologies: An approach to active learning. In F. J. G. Penalvo (Ed), *Advances in E-learning: Experiences and methodologies* (pp. 232–249). Hershey, PA: Information Science Reference.

Vito, G. F., Maahs, J. R., & Holmes, R. M. (2006). *Criminology: Theory, research, and policy* (2nd ed.). Boston: Jones & Bartlett.

CHAPTER

11

CAREER DEVELOPMENT

OBJECTIVES

After completing this chapter, the student will be able to:

- Discuss the average length of time new officers stay at their original police department and what influences their decision to leave.
- Describe the impact resignations have on an agency fiscally and morale-wise.
- Discuss the importance of compatibility between the organization and the employee.
- Explain the stages of career development.
- Describe the role patrol plays in preparing an officer for different positions roles within an agency.
- Describe some of the requirements before entering a specialty unit.
- Explain and identify career tracks and in-service training courses needed before being transferred from patrol.

KEY TERMS

career development – involves helping people to choose organizations and career paths and to attain career objectives.

Doc's Words of Wisdom

Career development has many meanings. However, if executed properly, a career development plan represents a commitment to the future of both the agency and the officer.

INTRODUCTION

Many enter law enforcement without an idea of what the future holds in store or the many opportunities that an agency may provide. Although the agencies do a great job of recruiting new officers, they fail miserably in the area of career development. As a result of this failure, agencies are left in wonderment as to why the new officers are leaving. The average stay with the organization is approximately thirty-four months in the state of North Carolina (Yearwood, 2003). Orrick (2008) notes that studies in Vermont, Alaska, and Florida reveal similar results. Martin and Jurik (2006) state that the reasons for turnover are dissatisfaction with promotional policies, transfer policies, opportunities, management style, agency practices, and the cost of housing in particular jurisdictions (p. 99).

Merchant (2004) states that new employees have to be recruited, selected, oriented, and trained. In fact, it is estimated that it costs an organization approximately one and one-half times the salary of the vacated position to replace an employee. He also argues that employee turnover can have a demoralizing effect on an organization, and it may also severely impact the overall efficiency of the organization (p. 1). This becomes even more critical in service organizations, such as police and firefighters, that require highly developed skills and competencies.

In Chapter 4, Police Socialization, there was a discussion regarding compatibility with an agency. Central to that discussion is the candidate personality and agency personality, and the compatibility between the two, similar to a marriage. Vasu, Stewart, and Garson (1998) posit that compatibility is consistent with values, education, and personality, all of which are relative to successfully assimilating into an organization. They note that in every organization, there needs to be differences in order for the organization to thrive, grow, and meet new challenges (p. 39). Other components of compatibility are agency philosophy; agency size (if an agency is small, it may limit one's promotional potential or the ability to laterally transfer); opportunities within the agency for either lateral transfers or promotions, depending on one's career path; and finally, career development programs.

A career development plan indicates that an agency is invested in the future of both the agency and the employees. *Career development* is a term that should be synonymous with a candidate's longevity, meeting the needs of the agency employees, transferability to specialty units, and promotions within an agency. Kovacich and Boni (1999) state that career development keeps individuals on track in meeting their specific career goals; in its simplest form, it is a road map for success within an organization (p. 118).

DEFINING CAREER DEVELOPMENT

Cummings and Worley (2008) provide that **career development** involves helping people to choose organizations and career paths and to attain career objectives (p. 429). However, employees need to be realistic and understand that there are certain limitations over which they will have no control. The limitations are defined by an employee's ability, budget constraints, opportunities and how often they become available, education and training, background, suitability, and whether there are any alternatives to the prescribed interests. Osborne, Brown, Niles, and Miner (1997) provide that the process of career development is a lifelong journey and is influenced by maturity and adaptability (p. 3). Examine Scenarios 11-1 and 11-2, and reflect on the concept of maturity as it applies to policing.

As much as employees would be thrilled to see that their agency is investing in them, it may not happen for any number of reasons. The beauty of law enforcement is that there are training facilities, the local police academy, and training companies that offer specific training and

career development

involves helping people to choose organizations and career paths and to attain career objectives.

SCENARIO 11-1: DANCING ON TABLE TOPS

Officer Smith is 21 years old and has been with your agency for one year today. He goes out to celebrate making probation at a local bar. Officer Smith gets intoxicated, removes his shirt, and begins dancing on the tables. During his dance, he takes out his badge and hands it to the crowd, stating, "I am a cop; I made it." Officer Smith is also the security officer at a local apartment complex and works there for reduced rent when off duty. During the summer months, it was reported that Officer Smith would go swimming nude in the complex's pool late at night. When Officer Smith is investigated by Internal Affairs, he advises the investigator that he sees nothing wrong with his actions and that cops do these things all the time. Officer Smith is terminated.

SCENARIO 11-2: CELEBRATING MY NEW JOB

Officer Johnson, who was sworn in on Friday, goes out drinking to celebrate with friends, and is found unconscious on a street corner, abandoned by her friends. She is transported to a local hospital, and hospital personnel identify her as a local police officer and notify the agency. Upon the shift commander's arrival, Officer Johnson becomes conscious, sees the shift commander, and runs from the emergency room. Once outside, she steals a car that has been left unattended and running when the driver took his pregnant wife into the emergency room. Officer Johnson drives one block and is found unconscious, slumped over the steering wheel, stopped at a red light. The investigation reveals that her friends believed that she would not be a good cop. In fact, they encouraged her to drink, and once she was too intoxicated to stand, they left her at the bar. Officer Johnson was sworn in on Friday and is terminated on Monday.

Analysis and Reflection

Take a moment and answer these questions regarding Scenarios 11-1 and 11-2. The conduct speaks for itself.

1. In either case, are there issues of maturity?

2. Where do you think both officers obtained their view of police conduct, and did this influence their decision making in these incidents?

3. Do you believe that either officer would have acted this way had they not been police officers?

4. As an administrator, how would you screen for such issues, or could you?

credentialing to meet an officer's particular interests. Two concerns may arise as an officer seeks professional development without the support of the agency:

1. Although the officer acquires the skill, it may never be realized with that agency for a number of reasons: politics; because someone else has been waiting longer than the candidate for a slot in that position; or because during the interview or test, the candidate has a poor showing that eliminates him or her.

2. To attend these schools without agency support requires that an officer use personal leave time and be responsible for all the expenses, such as travel, meals, and lodging, depending on the course location.

Kuijpers and Scheerens (2006) argue that emphasis in a career should be on the individual and self-management. In essence, this puts employees in control of their own destiny. However, we cannot forget that career development is a lifelong journey that has many highs and lows. Kuijpers et al. identify six career factors and competencies of career self-management that are relevant for career development: career development ability, reflection on capacities, reflection on motives, work exploration, career control, and networking (p. 313). Among the variables, the following should be considered as well: mobility perspective, career support at work, and private life (Super, 1990).

A point of consideration regarding career development in law enforcement: if a candidate desires to transfer from patrol to a specialty unit, then it is important to understand that each person is judged on his or her ability and aptitude for that position. In essence, a candidate will be judged on the quality of the work that he or she forwards to such divisions as detectives, narcotics, and traffic homicide. In addition to paying attention to the quality of work, it is a good idea to meet with the unit commander and officers to determine what skills and sacrifices are needed to make the transition.

Remember, some officers stay in patrol their entire career and have no desire to get promoted or try new things. Often these are the officers who become disenchanted and cynical. As discussed in Chapter 4, there are four stages in a police career. Osborne et al. (1997) note that many careers have highs and lows. Let's revisit the stages of a police career, with a new emphasis: the third stage is what all officers should attempt to avoid. One way to do so is to remember that policing is fluid, with constant change, so an officer may get an opportunity when a new supervisor comes into the picture or a change in administrative and organizational behaviors takes place.

- *Stage one/rookie years:* During this stage, officers are very optimistic. They enter policing with the idea that they are going to save the world, do everything by the book, and protect life and the rights of individuals. Niederhoffer (1967) describes these years as an indoctrination where the rookie learns the language, rituals, patrolling zones, discretion and keeping the peace, issuance of citations, the temptations of receiving payoffs, and making arrests (pp. 54–76). This stage can last between one and five years.

- *Stage two/productive years:* During this stage, officers have developed the necessary skills and are very proficient at their job. In fact, they are comfortable with their assignment and find a tremendous amount of job satisfaction. This is often where an officer is deciding on a career path, be it patrol, traffic, detectives, or promotions and administration. Niederhoffer (1967) describes this stage as the five-year officer, in many cases, looking beyond patrol to do something different (pp. 77–78). Although the officers are satisfied, they have developed some degree of cynicism as a result of two factors: crime and politics. This stage can begin as soon as the third year and last until the tenth year.

- *Stage three/cynical years:* These years can be created by several factors, such as being passed over for promotion or not getting an assignment the officer had planned for as part of his or her career development. In the cynical years, there is often resentment and bitterness that is born out of exchanges with the public and the administration. The cynicism impacts all officers, and what often brings about the change to a negative attitude is a new assignment, whether they want it or not. Every officer experiences cynicism, but it is unique to each individual based on the individual's personal feelings and satisfaction. This stage can begin as soon as the fifth year and last until the retirement.

- *Stage four/twilight years:* This is the end of an officer's career—the last four of five years. In most cases, officers have resolved any conflicts they had and their cynicism has leveled off. It would be safe to say that they have found their place within the organization and accept their role. Niederhoffer (1967) describes these officers as the old-timers who have put in fifteen or more years of service. Although these are called the twilight years, they can begin as soon as the tenth year and last until retirement.

See Figure 11-1 for a graphic illustration of these stages.

The stages of a law enforcement career are supported by Cummings et al. (1993) who provide a similar path of career development, the stages of which are associated with chronological age as opposed to years on the job: the establishment stage, ages 21–26; the advancement stage, ages 26–40; the maintenance stage, ages 40–60; and the withdrawal stage, age 60 and above (pp. 429–430).

In policing, career development has many meanings. In one agency, it may mean the opportunity to attend a specialty course, such as radar or terrorism. In another agency, it may mean that during an officer's annual evaluation, he or she has the opportunity to post a series of personal goals for the upcoming year. In any case, officers must take personal responsibility for creating and guiding their career development goals and objectives.

Some state training commissions have different levels of police officer certification. The state of Kentucky offers a series of career development tracks for law enforcement officers that begins with successful completion of the basic recruit academy and extends to the law enforcement executive. Following are the tracks specifically designated for officers and deputy sheriffs:

1. *Basic Law Enforcement Officer Certification* is awarded after successful completion of a 754-hour basic law enforcement academy (see Chapter 4, Police Socialization, for course descriptions).

2. *Intermediate Law Enforcement Officer* includes successful completion of the basic law enforcement certification course plus an additional 160 hours of in-service training. Ninety-six of those hours must be comprised of technical skill development courses, such as driving, firearms,

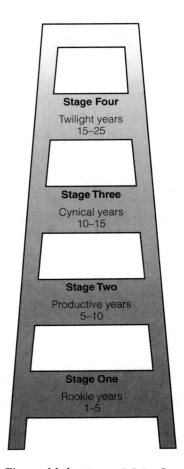

Figure 11-1 Stages of a Police Career

The stages of a police career are not etched in stone; they overlap and can begin and end at any point in an officer's career due to a number of variables that affect the officer's successes and failures.

computer crimes, and so on. Sixty-four hours must be comprised of human skill development courses, such as interview and interrogation, elderly abuse, domestic violence, law enforcement crisis team, and so on.

3. *Advanced Law Enforcement Officer* includes successful completion of the basic law enforcement certification course plus an additional 160 hours of in-service training. Sixty-four hours must be comprised of technical skill development courses (see 2 for examples), and 64 hours must be comprised of human skill development courses (see 2 for examples). Thirty-two hours must be comprised of conceptual skill development courses, such as ethics, leadership, grant writing, police supervision, and so on. At this level, you begin to see a difference in courses with the addition of supervision and/or administrative courses.

4. *Officer Investigator* includes successful completion of the basic law enforcement certification course plus an additional 200 hours of in-service training. The 200 hours of in-service training must include successful completion of the 80-hour Criminal Investigation I course or a Kentucky Law Enforcement Council (KLEC)–approved equivalent. The remaining 120 hours must be comprised of investigative courses identified by the KLEC, such as interview and interrogation, cybercrime, elderly abuse, human trafficking, identifying and seizure of electronic evidence, covert investigations, crime scene investigation, and so on. If you examine the course selections, they are designed to create a specialist in criminal investigation, and there are a number of specialties associated with criminal investigation.

5. *Traffic Officer* includes successful completion of the basic law enforcement certification course plus an additional 200 hours of in-service training. The 200 hours must include successful completion of the 80-hour Basic Accident Investigator course or a KLEC-approved equivalent. The remaining 120 hours must be comprised of traffic courses identified by the KLEC, such as Accident Investigation II, radar, breath test operator, DUI standardized field sobriety tests, commercial motor vehicle criminal interdiction, and so on. If you examine the course selections, they are designed to create a specialist in the area of traffic.

6. *Advanced Deputy Sheriff* includes successful completion of the basic law enforcement certification course plus an additional 160 hours of in-service training. Eighty hours of instruction are on topics specific to the sheriff's responsibilities, which can include such topics as court security, warrants, and the civil process, which are not traditional state/municipal law enforcement duties. Forty hours must be comprised of technical skill development courses (see 2 for examples), and 40 hours must be comprised of human skill development courses (see 2 for examples).

Kentucky's career development program is designed to provide an officer with a career track. In completing the additional training specified by the Kentucky Law Enforcement Commission (KLEC), officers are prepared to move to the next level in their career, either laterally, up through the chain of command, or by enhancing their ability and aptitude as a patrol officer.

It is important to understand that career objectives and specialties change due to promotion, needs of the organization, and reassignment. Some of the best managers in an organization have worked or been a supervisor in every division of a police/sheriff's department; such experience is of tremendous value to other officers as well as the department. See Figure 11-2, which illustrates the steps in the career development ladder.

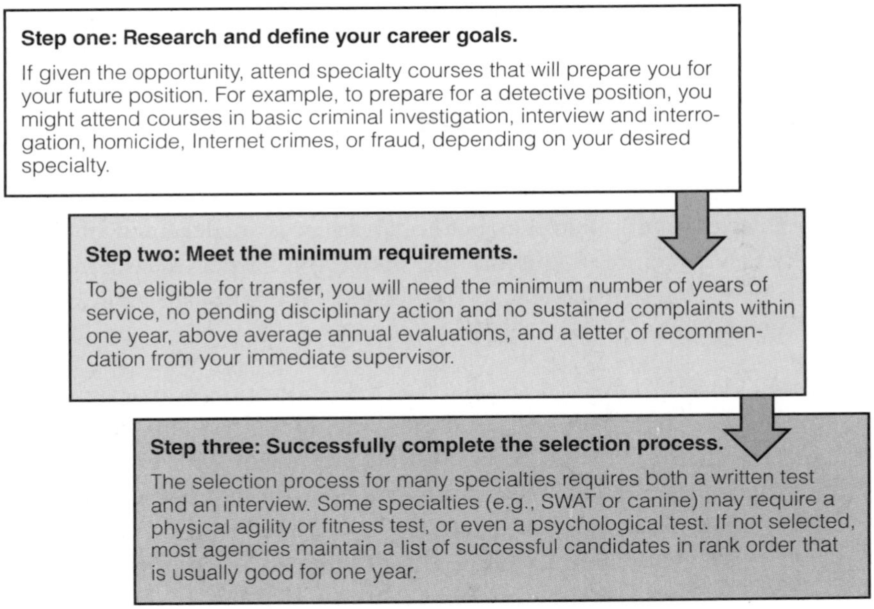

> **Step one: Research and define your career goals.**
>
> If given the opportunity, attend specialty courses that will prepare you for your future position. For example, to prepare for a detective position, you might attend courses in basic criminal investigation, interview and interrogation, homicide, Internet crimes, or fraud, depending on your desired specialty.

> **Step two: Meet the minimum requirements.**
>
> To be eligible for transfer, you will need the minimum number of years of service, no pending disciplinary action and no sustained complaints within one year, above average annual evaluations, and a letter of recommendation from your immediate supervisor.

> **Step three: Successfully complete the selection process.**
>
> The selection process for many specialties requires both a written test and an interview. Some specialties (e.g., SWAT or canine) may require a physical agility or fitness test, or even a psychological test. If not selected, most agencies maintain a list of successful candidates in rank order that is usually good for one year.

Figure 11-2   Stages of the Career Development Process

POLICE SPECIALTIES AND REQUIREMENTS

It is important to understand that sworn officers must spend time working the street in uniform patrol. As discussed in Chapter 4, a question that all candidates have is: how long do I need to be in patrol before I can transfer? The time frame is different for each agency; it could be as little as one year or as long as five years. Unless an officer has prior experience, leaving patrol after one or two years is a disservice to the agency and the officer, because new officers are just becoming comfortable with their newfound role. In fact, it takes about five years before new officers are considered seasoned/veterans because by this time they have experienced everything that patrol has to offer.

Detective/Investigator

To become a detective/investigator, an officer must meet the minimum requirements prescribed by the agency's departmental policy. Standards for most positions within an agency are posted with qualifications. In many cases, such standards will be a number of years in patrol, no pending disciplinary action or no sustained complaints within one year, above-average annual evaluations, a letter of recommendation from your immediate supervisor, and successful completion of a written exam and/or an oral interview.

If this is an officer's goal, then he or she should look to attend in-service training classes that will assist in specializing in investigations. Depending on the agency, an officer may be allowed to specialize in such areas as homicide, narcotics, auto theft, sex crimes, child abuse, or computer-related crimes. In fact, for larger agencies, this is the most efficient way to organize a detective bureau, because in many cases one suspect is responsible for multiple crimes before an arrest is made. Each of these specialties may require unique training above and beyond a basic investigators course. Some of the courses and course descriptions that an officer may look to take before applying for the position are:

1. *Basic Criminal Investigators* course is a 40-hour program designed for the new detective/investigator and includes classroom lectures and workshops on these topics: search and seizure, witness interviewing, arson investigation, forensic pathology, auto theft investigations, forensic artists, role of the crime lab, child abuse investigation, intelligence gathering and information processing, extremist groups, computer crimes, fraud and ID theft, and confidential informants.

2. *Interview and Interrogation* is an examination of the interviewing process and provides an officer with a structured interview format and allows him or her to obtain accurate information and detect deception. Topics that are covered are: the verbal communication process, witness memory enhancement, flow of information, the interviewing process, kinesics interview techniques, detecting deception, videotaping and recording interrogations, interview of rape victims, interview of child witnesses and victims, criminal personality profiling for interviews, the effective interrogator, legal aspects, and the psychology of interrogations.

Narcotics/Vice

In preparation to work narcotics/vice, a patrol officer may take these basic courses:

1. *Narcotic Identification and Investigations* course will explore the latest trends in street-level drug abuse as well as the common techniques used in drug trafficking. Officers will learn about the physiological effects of different drugs and what to expect when they encounter a person under the influence. Topics include: identification and recognition of commonly abused drugs, overview of illicit drug traffic and trends, the physiological effects of drugs, intelligence reports and case initiation,

informant utilization, raid planning and preparation, legal issues, drug laboratories, evidence and handling procedures, and officer safety.

2. *Methamphetamine and Clandestine Lab Investigations* course will teach the officer how to recognize methamphetamine and the common symptoms of abuse, and what clues to look for that may indicate a lab is present. The course explores the various crimes associated with addiction and the latest and most successful investigative strategies. Topics of instruction include: current trends and the spread of methamphetamine; techniques for the successful detection, investigation, and prosecution of methamphetamine-related crimes; first responder—dealing with a methamphetamine environment; special considerations for managing the crime scene; clean-up protocols; manufacturing—how to make a lab; precursor chemicals—controls and regulations; super labs; organization of a methamphetamine syndicate; methamphetamine abuse—psychological and physiological effects; property crimes and child endangerment as an element of methamphetamine addiction; public health and treatment programs; interagency relationships; and case studies and practical exercises.

3. *Undercover Operations* teaches the officer drug interception investigative techniques in an undercover setting for narcotic investigators in the field. The course discusses multijurisdictional standards and techniques utilized by investigators in undercover counterdrug operations. The officer will learn the skills utilized in advanced undercover roles while performing multijurisdictional task force operations. Included are the complexities of the selection process for undercover agents, the various roles and responsibilities of an undercover operation, planning an undercover operation, long-range undercover operations requiring the officer to function outside of an officer's immediate jurisdiction, undercover intelligence, basic surveillance techniques, the use and management of informants, the undercover operation process, flash roll management, undercover roles in reverse undercover settings, special concerns for women in undercover operations, dangers of undercover operations, psychological concerns for the undercover agent, and undercover operation risk management.

Gang Investigator

Egley and Major (2004) provide the following data concerning gang membership in the United States: an estimated 731,500 gang members and 21,500 gangs were active in the United States during the fiscal year

2002. They also note that larger cities and suburban counties accounted for approximately 85% percent of the gang membership in that year.

In response to the rise in gang violence, the sophistication of their organizations, and the criminal enterprises in which they are involved, many agencies have developed gang units/investigators to gather intelligence, track, and investigate crimes associated with gangs. It is not uncommon for gang and narcotics investigators to share intelligence information and investigate the same suspects because narcotics sale and distribution is a primary enterprise of gangs.

In preparing to become a gang investigator, an officer should consider these courses as a foundation:

1. *Criminal Street Gang Investigators* course is designed for the uniformed patrol officer or investigator. The officer will learn: the difference between tactical and strategic approaches toward gang investigations, the importance of law enforcement networking, the significance of good documentation and case file management on gangs and gang members, issues concerning expert witnesses and prosecution strategies, and the prevention of resurgent gang activity.

2. *Narcotic Identification and Investigation* course (see Narcotics/Vice for description).

3. *Tactical Operations* course is designed for the explicit purpose of officer safety for those officers involved in high-risk encounters with violent subjects usually associated with narcotics or gangs. Officers learn: operational planning, operational briefing, breaching, individual tactics and movement, the use of the ballistic shield, defensive tactics, building entries and clearing, vehicle assaults, and mental preparation for surviving high-risk encounters.

Special Weapons and Tactics (SWAT)/Emergency Response Team (ERT)

SWAT teams began in the late 1960s in response to a series of violent incidents that occurred throughout the United States. The Los Angeles Police Department is considered the first agency to begin such a unit. SWAT is a highly trained organization within the police department. Depending on the size of the organization, it may be a full-time assignment or, as it is in many agencies, a specialty team comprised of members from all divisions of the police department. Although it is most commonly known as SWAT, it goes by many monikers, including: Emergency Services Unit (ESU), Hostage Rescue Team (HRT), Special Response Team (SRT), and Emergency Response Team (ERT).

All SWAT teams are tasked with the same job. Some of the specialties within SWAT are: entry teams, snipers and spotters, medics, and in some cases bomb technicians. Besides all the basic qualifications, SWAT has its own unique qualifications that require a candidate to compete in the areas of physical fitness, firearms, and an oral interview performed by team members. Candidates must also successfully pass a psychological examination. Team members are on call 24 hours a day.

The basic fitness test that many agencies use is from the Institute of Aerobics Research (Cooper Institute). This battery of tests was discussed briefly in Chapter 4 but is revisited here. The test developed by the Cooper Institute is but one test an agency may use. The benefit of using the Cooper test is that it has been researched and validated, and the standards are court-defensible if a candidate challenges the test as being biased. These standards were developed with the understanding that age and gender are not taken into consideration; the standards are universal for everyone based on the Civil Rights Act of 1991, Section 106, which is entitled Prohibition Against Discriminatory Use of Test Scores. Section 106(1) reads:

> It shall be an unlawful employment practice for a respondent, in connection with the selection or referral of applicants or candidates for employment or promotion, to adjust the scores of, use different cutoff scores for, or otherwise alter the results of, employment related tests on the basis of race, color, religion, sex or national origin.

Many agencies use this same battery of tests and the same cutoff scores as a preemployment screening tool. The standards provided by Cooper are:

- 1.5-mile run, 14:40–15:54 minutes. The 1.5-mile run evaluates aerobic capacity and is highly predictive of one's ability to perform job tasks in all cases.
- 300-meter run, 64.3–66.0 seconds. The 300-meter run evaluates anaerobic power and is highly predictive of one's ability to perform job tasks in all cases.
- One-repetition maximum bench press, raw score 151–165 pounds, convert one-repetition maximum bench press ratio 0.78–0.84 of body weight. The one-repetition bench press evaluates muscular strength and is highly predictive of one's ability to perform job tasks in all cases.
- Vertical jump, 15.5–16 inches. The vertical jump evaluates explosive leg power and is highly predictive of one's ability to perform job tasks in all cases.

- Push-ups, 25–34 performed in one minute. The one-minute push-up test evaluates muscular endurance and is predictive of one's ability to perform job tasks in most cases.

- Sit-ups, 30–38 performed in one minute. The one-minute sit-up test evaluates core body muscular endurance and is predictive of one's ability to perform job tasks in most cases.

In addition to this fitness test, agencies may add other tests such as swimming, an obstacle course, and/or a rope climb. To complete the skill set, there is usually a firearms test. It may be as simple as scoring 90% or better after the completion of the fitness test using the standard agency qualification course, or it may be a series of qualifying exercises that deal with decision making, shooting on the move, and tactics.

Upon successful completion of the process, team members make the selection, taking into consideration the candidate's compatibility with team members, goals, and philosophy. Once selected, the candidate is not automatically on the team. He or she must first successfully complete a SWAT course. There are many versions: some teams send officers to the local academy where the officer will acquire basic team skills, which are then refined in training, while other agencies hold in-house training programs.

- *Basic SWAT School:* In almost every case, candidates receive training in the following areas: team weapons systems (anywhere from two to five); tactics for handling barricaded gunmen, building entries, raid entries, and hostage incidents on buses, planes, and so on; executive protection; tactical rappelling; land navigation; hostage negotiation; counterterrorism; driving; and a basic sniper course.

Depending on the jurisdiction, training also may include agency-specific topics (e.g., diving in the Miami-Dade Police Department). The agency's needs are influenced by: geography, buildings, population, mass transit systems, infrastructure, sea ports, airports, school system, nature of the crimes, and so on.

Hostage Negotiation Team (HNT)

The first Hostage Negotiation Team was formed in the early 1970s by the New York City Police Department following a botched robbery and a 47-hour standoff at John & Al's Sporting Goods store in Brooklyn, New York (Louden, 2004). The team was developed because then NYPD Commissioner Patrick Murphy recognized the necessity for ending such incidents with little or no violence. In any hostage situation, the commander of the scene has four options: (1) confrontational entry of the building without regard for the hostages or hostage-taker; (2) use of a sniper to eliminate the hostage-taker; (3) use of chemical agents, such as tear gas, to force the hostage-taker from the building; or (4) contain the area and give a negotiator the opportunity to end the incident without the use of force. In either of the first three, the potential for serious injury or death increases exponentially because those options are confrontational.

Negotiators are used to resolve a myriad of incidents such as a barricaded subject, trapped armed robbers, hostage situations, stalking victims and perpetrators, high-risk suicide, mental health warrants, high-risk warrants, gang violence, and applying stress-reducing debriefing techniques to crisis victims, police officers, and other public service employees (IACP & FLETC, 2003). Like the SWAT teams, hostage negotiators are on call 24 hours a day. In most cases, a negotiator is assigned to patrol and on duty. However, when an incident becomes protracted, the team will be called out to assist. The team is needed to give the primary negotiator a break in the negotiations, which can become psychologically draining. The team members provide a number of services along with suggestions in resolving the situation. This is probably one of the most difficult jobs because the negotiator, along with on-scene commanders, sometimes must decide to end negotiations and turn the scene over to SWAT, with the understanding that someone will probably get injured or die.

After all the successes that law enforcement has had with hostage negotiations over the years, the selection process and the quality of training still vary widely because there is no uniform standard. Louden (2004) states that of the 271 agencies that participated in a survey regarding the selection and training of negotiators, 150 did not have a written policy for the selection of negotiators. He reports that candidates were selected in one of three ways: responded to a departmental posting for the position; encouraged to apply by someone in the agency; or volunteered without being prompted (p. 51). This is very interesting because the process of a negotiation is draining and can last for days, with the hostages' lives on the line. Negotiators are burdened with the loss of life if they fail, which will probably impact them negatively for the rest of their career. Two of the courses that help prepare officers to become negotiators are:

- *Hostage Negotiation* course will provide a candidate with many skills, with each being reinforced through practical exercises. The student will learn crisis negotiation; preincident planning, effective communication, active listening, team responsibilities, intelligence gathering, negotiation team responsibilities, psychological principles, and suicide prevention.

- *Critical Incident Stress Management* is designed to teach participants the fundamentals of, and a specific protocol for, individual intervention. The audience for this class includes emergency services, military, and business/industrial peer support personnel without formal training in mental health, as well as mental health professionals who desire to increase their knowledge of individual (one-on-one) crisis intervention techniques. (Retrieved January 7, 2008, from http://www.icisf.org/)

Drug Abuse Resistance Education (DARE) Instructor

DARE was founded in 1983 in Los Angeles in response to the proliferation of drugs and their impact on juveniles. The program is taught by specially trained officers, and the curriculum is designed for grades kindergarten through 12. The program's design is to teach school-aged children to resist peer pressure and to live violence-free. Officers receive 80 hours of training in such areas as child development, classroom management, teaching techniques, and communication skills. They receive an additional 40 hours of training to prepare them to teach the high school curriculum, which can be especially difficult, since this is where many have started to experiment and have developed some of the negative peer relationships the program is attempting to address (POLICY 03-02 thru 04-03).

Gang Resistance Education and Training (GREAT) Instructor

The GREAT program is modeled after the DARE program. It was initially developed in 1991 as a combined effort of the U.S. Bureau of Alcohol, Tobacco, Firearms, and Explosives (ATF) and the Phoenix Police Department (PPD) (U.S. Bureau of Justice Administration, 2005). The GREAT curriculum, which is designed for middle school students or grades 6 through 8, consists of thirteen lessons. There is also an optional elementary curriculum designed for grades 4 and 5. The GREAT program provides officers with two options in becoming certified:

- The 40-hour GREAT Officer Training (GOT) is meant for candidates with a minimum of one year of full-time experience as law enforcement officers who:
    - **a.** Have a minimum of one full semester of classroom teaching experience or equivalent public-speaking experience and have

received instructor training certification, which includes classroom management and teaching/training methodologies, or its equivalent in practical, documented experience; or

b. Have a valid elementary, secondary, or high school teaching certificate with recent teaching experience.

- The 80-hour GOT is meant for candidates with a minimum of two years of full-time experience as law enforcement officers but with little or no classroom teaching experience. (p. 8)

Police Canine (K-9)

Canine units are usually assigned to patrol. This is the most unusual unit in policing in that the dog goes home with the officer at the end of their shift. In fact, the dog is considered a part of the family and is trained to know the difference between work and home. Canine handlers refer to the dogs as their partners; the dogs are actual officers in the department and are protected by state statute. Police canines have many uses: building searches, narcotics detection, tracking, explosives detection, article searches, and protection.

The selection process for a canine officer begins with compatibility with the officer's residence. Will the dog be accepted as a family member? In addition to the family, in many instances, the department requires that the officer have the ability to have a secure pen for the dog outside of the house.

Often the officer has to successfully pass a fitness test similar to that of SWAT. The canine tryouts will probably include: a fitness test, compass reading, a swimming test, and firearms qualification. The officer also may have to lift his or her dog over a fence, run a track with the dog on a leash for two or three miles, and control the dog when encountering a suspect. Depending on the breed, the dogs can weigh as much as 90 pounds.

- *Canine Handler Training* course: The Criminal Justice Training Standards and Training Commission in the State of Florida have established mandatory guidelines for what they describe as Patrol Canine Teams in Rule 11B27.013. The rule establishes a minimum of 400 hours of team training (meaning both the handler and the canine). The basic certification course for patrol canines includes training and evaluation in: obedience and control, evidence search, area search, building search, vehicle stops, and criminal apprehension. A team can hold more than one specialty and be dual certified in such areas as: patrol/tracking, patrol/narcotics, and patrol/explosives. Another specialty category is an arson canine, most often used by arson investigators searching for accelerants at an arson scene.

One point of interest with police canines: many are trained to respond to commands in German. The key to the success of a canine team is training all the time.

For many small agencies, a canine unit may be cost prohibitive. A dog can cost as much as $10,000, depending on the dog's breed and the training the dog receives before arriving at the agency. This cost is on top of the cost of the 400 hours of team training.

Crime Scene Technician

Crime scene investigation has exploded with the advent of such television shows as *CSI*, the Discovery Channel's *Bone Detectives*, and truTV's *Body of Evidence, Forensic Files, Murder by the Book*, and *The Investigators*. All these shows are compelling and motivate their viewers to choose the profession. What is depicted on television, however, is not necessarily the job. You will not find the technicians in high heels and well-dressed; many wear fatigues as their work clothes simply because the job is so dirty. Understand that the crime scene technician's job is to locate evidence, and it may be anywhere: gutters, trees, sewers, crawl spaces under houses, attics, landfills, dumpsters, and so on. The bottom line is that this is not a glamorous profession, but it is very rewarding when the pieces of the puzzle come together.

There are two types of technicians: those who are sworn officers, and civilians who have been trained and certified. Many units have both. There is a difference between the technicians who process the crime scene and collect the evidence and those who work in the lab. The primary difference is education; those who work in the lab must have a minimum of a bachelor's degree in the natural or physical sciences. The Washington State Patrol mandates the following qualifications before applying for the position of Forensic Scientist I:

- A bachelor of science degree in forensic science or in one of the natural sciences such as biology or chemistry in addition to having a number of credits in physics (Retrieved January 9, 2008, from http://careers.wa.gov/)

In most states, the crime lab is managed by the state police or state bureau of investigations. Many large agencies have an in-house lab, which means that the evidence is a priority, as opposed to that sent to the state crime lab or the FBI where it is on a first-come, first-serve basis and may be backlogged for months. The state of Iowa's Division of Criminal Investigation Crime Lab provides the following services to law enforcement

agencies in their state: arson and explosives, controlled substance identification, DNA profiling, document examination, evidential breath testing,
firearm and tool mark identification, forensic photography, latent prints
and impressions, and trace evidence.

Crime scene technicians collect the evidence that is processed in the
lab, which means that their handling of the evidence must meet all the
rules of evidence in the collection, documentation, packaging, and transporting of the evidence to the state or local crime lab. Their job involves:
dusting for and lifting fingerprints, taking crime scene photographs,
collecting DNA evidence, photographing autopsies, and collecting trace
evidence.

- *Basic Crime Scene Technicians* course is usually an 80-hour course and
  is designed for police officers with the fundamentals of evidence
  processing and the skills necessary to properly investigate a crime
  scene. Much of the class is hands-on and addresses such topics as:
  photography; arson investigation; fingerprint development; casting
  and footwear/tire impressions; legal aspects; collection of evidence;
  major crimes investigation; recording the scene; death investigation
  road traffic victim; crime scene sketching; handling of blood evidence
  and other bodily fluids; handling of hair, fiber, and trace evidence;
  firearms distance determination; and gunshot residue collection.

For the civilian who would like to become a technician, there are a
number of college programs that can prepare a candidate to become certified. The programs offer both bachelor's and associate's degrees. A well-
rounded bachelor's program should introduce a student to such courses as:
criminal law, forensic sciences and physical or natural science, criminalistics,
forensic psychology, ethics, criminal behavior, and forensic anthropology.

CONCLUSION

The concept of career development in policing means different things to
different agencies. Some agencies or states have plans similar to that of
the state of Kentucky, while others offer no guidelines and leave officers
wondering about their future. As a candidate, it is important to define your
career objectives. You do not have to do so immediately, but at least upon
entering an agency. However, take the time to explore the many options.

One thing to consider is: the larger the organization, the greater the
opportunity. An agency such as NYPD offers opportunities that are too
vast to list, but in an agency with ten officers, the opportunities are limited.

Remember, the average time a new officer stays at an agency is thirty-four months. Finally, keep in mind that this is law enforcement, so nothing is perfect; in many cases, the mission of the organization will come first.

To be successful, you need to have a career plan. There is nothing wrong with taking control of your future and not relying on the agency for your career development. The principles of professionalism should always be an individual priority even if they are not supported by the organization.

 ## DISCUSSION QUESTIONS

1. Discuss the average length of time a new officer stays at his or her original department, and describe the factors that influence the officer's decision to leave.

2. What variables influence the level of compatibility between the department and the officer?

3. What is career development? Describe its stages, and discuss their individual importance.

4. Does patrol prepare an officer to undertake different assignments within the agency? Cite examples of some of the criteria officers must meet before entering specialty units.

5. Describe the state of Kentucky's career development program. How does it relate to self-management? Defend your answer.

 ## RESEARCH TOPICS

Following are two topics that are central to this chapter. Choose one, and research the topic based on the instructions of your professor.

- *Future career goals.* This chapter has provided a road map for career development and the specialty training that may be needed to move from patrol throughout the department, with the most important statement being that career development is your personal responsibility. Examine the many opportunities in law enforcement, and decide on a path that you would like to take during a 25-year career. Research the positions, find out what training is necessary, and outline your career development plan for the next 25 years. Explain why you chose this path.

- *Maturity and policing.* This chapter offered some insight into the issue of maturity and policing and illustrated two catastrophes in Scenarios 11-1 and 11-2. Research the issue of maturity in policing as it relates to the selection process. Based on the two scenarios that were presented, would you raise the minimum age for candidates from 21 years old to, say, 25? Defend your answer.

 # BIBLIOGRAPHY

Browning, M. (2002). Kentucky law enforcement career development program. *Kentucky Law Enforcement News, 1*(3).

Cooper Institute for Aerobics Research. (2002). *Procedures and sequencing of physical fitness tests in law enforcement.* Dallas, TX: Author.

Criminal Justice Training and Standards Commission. (2007). *Canine team and evaluators certification procedures.* Tallahassee, FL: Author.

Cummings, T. G., & Worley, C. G. (2008). *Organization development and change.* Mason, OH: South Western Cengage Learning.

D.A.R.E. America. (1996). *National D.A.R.E. policies.* Los Angeles: Author.

Egley, A., & Major, A. K. (2004). *Highlights of the 2002 national youth gang survey.* Washington, DC: Office of Juvenile Delinquency and Prevention.

International Association of Chiefs of Police (IACP) & Federal Law Enforcement Training Center (FLETC). (2003). *Hostage negotiation study guide.* Alexandra, VA: Authors.

Kovacich, G. L., & Boni, W. C. (1999). *High-technology-crime investigators handbook: Working in the global information environment.* Burlington, MA: Elsevier Science.

Kuijpers, M. C. A. T., & Scheerens, J. (2006). Career competencies for the modern career. *Journal of Career Development, 32*(4), 303–319.

Louden, R. L. (2004). Selection and training of police hostage negotiators: What's missing? *Law Enforcement Executive Forum Journal, 4*(2).

Martin, S. E., & Jurik, N. C. (2006). *Doing justice, doing gender: Women in legal and criminal justice occupations.* Thousand Oaks, CA: Sage.

Merchant, R. C. (2004). *The role of career development in improving organizational effectiveness and employee development.* Tallahassee: Florida Department of Law Enforcement.

Niederhoffer, A. (1967). *Behind the shield: The police in urban society.* Garden City, NY: Doubleday Books.

Orrick, D. (2008). *Recruitment, retention, and turnover of police personnel: Reliable, practical, and effective solutions.* Springfield, IL: Charles C. Thomas.

Osborne, W. L., Brown, S., Niles, S., & Miner, C. U. (1997). *Career development, assessment, and counseling: Applications of Donald E. Super c–dac approach.* Alexandria, VA: American Counseling Association.

State of Iowa. (2008). *Division of criminal investigation employment opportunities.* Retrieved January 9, 2008, from http://careers.wa.gov/.

Super, D. E. (1990). A life span, life space approach to career development. In D. Brown & L. Brooks and Associates (Eds.), *Career choice and development* (pp. 167–261). San Francisco: Jossey-Bass.

U.S. Bureau of Justice Administration. (2005). *Gang resistance education and training policy manual.* Washington, DC: Author.

U.S. Congress. (1991). *Civil rights act of 1991.* Washington, DC: Author.

Vasu, M. L., Stewart, D. W., & Garson, G. D. (1998). *Organizational behavior and public management* (3rd ed.). Boca Raton, FL: CRC Press.

Yearwood, D. (2003). *Recruitment and retention study series sworn police personnel.* Raleigh: North Carolina's Governor's Crime Commission.

CHAPTER

FUTURE OF LAW ENFORCEMENT

12

KEY TERMS

categories of transnational crime – include smuggling—commodities, drugs, and protected species; contraband (goods subject to tariffs or quotas)—stolen cars and tobacco products; and services—prostitution, immigrants, money laundering, indentured servitude, and fraud.

human trafficking – sex trafficking in which a commercial sex act is induced by force, fraud, or coercion, or in which the person induced to

perform such an act has not attained 18 years of age; or the recruitment, harboring, transportation, provision, or obtaining of a person
for labor or services, through the use of force, fraud, or coercion for
the purpose of subjection to involuntary servitude, peonage, debt
bondage, or slavery.

National Center for Missing and Exploited Children – assists
in the location of children who are missing and exploited. It also
provides data on the numbers of children missing in the United States,
as well as resources for law enforcement and communities when
dealing with a missing child.

Trafficking in Persons (TIP) Report – a U.S. State Department
document that provides a yearly analysis of the human trafficking
problem in the United States and the world.

transnational crime – people in more than one country maintaining a system of operation and communication that is effective enough
to perform criminal transactions, sometimes repeatedly.

Doc's Words of Wisdom

*Law enforcement hasn't changed in the last fifty years. There is an expectation
by the public that when they need service, police will respond. However, the
future of policing is predicated by its past; the problems remain the same, with
additional responsibilities.*

INTRODUCTION

The traditional responsibilities of police in the United States were
outlined by the American Bar Association (1972): identify criminal
activity and offenders and apprehend where appropriate; reduce
the opportunity for some crimes through patrol; aid those who are
in danger; protect constitutional guarantees; facilitate movement
of people and vehicles (traffic control); assist those who cannot
care for themselves; resolve conflict; identify potentially serious
problems for police or government; maintain a feeling of security
in the community; promote and preserve civil order; and provide
emergency services (p. 9).

However, the opening quotation says it all. Policing has made very
few changes. The advances that have been made are based on legal
mandates and technology, with technology having the greatest impact
with new tools for crime fighting. The same tools that police covet as

advancing their cause in crime fighting are the very same tools that criminals have used in the development of new criminal enterprises such as transnational crime, cybercrime, the exploitation of children, human trafficking, white-collar crime, and narcotics (Ferraro & Sudol, 2006; Kovacich & Jones, 2006; Lee III, 1999; Norman, 2001). In addition to the new frontier, policing in the United States will still be responsible for meeting the needs of their community and will have to face the organizational challenges associated with professionalism.

The plague of modern policing is limited budgets; therefore, police will have to choose their battles because they cannot be successful at fighting all of them. One issue that continues to be revisited by politicians and communities alike is consolidation of police services. Even though municipal governments have the right of home rule, it can be argued that there is a duplication of services, with the ultimate question being whether consolidation would allow police to provide effective and efficient law enforcement for less money. Dantzker (2005) argues that the fragmentation of law enforcement causes a lack of cooperation, a duplication of services, jurisdictional disputes, and a lack of conformity and uniformity within jurisdictions (pp. 34–35).

Vollmer (1936) recognized that often local agencies are pitted against advanced criminals who move across jurisdictional lines, which limits police in their ability to pursue them. Vollmer argued that rather than being fragmented, all agencies should become one unified body under the state police (p. 8). Today agencies are not disbanding to become a part of the state police; however, there is a trend to disband agencies for consolidation into regional or metropolitan organizations in an effort to pool resources and save money (Johnson, 2009).

TRANSNATIONAL CRIME

The United Nations (2005) defines **transnational crime** as people in more than one country maintaining a system of operation and communication that is effective enough to perform criminal transactions, sometimes repeatedly (p. 14). Mueller (2001) notes that transnational crime is an enterprise that has many tentacles, including: business, white-collar crime and corruption, works of art and other cultural property, narcotics, and violence (p. 14). Reuter and Petrie (1999) provide **categories of transnational crime** they deem to be significant, which correspond to those in Mueller's discussion: smuggling, contraband, and services (pp. 11–12).

transnational crime

people in more than one country maintaining a system of operation and communication that is effective enough to perform criminal transactions, sometimes repeatedly.

categories of transnational crime

include smuggling—commodities, drugs, and protected species; contraband (goods subject to tariffs or quotas)—stolen cars and tobacco products; and services—prostitution, immigrants, money laundering, indentured servitude, and fraud.

These types of crimes may fluctuate based on the successful level of enforcement. In addition, although these acts are viewed from a global perspective, it is difficult for local law enforcement to look beyond their jurisdictional boundaries. One example of such a crime is the sale and abuse of narcotics. Beare (2003) argues that transnational organized crime can be seen as a chain of local criminal transactions that have a direct impact on communities (p. xxxvi). Passas (2001) makes an interesting point that not all criminal activity has reached the point of being transnational; some may occur only at the local level. However, the local market is best understood as becoming the retail end of large transnational markets.

Commodities that have a direct impact on the United States are narcotics, child porn, and human trafficking (Liddick, 2004; Miko, 2007). Thachuk (2007) makes a clear distinction between quality of citizens' lives and transnational threats.

HUMAN TRAFFICKING

human trafficking

sex trafficking in which a commercial sex act is induced by force, fraud, or coercion, or in which the person induced to perform such an act has not attained 18 years of age; or the recruitment, harboring, transportation, provision, or obtaining of a person for labor or services, through the use of force, fraud, or coercion for the purpose of subjection to involuntary servitude, peonage, debt bondage, or slavery.

Trafficking in Persons (TIP) Report

a U.S. State Department document that provides a yearly analysis of the human trafficking problem in the United States and the world.

Human trafficking is defined by the U.S. State Department as "sex trafficking in which a commercial sex act is induced by force, fraud, or coercion, or in which the person induced to perform such an act has not attained 18 years of age; or the recruitment, harboring, transportation, provision, or obtaining of a person for labor or services, through the use of force, fraud, or coercion for the purpose of subjection to involuntary servitude, peonage, debt bondage, or slavery" (p. 6).

The magnitude of this problem is not clear. The **Trafficking in Persons (TIP) Report** in 2008 (U.S. State Department, 2008) offers that in 2006, an estimated 800,000 people were trafficked across borders. In the fiscal year 2007, the Department of Justice initiated 182 investigations, charged 89 individuals, and obtained 103 convictions for human trafficking (p. 51). In contrast, between 2000 and 2007, Health and Human Services certified 1,379 victims of human trafficking who were granted protection in the United States (p. 51). Clearly a discrepancy in numbers exists, and there is no clear way to identify the magnitude of the problem.

The question that analysts and intelligence must address in regard to human trafficking is: What is the significance of this problem in relationship to terrorism and terrorist cells, narcotics and narcotics distribution, and the other problems that threaten the U.S. quality of life or stability of the country? Because of the uncertainty of the magnitude of this problem, it remains an issue for local, state, and federal law enforcement. (See Scenario 12-1.)

SCENARIO 12-1: PROSTITUTION

You are working undercover vice, and today your unit is working street prostitution. One of the arrests you make is of a Russian prostitute. Once she is transported to the station, you interview her and she informs you that she has been kidnapped and brought to this country illegally. She also informs you that she is one of approximately twenty-five other teenage girls who were brought here illegally. In addition to prostitution, her handlers are involved in the distribution of heroin, gambling, extortion, murder, protection, weapons, pornography, and the sexual exploitation of children. She advises that she will cooperate, show you the houses, and give you delivery dates of future shipments of drugs. What she is asking for in exchange is U.S. citizenship and to be relocated.

You check with your sources at the DEA, FBI, and ATF, and each of the organizations confirms some part of the story. Also, Immigration and Naturalization confirms that she is in the country illegally. Finally, you check with INTERPOL, and they confirm the story, identifying the known members of the gang.

Analysis and Reflection

1. Should you be skeptical of the information that you have received? Yes, even though much of it checks out. You have to wonder why you do not know about this gang. Much of what police do is not intelligence gathering, however, and in many cases these crimes go unreported or there are no leads.

2. Who will you need to get approval from in order to work a case like this? This is an interesting case because it has many tentacles; you have the ability to make an arrest at the local level, but that barely touches the surface of this problem. Beyond the local criminal activity, this case could have state, national, and international implications. For example, it will require that U.S. law enforcement agencies interface with Russian authorities, especially since one of the crimes is child pornography. This case will most likely require a task force of some kind to meet the various needs presented by it.

3. Do you have the ability to promise her citizenship and dismissal of criminal charges? If the case is at the local level, you can probably work a deal with the state attorney's office. However, decisions regarding citizenship will have to be worked out with federal prosecutors and Immigration.

4. Since you started this case, will you be allowed to stay with it? This is a decision that will be made by those above your pay grade. If a task force is formed, you will probably have the opportunity to remain with the case; after all, it was your arrest that opened this door. In addition, informants will often agree to work only with their local contacts because they trust them and not anyone else.

EXPLOITATION OF CHILDREN

There is clearly a world market for children who are missing and exploited. Many of these children come from third world countries where large numbers of children are homeless, begging, and on the street, which makes them easy prey (Montgomery, 2001; U.S. State Department, 2008).

In the United States and in most modern societies, there is an additional variable that is not available to children of the third world—the Internet, which also makes children easy prey. This has become such a problem that law enforcement agencies have developed cybercrimes units to deal specifically with it, along with other computer-related crimes, and in doing so have had to join forces with agencies around the world to successfully prosecute individuals. Akdeniz (2008) notes that these crimes are often transnational in nature because the Internet is global and has no borders; because of this, we need to harmonize child pornography laws as well policies and procedural laws (pp. 275–276).

Independent of the Internet, the United States has found the exploitation of children to be a serious problem. Crimes against children have been brought to the forefront because of their brutality and the loss of innocence that the victims suffer. It is because of these acts that state and federal legislation has been passed in an attempt to protect children from sexual predators. Not all of these laws, however, have been successful. Zogba, Witt, Dalesaandro, and Veysey (2008) note that Megan's Law, which requires the registration of sex offenders, has had no impact or deterrence effect on sex offenses and sexual offenders (p. 2).

National Center for Missing and Exploited Children

assists in the location of children who are missing and exploited. It also provides data on the numbers of children missing in the United States, as well as resources for law enforcement and communities when dealing with a missing child.

To understand the magnitude of the problem in the United States, examine the following data from the **National Center for Missing and Exploited Children** (2006). The most recent data available are from 1999, when a frightening estimated total of 58,200 children were abducted by a nonfamily perpetrator. Of that total, an estimated 115 children were victims of stereotypical kidnappings; and in the stereotypical kidnappings, 40% of the children were killed. In only 21% (12,100) of these cases was the child reported missing and law enforcement became involved while the child was still missing. Youth ages 15 to 17 were the most frequent victims of these nonfamily abductions (59%); girls were more frequent victims than boys in this study, making up about two-thirds all victims; and nearly half of these victims (46%) were sexually assaulted by the perpetrator (p. 53).

NARCOTICS

The United States has been in a "War on Drugs" since the early 1980s. The fundamental theme has been to stop the flow of drugs into the country (O'Block, Donnermeyer, & Doeren, 1991; Youngers & Rosin, 2005). However, law enforcement has encountered a host of cartels with the skills and resources to get drugs into the United States as well as the ability to receive their profits. The drug trade in the United States is a multibillion-dollar industry, and as much as 30% of the profits finds its way back to the cartels through money laundering (McCollum, 1997, p. 110). Chambliss (1992) notes that opium, cocaine, marijuana, and heroin gross in excess of $130 billion dollars per year in the United States. In addition, the importation, sale, and distribution of narcotics generate more revenue than any multinational corporation in the world (p. 16).

Criminologists argue that the War on Drugs has failed because the kingpin is rarely arrested; in the United States, those most often arrested are abusers and low-level dealers during street transactions (Beare, 2003; Bertram, Sharpe, & Andreas, 1996; Steinbock, 1999). Although dated, a study conducted by the National Institute on Drug Abuse (Gerstein et al., 1990), which completed a meta-analysis of data regarding substance abuse, offers some insight into the substance abuse problem in the United States. The study estimated that 5.5 million people need drug treatment in the United States; 1.1 million who are dependent on drugs are supervised or incarcerated by the criminal justice system; 1.4 million are dependent and not supervised by criminal justice organizations; and another 3 million are dependent in households and need some form of treatment (p. 91). Although this issue will continue to be a battle for law enforcement, it is a societal issue that cannot be resolved by incarceration alone. Considering that this issue is transnational but the end sale is on our streets, and that our strategies to date have failed, reflect on this question: What direction would you take if you were a policy maker?

CYBERCRIME

Cybercrime is the new challenge for police who traditionally have been about answering calls for service. In the case of cybercrime, the investigations occur in cyberspace, which is the new beat; the crimes are child porn, stalking, money laundering, white-collar crime, fraud, and a host of others (Boni & Kovacich, 1999; Jewkes, 2007).

The inherent problem is that cyberspace knows no jurisdictional boundaries. Wall (2007) posits that there are three order-of-maintenance issues associated with the public police and cybercrime: public law enforcement agencies must resolve their differences to forge a working relationship at the local, state, national, and international level (one such issue may be trust); public-to-private relationships and the relationship that public law enforcement has with private industry (in this case, vendors or Internet providers and the issue is trust and limits on privacy); and relationships that arise between private agencies that may exclude police (p. 179).

Since cybercrime knows no boundaries, in 2001 the Council of Europe adopted a treaty entitled the Convention on Cybercrime. As of July 2002, the treaty was signed by twenty-nine of the Council of Europe states along with the United States, Canada, South Africa, and Japan (Westby & American Bar Association, 2003). The treaty contains forty-eight articles that detail every aspect of an investigation including jurisdiction, search and seizure, as well as the types of crimes to be investigated. In addition to the international treaty, the United States has federal legislation that eliminates boundaries in state and local investigations, and each state has a set of similar laws (Crumbley, Heitger, & Smith, 2005; Shinder & Cross, 2008).

Most if not all of the advances in policing have to do with technology, which has had the greatest impact on policing beginning with two-way radios in patrol cars, body armor, weapons, computers, and the contributions of science with DNA analysis. Today, we take all these things for granted and act as if the "good old days" never existed. However, if we examine the last fifty or sixty years and the expanse of technology, the future of crime fighting will be dependent upon an agency's ability to adapt to change and stay ahead of the technological curve. Fiscal restraints will always be a primary consideration in a department's ability to acquire the necessary resources.

POLICING IN THE FUTURE

Policing has spent most of its years attempting to meet the needs of its constituents. White (2004) argues that police present a myth that they are set aside from society with the purpose of controlling crime; however, nothing could be further from the truth because police are a part of society and they cannot control crime (p. 53). White's theory is very true. The tenets of community policing are partnerships that are formed with the community; police need the community to be effective. Stansfield (2005) theorizes that the future of policing may be community policing, but it will not be any of the current models. Stansfield's belief is that policing will be informational ordered and private (p. 70). Stansfield's argument is supported by Bayley and Shearing (1996), who argue that traditional models of policing as we know them will succumb to three changes that are already taking place: public policing will no longer be a monopoly; public policing is suffering an identity crisis; and public policing is restructuring and becoming plural (pp. 585–586).

As each of these theorists have discussed, the emerging trends and partnerships between private industry and law enforcement have already begun. In the past, police were reluctant to share information or have a liaison with the private sector, in particular, private security. Law enforcement officials expressed their concern based on lack of professionalism and the quality of the private firm's employees. Kakalik and Wildhorn (1971) provide a profile of private security officers as middle-aged white males, with a poor education, and earning minimum wage. In contrast, Bowman (2007) offers a much different profile of today's security contract officers, stating that they are in their 30s with improved training. Propriety officers—those who are hired directly by the company—are better trained and receive higher pay (p. 1301).

Scarborough and Collins (2002) note that the American Society for Industrial Security (ASIS) has 32,000 members; 70% of them hold bachelor's degrees, and 25% have graduate degrees. Security is still an industry with little or no mandated training. However, a number of changes have been introduced since the computer age and the Internet (Brislin, 1998; Fischer, Halibozek, & Green, 2008).

The financial industry has had to protect its interests by maintaining a staff of security experts who specialize in Internet crimes. In doing so, private security has participated in task forces that are a mix of federal, state, and local law enforcement. In 2006, the U.S. Secret Service formed nine such task forces called the Electronic Crimes Task Forces (Hunter, 2002; Stana, 2004). The task forces are a collaborative effort between law enforcement, private industry, and academia. With law enforcement resources being stretched to the limit, it is clear that they cannot protect every asset within a community. Therefore, private industry must provide its own security, be it uniformed officers or the use of biometrics, closed-circuit television, alarms, access control, and so on.

Take a moment and reflect on potential targets in your area. They will include: stadiums/arenas, power/water plants, chemical plants, large financial districts, bridges, tunnels, public transportation, military installations, university campuses that have nuclear capability, port authorities, malls, media, and so on. A comparison of your local list to the number of national and international targets will define the need for collaboration between private and public police. Dixon and Reville (2006) argue that terrorism is an evolving risk, with government targets making every effort to harden. The burden then shifts from public institutions to private enterprise, which may have soft targets (pp. 297–298).

Youngs (2004) notes that police are faced with difficult times ahead, most notably increased equipment costs and a decrease in tax revenue. Youngs argues that the privatization of some police department functions is a solution and is already occurring around the country, with private security transporting prisoners and providing court security and traffic control (pp. 7–9). Westgate (2007) notes that similar partnerships exist with federal agencies where threat assessments, executive protection, international access control, security protocol development, rapid response teams, and the monitoring of detection equipment are outsourced in some cases. The qualifications of these officers are mandated by the agency for which they provide services (pp. 232–233).

FUTURE OF POLICING AND SOCIETY

Stephens (2005) states that the future of policing will depend on the type of society being policed—meaning the social, economic, political, and technological sophistication of the populace (p. 51). What is missing in his observation is: regardless of those conditions, policing has to deal with the cultural nuances of a society, and the change in these, along with other issues, has had a great impact on the profession.

Williams and Arrigo (2008) present the theory of Thomas Hobbes, arguing that humans are in a constant struggle to obtain the basic necessities of life, along with money and power; that they are limited; and that without government, police, laws, and the court, we would likely cheat, steal, or murder to get what we want. Theoretically, all members of society enter into a social contract, and in doing so, we give up our free will and agree to civility (p. 191).

However, the concept of a social contract within a society loses some of its meaning when we are faced with transnational crime. More importantly, the demographics of a nation, a state, a county, and a city or village within the United States may determine that culture's perception of the social contract. In the United States, what was traditionally clear-cut regarding right and wrong has changed dramatically. Now there are many different points of view, and police need to understand that with the cultural changes have come different value systems, and thus a change in the social contract.

Passel and Cohn (2008) state that the U.S. population will soar to 438 million by 2050; however, the most startling change can be found in the demographics: one in five Americans will have been born outside the United States; Whites will become the minority population at 47%; Latinos/Hispanics will increase to 29%; African Americans will remain at 13%; and other Nonwhite nationalities will make up the other 11% of the U.S. population. By the year 2050, 53% of U.S. citizens will be people of color (p. i). (See Figure 12-1.)

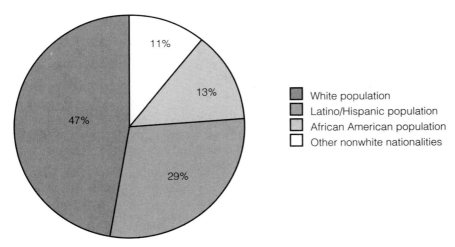

Figure 12-1   Projected Demographic Picture of the United States, Year 2050

Projections are that the U.S. population will soar to 438 million by 2050. One in five Americans will have been born outside the United States; Whites will become the minority population at 47%; Latinos/Hispanics will increase to 29%; African Americans will remain at 13%; and other Nonwhite nationalities will make up the other 11% of the U.S. population. By the year 2050, 53% of U.S. citizens will be people of color.

(Data source: Passel & Cohn, 2008.)

In contrast to the future, the 2000 census of the United States (U.S. Census Bureau, 2000) provided the following demographic portrait of the population: White, 75%; Black, 12.3%; American Indian/Alaskan Native, 0.9%; Asian, 3.9%; Native Hawaiian/Other Pacific Islander, 0.1%; Some Other Race, 5.5%; Two or More Races, 2.4%; and Hispanic/Latino, 12.5% (p. 3).

To paraphrase the quotation at the beginning of the chapter: the future of policing can be found in its past. Undoubtedly, there are numerous new challenges in policing, and yet very little will change when it comes to contact with the public. The research shows that although there are subcultures within the ranks, the police personality is much the same, regardless of race and gender. Skolnick (2004) notes that a police officer's personality may be summarized by two principles: danger and authority. Stephens (2005) also supports the idea that the future of policing can be found in its past, arguing that the threats to policing in the future are: unqualified leadership; aggressive policing and racial profiling; misuse of power and feelings of entitlement; community pressure to return to the warrior officer; a lack of positive true leaders; terrorist tactics used by domestic criminals; federalization of policing; entangling alliances with the private sector where there is no accountability; and not seeking alternative policing models to address the terrorism problem (p. 54).

CONCLUSION

Policing in the future faces many challenges. It is unknown what future initiatives may arise from further globalization of third world countries. Stephens (2005) provides a glimpse into the challenges of the future, and in most cases they are not new.

The bottom line is that policing will continue to strive for professionalism, and yet the demands will be ever-changing because of politics and the globalization of crime. The challenges of the future can be found in the past; however, the success of the profession will lie in innovative leadership that has vision, is not afraid to experiment, and is willing to meet both old and new challenges head-on.

 ## DISCUSSION QUESTIONS

1. Describe the impact that budgets will have on local law enforcement and its ability to address the issues of the future.

2. It is said that transnational crime knows no boundaries and that the end user is the local market. In order to be successful, does policing in the United States need to change to a state or federal police organization as suggested by Vollmer in 1936? Defend your answer.

3. Narcotics have been an issue in the United States since the 1800s, and since that time, we have not been successful in stopping the problem with enforcement efforts. What policy do you believe that we as a society should develop in dealing with this problem? Defend your answer.

4. It has been proposed that policing in the future will become a plural institution, meaning that it will partner with private industry and communities. What are some of the problems that might arise through such associations? Would this be a good thing for the future of policing? Defend your answer.

5. American society is changing, and will change even more dramatically in the future based on demographic projections. With that understanding, what will policing need to do to meet the needs of this ever-changing environment? Defend your answer.

RESEARCH TOPICS

Following are two topics that are central to this chapter. Choose one, and research the topic based on the instructions of your professor.

- *Skill sets.* Many of the old-timers in policing are frustrated with the new generation of police. The primary criticism of this new generation is that they lack interpersonal skills and prefer the computer over people. Research the topic of generational differences and how they might impact the future of policing. In your research, determine if the old-timers have a legitimate complaint; if so, offer solutions, and if not, explain why not. Defend your answer.

- *Transnational crime.* Crime is becoming a borderless institution. Today the hot topics are the Mexican drug cartels and open warfare on the streets of Mexico. An interesting aspect of this warfare is that the guns are purchased in the United States and transported to Mexico for battle. Research the Mexican drug cartels and attempt to find a solution to stopping the war on the streets of Mexico, understanding that this war will end up on the streets of America. Defend your answer.

BIBLIOGRAPHY

Akdeniz, Y. (2008). *Internet child pornography and the law: National and international responses.* Burlington, VT: Ashgate.

American Bar Association (1972). *Standards relating to the urban police function.* New York: Institute of Judicial Administration.

Bayley, D. H., & Shearing, C. D. (1996). The future of policing. *Law and Society Review, 30*(3), 585–605.

Beare, M. E. (2003). *Critical reflections on transnational organized crime, money laundering and corruption.* Toronto, ON: University of Toronto Press.

Bertram, E., Sharpe, K., & Andreas, P. (1996). *Drug war politics: The price of denial.* Berkeley: University of California Press.

Boni, W. C., & Kovacich, G. L. (1999). *I-way robbery: Crime on the Internet.* Boston: Butterworth-Heinemann.

Bowman, G. (2007). Physical security for mission critical facilities and data centers. In H. F. Tipton & M. Krause (Eds.), *Information security management handbook* (6th ed., pp. 1293–1316). Boca Raton, FL: Auerbach.

Brislin, R. F. (1998). *The effective security officer's manual* (2nd ed.). Boston: Butterworth-Heinemann.

Carte, G. E., & Carte, E. H. (1975). *Police reform in the United States: The era of August Vollmer, 1905–1932.* Berkeley: University of California Press.

Chambliss, W. J. (1992). The consequences of prohibition: Crime, corruption and international narcotics control. In H. Traver & M. S. Gaylord (Eds.), *Drugs, law, and the state* (pp. 15–32). New Brunswick, NJ: Transaction.

Crumbley, D. L., Heitger, L. E., & Smith, G. S. (2005). *Forensic and investigative accounting* (2nd ed.). Chicago: CCH Incorporated.

Dantzker, M. L. (2005). *Understanding today's police* (4th ed.). Monsey, NY: Criminal Justice Press.

Dixon, L., & Reville, R. T. (2006). *National security and private-sector risk management for terrorism.* Santa Monica, CA: Rand Corporation.

Ferraro, M. M., & Sudol, J. (2006). Internet crimes against children. In T. A. Johnson (Ed.), *Forensic computer crime investigation* (pp. 129–148). Boca Raton, FL: CRC Press.

Fischer, R., Halibozek, E., & Green, G. (2008). *Introduction to security* (6th ed.). Burlington, MA: Butterworth-Heinemann.

Fisher, B. A. J. (2000). *Techniques of crime scene investigation* (6th ed.). New York: CRC Press.

Florida Department of Law Enforcement. (2002). *Discriminatory profiling and professional traffic stops.* Tallahassee, FL: Author.

Gerstein, D. R., Harwood, H. J., U.S. Institute of Medicine Committee for the Substance Abuse Coverage Study, & National Institute on Drug Abuse. (1990). *Treating drug problems.* Washington, DC: National Academy of Sciences.

Hunter, R. (2002). *World without secrets: Business, crime, and privacy in the age of ubiquitous computing.* New York: John Wiley & Sons.

Jewkes, Y. (2007). *Crime online: Committing, policing, and regulating cybercrime.* Portland, OR: Willan.

Johnson, C. (2009, February 8). Economic woes hit police departments: The budget and staff cuts as property crime rises. *Washington Post,* in *Gainesville Sun,* p. 7A.

Kakalik, J. S., & Wildhorn, S. (1971). *Current regulation of private police: Regulatory agency experience and views.* Santa Monica, CA: Rand Corporation.

Kovacich, G. L., & Jones, A. (2006). *High technology crime investigator's handbook.* Burlington, MA: Butterworth-Heinemann.

Lee III, R. W. (1999). Transnational organized crime: An overview. In T. Farer (Ed.), *Transnational crime in the Americas* (pp. 1–38). New York: Routledge.

Legal Community Against Violence. (2006). *Regulating guns in America: An evaluation and comparison of federal, state, and selected gun laws.* San Francisco: Author.

Liddick, D. R. (2004). *The global underworld.* Westport, CT: Greenwood.

Litchblau, E. (2005, August 24). Profiling report leads to a demotion. *New York Times,* p. A1.

McCollum, B. (1997). *Taking the profit out of drug trafficking: The battle against money laundering.* Darby, PA: Diane.

Miko, F. T. (2007). International human trafficking. In K. L. Thachuk (Ed.), *Transnational threats: Smuggling and trafficking in arms, drugs, and human life* (pp. 36–52). Westport, CT: Praeger Security.

Montgomery, H. K. (2001). *Modern Babylon? Prostituting children in Thailand.* New York: Berghahn Books.

Mueller, G. O. W. (2001). Transnational crime: Definitions and concepts. In P. Williams & W. Vlassis (Eds.), *Combating transnational crime: Concepts, activities, and responses* (pp. 13–21). New York: Routledge.

National Center for Missing and Exploited Children. (2006). *Missing and abducted children: A law enforcement guide to case investigation and program management.* Alexandria, VA: Author.

Norman, P. (2001). Policing high-tech crime within the global context: The role of transnational policy networks. In D. Wall (Ed.), *Cybercrimes and cyberfears* (pp. 184–194). New York: Routledge.

O'Block, R. L., Donnermeyer, J. F., & Doeren, S. E. (1991). *Security and crime prevention.* Newton, MA: Butterworth-Heinemann.

Passas, N. (2001). Globalization and transnational crime: Effects of criminogenic asymmetries. In P. Williams & W. Vlassis (Eds.), *Combating transnational crime: Concepts, activities, and responses* (pp. 24–56). New York: Routledge.

Passel, J., & Cohn, D. (2008). *Immigration to play lead role in future U.S. growth: U.S. population projections: 2005–2050.* Washington, DC: Pew Research Center.

Reuter, P., & Petrie, C. (1999). *Transnational organized crime: Summary of a workshop.* Washington, DC: National Academy Press.

Scarborough, K. E., & Collins, P. A. (2002). *Women in public and private law enforcement.* Boston: Butterworth-Heinemann.

Shinder, D. L., & Cross, M. (2008). *Scene of the cybercrime* (2nd ed.). Burlington, MA: Snygress.

Skolnick, J. (2004). A sketch of the police officer's "working personality." In B. W. Hancock & P. M. Sharp (Eds.), *Criminal justice in America: Theory, practice, and policy* (pp. 100–124). Upper Saddle River, NJ: Prentice Hall.

Stana, R. M. (2004). Awareness and use of existing data on identity theft. In C. L. Hayward (Ed.), *Identity theft* (pp. 92–128). Hauppauge, NY: Novinka Press.

Stansfield, R. (2005). Policing in the information age: The evolution of the 21st century police reform. In J. F. Hodgson & C. Orban (Eds.), *Public policing in the 21st century: Issues and dilemmas in the U.S. and Canada* (pp. 61–82). Monsey, NY: Criminal Justice Press.

Steinbock, B. (1999). Drug prohibition: A public health perspective. In D. E. Beauchamp & B. Steinbock (Eds.), *New ethics for public health* (pp. 150–163). New York: Oxford University Press.

Stephens, G. (2005). Policing the future: Law enforcement's new challenge. *The Futurist, 39*(2), 51–57.

Thachuk, K. (2007). *Transnational threats: Smuggling and trafficking in arms, drugs and human life.* Westport, CT: Praeger.

United Nations Office on Drugs and Crime. (2005). *Transnational organized crime in the West African region.* New York: Author.

U.S. Census Bureau. (2000). *The United States 2000 census.* Washington, DC: Author.

U.S. State Department. (2008). *Trafficking in persons report 2008.* Washington, DC: Author.

Vollmer, A. (1936). *The police and modern society.* Berkeley: Regents of University of California.

Wall, D. S. (2007). *Cybercrime: The transformation of crime in the information age.* Malden, MA: Polity Press.

Westby, J. R., & American Bar Association Privacy and Computer Crime Committee, International Cybercrime Project. (2003). *International guide to combating cybercrime.* Chicago: American Bar Association.

Westgate, D. (2007). Private security for public purposes. In. R. L. Kemp (Ed.), *Homeland security for the private sector: A handbook* (pp. 232–234). Jefferson, NC: McFarland.

White, J. R. (2004). *Defending the homeland: Domestic intelligence, law enforcement, and security.* Belmont, CA: Thomson/Wadsworth.

Williams, C. R., & Arrigo, B. A. (2008). *Ethics, crime, and criminal justice.* Upper Saddle River, NJ: Pearson/Prentice Hall.

Youngers, C. A., & Rosin, E. (2005). The U.S. war on drugs: Its impact in Latin America and the Caribbean. In C. A. Youngers & E. Rosin (Eds.), *Drugs and democracy in Latin America: The impact of U.S. policy* (pp. 1–14). Boulder, CO: Lynne Reinner.

Youngs, A. (2004). The future of public/private partnerships. *FBI Law Enforcement Bulletin, 73*(1), 7–11.

Zogba, K., Witt, P., Dalesaandro, M., & Veysey, B. (2008). *Megan's law: Assessing the practical and monetary efficacy.* Washington, DC: National Institute of Justice.

APPENDIX A

ORGANIZATIONS OF INTEREST

INTRODUCTION

As a student, you may have an interest in a particular field and would like to see what the specialists in that field are studying that goes beyond your studies at school. Or perhaps you would like more information about a variety of specialized areas to help you decide on a particular field. Exploring areas of interest may help you specialize, even when your academic advisor and professors have no concept of what you are attempting to accomplish in your career development plans.

PROFESSIONAL ORGANIZATIONS OF INTEREST

Following you will find a host of professional organizations, their mission statements, and the guidelines for becoming a member. Many offer student membership and have annual conferences, which provide specialized training. This information is offered to allow you to explore the possibilities.

American Criminal Justice Association LAMBDA ALPHA EPSILON (ACJA-LAE)

This organization has a history that dates back to 1939. It is a national fraternity, and its membership is composed of individuals employed in the criminal justice system as well as students who are taking courses in the field of criminal justice from an accredited college. The goals of LAE are to promote a greater fraternal relationship among graduates of technical and professional police schools; higher standards of educational attainment among peace officers; the institution of courses of police science by recognized colleges and universities; research projects in the field of police science; a better understanding by the public of the aims and ideals of peace officer organizations; the selection of properly trained personnel for law enforcement positions; standard modern methods in the field of law enforcement; and unity of action among law enforcement agencies. The organization promotes its goals and objectives through a series of national and regional conferences, which offer seminars regarding the latest advancements in the field of criminal justice. In addition, LAE offers something that is unique to this organization—national and regional competitions in the following technical areas of criminal justice:

- *Written examinations:* criminal law, police management and operations, juvenile justice, corrections, and LAE knowledge. The written competition is an examination designed specifically for each field of study based on federal statutes or nationally recognized practices.

- *Crime scene investigation:* designed to test preliminary investigative skills in a situation, which requires that specific actions be taken and procedures be followed.

- *Physical agility:* a course designed similar to that which most police agencies require in the preemployment process; it may require long runs, negotiating obstacles, and scaling walls. Competitors are classified by age and gender.

- *Firearms competition:* designed similar to any police combat qualification course with four stages of fire, beginning at the 7-yard line with the final stage of fire from the 25-yard line.

The ACJA-LAE can be contacted in the following ways:

Mail: ACJA-LAE, P.O. Box 601047, Sacramento, CA 95860-1047
E-mail: acjalae@aol.com
Phone: (916) 484-6553
Web address: http://www.acjalae.org/ (Retrieved December 8, 2009)

The Academy of Criminal Justice Sciences (ACJS)

This is an international association established in 1963 to foster professional and scholarly activities in the field of criminal justice. The ACJS promotes criminal justice education, research, and policy analysis within the discipline of criminal justice for both educators and practitioners. The organization provides several forums for disseminating information; two are peer-reviewed journals, the *Justice Quarterly (JQ)* and the *Journal of Criminal Justice Education (JCJE)*. The ACJS hosts an annual conference on a variety of hot topics presented by leading experts in the field of criminal justice. The organization's membership is composed of scholars, professionals, and students. The ACJS can be contacted in the following ways:

Mail: ACJS, P.O. Box 960, Greenbelt, MD 20768-0960

E-mail: ExecDir@acjs.org

Phone: (301) 446-6300 or (800) 757-ACJS (2257)

Web address: http://www.acjs.org/ (Retrieved December 8, 2009)

American Society of Criminology (ASC)

This international organization is concerned with criminology and embraces scholarly, scientific, and professional knowledge concerning the etiology, prevention, control, and treatment of crime and delinquency. This includes the measurement and detection of crime, a review of legislation and the practice of law, as well as an examination of the law enforcement, judicial, and correctional systems. The ASC disseminates information through several forums, including two peer-reviewed journals, *Criminology* and *Criminology & Public Policy*, and a newsletter, *The Criminologist*. The organization hosts an annual conference on a variety of hot topics presented by leading experts in the field of criminology. In addition, the ASC has divisions of interests for its membership, which include Corrections and Sentencing, Critical Criminology, Women and Crime, International Criminology, and People of Color and Crime. Each of these specialized divisions distributes newsletters, journals, and announcements to its membership on a regular basis. The ASC membership is composed of scholars, professionals, and students. The organization can be contacted in the following ways:

Mail: American Society of Criminology, 1314 Kinnear Road, Suite 212, Columbus, OH 43212-1156

E-mail: asc2@osu.edu

Phone: (614) 292-9207

Web address: https://www.asc41.com/index.htm (Retrieved December 8, 2009)

American Academy of Forensic Sciences (AAFS)

The AAFS was established in 1948 with the mission of improving the administration and achievement of justice through the application of science to the process of law. The AAFS is divided into ten sections spanning the forensic enterprise. Included among the members are physicians, attorneys, dentists, toxicologists, physical anthropologists, document examiners, psychiatrists, physicists, engineers, criminalists, educators, and others. The AAFS disseminates information through several forums, including a peer-reviewed journal entitled *Journal of Forensic Sciences,* newsletters, annual meetings, and seminars. The membership is composed of scholars, professionals, and students, with three distinct categories of membership: Associate Member, Trainee Affiliate, and Student Affiliate. The AAFS can be contacted in the following ways:

Mail: AAFS, 410 North 21st Street, Colorado Springs, CO 80904
E-mail: awarren@aafs.org
Phone: (719) 636-1100
Web address: http://www.aafs.org/ (Retrieved December 8, 2009)

International Association of Computer Investigative Specialists (IACIS)

This is an international volunteer nonprofit corporation composed of law enforcement professionals dedicated to education in the field of forensic computer science. The IACIS members represent federal, state, local, and international law enforcement professionals. Regular IACIS members have been trained in the forensic science of seizing and processing computer systems. Membership to this organization is limited to law enforcement officers and, in some cases, will be extended to retired law enforcement officers as well as contract employees working in a law enforcement environment. The IACIS can be contacted in the following ways:

Mail: IACIS, P.O. Box 1728, Fairmont, WV 26555
Phone: (888) 884-2247
Web address: http://www.iacis.info/ (Retrieved December 8, 2009)

International Association of Crime Analysts (IACA)

The IACA was formed in 1990 to help crime analysts around the world improve their skills and make valuable contacts, to help law enforcement agencies make the best use of crime analysis, and to advocate for standards of performance and techniques within the profession itself. The organization accomplishes these goals through training, networking, and publications. The IACA provides standards for certification in becoming a crime analyst. Membership is open to students and practitioners alike. The IACA can be contacted in the following ways:

Mail: International Association of Crime Analysts, 9218 Metcalf Avenue, #364, Overland Park, KS 66212

E-mail: iaca@iaca.net

Phone: (800) 609-3419

Web address: http://www.iaca.net/ (Retrieved December 8, 2009)

CONCLUSION

A number of professional organizations restrict membership due to the sensitive nature of their work. There are professional law enforcement organizations specializing in Explosives, SWAT, Training, Fraud/Financial Crimes, Auto Theft, Firearms Training, Police Canines, Narcotics Enforcement, Crime Scene Investigation and Reconstruction, Police Psychology, Profiling and Behavioral Analysis, Police Stress, and Law Enforcement Executives. Examining these organizations' requirements for becoming certified in a particular field or specialization may assist you in outlining your future career path.

APPENDIX B

TERRORISM RESOURCES

RESOURCES FOR INTERNATIONAL AND DOMESTIC TERRORIST GROUPS

The FBI is responsible for tracking and publishing data concerning terrorist activity and incidents that they investigate both domestically and on the international front. However, their published data are limited because they include only cases where the investigations are complete. Following is a list of other resources that identify and provide detailed information on international terrorists and their organizations.

Terrorism Research Center (TRC)

Founded in 1996, the Terrorism Research Center, Inc. (TRC) is an independent institute dedicated to the research of terrorism, information warfare and security, critical infrastructure protection, and other issues of low-intensity political violence and gray-area phenomena. The TRC provides core expertise in terrorism, counterterrorism, critical infrastructure protection, information warfare and security (including design review, technical assessments, policy development and review, and training), vulnerability and threat assessment (red teaming), systems engineering, encryption, intelligence analysis, and national security and defense policy. The Web address for the TRC is: http://www.terrorism.com/index.php (retrieved December 9, 2009).

Memorial Institute for the Prevention of Terrorism (MIPT), Terrorism Knowledge Base (TKB)

This nonprofit organization is dedicated to preventing terrorism on U.S. soil or mitigating its effects. The MIPT was established after the April 1995 bombing of the Murrah Federal Building in Oklahoma City. The

TKB is a one-stop resource for comprehensive research and analysis on global terrorist incidents, terrorism-related court cases, and terrorist groups and leaders. The TKB covers the history, affiliations, locations, and tactics of terrorist groups operating across the world, with more than thirty-five years of terrorism incident data and hundreds of group and leader profiles and trials. The TKB also features interactive maps, statistical summaries, and analytical tools that can be used to create custom graphs and tables. The Web address for the TKB is: http://www.mipt.org/ (retrieved December 9, 2009).

FBI Counterterrorism Division

This division of the FBI provides a series of publications that detail their responsibility and investigations since 1996. The Web address for the FBI publications is: http://www.fbi.gov/publications.htm (retrieved December 9, 2009).

National Counterterrorism Center (NCTC)

The NCTC was established in August 2004 to serve as the primary organization in the U.S. Government (USG) for integrating and analyzing all intelligence pertaining to terrorism and counterterrorism (CT) and to conduct strategic operational planning by integrating all instruments of national power. In December 2004, Congress codified the NCTC in the Intelligence Reform and Terrorism Prevention Act (IRTPA) and placed the NCTC in the Office of the Director of National Intelligence. Located at the Liberty Crossing Building in Northern Virginia, the NCTC is a multiagency organization dedicated to eliminating the terrorist threat to U.S. interests at home and abroad. The Web address for the NCTC is: http://www.nctc.gov/ (retrieved December 9, 2009).

Rand Corporation

The Rand Corporation is a private entity that provides research in a plethora of fields, including: the arts, child policy, civil justice, education, energy, health care, international affairs, national security, population/aging, public safety, substance abuse, science/technology, transportation, workforce, and terrorism and homeland security. Rand has been researching terrorism for more than thirty years. As a public service, RAND disseminates all unclassified research as printed documents or online. The Web address for Rand's terrorism research is: http://www.rand.org/research_areas/terrorism/ (retrieved December 31, 2007).

U.S. Department of State Terrorist Watch List

This is a list of organizations that are considered a threat to the United States. The Web address of the watch list is: http://www.state.gov/s/ct/rls/fs/2001/6531.htm (retrieved December 9, 2009).

Anti-Defamation League (ADL)

The ADL was founded in 1913 with the platform of stopping the defamation of the Jewish people and to secure justice and fair treatment for all. From a researcher's perspective, it is important to remain objective in the analysis of the data and, if uncertain, to balance the findings with other sources. However, this does not discount the importance of the ADL's research or the contribution that the group has made to the study of extremism in the United States. Since the organization is Jewish, it is under constant attack from the far right as well as the *jihadists*. The ADL maintains a database of extremist incidents in both the United States and internationally. In addition, the organization pays particular attention to such groups as Skin Heads, the KKK, and Black Muslims in the United States. The ADL Web address is: http://www.adl.org/ (retrieved December 9, 2009).

Southern Poverty Law Center (SPLC)

This is another group that has been active in its effort to track and fight the far right. The SPLC was founded in 1971 as a small civil rights law firm. In 1981, the SPLC began investigating hate activity in response to a resurgence of groups like the Ku Klux Klan. Today the SPLC Intelligence Project monitors hate groups and tracks extremist activity throughout the United States. It provides comprehensive updates to law enforcement, the media, and the public through its quarterly magazine *Intelligence Report*. As with the ADL, from a researcher's perspective, it is important to remain objective in the analysis of the data and, if uncertain, to balance the findings with other sources, but this does not discount the importance of the SPLC's research or the group's contribution to the study of extremism in the United States. The SPLC's list showing the number of active groups in the United States by category for 2009 included: Black Separatists, 88; Christian Identity, 37; General Hate, 73; Ku Klux Klan, 165; Neo-Confederate, 102; Neo-Nazi, 191; Racist Skinhead, 78; and White Nationalist, 110. This list is probably the most comprehensive list that is unclassified and available to the public. The Web address of the SPLC is: http://www.splcenter.org/ (retrieved December 9, 2009).

INDEX